T0183491

The series Lecture Notes in Computer Science (LNCS), including its subseries Lecture Notes in Artificial Intelligence (LNAI) and Lecture Notes in Bioinformatics (LNBI), has established itself as a medium for the publication of new developments in computer science and information technology research, teaching, and education.

LNCS enjoys close cooperation with the computer science R & D community, the series counts many renowned academics among its volume editors and paper authors, and collaborates with prestigious societies. Its mission is to serve this international community by providing an invaluable service, mainly focused on the publication of conference and workshop proceedings and postproceedings. LNCS commenced publication in 1973.

Lecture Notes in Computer Science 14330

Robert Glück · Bishoksan Kafle
Editors

Logic-Based Program Synthesis and Transformation

33rd International Symposium, LOPSTR 2023 Cascais, Portugal, October 23–24, 2023 Proceedings

Editors
Robert Glück
University of Copenhagen
Copenhagen, Denmark

Bishoksan Kafle
IMDEA Software Institute
Madrid, Spain

ISSN 0302-9743 ISSN 1611-3349 (electronic)
Lecture Notes in Computer Science
ISBN 978-3-031-45783-8 ISBN 978-3-031-45784-5 (eBook)
https://doi.org/10.1007/978-3-031-45784-5

This Springer imprint is published by the registered company Springer Nature Switzerland AG
The registered company address is: Gewerbestrasse 11, 6330 Cham, Switzerland

Preface

This volume is a compilation of the papers selected for presentation at LOPSTR 2023, the *33rd International Symposium on Logic-Based Program Synthesis and Transformation.* This event took place on October 23–24, 2023, in Cascais (Lisbon), Portugal. The symposium was held in conjunction with PPDP 2023, the 25th International Symposium on Principles and Practice of Declarative Programming.

With a history spanning over three decades, LOPSTR has maintained its prominence in the field. Its inaugural meeting was hosted in Manchester, UK, in 1991. Information about previous symposia can be found at https://lopstr.webs.upv.es/ and about the current symposium at https://lopstr.github.io/2023/.

In response to the call for papers, a total of 29 contributions were submitted by 88 authors from 12 countries. Following a meticulous evaluation process by the program committee, 12 submissions were chosen for presentation, encompassing 8 Regular Papers and 4 Short Papers. Each submission went through a rigorous single-blind review process, receiving at least three reviews. This was followed by an online discussion among the program committee members, where the pros and cons of each submission were discussed, sometimes extensively.

We are very grateful to all authors of the submitted papers and to the invited speakers. Their contributions and active participation remain fundamental to the success of this symposium. The symposium program included two distinguished invited speakers, Maribel Fernández and Manuel Hermenegildo, kindly sponsored by the Association of Logic Programming (ALP). Maribel will be co-presenting with PPDP. Additionally, thanks to Springer's sponsorship, two best paper awards (one for each submission category) were given at the symposium.

We extend our sincere gratitude to the dedicated members of the program committee, who invested their efforts in generating excellent reviews for the submitted papers. We also extend it to the external reviewers who played a pivotal role in the paper selection process. Recognition is also due to Daniel Jurjo, the publicity chair, and to Maurizio Prioetti, the chairperson of the LOPSTR Steering Committee. The organizing committee of SPLASH 2023, led by general chair Vasco Thudichum Vasconcelos, receives commendation for their event management.

The invaluable support provided by EasyChair in facilitating the submission and review process is greatly acknowledged. Last, but not least, the collaboration with Springer in preparing this volume was very efficient and pleasant.

August 2023

Robert Glück
Bishoksan Kafle

Organization

Program Committee Chairs

Robert Glück	University of Copenhagen, Denmark
Bishoksan Kafle	IMDEA Software Institute, Spain

Steering Committee

Emanuele De Angelis	National Research Council, Italy
Maribel Fernández	King's College London, UK
Fabio Fioravanti	Università degli Studi G. d'Annunzio, Italy
Maurizio Gabbrielli	University of Bologna, Italy
John Gallagher	Roskilde University, Denmark
Fred Mesnard	Université de La Réunion, France
Maurizio Proietti (Chair)	National Research Council, Italy
Peter Stuckey	Monash University, Australia
Wim Vanhoof	University of Namur, Belgium
Germán Vidal	Universitat Politècnica de València, Spain
Alicia Villanueva	Universitat Politècnica de València, Spain

Program Committee

Slim Abdennadher	German International University, Egypt
José Júlio Alferes	Universidade NOVA de Lisboa, Portugal
Roberto Amadini	University of Bologna, Italy
William Byrd	University of Alabama at Birmingham, USA
Michael Codish	Ben-Gurion University of the Negev, Israel
Gregory Duck	National University of Singapore, Singapore
Isabel Garcia-Contreras	University of Waterloo, Canada
Ashutosh Gupta	IIT Bombay, India
Gopal Gupta	University of Texas at Dallas, USA
Michael Hanus	Kiel University, Germany
Temesghen Kahsai	Amazon, USA
Maja Hanne Kirkeby	Roskilde University, Denmark
Michael Leuschel	Heinrich Heine University Düsseldorf, Germany
Nai-Wei Lin	National Chung Cheng University, Taiwan

Fred Mesnard	Université de La Réunion, France
José F. Morales	IMDEA Software Institute, Spain
Carlos Olarte	Université Sorbonne Paris Nord, France
Alberto Pettorossi	Università di Roma Tor Vergata, Italy
Christoph Reichenbach	Lund University, Sweden
Peter Schachte	University of Melbourne, Australia
Helge Spieker	Simula Research Laboratory, Norway
Theresa Swift	Universidade NOVA de Lisboa, Portugal
Laura Titolo	NASA Langley Research Center, USA
Kazunori Ueda	Waseda University, Japan
Germán Vidal	Universitat Politècnica de València, Spain
Nisansala Yatapanage	Australian National University, Australia
Florian Zuleger	Vienna University of Technology, Austria

Publicity Chair

Daniel Jurjo	IMDEA Software Institute, Spain

Additional Reviewers

Alia El Bolock
Sopam Dasgupta
Moreno Falaschi
Marco A. Feliu
Louis Rustenholz
Caroline Sabty
Ken Sakayori
Elmer Salazar

On-The-Fly Verification via Incremental, Interactive Abstract Interpretation with CiaoPP and VeriFly (Invited Talk)

M. V. Hermenegildo[1,2], I. Garcia-Contreras[1,2], J. F. Morales[1,2], P. Lopez-Garcia[1,4], L. Rustenholz[1,2], D. Ferreiro[1,2] and D. Jurjo[1,2]

[1] IMDEA Software Institute, Spain
[2] Universidad Politécnica de Madrid (UPM), Spain
[3] University of Waterloo, Canada
[4] Spanish Council for Scientific Research (CSIC), Spain

Ciao Prolog pioneered the idea of being able to optionally and gradually add assertions or contracts to programs in order to offer formal guarantees, a now very popular solution for solving the classic trade-offs between dynamic and static languages. This approach is enabled by Ciao's program analysis and verification framework, CiaoPP, which performs abstract interpretation-based, context- and path-sensitive analysis to infer information against which assertions are checked to achieve verification or flag errors statically.

The framework supports multiple other languages in addition to Prolog, from machine code to smart contracts, by translation into Horn clauses. Program semantics is computed over different user-definable abstract domains, via efficient fixpoint computation. This allows inference and verification of both functional and non-functional properties, including, e.g., energy or 'gas' consumption.

While this type of verification can be performed offline (e.g., as part of continuous integration) it is very useful when it occurs interactively during software development, flagging errors as the program is written. However, while context- and path-sensitive global analysis over complex domains can provide the precision needed for effective verification and optimization, it can also be expensive when applied to large code bases, sometimes making interactive use impractical. On the other hand, in many program development situations modifications are small and isolated within a few components. The modular and incremental fixpoint algorithms used by CiaoPP take advantage of this to reuse as much as possible previous analysis results, reducing response times in interactive use.

In this talk we will review these ideas and show how the integration of the Ciao abstract interpretation framework within different IDEs takes advantage of our efficient and incremental fixpoint to achieve effective verification on-the-fly, as the program is developed. We also demonstrate a number of embeddings of this framework within the browser, and show as an example an application for building interactive tutorials, which we have used for teaching verification and abstract interpretation.

Partially funded by MICINN PID2019-108528RB-C21 *ProCode*, TED2021-132464B-I00 *PRODIGY*, FJC2021-047102-I, and by the Tezos foundation. Thanks also to M.A. Sánchez-Ordaz and V. Pérez-Carrasco for previous contributions to this work.

Contents

Keynote

Unification Modulo Equational Theories in Languages with Binding Operators (Invited Talk) 3
Maribel Fernández

Horn Clauses Analysis, Transformation and Synthesis

Design Datalog Templates for Synthesizing Bidirectional Programs from Tabular Examples 9
Bach Nguyen Trong, Kanae Tsushima, and Zhenjiang Hu

Transforming Big-Step to Small-Step Semantics Using Interpreter Specialisation 28
John P. Gallagher, Manuel Hermenegildo, José Morales, and Pedro Lopez-Garcia

Constrained Horn Clauses Satisfiability via Catamorphic Abstractions 39
Emanuele De Angelis, Fabio Fioravanti, Alberto Pettorossi, and Maurizio Proietti

Static Analysis and Type Systems

A Reusable Machine-Calculus for Automated Resource Analyses 61
Hector Suzanne and Emmanuel Chailloux

A Rule-Based Approach for Designing and Composing Abstract Domains 80
Daniel Jurjo, José Morales, Pedro Lopez-Garcia, and Manuel Hermenegildo

A Logical Interpretation of Asynchronous Multiparty Compatibility 99
Marco Carbone, Sonia Marin, and Carsten Schürmann

Relational Solver for JAVA Generics Type System 118
Peter Lozov, Dmitry Kosarev, Dmitry Ivanov, and Dmitry Boulytchev

Unification and Substitution in (C)LP

Predicate Anti-unification in (Constraint) Logic Programming 131
Gonzague Yernaux and Wim Vanhoof

A Term Matching Algorithm and Substitution Generality 150
Marija Kulaš

Knowledge Representation and AI-Based Learning

A Novel EGs-Based Framework for Systematic Propositional-Formula Simplification 169
Jordina Francès de Mas and Juliana Bowles

From Static to Dynamic Access Control Policies via Attribute-Based Category Mining 188
Anna Bamberger and Maribel Fernández

Towards a Certified Proof Checker for Deep Neural Network Verification 198
Remi Desmartin, Omri Isac, Grant Passmore, Kathrin Stark, Ekaterina Komendantskaya, and Guy Katz

Author Index 211

Keynote

Unification Modulo Equational Theories in Languages with Binding Operators (Invited Talk)

Maribel Fernández(✉)

Department of Informatics, King's College London, London, UK
Maribel.Fernandez@kcl.ac.uk

Abstract. Unification (i.e., solving equations between terms) is a key step in the implementation of logic programming languages and theorem provers, and is also used in type inference algorithms for functional languages and as a mechanism to analyse rewrite-based specifications (e.g., to find critical pairs). Matching is a version of unification in which only one of the terms in the equation can be instantiated. In this talk, we present matching and unification algorithms for languages that include binding operators as well as operators that satisfy equational axioms, such as associativity and commutativity.

Keywords: Binding Operator · Nominal Logic · Unification · Matching · Equational Axioms

Overview

Unification is a key step in the implementation of logic programming languages and theorem provers, and is also used in type inference algorithms for functional languages and as a mechanism to analyse rewrite-based specifications (e.g., to find critical pairs). In its simplest form, a unification problem consists of two first-order terms, which may have variables, and a solution to a unification problem is a substitution that makes the two terms syntactically equal. Matching is a version of unification in which only one of the terms in the equation can be instantiated; it has many applications (e.g., to define the rewriting relation generated by a set of rules or to implement functional language evaluators).

Often, operators satisfy equational axioms (e.g., associativity, commutativity), which must be taken into account during the unification or matching process. In addition, when the expressions to be unified involve binding operators (as is the case when representing programs, logics, computation models, etc.), unification must take into account the α-equivalence relation generated by the binders.

Partially funded by the Royal Society (International Exchanges, grant number IES\R2\212106).

R. Glück and B. Kafle (Eds.): LOPSTR 2023, LNCS 14330, pp. 3–6, 2023.
https://doi.org/10.1007/978-3-031-45784-5_1

To specify binding operators, various approaches have been proposed: encoding bound names by indices (as in De Bruijn versions of explicit substitution calculi for the λ-calculus [10,20,27]), or using the λ-calculus itself as meta-language (as in higher-order abstract syntax [18] and higher-order rewriting sytems [19,22]), or using the nominal approach introduced by Gabbay and Pitts, [16,17,26]. The latter has its roots in nominal set theory [25] and has a first-order presentation that makes formal reasoning about binding operators similar to conventional on-paper reasoning. Nominal logic [23,24] uses the well-understood concept of *permutation groups acting on sets* to provide a rigorous, first-order treatment of common informal practice to do with fresh and bound names. Importantly, nominal matching and nominal unification [31,32], which work modulo α-equivalence, are decidable and unitary (there is a most general solution for any solvable unification or matching problem). Moreover, efficient algorithms exist [6–8,21], which are the basis for efficient implementations of nominal rewriting [13–15,30] and nominal logic programming [9].

In this talk, we first give an overview of the nominal approach to the representation of languages with binders and then focus on solving equations (i.e., unification problems) modulo α-equivalence and equational axioms. In practice unification problems arise in the context of axioms such as associativity and commutativity (AC) [5,11,12,28,29]. We will discuss notions of α-equivalence modulo AC [1], extensions of nominal matching and unification to deal with AC operators [2,4], and the use of nominal narrowing [3] to deal with equational theories presented by convergent nominal rewriting rules.

The talk is structured as follows: we will start with the definition of nominal logic (including the notions of fresh atom and α-equivalence) followed by a brief introduction to nominal matching and unification. We will then define nominal rewriting, a generalisation of first-order rewriting that provides in-built support for α-equivalence following the nominal approach. Finally, we will discuss algorithms for nominal unification and rewriting modulo AC operators.

References

1. Ayala-Rincón, M., de Carvalho Segundo, W., Fernández, M., Nantes-Sobrinho, D., Oliveira, A.: A formalisation of nominal α-equivalence with A, C, and AC symbols. Theoret. Comput. Sci. **781**, 3–23 (2019). https://doi.org/10.1016/j.tcs.2019.02.020
2. Ayala-Rincón, M., de Carvalho Segundo, W., Fernández, M., Silva, G.F., Nantes-Sobrinho, D.: Formalising nominal C-unification generalised with protected variables. Math. Struct. Comput. Sci. **31**(3), 286–311 (2021). https://doi.org/10.1017/S0960129521000050
3. Ayala-Rincón, M., Fernández, M., Nantes-Sobrinho, D.: Nominal narrowing. In: Kesner, D., Pientka, B. (eds.) 1st International Conference on Formal Structures for Computation and Deduction, FSCD 2016, June 22–26, 2016, Porto, Portugal. LIPIcs, vol. 52, pp. 11:1–11:17. Schloss Dagstuhl - Leibniz-Zentrum für Informatik (2016). https://doi.org/10.4230/LIPIcs.FSCD.2016.11
4. Ayala-Rincón, M., Fernández, M., Silva, G.F., Kutsia, T., Nantes-Sobrinho, D.: Nominal AC-matching. In: Dubois, C., Kerber, M. (eds.) Proceedings of the 16th

Conference on Intelligent Computer Mathematics (CICM 2023). LNAI, Springer, Cham (2023). https://doi.org/10.1007/978-3-031-42753-4_4
5. Boudet, A., Contejean, E., Devie, H.: A new AC unification algorithm with an algorithm for solving systems of diophantine equations. In: Proceedings of the Fifth Annual Symposium on Logic in Computer Science (LICS 1990), Philadelphia, Pennsylvania, USA, 4–7 June 1990, pp. 289–299. IEEE Computer Society (1990)
6. Calvès, C., Fernández, M.: A polynomial nominal unification algorithm. Theoret. Comput. Sci. **403**, 285–306 (2008)
7. Calvès, C., Fernández, M.: Matching and alpha-equivalence check for nominal terms. J. Comput. Syst. Sci. **76**(5), 283–301 (2010)
8. Calvès, C., Fernández, M.: The first-order nominal link. In: Alpuente, M. (ed.) LOPSTR 2010. LNCS, vol. 6564, pp. 234–248. Springer, Heidelberg (2011). https://doi.org/10.1007/978-3-642-20551-4_15
9. Cheney, J., Urban, C.: Alpha-prolog: a logic programming language with names, binding and alpha-equivalence. In: Demoen, B., Lifschitz, V. (eds.) ICLP 2004. LNCS, vol. 3132, pp. 269–283. Springer, Heidelberg (2004). https://doi.org/10.1007/978-3-540-27775-0_19
10. Curien, P.L., Hardin, T., Lévy, J.J.: Confluence properties of weak and strong calculi of explicit substitutions. J. ACM **43**(2), 362–397 (1996). https://citeseer.ist.psu.edu/curien96confluence.html
11. Fages, F.: Associative-commutative unification. In: Shostak, R.E. (ed.) CADE 1984. LNCS, vol. 170, pp. 194–208. Springer, New York (1984). https://doi.org/10.1007/978-0-387-34768-4_12
12. Fages, F.: Associative-commutative unification. J. Symbolic Comput. **3**(3), 257–275 (1987)
13. Fernández, M., Gabbay, M., Mackie, I.: Nominal rewriting systems. In: Moggi, E., Warren, D.S. (eds.) Proceedings of the 6th International ACM SIGPLAN Conference on Principles and Practice of Declarative Programming, 24–26 August 2004, Verona, Italy, pp. 108–119. ACM (2004). https://doi.org/10.1145/1013963.1013978
14. Fernández, M., Gabbay, M.J.: Nominal rewriting. Inf. Comput. **205**(6), 917–965 (2007)
15. Fernández, M., Gabbay, M.J.: Closed nominal rewriting and efficiently computable nominal algebra equality. In: Crary, K., Miculan, M. (eds.) Proceedings 5th International Workshop on Logical Frameworks and Meta-languages: Theory and Practice, LFMTP 2010, Edinburgh, UK, 14th July 2010. EPTCS, vol. 34, pp. 37–51 (2010). https://doi.org/10.4204/EPTCS.34.5
16. Gabbay, M.J.: Foundations of nominal techniques: logic and semantics of variables in abstract syntax. Bull. Symbolic Logic **17**, 161–229 (2011)
17. Gabbay, M.J., Pitts, A.M.: A new approach to abstract syntax with variable binding. Formal Aspects Comput. **13**(3–5), 341–363 (2001)
18. Harper, R., Honsell, F., Plotkin, G.: A framework for defining logics. JACM **40**(1), 143–184 (1993)
19. Klop, J.W., van Oostrom, V., van Raamsdonk, F.: Combinatory reduction systems: introduction and survey. Theor. Comput. Sci. **121**(1&2), 279–308 (1993)
20. Lescanne, P.: From lambda-sigma to lambda-upsilon: a journey through calculi of explicit substitutions. In: POPL, pp. 60–69. ACM (1994)
21. Levy, J., Villaret, M.: An efficient nominal unification algorithm. In: Proceedings of the 21st International Conference on Rewriting Techniques and Applications (RTA 2010). Leibniz International Proceedings in Informatics (LIPIcs), vol. 6, pp. 209–226. Schloss Dagstuhl-Leibniz-Zentrum fuer Informatik (2010)

22. Mayr, R., Nipkow, T.: Higher-order rewrite systems and their confluence. Theor. Comp. Sci. **192**, 3–29 (1998)
23. Pitts, A.M.: Nominal logic: a first order theory of names and binding. In: Kobayashi, N., Pierce, B.C. (eds.) TACS 2001. LNCS, vol. 2215, pp. 219–242. Springer, Heidelberg (2001). https://doi.org/10.1007/3-540-45500-0_11
24. Pitts, A.M.: Nominal logic, a first order theory of names and binding. Inf. Comput. **186**(2), 165–193 (2003)
25. Pitts, A.M.: Nominal Sets: Names and Symmetry in Computer Science. Cambridge UP (2013)
26. Pitts, A.M., Gabbay, M.J.: A metalanguage for programming with bound names modulo renaming. In: Backhouse, R., Oliveira, J.N. (eds.) MPC 2000. LNCS, vol. 1837, pp. 230–255. Springer, Heidelberg (2000). https://doi.org/10.1007/10722010_15
27. Stehr, M.O.: CINNI - a generic calculus of explicit substitutions and its application to λ-, ς- and π-calculi. ENTCS **36**, 70–92 (2000), Proceedings of 3rd International Workshop on Rewriting Logic and its Applications
28. Stickel, M.: A unification algorithm for associative-commutative functions. J. ACM **28**(3), 423–434 (1981)
29. Stickel, M.E.: A complete unification algorithm for associative-commutative functions. In: Advance Papers of the Fourth International Joint Conference on Artificial Intelligence, Tbilisi, Georgia, USSR, 3–8 September 1975, pp. 71–76 (1975)
30. Suzuki, T., Kikuchi, K., Aoto, T., Toyama, Y.: Confluence of orthogonal nominal rewriting systems revisited. In: Fernández, M. (ed.) 26th International Conference on Rewriting Techniques and Applications (RTA 2015). Leibniz International Proceedings in Informatics (LIPIcs), vol. 36, pp. 301–317. Schloss Dagstuhl-Leibniz-Zentrum fuer Informatik, Dagstuhl, Germany (2015). https://doi.org/10.4230/LIPIcs.RTA.2015.301, https://drops.dagstuhl.de/opus/volltexte/2015/5204
31. Urban, C., Pitts, A., Gabbay, M.: Nominal unification. In: Baaz, M., Makowsky, J.A. (eds.) CSL 2003. LNCS, vol. 2803, pp. 513–527. Springer, Heidelberg (2003). https://doi.org/10.1007/978-3-540-45220-1_41
32. Urban, C., Pitts, A.M., Gabbay, M.J.: Nominal unification. Theoret. Comput. Sci. **323**(1–3), 473–497 (2004)

Horn Clauses Analysis, Transformation and Synthesis

Design Datalog Templates for Synthesizing Bidirectional Programs from Tabular Examples

Bach Nguyen Trong[1,2(✉)], Kanae Tsushima[1,2], and Zhenjiang Hu[2,3]

[1] The Graduate University for Advanced Studies, SOKENDAI, Kanagawa, Japan
[2] National Institute of Informatics, Tokyo, Japan
{bach,k_tsushima}@nii.ac.jp
[3] School of Computer Science, Peking University, Beijing, China
huzj@pku.edu.cn

Abstract. In the database community, many synthesizers have been proposed to synthesize unidirectional programs (queries) from tabular examples, but it remains as a challenge to synthesize *bidirectional programs* (view update strategies) from examples over tables that have internal functional dependencies. In this work, we propose a systematic method to synthesize bidirectional programs from examples with functional dependencies using ProSynth. By forward propagation of functional dependencies from the source through intermediate relations to the view via a set of atomic forward programs, we show how to design Datalog templates encoding the *well-behaved view update strategies* with *minimal effects* as well as the *constraints* and *effects* imposed by the specified functional dependencies, to guide the synthesis of atomic backward programs which could be combined into a complete backward program. We have fully implemented our proposed approach in a tool called SynthBP, which is capable of automatically synthesizing bidirectional programs for 31 out of 32 practical benchmarks.

Keywords: program synthesis · bidirectional program · Datalog

1 Introduction

Datalog [5], a declarative logic programming language, is broadly used in artificial intelligence and database management due to its ability to represent complex logical rules and relationships between data. Several different techniques for synthesizing Datalog programs from examples have been proposed to help non-experts in many relation-related areas, such as relational query synthesis [23,24,28,31], data wrangling [8,16], and data migration [32,33].

One of the state-of-the-art Datalog synthesizers is ProSynth [23], which is able to use a tabular input–output example to synthesize a program written in Datalog. Since a Datalog program is largely a set of rules, ProSynth reduces the synthesis problem to a rule-selection problem by (1) requiring the preparation of

R. Glück and B. Kafle (Eds.): LOPSTR 2023, LNCS 14330, pp. 9–27, 2023.
https://doi.org/10.1007/978-3-031-45784-5_2

a fixed finite set of candidate rules by using *templates* and enumerations, and (2) selecting a subset of the prepared set that satisfies the given example. Preparing a "good" set of templates and candidate rules is very important because it forms a "good" search space where ProSynth can find an expected program.

However, ProSynth and many other synthesizers on relations cannot directly and efficiently synthesize bidirectional programs that express an important data synchronization mechanism called a *bidirectional transformation* [9]. Bidirectional transformations are used widely in many fields of computing, such as relational databases, programming languages, and software development, to provide a reliable way to maintain consistency between multiple representations [7]. A bidirectional program is normally a *well-behaved* pair of transformation programs: a *get*, which is a *forward/query* program that produces a view by querying over a source, and a *put*, which is a *backward/view update* program that produces an updated source from an original source and an updated view. The *get* and *put* programs must satisfy well-behavedness properties (Sect. 2.2) to ensure consistency [9]. In practice, many well-behaved bidirectional programs are written in Datalog [29], but it is really not easy to write them. Program synthesis with ProSynth may help overcoming the difficulty, but the tough challenge that keeps ProSynth from synthesizing a bidirectional program (get, put) is that ProSynth cannot guarantee the well-behavedness between two independently synthesized programs *get* and *put*. Naively enumerating all *get*s and *put*s and then verifying well-behavedness is typically difficult because the well-behavedness is often difficult to achieve.

We may tackle the challenge by two steps: first, we use ProSynth to synthesize *get* from examples as a set of atomic queries get_as, then, we just focus on synthesizing the corresponding well-behaved view update programs put_a by templatizing the existing *minimal well-behaved view update strategies* [13–15] as candidate rules and adapting ProSynth. The combination of all well-behaved (get_a, put_a)s is an expected well-behaved pair (get, put). Things become more complicated and difficult when the examples are defined over tables (relations) that have internal dependencies such as *functional dependencies* (FDs). If there are FDs on relation schemas, they impose some specific internal *constraints*, such as that data on a relation r must agree on the FDs of r. FDs also cause *effects* when reflecting view updates into source updates: If we run a bidirectional program backward, more changes would occur in the source so that all the data on the source would match the FDs.

In this paper, we aim at the synthesis of bidirectional programs from examples and FDs. We attach FDs to the source and forward-propagate FDs from the source to the view via the atomic get_as. Then, for each atomic part, we obtain the FDs of the corresponding source and view. Besides templates of minimal well-behaved view update strategies, we also prepare templates for the constraints and effects of FDs to enhance the search spaces of the synthesis of put_as.

The main contributions of this paper are summarized as follows:

- We introduce an algorithm to forward-propagate FDs in tree form from a source through intermediate relations to a view via get_as (Sect. 4). The FDs obtained on the source, the view and intermediate relations restrict invalid updates.
- We design Datalog templates that encode the minimal-effect view update strategies (Sect. 5) as well as the constraints and effects of FDs on relations (Sect. 6). These templates help to adapt ProSynth to synthesize the corresponding well-behaved put_as.
- We implement our proposed approach in a powerful tool called SynthBP that can automatically solve 31/32 practical synthesis benchmarks (Sect. 7).

2 Background

In this section, we briefly overview relational databases [1], non-recursive Datalog [5] and bidirectional programs [9]. We then review the concepts of FDs, the tree structure of FDs, and relation revisions over that structure when updating relational views [4]. Finally, we present the Datalog synthesizer ProSynth [23].

2.1 Relational Databases and NR-Datalog

- *Relational databases* A database $\mathcal{D}$ is a finite map from relation schemas $\mathbb{R}$ to relations r. A *relation schema* is a finite nonempty set $\mathbb{R}$ of *attributes*. Each attribute A of a relation schema $\mathbb{R}$ is associated with a domain $dom(A)$ (or $\mathbb{A}$), which represents the possible values a that could appear in column A. If X and Y are attribute sets, we may write XY for the union $X \cup Y$. If $X = \{A_1, A_2, \ldots, A_m\}$, we may write $A_1 A_2 \ldots A_m$ for X. The singleton $\{A\}$ may be written as simply A. A *tuple* t (alternatively written as $\langle t_1, \ldots, t_k \rangle$) over $\mathbb{R}$, written $t :: \mathbb{R}$, is a function $t : \mathbb{R} \to \bigcup_{A \in \mathbb{R}} \mathbb{A}$, where $\forall A \in \mathbb{R}.\ t(A) \in \mathbb{A}$. We write $t[X]$ for the projection of a tuple t over X of $\mathbb{R}$ if $X \subseteq \mathbb{R}$. A *relation* R over $\mathbb{R}$, written $R :: \mathbb{R}$, is a finite set of tuples over $\mathbb{R}$. We sometimes write $R(A_1 : \mathbb{A}_1, \ldots, A_m : \mathbb{A}_m)$ for $R :: A_1 \ldots A_m$.
- *NR-Datalog* NR-Datalog [5] is a fragment of Datalog with negation, built-in predicates of comparison, and no direct or indirect recursion. An NR-Datalog program P is a finite nonempty set of *clauses*, where each clause is either a *fact* "$R(c_1, \ldots, c_n)$." or a *rule* "H :− $B_1, \ldots, B_n$.", where R is a *relation symbol*, the c_is are constants, H is a *head*, and $\{B_1, \ldots, B_n\}$ is a *body*. The head H is a *positive literal* (or *atom*) of the form $R(t_1, \ldots, t_n)$ (or written as $R(\overrightarrow{t})$), where R is a relation symbol and each argument t_i is either a variable or a constant. Each B_i in the body is either a positive literal $R(\overrightarrow{t})$, or a *negative literal* $\neg\ R(\overrightarrow{t})$, or a *constraint* $t_1 \oplus t_2$ (i.e., a literal $\oplus(t_1, t_2)$ where $\oplus$ is a built-in relational symbol of comparisons). A variable occurring exactly once in a rule could be conventionally replaced by an anonymous variable denoted as "_". A single-line rule of form "H :− $B_1; \ldots; B_n$." is a short expression of n rules "H :− B_1.",…,"H :− B_n.".

2.2 Bidirectional Program

A bidirectional program [9,30] consists of a pair of transformation programs – a forward $get :: \mathbb{S} \rightarrow \mathbb{V}$, which produces a view over a source, and a backward $put :: \mathbb{S} \times \mathbb{V} \rightarrow \mathbb{S}$, which reflects the changes to a view back to the source – and this pair must satisfy the following *well-behavedness* properties:

$$\forall S.\ put(S,\ get(S)) = S \quad [\text{GETPUT}]$$
$$\forall S, V'.\ get(put(S, V')) = V' \quad [\text{PUTGET}]$$

The GETPUT states that if one gets a view $V = get(S)$ from a source S and puts it back again, S will not change; the PUTGET states that an updated view V' can be fully restored by applying *get* over the updated source $S' = put(S, V')$.

A bidirectional program (get, put) can be written in NR-Datalog [29], where writing a *get* is like writing a relational query, while writing a *put* requires the use of delta relations [10,11,29] to represent updates to the source. A delta relation $\Delta R :: \Delta\mathbb{R}$ is a pair $(\Delta R^-, \Delta R^+)$ where $\Delta R^- :: \mathbb{R}$ and $\Delta R^+ :: \mathbb{R}$, respectively, capture insertions and deletions against R.

Example 1. We can write a program $get = \{r_1^b\}$ to define a view $V = \{\langle 1\rangle, \langle 3\rangle\}$ of schema $V(Num)$ over a source $S = \{\langle 1, 2\rangle, \langle 3, 4\rangle\}$ of schema $S(Num,\ Num)$.

$$r_1^b\ \ V(v_1)\ :-\ S(v_1, v_2).$$

If the view is changed to $V' = \{\langle 1\rangle, \langle 5\rangle)\}$, to propagate the update, we can write a program $put = \{r_2^b, r_3^b, r_4^b\}$ that takes S and V' as input where

$$r_2^b\ \ \Delta S^-(v_1, v_2)\ :-\ S(v_1, v_2)\ ,\ \neg\ V'(v_1).$$
$$r_3^b\ \ \Delta S^+(v_1, v_2)\ :-\ V'(v_1)\ ,\ \neg\ S(v_1, v_2)\ ,\ v_2 = 0.$$
$$r_4^b\ \ S'(v_1, v_2)\ :-\ S(v_1, v_2),\ \neg\ \Delta S^-(v_1, v_2)\ ;\ \Delta S^+(v_1, v_2).$$

Each rule for computing ΔS (e.g. r_2^b and r_3^b) describes a *view update strategy.* A run of *put* evaluates $\Delta S^- = \{\langle 3, 4\rangle\}$ and $\Delta S^+ = \{\langle 5, 0\rangle\}$, then outputs $S' = \{\langle 1, 2\rangle, \langle 5, 0\rangle\}$. We can either manually verify the well-behavedness or adapt an automated tool called BIRDS [29] to perform the verification. ▲

2.3 Functional Dependencies: Constraints and Effects

A *functional dependency* over $\mathbb{R}$ is written as $X \rightarrow Y :: \mathbb{R}$, where $X \subseteq \mathbb{R}$ and $Y \subseteq \mathbb{R}$. If $X \rightarrow Y :: \mathbb{R}$ and $R :: \mathbb{R}$, we say that R satisfies *constraints* $X \rightarrow Y$, written $R \models X \rightarrow Y$, if $t_1[X] = t_2[X]$ implies $t_1[Y] = t_2[Y]$ for all $t_1, t_2 \in R$. It is conventional to write FD $A \rightarrow BC$ to mean FD $\{A\} \rightarrow \{B, C\}$. Let $\mathcal{F}$ be a set of FDs over $\mathbb{R}$, written $\mathcal{F} :: \mathbb{R}$. We write $R \models \mathcal{F}$ to mean that $\forall X \rightarrow Y \in \mathcal{F}.\ R \models X \rightarrow Y$. We can normalize $X \rightarrow Y$ as $\{X \rightarrow A_i\}_{A_i \in Y}$.

Bohannon et al. [4] introduced a special structure of FDs called a *tree form,* in which they can construct properly bidirectional programs with FDs. Given an FD set $\mathcal{F}$, let $V_{\mathcal{F}} = \{X \mid X \rightarrow Y \in \mathcal{F}\} \cup \{Y \mid X \rightarrow Y \in \mathcal{F}\}$ and $E_{\mathcal{F}} =$

$\{(X,Y) \mid X \to Y \in \mathcal{F}\}$; then, we say $\mathcal{F}$ is in *tree form* if the directed graph $T_{\mathcal{F}} = (V_{\mathcal{F}}, E_{\mathcal{F}})$ is a forest and no distinct nodes of T_F have common attributes. If $\mathcal{F}$ is in tree form, we write $roots(\mathcal{F})$ and $leaves(\mathcal{F})$ for the sets of root and leaf nodes in $T_{\mathcal{F}}$, respectively. Every $\mathcal{F}$ in tree form has a unique *canonical tree from* $\mathcal{F}^*$ where $size(X) = 1$ for all $X \in leaves(\mathcal{F})$.

To calculate the *effects* of FDs putting changes from a view to a source, Bohannon et al. [4] introduced revision operators. Given an FD set $\mathcal{F} :: \mathbb{R}$ and relations $R_1, R_2 :: \mathbb{R}$ such that $R_1 \models \mathcal{F}$, a relation revision $R_1 \leftarrow_{\mathcal{F}} R_2$ [4] computes a new relation $R_1^* :: \mathbb{R}$ similar to R_1 whose tuples do not conflict with those of R_2 on $\mathcal{F}$. For example, given $\mathbb{R} = AB$, $\mathcal{F} = \{A \to B\}$, $R_1 = \{\langle 1, b_2\rangle, \langle 2, b_1\rangle, \langle 3, b_3\rangle\}$, and $R_2 = \{\langle 2, b_2\rangle, \langle 4, b_4\rangle\}$, we have that $R_1 \leftarrow_{\mathcal{F}} R_2$ computes $R_1^* = \{\langle 1, b_2\rangle, \underline{\langle 2, b_2\rangle}, \langle 3, b_3\rangle\}$.

The relation revision operation $R_1 \leftarrow_{\mathcal{F}} R_2 = \{t_1 \leftarrow_{\mathcal{F}} R_2 \mid t_1 \in R_1\}$ is expressed by a set of tuple revisions $t_1 \leftarrow_{\mathcal{F}} R_2$, where $t_1 \in R_1$, $R_1 :: \mathbb{R}, R_2 :: \mathbb{R}$, and $\mathcal{F} :: \mathbb{R}$ is an FD set in tree form such that $R_1 \models \mathcal{F}$. Tuple revision $t_1 \leftarrow_{\mathcal{F}} R_2$ [4] can be defined by recursion over the forest $T_{\mathcal{F}}$ that indicates the update propagation from the roots to the leaves:

$$
\begin{aligned}
& t_1 \leftarrow_{\emptyset} R_2 = t_1 \\
& t_1 \leftarrow_{\{X \to Y\} \cup \mathcal{F}'} R_2 = \begin{cases} (t_1 \leftharpoondown t_2[Y]) \leftarrow_{\mathcal{F}'} R_2 & \text{if } \exists\, t_2 \in R_2.\ t_1[X] = t_2[X] \\ t_1 \leftarrow_{\mathcal{F}'} R_2 & \text{otherwise} \end{cases} \\
& \text{where } X \in roots(\mathcal{F}) \text{ and } \mathcal{F} = \{X \to Y\} \cup \mathcal{F}'
\end{aligned}
$$

If $\mathcal{F}$ is empty, tuple revision simply returns t_1. Otherwise, there must be at least one FD $X \to Y$ where $X \in roots(T_{\mathcal{F}})$. If t_1 and some $t_2 \in R_2$ have the same values against X, we return a copy of t_1 whose $t_1[Y]$ has been updated according to $t_2[Y]$ (written as $t_1 \leftharpoondown t_2[Y]$); otherwise, t_1 is returned. The remaining FDs continue to be considered recursively.

From the definitions of revisions, we have:

$$
\begin{aligned}
& R_1 \leftarrow_{\emptyset} R_2 = R_1 \\
& R_1 \leftarrow_{\{X \to Y\} \cup \mathcal{F}'} R_2 = (R_1 \leftarrow_{\{X \to Y\}} R_2) \leftarrow_{\mathcal{F}'} R_2
\end{aligned}
$$

2.4 ProSynth

ProSynth [23] is a modern program-by-example tool for synthesizing a Datalog program P, which is consistent with one tabular input–output example E on relations. ProSynth asks the user to provide a fixed finite set of candidate rules P_{all}, then reduces the synthesis to selecting a subset P of P_{all} such that P satisfies E. Each rule in P_{all} is associated with a Boolean variable that describes whether the rule is selected or not. ProSynth uses counterexample-guided inductive synthesis (CEGIS) [26] with a SAT solver to suggest a selection of rules and a Datalog solver Souffle [12] to check whether the selection agrees on E. Its algorithm uses provenances obtained from Souffle to learn the constraints for the SAT solver. A difficult challenge when using ProSynth is to prepare a "good" P_{all} for a specific problem. In fact, PROSYNTH only prepares candidate rules by instantiating meta-rules (*templates*) that describe common Datalog rules and enumerating the body of meta-rules by length [23]. PROSYNTH cannot trivially synthesize bidirectional programs on relations. It also cannot directly deal with the constraints and effects of FDs if the prepared set P_{all} is not good enough.

3 Overview

In this section, we present an overview of our proposed approach. Consider a specification $(\mathcal{S}, \mathcal{E})$, where $\mathcal{S}$ includes two schemas, a source S and a view V,

$$s_1^o \;\; S(A:\mathbb{A}, B:\mathbb{B}, C:\mathbb{C}, D:\mathbb{D}, \mathcal{F}_S = \{A \to B, A \to D\})$$
$$s_2^o \;\; V(A_V:\mathbb{A}, B_V:\mathbb{B}, C_V:\mathbb{C})$$

and $\mathcal{E}$ is a tabular example including the original source table T_S, the updated source table $T_{S'}$, the original view table T_V and the updated view table $T_{V'}$. Based on $\mathcal{E}$, we have two examples of *get*: $(input = T_S, output = T_V)$ and $(input = T_{S'}, output = T_{V'})$ and one example of *put*: $(input = (T_S, T_{V'}), output = T_{S'})$. We require the user to explicitly provide the possible FDs in tree form for relation S of the source to avoid delving into the efficient discovery of essential FDs, which is a well-known difficult challenge in database research [22].

Suppose we have a set of atomic queries get_as that constitute a query *get*, which satisfies two given examples, for instance,

$$r_1^o \;\; M_1(v_0, v_1, v_2) :- S(v_0, v_1, v_2, v_3).$$
$$r_2^o \;\; M_2(v_0, v_1, v_2) :- M_1(v_0, v_1, v_2)\ ,\ v_2 = \text{“}T\text{”}.$$
$$r_3^o \;\; V(v_0, v_1, v_2) \;\; :- M_2(v_0, v_1, v_2).$$

We possibly achieve this by adapting PROSYNTH with a set of candidate rules for relational queries and then decomposing the resulting synthesized query into atomic queries. If we evaluate the set of get_as on the original and updated source tables, one by one, we can obtain examples of all atomic pairs (get_a, put_a)s.

Our approach is to adapt PROSYNTH to synthesize the corresponding atomic put_as that could be then combined into a complete view update program *put*. To perform such synthesis, we design the well-behaved templates for put_a given get_a and generate candidates from these templates. A put_a synthesized from such candidates would form with the corresponding get_a a well-behaved bidirectional program. The combination of all well-behaved (get_a, put_a)s is an expected well-behaved pair (get, put) [9]. We focus on three main procedures in this paper.

1. Forward-propagating FDs from the source to the view via atomic queries. We can obtain the following schemas with FDs using $\mathcal{F}_S$ and $\{r_1^o, r_2^o, r_3^o\}$:

$$s_3^o \;\; M_1(A_{M_1}:\mathbb{A}, B_{M_1}:\mathbb{B}, C_{M_1}:\mathbb{C}, \mathcal{F}_{M_1} = \{A_{M_1} \to B_{M_1}\})$$
$$s_4^o \;\; M_2(A_{M_2}:\mathbb{A}, B_{M_2}:\mathbb{B}, C_{M_2}:\mathbb{C}, \mathcal{F}_{M_2} = \{A_{M_2} \to B_{M_2}\})$$
$$s_5^o \;\; V(A_V:\mathbb{A}, B_V:\mathbb{B}, C_V:\mathbb{C}, \mathcal{F}_V = \{A_V \to B_V\})$$

Table 1. An example of an atomic program (get_a, put_a)

M_1

A	B	C
1	b_1	F
1	b_1	T
2	b_2	T

M_2

A	B	C
1	b_1	T
2	b_2	T

M'_1

A	B	C
1	b_2	F
1	b_2	T
2	b_2	T

M'_2

A	B	C
1	b_2	T
2	b_2	T

We use the terms A_{M_1} and B_{M_2} to precisely describe attributes in the intermediate relations, but they could be correspondingly simplified as A and B.

2. Templatizing view update strategies with minimal effects for well-behaved put_a given get_a. This is based on the existing set of minimal strategies for updating atomic views in [13–15]. Let us consider the atomic query r_2^o (temporarily called get_a) that defines the view M_2 by a selection on the source M_1. Suppose we want to find a put_a such that (get_a, put_a) is well-behaved and satisfies the example in Table 1. We prepare candidate clauses for minimal (basic) view update strategies against a σ-rule (Table 2) described by get_a as follows:

$$
\begin{array}{lll}
r_4^o & Fr(\text{“\_r\_”}) & :-\ M'_2(\_, \_, v_2)\ ,\ v_2 \neq \text{“}T\text{”}. \\
r_5^o & \Delta M_1^-(v_0, v_1, v_2) & :-\ \neg M'_2(v_0, v_1, v_2)\ ,\ M_1(v_0, v_1, v_2)\ ,\ v_2 = \text{“}T\text{”}. \\
r_6^o & \Delta M_1^+(v_0, v_1, v_2) & :-\ M'_2(v_0, v_1, v_2)\ ,\ \neg M_1(v_0, v_1, v_2)\ ,\ v_2 = \text{“}T\text{”}. \\
r_7^o & M'_1(v_0, v_1, v_2) & :-\ M_1(v_0, v_1, v_2)\ ,\ \neg \Delta M_1^-(v_0, v_1, v_2)\ ;\ \Delta M_1^+(v_0, v_1, v_2).
\end{array}
$$

Note that a special relation Fr will flag a rejection with the value "_r_" if there is a tuple in M'_2 violating the constraints imposed on the view by the query get_a.

3. Templatizing constraints and effects of the specified FDs against put_a. We first prepare additional rules describing the constraints of $\mathcal{F}_{M_1}$, for instance,

$$
\begin{array}{ll}
r_8^o & Fr(\text{“\_r\_”}) :-\ M_1(v_1, v_2, \_)\ ,\ M_1(v_1, v_2^x, \_)\ ,\ v_2 \neq v_2^x. \\
r_9^o & Fr(\text{“\_r\_”}) :-\ M'_1(v_1, v_2, \_)\ ,\ M'_1(v_1, v_2^x, \_)\ ,\ v_2 \neq v_2^x.
\end{array}
$$

Rule r_8^o means that a rejection will occur if there are two tuples in M_1 such that the first attribute values are the same but the second attribute values are different. This is similar to the meaning of FD $A_{M_1} \rightarrow B_{M_1}$ in $\mathcal{F}_{M_1}$. Rule r_9^o can be understood similarly, but for M'_1, which shares the same schema as M_1.

The effects of $\mathcal{F}_{M_1} = \{A_{M_1} \rightarrow B_{M_1}\}$ when performing the view update could be interpreted as follows: if there is a new tuple t added to M_1, then all other tuples in M'_1 should follow t on $\mathcal{F}_{M_1}$. In other words, if a tuple t^x in M_1 conflicts with t, then we need strategies to resolve the conflict so that all data in M'_1 agree on $\mathcal{F}_{M_1}$. Essentially, such a conflict could be resolved by either deleting t^x from M_1 or revising t^x as revision operators do (Sect. 2.3).

To templatize these strategies, we design templates encoding the effects of FDs over the source delta, which have been computed from the basic (minimal-effect) candidate rules. Simply put, we consider the generated basic rules as the base rules ΔS_b (e.g. change ΔM_1^- and ΔM_1^+ in r_5^o and r_6^o into ΔM_{1b}^- and ΔM_{1b}^+, respectively), and we add more rules about the effects of FDs over the data in ΔS_b. We could templatize the strategy of deleting the conflicts as $\mathcal{F}_{M_1} = \{A_{M_1} \rightarrow B_{M_1}\}$ with the following rules:

$$
\begin{array}{lll}
r_{10}^o & M_{1d}^{\mathcal{F}}(v_0, v_1, v_2) & :-\ \Delta M_{1b}^+(v_0, v_1^x, \_)\ ,\ M_1(v_0, v_1, v_2)\ ,\ v_1 \neq v_1^x. \\
r_{11}^o & \Delta M_1^-(v_0, v_1, v_2) & :-\ \Delta M_{1b}^-(v_0, v_1, v_2). \\
r_{12}^o & \Delta M_1^-(v_0, v_1, v_2) & :-\ M_{1d}^{\mathcal{F}}(v_0, v_1, v_2).
\end{array}
$$

Rule r_{10}^o computes $M_{1d}^{\mathcal{F}}$ containing all tuples in M_1 that conflict with some basic inserted tuple to M_1 (in ΔM_{1b}^+) on FD $A_{M_1} \rightarrow B_{M_1}$. There will be more rules like r_{10}^o if $\mathcal{F}_{M_1}$ has more FDs. The next two rules say that a tuple in ΔM_1^- (i.e., a tuple that should be deleted from M_1) is in either ΔM_{1b}^- (which keeps the basic deletions) or $M_{1d}^{\mathcal{F}}$ (which keeps the conflicting tuples).

Algorithm 1: Forward-Propagating FDs

procedure FORWARDPROPAGATEFDS($\mathcal{S}, \mathcal{D}$):
  $visited \leftarrow dict\{r : False \text{ for } r \in \mathcal{D}\}$
  $Q \leftarrow \emptyset$
  $R \leftarrow$ a set of relation names occurring in $\mathcal{D}$
  for $r \in \mathcal{S}$ **do**
    if r *is a source* **then** $Q, R \leftarrow Q \cup \{\text{NAME}(r)\}, R - \{\text{NAME}(r)\}$
  while $R \neq \emptyset$ **do**
    $R_f \leftarrow \{r \mid r \in \mathcal{D} \wedge visited[r] = False\}$
    for $r \in R_f$ **do**
      if $\text{NAME}(\text{HEAD}(r)) \notin Q \wedge \text{NAME}(\text{BODYLITERAL}(r)) \subseteq Q$ **then**
        $\mathcal{S} \leftarrow \text{PROPAGATEFDS-A}(\mathcal{S}, r)$
        $Q, R \leftarrow Q \cup \{\text{NAME}(\text{HEAD}(r))\}, R - \{\text{NAME}(\text{HEAD}(r))\}$
        $visited[r] = True$
  return $\mathcal{S}$ *as* $\mathcal{S}_f$

Templatizing strategies for revising conflicts is more complex since we have to translate the formal implementation of revision operators defined recursively over FDs in tree form to NR-Datalog rules, which have no tree form. We will be more specific regarding the gaps in Sect. 6.2.

4 Forward-Propagating FDs

Suppose that we have a set $\mathcal{D}$ of atomic queries get_as that form a query *get* satisfying the given example. The first two columns of Table 2 show possible forms of atomic rules in $\mathcal{D}$, including the ρ-*rule*, $\cup$-*rule*, $\backslash$-*rule*, $\cap$-*rule*, σ-*rule*, π-*rule*, $\bowtie$-*rule*, and $\times$-*rule*, which define renaming, union, difference, intersection, selection, projection, and natural join and cross product views, respectively. Note in particular that (1) each constraint in a σ-*rule* is a comparison between a variable and a constant; (2) a π-*rule* only defines a proper projection; and (3) a $\times$-*rule* defines the cross product between a general relation S and a relation $V^{1\times m}$, which is expressed by equality constraints.

Algorithm 1 describes how to forward-propagate FDs from the source to the view. The procedure FORWARDPROPAGATEFDS takes as input a set of schemas $\mathcal{S}$ (of the source, the view and intermediate relations) and a set of atomic rules $\mathcal{D}$ and produces as output the updated set of schemas $\mathcal{S}_f$ with FDs computed for each relation. We say a relation is *processed* (*unprocessed*) if its FDs are (not) computed, and a rule is *visited* (*unvisited*) if (not) all relations appearing in the rule are processed.

FORWARDPROPAGATEFDS uses a key-value dictionary *visited* to check if a rule has been visited and two sets R and Q that include the names of unprocessed and processed relations, respectively. Initially, all values of *visited* are *False*, Q is empty, and R contains all relation names in $\mathcal{D}$ (lines 2–4). Because source relations have FDs given by users, those source names are added to Q and removed from R (lines 5–6). Then, as long as there is an unprocessed relation, a loop of propagating FDs (lines 7–13) will be executed. For each atomic and unvisited rule r in $\mathcal{D}$, if all relations appearing in the body of r (*rhs*) are processed and the relation appearing in the head of r (*lhs*) is unprocessed, PROPAGATEFDS-A is invoked to propagate FDs from the *rhs* to the *lhs* of the atomic rule r. Then, the relation in *lhs* is processed, and its name should be added to Q and removed from R. The rule r is also set to be visited.

Table 2. Forward propagation of FDs for atomic rules

Type	Atomic Rule r	Schema & Mapping	FDs: $\mathcal{F}_V$
ρ	$V(x_1,\ldots,x_n) :- S(y_1,\ldots,y_n).$ where $(x_1,\ldots,x_n) = \rho(y_1,\ldots,y_n)$ ρ is a permutation function	$\mathbb{S} = A_1^y A_2^y \ldots A_n^y$ $\mathbb{V} = A_1 A_2 \ldots A_n$ $\mathcal{M}_r[A_j^y] = A_i$ if $\exists i.\ y_j = x_i$	$\mathcal{F}_V = \text{ADAPTATTR}(\mathcal{F}_S, \mathcal{M}_r)$
$\cup$	$V(x_1,\ldots,x_n) :- S_1(x_1,\ldots,x_n);$ $S_2(x_1,\ldots,x_n).$	$\mathbb{S}_1 = \mathbb{S}_2 = \mathbb{V} = A_1 A_2 \ldots A_n$ $\mathcal{M}_r[A_j] = A_j$	$\mathcal{F}_V = \emptyset$
$\setminus$	$V(x_1,\ldots,x_n) :- S_1(x_1,\ldots,x_n),$ $\neg\ S_2(x_1,\ldots,x_n).$	$\mathbb{S}_1 = \mathbb{S}_2 = \mathbb{V} = A_1 A_2 \ldots A_n$ $\mathcal{M}_r[A_j] = A_j$	$\mathcal{F}_V = \text{ADAPTATTR}(\mathcal{F}_{S_1}, \mathcal{M}_r)$
$\cap$	$V(x_1,\ldots,x_n) :- S_1(x_1,\ldots,x_n),$ $S_2(x_1,\ldots,x_n).$	$\mathbb{S}_1 = \mathbb{S}_2 = \mathbb{V} = A_1 A_2 \ldots A_n$ $\mathcal{M}_r[A_j] = A_j$	$\mathcal{F}_V = \text{ADAPTATTR}(\mathcal{F}_{S_1}, \mathcal{M}_r)$ $\cup\text{ADAPTATTR}(\mathcal{F}_{S_2}, \mathcal{M}_r)$
σ	$V(x_1,\ldots,x_n) :- S(x_1,\ldots,x_n),$ $v_1 \oplus c_1,\ldots,v_m \oplus c_m.$ where $m > 0, \{v_1,\ldots,v_m\} \subseteq \{x_1,\ldots,x_n\}$	$\mathbb{S} = \mathbb{V} = A_1 A_2 \ldots A_n$ $\mathcal{M}_r[A_j] = A_j$	$\mathcal{F}_V = \text{ADAPTATTR}(\mathcal{F}_S, \mathcal{M}_r)$
π	$V(x_1,\ldots,x_m) :- S(y_1,\ldots,y_n).$ where $\{x_1,\ldots,x_m\} \subsetneq \{y_1,\ldots,y_n\}$	$\mathbb{S} = A_1^y A_2^y \ldots A_n^y$ $\mathbb{V} = A_1 A_2 \ldots A_n$ $\mathcal{M}_r[A_j^y] = A_i$ if $\exists i. y_j = x_i$ else *null*	$\mathcal{F}_V = \text{ADAPTATTR}($ $\text{REPAIRTREE}(\mathcal{F}_S, \mathcal{M}_r)$ $)$
$\bowtie$	$V(x_1,\ldots,x_m) :- S_1(y_1,\ldots,y_n),$ $S_2(v_1,\ldots,v_o).$ where $\{y_1,\ldots,y_n\} \cup \{v_1,\ldots,v_o\} = \{x_1,\ldots,x_m\},$ $\{y_1,\ldots,y_n\} \cap \{v_1,\ldots,v_o\} \neq \emptyset$	$\mathbb{S}_1 = A_1^y A_2^y \ldots A_n^y$ $\mathbb{S}_2 = A_1^v A_2^v \ldots A_o^v$ $\mathbb{V} = A_1 A_2 \ldots A_m$ $\mathcal{M}_r[A_j^y] = A_i$ if $\exists i.\ y_j = x_i$ $\mathcal{M}_r[A_j^v] = A_i$ if $\exists i.\ v_j = x_i$	$\mathcal{F}_V = \text{ADAPTATTR}(\mathcal{F}_{S_1}, \mathcal{M}_r)$ $\cup\text{ADAPTATTR}(\mathcal{F}_{S_2}, \mathcal{M}_r)$
$\times$	$V(x_1,\ldots,x_{m+n}) :- S_1(y_1,\ldots,y_n),$ $v_1 = c_1,\ldots,v_m = c_m.$ where $\{y_1,\ldots,y_n\} \cup \{v_1,\ldots,v_m\} = \{x_1,\ldots,x_{m+n}\},$ $\{y_1,\ldots,y_n\} \cap \{v_1,\ldots,v_m\} = \emptyset$	$\mathbb{S}_1 = A_1^y A_2^y \ldots A_n^y$ $dom(v_1) = A_1^v,\ldots,dom(v_m) = A_m^v$ $\mathbb{V} = A_1 A_2 \ldots A_{m+n}$ $\mathcal{M}_r[A_j^y] = A_i$ if $\exists i.\ y_j = x_i$ $\mathcal{M}_r[A_j^v] = A_i$ if $\exists i.\ v_j = x_i$	$\mathcal{F}_V = \text{ADAPTATTR}(\mathcal{F}_S, \mathcal{M}_r)$

Table 2 denotes the result of invoking the subprocedure PROPAGATEFDS-A for each atomic rule r with view V and source S (or (S_1, S_2)). We write $\mathcal{F}_X$ as the FD set against a relation X, $\mathcal{M}_r$ as an attribute mapping of a rule r that maps attributes in the rule body to attributes in the rule head, and ADAPTATTR$(\mathcal{F}_{\mathcal{X}}, \mathcal{M}_r)$ as a function that revises $\mathcal{F}_{\mathcal{X}}$ following $\mathcal{M}_r$.

Example 2. ($\pi - rule$) $V(v_1, v_2, v_3)$: $-S(v_0, v_1, v_2, v_3)$ where $\mathbb{S} = ABCD$, $\mathcal{F}_S = \{B \to A, B \to C, A \to D\}$, $\mathbb{V} = A_1A_2A_3$. We have $\mathcal{M}_r[A] = null, \mathcal{M}_r[B] = A_1, \mathcal{M}_r[C] = A_2, \mathcal{M}_r[D] = A_3$, and $\mathcal{F}_V = \{A_1 \to A_2, A_1 \to A_3\}$. When attribute A is dropped from the source S, before adapting the attributes with respect to the view V, we need to repair the tree form of the FDs by deleting all edges related to A (e.g., $B \to A$, $A \to D$) and possibly adding edges from A's parents to A's children (e.g., $B \to D$) if A is not at a root. ▲

5 Templatizing Minimal-Effect View Update Strategies

Based on the domain knowledge in the database community [13–15], there is a complete and finite set of strategies with *minimal effects* for well-behaved put_a if get_a is an atomic query. We will encode these minimal-effect view update strategies as Datalog templates and use the templates to generate a fixed set of candidate rules for the synthesis of put_a with PROSYNTH.

Given a $get_a :: \mathbb{S} \to \mathbb{V}$, the program $put_a :: (\mathbb{S}, \mathbb{V}) \to \mathbb{S}$, which takes (S, V') as input, could be constructed as a set $P_{\Delta S}$ including Datalog clauses that compute ΔS from (S, V'), and one more rule to compute the updated source S' as follows:

$$r_1^m \;\; S'(\overrightarrow{x}) : -\; S(\overrightarrow{x}),\; \neg\; \Delta S^-(\overrightarrow{x})\; ;\; \Delta S^+(\overrightarrow{x}).$$

Figure 1 details our well-designed templates for minimal-effect strategies. For an atomic query of type α, there are three basic types of templates: (1) $(\text{SDR})^\alpha$ including rules that describe strategies for $P_{\Delta S}$; (2) $(\text{AR})^\alpha$ including *possible* facts of auxiliary relations used in $(\text{SDR})^\alpha$; and (3) $(\text{FR})^\alpha$ including *possible* rules against a special flag relation Fr for verifying the imposed constraints. While the clauses in $(\text{AR})^\alpha$ and $(\text{FR})^\alpha$ are all fixed in a possible result, the rules in $(\text{SDR})^\alpha$ are selectable and only selected in the output by synthesis.

In Sect. 3, we follow these templates to generate Datalog clauses that describe minimal-effect view update strategies against a σ-rule. Next, we explore templates for a $\cup$-*rule* defining a union view V from two sources S_1 and S_2. Each rule in $(\text{SDR})^\cup$ describes a view update strategy. If a tuple $\overrightarrow{x}$ is not in the updated view V', $\overrightarrow{x}$ should disappear from both S_1 and S_2, which is encoded in the first rule of $(\text{SDR})^\cup$:

$$r_2^m \;\; \Delta S_i^-(\overrightarrow{x}) : -\; \neg\; V'(\overrightarrow{x})\; ,\; S_i(\overrightarrow{x}).$$

If $\overrightarrow{x}$ is in V', $\overrightarrow{x}$ should either appear in S_1 or appear in S_2 or appear in both S_1 and S_2. If $\overrightarrow{x}$ is newly inserted into the view, there are three different update

ρ-rule $V(\overrightarrow{x}) :- S(p(\overrightarrow{x}))$.
$(\text{SDR})^{\rho} : \Delta S^{+}, \Delta S^{-}$
$\Delta S^{+}(p(\overrightarrow{x})) :- V'(\overrightarrow{x}) , \neg S(p(\overrightarrow{x}))$.
$\Delta S^{-}(p(\overrightarrow{x})) :- \neg V'(\overrightarrow{x}) , S(p(\overrightarrow{x}))$.

∪-rule $V(\overrightarrow{x}) :- S_1(\overrightarrow{x}) ; S_2(\overrightarrow{x})$.
$(\text{SDR})^{\cup} : \Delta S_i^{+}, \Delta S_i^{-}, i \in \{1,2\}$
$\Delta S_i^{-}(\overrightarrow{x}) :- \neg V'(\overrightarrow{x}) , S_i(\overrightarrow{x})$.
$\Delta S_i^{+}(\overrightarrow{x}) :- V'(\overrightarrow{x}) , \neg S_i(\overrightarrow{x}) , \neg S_{3-i}(\overrightarrow{x})$.
$\Delta S_i^{+}(\overrightarrow{x}) :- V'(\overrightarrow{x}) , \neg S_i(\overrightarrow{x}) , \neg S_{3-i}(\overrightarrow{x}) , Au_{\cup}^{*}(\overrightarrow{x})$.
$\Delta S_i^{+}(\overrightarrow{x}) :- V'(\overrightarrow{x}) , \neg S_i(\overrightarrow{x}) , \neg S_{3-i}(\overrightarrow{x}) , \neg Au_{\cup}^{*}(\overrightarrow{x})$.
$(\text{AR})^{\cup} : Au_{\cup}^{*} \in \{Au_{\cup}^{1}, Au_{\cup}^{2}, Au_{\cup}^{12}\}$
$Au_{\cup}^{1} = \{t \text{ for } t \in \mathcal{E}_{\cup}|_{V'} - \mathcal{E}_{\cup}|_{V} \text{ if } t \in \mathcal{E}_{\cup}|_{\Delta S_1^{+}} \wedge t \notin \mathcal{E}_{\cup}|_{\Delta S_2^{+}}\}$
$Au_{\cup}^{2} = \{t \text{ for } t \in \mathcal{E}_{\cup}|_{V'} - \mathcal{E}_{\cup}|_{V} \text{ if } t \in \mathcal{E}_{\cup}|_{\Delta S_2^{+}} \wedge t \notin \mathcal{E}_{\cup}|_{\Delta S_1^{+}}\}$
$Au_{\cup}^{12} = \{t \text{ for } t \in \mathcal{E}_{\cup}|_{V'} - \mathcal{E}_{\cup}|_{V} \text{ if } t \in \mathcal{E}_{\cup}|_{\Delta S_1^{+}} \wedge t \in \mathcal{E}_{\cup}|_{\Delta S_2^{+}}\}$

\\-rule $V(\overrightarrow{x}) :- S_1(\overrightarrow{x}) , \neg S_2(\overrightarrow{x})$.
$(\text{SDR})^{\setminus} : \Delta S_i^{+}, \Delta S_i^{-}, i \in \{1,2\}$
$\Delta S_1^{+}(\overrightarrow{x}) :- V'(\overrightarrow{x}) , \neg S_1(\overrightarrow{x})$.
$\Delta S_2^{-}(\overrightarrow{x}) :- V'(\overrightarrow{x}) , S_2(\overrightarrow{x})$.
$\Delta S_1^{-}(\overrightarrow{x}) :- \neg V'(\overrightarrow{x}) , S_1(\overrightarrow{x}) , \neg S_2(\overrightarrow{x})$.
$\Delta S_2^{+}(\overrightarrow{x}) :- \neg V'(\overrightarrow{x}) , \neg S_2(\overrightarrow{x}) , S_1(\overrightarrow{x})$.
$\Delta S_1^{-}(\overrightarrow{x}) :- \neg V'(\overrightarrow{x}) , S_1(\overrightarrow{x}) , \neg S_2(\overrightarrow{x}) , Au_{\setminus}^{*}(\overrightarrow{x})$.
$\Delta S_1^{-}(\overrightarrow{x}) :- \neg V'(\overrightarrow{x}) , S_1(\overrightarrow{x}) , \neg S_2(\overrightarrow{x}) , \neg Au_{\setminus}^{*}(\overrightarrow{x})$.
$\Delta S_2^{+}(\overrightarrow{x}) :- \neg V'(\overrightarrow{x}) , \neg S_2(\overrightarrow{x}) , S_1(\overrightarrow{x}) , Au_{\setminus}^{*}(\overrightarrow{x})$.
$\Delta S_2^{+}(\overrightarrow{x}) :- \neg V'(\overrightarrow{x}) , \neg S_2(\overrightarrow{x}) , S_1(\overrightarrow{x}) , \neg Au_{\setminus}^{*}(\overrightarrow{x})$.
$(\text{AR})^{\setminus} : Au_{\setminus}^{*} \in \{Au_{\setminus}^{1}, Au_{\setminus}^{2}, Au_{\setminus}^{12}\}$
$Au_{\setminus}^{1} = \{t \text{ for } t \in \mathcal{E}_{\setminus}|_{V} - \mathcal{E}_{\setminus}|_{V'} \text{ if } t \in \mathcal{E}_{\setminus}|_{\Delta S_1^{-}} \wedge t \notin \mathcal{E}_{\setminus}|_{\Delta S_2^{+}}\}$
$Au_{\setminus}^{2} = \{t \text{ for } t \in \mathcal{E}_{\setminus}|_{V} - \mathcal{E}_{\setminus}|_{V'} \text{ if } t \in \mathcal{E}_{\setminus}|_{\Delta S_2^{+}} \wedge t \notin \mathcal{E}_{\setminus}|_{\Delta S_1^{-}}\}$
$Au_{\setminus}^{12} = \{t \text{ for } t \in \mathcal{E}_{\setminus}|_{V} - \mathcal{E}_{\setminus}|_{V'} \text{ if } t \in \mathcal{E}_{\setminus}|_{\Delta S_1^{-}} \wedge t \in \mathcal{E}_{\setminus}|_{\Delta S_2^{+}}\}$

∩-rule $V(\overrightarrow{x}) :- S_1(\overrightarrow{x}) , S_2(\overrightarrow{x})$.
$(\text{SDR})^{\cap} : \Delta S_i^{+}, \Delta S_i^{-}, i \in \{1,2\}$
$\Delta S_i^{+}(\overrightarrow{x}) :- V'(\overrightarrow{x}) , \neg S_i(\overrightarrow{x})$.
$\Delta S_i^{-}(\overrightarrow{x}) :- \neg V'(\overrightarrow{x}) , S_i(\overrightarrow{x}) , S_{3-i}(\overrightarrow{x})$.
$\Delta S_i^{-}(\overrightarrow{x}) :- \neg V'(\overrightarrow{x}) , S_i(\overrightarrow{x}) , S_{3-i}(\overrightarrow{x}) , Au_{\cap}^{*}(\overrightarrow{x})$.
$\Delta S_i^{-}(\overrightarrow{x}) :- \neg V'(\overrightarrow{x}) , S_i(\overrightarrow{x}) , S_{3-i}(\overrightarrow{x}) , \neg Au_{\cap}^{*}(\overrightarrow{x})$.
$(\text{AR})^{\cap} : Au_{\cap}^{*} \in \{Au_{\cap}^{1}, Au_{\cap}^{2}, Au_{\cap}^{12}\}$
$Au_{\cap}^{1} = \{t \text{ for } t \in \mathcal{E}_{\cap}|_{V} - \mathcal{E}_{\cap}|_{V'} \text{ if } t \in \mathcal{E}_{\cap}|_{\Delta S_1^{-}} \wedge t \notin \mathcal{E}_{\cap}|_{\Delta S_2^{-}}\}$
$Au_{\cap}^{2} = \{t \text{ for } t \in \mathcal{E}_{\cap}|_{V} - \mathcal{E}_{\cap}|_{V'} \text{ if } t \in \mathcal{E}_{\cap}|_{\Delta S_2^{-}} \wedge t \notin \mathcal{E}_{\cap}|_{\Delta S_1^{-}}\}$
$Au_{\cap}^{12} = \{t \text{ for } t \in \mathcal{E}_{\cap}|_{V} - \mathcal{E}_{\cap}|_{V'} \text{ if } t \in \mathcal{E}_{\cap}|_{\Delta S_1^{-}} \wedge t \in \mathcal{E}_{\cap}|_{\Delta S_2^{-}}\}$

σ-rule $V(\overrightarrow{x}) :- S(\overrightarrow{x}) , v_1 \oplus_1 c_1 , \ldots , v_m \oplus_m c_m$. where $\{v_1 , \ldots , v_m\} \subseteq set(\overrightarrow{x})$
$(\text{SDR})^{\sigma} : \Delta S^{+}, \Delta S^{-}$
$\Delta S^{-}(\overrightarrow{x}) :- \neg V'(\overrightarrow{x}) , S(\overrightarrow{x}) , v_1 \oplus_1 c_1, \ldots, v_m \oplus_m c_m$.
$\Delta S^{+}(\overrightarrow{x}) :- V'(\overrightarrow{x}) , \neg S(\overrightarrow{x}) , v_1 \oplus_1 c_1, \ldots, v_m \oplus_m c_m$.
$\Delta S^{+}(\overrightarrow{x^r}) :- \neg V'(\overrightarrow{x}) , S(\overrightarrow{x}) , \neg S(\overrightarrow{x^r}) , Au_{\sigma}^{0}(\overrightarrow{y_\sigma^r}) , v_1 \oplus_1 c_1, \ldots, v_m \oplus_m c_m$.
$\Delta S^{+}(\overrightarrow{x^r}) :- \neg V'(\overrightarrow{x}) , S(\overrightarrow{x}) , \neg S(\overrightarrow{x^r}) , Au_{\sigma}^{1}(\overrightarrow{x^r}) , v_1 \oplus_1 c_1, \ldots, v_m \oplus_m c_m$.
where $\overrightarrow{x^r} = ara(\overrightarrow{x}, \overrightarrow{y_\sigma}, \overrightarrow{y_\sigma^r}), \overrightarrow{y_\sigma} = \langle u_1, \ldots, u_k\rangle, \overrightarrow{y_\sigma^r} = \langle u_1^r, \ldots, u_k^r\rangle$
$\langle u_1, \ldots, u_k\rangle = tuple(set(\{v_1, \ldots, v_m\}))$
$(\text{AR})^{\sigma} : Au_{\sigma}^{*} \in \{Au_{\sigma}^{0}, Au_{\sigma}^{1}\}$
$Au_{\sigma}^{0} = \{\Pi_{pos(\overrightarrow{y_\sigma}, \overrightarrow{x})} t \text{ for } t \in D_\sigma\}$
$Au_{\sigma}^{1} = D_\sigma$
where $D_\sigma = \{t \text{ for } t \in \mathcal{E}_\sigma|_{\Delta S+} \text{ if } \Pi_{pos(ad(\overrightarrow{x}, \overrightarrow{y_\sigma}), \overrightarrow{x})} t \in \Pi_{pos(ad(\overrightarrow{x}, \overrightarrow{y_\sigma}), \overrightarrow{x})}(\mathcal{E}_\sigma|_{\Delta S-})\}$
$(\text{FR})^{\sigma} : Fr$
$Fr(\text{“\_r\_”}) :- V^{*}(awa(\overrightarrow{x}, \{v_i\})), v_i \neg\oplus_i c_i$.
where $V^{*} \in \{V, V'\}, i \in \{1, \ldots, m\}$

π-rule $V(\overrightarrow{x}) :- S(\overrightarrow{y})$. where $set(\overrightarrow{x}) \subsetneq set(\overrightarrow{y})$
$(\text{SDR})^{\pi} : \Delta S^{+}, \Delta S^{-}$
$\Delta S^{-}(\overrightarrow{y}) :- \neg V'(\overrightarrow{x}) , S(\overrightarrow{y})$.
$\Delta S^{+}(\overrightarrow{y}) :- V'(\overrightarrow{x}) , \neg S(awa(\overrightarrow{y}, \overrightarrow{x})) , Au_{\pi}^{0}(ad(\overrightarrow{y}, \overrightarrow{x}))$.
$\Delta S^{+}(\overrightarrow{y}) :- V'(\overrightarrow{x}) , \neg S(awa(\overrightarrow{y}, \overrightarrow{x})) , Au_{\pi}^{1}(\overrightarrow{y})$.
$\Delta S^{+}(\overrightarrow{y}) :- V'(\overrightarrow{x}) , \neg S(awa(\overrightarrow{y}, \overrightarrow{x})) , Au_{\pi}^{0}(ad(\overrightarrow{y}, \overrightarrow{x})) , \neg Au_{\pi}^{1}(awa(\overrightarrow{y}, \overrightarrow{x}))$.
$(\text{AR})^{\pi} : Au_{\pi}^{*} \in \{Au_{\pi}^{0}, Au_{\pi}^{1}\}$
$Au_{\pi}^{0} = \{most\_common(\langle \Pi_{pos(ad(\overrightarrow{y}, \overrightarrow{x}), \overrightarrow{y})} t \text{ for } t \in D_\pi\rangle)\}$
$Au_{\pi}^{1} = \{t \text{ for } t \in D_\pi \text{ if } \Pi_{pos(ad(\overrightarrow{y}, \overrightarrow{x}), \overrightarrow{y})} t \notin Au_{\pi}^{0}\}$
where $D_\pi = \{t \text{ for } t \in \mathcal{E}_\pi|_{\Delta S+} \text{ if } \Pi_{pos(\overrightarrow{x}, \overrightarrow{y})} t \in (\mathcal{E}_\pi|_{V'} - \mathcal{E}_\pi|_{V})\}$

⋈-rule $V(\overrightarrow{x}) :- S_1(\overrightarrow{y_1}) , S_2(\overrightarrow{y_2})$. where $set(\overrightarrow{y_1}) \cup set(\overrightarrow{y_2}) = set(\overrightarrow{x})$
| and $set(\overrightarrow{y_1}) \cap set(\overrightarrow{y_2}) \neq \emptyset$
$(\text{SDR})^{\bowtie} : \Delta S_i^{+}, \Delta S_i^{-}, i \in \{1,2\}$
$\Delta S_i^{+}(\overrightarrow{y_i}) :- V'(awa(\overrightarrow{x}, \overrightarrow{y_i})) , \neg S_i(\overrightarrow{y_i})$.
$\Delta S_i^{-}(\overrightarrow{y_i}) :- \neg V'(awa(\overrightarrow{x}, \overrightarrow{y_i})) , S_i(\overrightarrow{y_i}) , S_{3-i}(\overrightarrow{y_{3-i}})$.
$\Delta S_i^{-}(\overrightarrow{y_i}) :- \neg V'(awa(\overrightarrow{x}, \overrightarrow{y_i})) , S_i(\overrightarrow{y_i}) , S_{3-i}(\overrightarrow{y_{3-i}}) , Au_{\bowtie}^{*}(awa(\overrightarrow{x}, \overrightarrow{y_i}))$.
$\Delta S_i^{-}(\overrightarrow{y_i}) :- \neg V'(awa(\overrightarrow{x}, \overrightarrow{y_i})) , S_i(\overrightarrow{y_i}) , S_{3-i}(\overrightarrow{y_{3-i}}) , \neg Au_{\bowtie}^{*}(awa(\overrightarrow{x}, \overrightarrow{y_i}))$.
$(\text{AR})^{\bowtie} : Au_{\bowtie}^{*} \in \{Au_{\bowtie}^{1}, Au_{\bowtie}^{2}, Au_{\bowtie}^{12}\}$
$Au_{\bowtie}^{1} = \{t \text{ for } t \in \mathcal{E}_{\bowtie}|_{V} - \mathcal{E}_{\bowtie}|_{V'} \text{ if } \Pi_{pos(\overrightarrow{y_1}, \overrightarrow{x})} t \in \mathcal{E}_{\bowtie}|_{\Delta S_1^{-}} \wedge \Pi_{pos(\overrightarrow{y_2}, \overrightarrow{x})} t \notin \mathcal{E}_{\bowtie}|_{\Delta S_2^{-}}\}$
$Au_{\bowtie}^{2} = \{t \text{ for } t \in \mathcal{E}_{\bowtie}|_{V} - \mathcal{E}_{\bowtie}|_{V'} \text{ if } \Pi_{pos(\overrightarrow{y_2}, \overrightarrow{x})} t \in \mathcal{E}_{\bowtie}|_{\Delta S_2^{-}} \wedge \Pi_{pos(\overrightarrow{y_1}, \overrightarrow{x})} t \notin \mathcal{E}_{\bowtie}|_{\Delta S_1^{-}}\}$
$Au_{\bowtie}^{12} = \{t \text{ for } t \in \mathcal{E}_{\bowtie}|_{V} - \mathcal{E}_{\bowtie}|_{V'} \text{ if } \Pi_{pos(\overrightarrow{y_1}, \overrightarrow{x})} t \in \mathcal{E}_{\bowtie}|_{\Delta S_1^{-}} \wedge \Pi_{pos(\overrightarrow{y_2}, \overrightarrow{x})} t \in \mathcal{E}_{\bowtie}|_{\Delta S_2^{-}}\}$
$(\text{FR})^{\bowtie} : Fr$
$Fr(\text{“\_r\_”}) :- \Delta S_i^{+}(awa(\overrightarrow{y_i}, \overrightarrow{y_{3-i}})) , S_i(awa(\overrightarrow{y_i}, \overrightarrow{y_{3-i}}))$.
$Fr(\text{“\_r\_”}) :- \Delta S_i^{-}(awa(\overrightarrow{y_i}, \overrightarrow{y_{3-i}})) , S'_i(awa(\overrightarrow{y_i}, \overrightarrow{y_{3-i}}))$.

×-rule $V(\overrightarrow{x}) :- S(\overrightarrow{y}) , v_1{=}c_1 , \ldots , v_m{=}c_m$. where $set(\overrightarrow{y}) \cup \{v_1, \ldots, v_m\} = set(\overrightarrow{x})$
| and $set(\overrightarrow{y}) \cap \{v_1, \ldots, v_m\} = \emptyset$
$(\text{SDR})^{\times} : \Delta S^{+}, \Delta S^{-}$
$\Delta S^{+}(\overrightarrow{y}) :- V'(\overrightarrow{x}) , \neg S(\overrightarrow{y}) , v_1 = c_1 , \ldots, v_m = c_m$.
$\Delta S^{-}(\overrightarrow{y}) :- \neg V'(\overrightarrow{x}) , S(\overrightarrow{y}) , v_1 = c_1 , \ldots, v_m = c_m$..
$(\text{FR})^{\times} : Fr$
$Fr(\text{“\_r\_”}) :- V^{*}(awa(\overrightarrow{x}, \{v_i\})) , v_i \neq c_i$.
where $V^{*} \in \{V, V'\}, i \in \{1, \ldots, m\}$

$(\text{SDR})^{\alpha}$, $(\text{AR})^{\alpha}$ and $(\text{FR})^{\alpha}$ are sets of template-based clauses for source delta, auxiliary and flag relations, respectively.
Each Au_{α}^{*} in $(\text{AR})^{\alpha}$ is an auxiliary relation that holds necessary ground tuples/facts.
$\mathcal{E}_\alpha$ is an example of form $(T_S, T_{S'}, T_V, T_{V'})$ against an *α-rule*, and $\mathcal{E}_\alpha|_X$ contains tuples in X that can be calculated from $\mathcal{E}_\alpha$.
Fr is a flag relation that checks constraints imposed on the sources and views. $\langle\text{“\_r\_”}\rangle \in Fr$ expresses a rejection.
$\{\ldots\}$ and $\langle\ldots\rangle$ respectively represent a set and a tuple. $set(X)$ and $tuple(X)$ respectively convert X to a set and a tuple.
If X is a tuple, $X[i]$ returns the i-th element, $index(v, X)$ returns the index of an element v, and $most\_common(X)$ returns the most common element, in X.
If X and Y are tuples and $set(Y) \subseteq set(X)$, *(POSition function)* $pos(Y, X) := \langle index(v, X) \text{ for } v \in Y\rangle$.
If t is a tuple, $\Pi_{pos(Y,X)} t$ returns a new tuple by projecting t at $pos(Y, X)$. If R is a set of tuples, $\Pi_{pos(Y,X)} R := \{\Pi_{pos(Y,X)} t \text{ for } t \in R\}$.
(Argument function) $arg(X)$ returns a tuple of variables appearing in literal/constraint/set/tuple X.
(Argument-Difference function) $ad(X, Y) := \langle v \text{ for } v \in arg(X) \text{ if } v \notin arg(Y)\rangle$
(Argument-With-Anonymous function) $awa(X, Y) := \langle v \text{ if } v \in arg(Y) \text{ else } \_ \text{ for } v \in arg(X)\rangle$
(Argument-Replacing-Argument function) $ara(X, V_1, V_2) := \langle v \text{ if } v \notin V_1 \text{ else } V_2[index(v, V_1)] \text{ for } v \in arg(X)\rangle$ if $set(V_1) \subseteq set(arg(X))$ and $|V_1| = |V_2|$
Example: If $X = \langle v_0, v_1, v_2, v_3\rangle, Y = \langle v_2, v_3, v_0\rangle$, then $pos(Y, X) = \langle 2, 3, 0\rangle, \Pi_{pos(Y,X)}\{\langle\text{“a”}, \text{“b”}, \text{“c”}, \text{“d”}\rangle\} = \{\langle\text{“c”}, \text{“d”}, \text{“a”}\rangle\}$
If $X = \langle v_0, v_1, v_2, v_3\rangle, Y = \langle v_0, v_4\rangle$, then $arg(X) = \langle v_0, v_1, v_2, v_3\rangle, arg(Y) = \langle v_0, v_4\rangle, ad(X, Y) = \langle v_1, v_2, v_3\rangle, awa(X, Y) = \langle v_0, \_, \_, \_\rangle$
If $X = \langle v_0, v_1, v_2, v_3\rangle, V_1 = \langle v_1, v_3\rangle, V_2 = \langle v_4, v_5\rangle$, then $ara(X, V_1, V_2) = \langle v_0, v_4, v_2, v_5\rangle$

Fig. 1. Datalog templates encoding minimal-effect view update strategies

strategies: inserting $\overrightarrow{x}$ into either only S_1 or only S_2 or both S_1 and S_2. The different inserted tuples could follow different strategies. The next three rules of $(\text{SDR})^{\cup}$ encode different cases of combining these strategies:

$$r_3^m \quad \Delta S_i^{+}(\overrightarrow{x}) :- V'(\overrightarrow{x}) , \neg S_i(\overrightarrow{x}) , \neg S_{3-i}(\overrightarrow{x}).$$
$$r_4^m \quad \Delta S_i^{+}(\overrightarrow{x}) :- V'(\overrightarrow{x}) , \neg S_i(\overrightarrow{x}) , \neg S_{3-i}(\overrightarrow{x}) , Au_{\cup}^{*}(\overrightarrow{x}).$$
$$r_5^m \quad \Delta S_i^{+}(\overrightarrow{x}) :- V'(\overrightarrow{x}) , \neg S_i(\overrightarrow{x}) , \neg S_{3-i}(\overrightarrow{x}) , \neg Au_{\cup}^{*}(\overrightarrow{x}).$$

where r_3^m describes that all inserted tuples follow the same update strategy while r_4^m and r_5^m use auxiliary relations $Au_{\cup}^*$ to cover the tuples following the most common strategy and other specific strategies (like an if-then-else statement). The auxiliary relations are defined in $(\mathrm{AR})^{\cup}$ using set comprehensions as:

$$\begin{aligned}
a_1^m \ Au_{\cup}^1 &= \{t \text{ for } t \in \mathcal{E}_{\cup}|_{V'} - \mathcal{E}_{\cup}|_V \text{ if } t \in \mathcal{E}_{\cup}|_{\Delta S_1^+} \wedge t \notin \mathcal{E}_{\cup}|_{\Delta S_2^+}\} \\
a_2^m \ Au_{\cup}^2 &= \{t \text{ for } t \in \mathcal{E}_{\cup}|_{V'} - \mathcal{E}_{\cup}|_V \text{ if } t \in \mathcal{E}_{\cup}|_{\Delta S_2^+} \wedge t \notin \mathcal{E}_{\cup}|_{\Delta S_1^+}\} \\
a_3^m \ Au_{\cup}^{12} &= \{t \text{ for } t \in \mathcal{E}_{\cup}|_{V'} - \mathcal{E}_{\cup}|_V \text{ if } t \in \mathcal{E}_{\cup}|_{\Delta S_1^+} \wedge t \in \mathcal{E}_{\cup}|_{\Delta S_2^+}\}
\end{aligned}$$

where $\mathcal{E}_{\cup}|_X$ is a set of tuples in X that could be computed from the specified example $\mathcal{E}_{\cup}$. $Au_{\cup}^1$, $Au_{\cup}^2$ and $Au_{\cup}^{12}$ store tuples related to the three aforementioned insertion strategies. There is no clause for $(\mathrm{FR})^{\cup}$ if there is no constraint for S_1, S_2 or V.

For other atomic queries of type α, $(\mathrm{SDR})^{\alpha}$ and $(\mathrm{AR})^{\alpha}$ could be interpreted in a similar way as above. Tuple comprehensions are used to define some attribute functions (e.g., *ad*, *awa*, *ara*) that compute specific tuples of variables to form the body of template rules, which makes the rules safe and correct.

To prevent invalid updates, we use a special relation Fr (whose semantic is like $\perp$) that is described in $(\mathrm{FR})^{\alpha}$. If there is a tuple that violates the imposed constraints, Fr will flag a rejection with the value "_r_". Rather than heavily interfering inside SOUFFLE for immediately rejecting update propagation, we simply use Fr to monitor the rejection. Data may be restored to the original state if $\langle$"_r_"$\rangle$ is found in Fr. For a *σ-rule*/*×-rule* r, the negation of each constraint in the body of r is used as a constraint in a flag rule of $(\mathrm{FR})^{\sigma}/(\mathrm{FR})^{\times}$. For a *⋈-rule*, rejects are flagged if in the join positions, the inserted data are already in the original source or the deleted data are still in the update source.

6 Templatizing Constraints and Effects of FDs

Using specified FD information for the source and the view against an atomic query get_a, we can prepare templates encoding the constraints and effects of the FDs and enrich the search space of the synthesis of the corresponding put_a.

6.1 Templatizing the Constraints of FDs

If a relation r has internal dependencies described by the FDs, both the original and updated data on r are *constrained* to agree on the FDs.

Example 3. Consider relation $S :: ABCD$ satisfying $\mathcal{F}_S = \{A \to B, A \to D\}$. For FD $A \to B$, we can use the relation Fr to encode the constraints as follows:

$$\begin{aligned}
&r_1^c \ Fr(\text{“_r_”}) :- S(v_1, v_2, _, _), S(v_1, v_2^x, _, _), v_2 \neq v_2^x. \\
&r_2^c \ Fr(\text{“_r_”}) :- S'(v_1, v_2, _, _), S'(v_1, v_2^x, _, _), v_2 \neq v_2^x.
\end{aligned}$$

The meaning of these two rules is similar to the explanation of the constraints of FDs in Sect. 3. We can prepare a similar pair of flag rules for FD $A \to D$. ▲

Algorithm 2: Templatizing the Constraints of FDs

```
procedure TemplatizeConstraintFDs(S_f):
    C ← ∅
    for R :: A_1 A_2 ... A_n ∈ S_f do
        for s ∈ {original, updated} do
            for X → A_k ∈ F_R do
                ars_1, ars_2 ← [_] * n, [_] * n
                for i ∈ [1, ..., n] do
                    if A_i ∈ X then ars_1[i], ars_2[i] ← v_i, v_i
                    if A_i = A_k then ars_1[i], ars_2[i] ← v_k, v_k^x
                Add the following rule to C: Fr("_r_") : −r^s(ars_1), r^s(ars_2), v_k ≠ v_k^x.
    return C
```

Algorithm 2 describes how we can templatize the constraints of the FDs in NR-Datalog. TemplatizeConstraintFDs takes as input a set $\mathcal{S}_f$ of schemas of relations with computed FDs and produces as output a set C of flag rules describing the constraints of the FDs. The procedure executes nested loops where the relation R iterates over $\mathcal{S}_f$, state s iterates over a set of original and updated states, and FD $X \rightarrow A_k$ iterates over $\mathcal{F}_R$. Then, we prepare the variables in the body of the flag rule and build a complete rule expressing the constraint of the considered FD. Informally, in such a flag rule against FD f, we need to prepare two positive literals L_1 and L_2 that have the same variables in the positions on the *lhs* of f, different variables in the positions on the *rhs* of f, and anonymous variables for the remaining positions.

6.2 Templatizing the Effects of FDs

The *effects* of FDs could appear in $P_{\Delta S}$, where an updated tuple in ΔS could conflict with an original tuple t of S on an FD. If such conflicts are not handled, the result S' would contain data inconsistencies on the FD. There are two strategies for resolving the conflict: deleting t from S and revising t based on specified FDs with revision operators. The former could be simply done by templatizing rules for adding the conflicting tuple t to ΔS^-. The latter is more complicated since revision operators (Sect. 2.3) are recursive structures with FDs that have never been defined in NR-Datalog. Moreover, an NR-Datalog program has no information on how the FDs are structured. We need to develop an intermediary that converts revision operators into NR-Datalog clauses.

Assume that we have generated Datalog rules for $P_{\Delta S}$ from the base templates with minimal effects. We slightly rename the heads of the rules to ΔS_b^- and ΔS_b^+ as appropriate. We use $\Delta S_b \equiv (\Delta S_b^-, \Delta S_b^+)$ to hold the updated data with minimal effects and use ΔS to hold the updated data after accounting for the effects of the FDs. The templates encoding effects of the FDs will be designed over ΔS_b; i.e., we expect to obtain a put_a program that computes the updated data as usual and then resolves the conflicts.

Example 4. Consider templatizing the effects of FDs in Sect. 3. First, we replace the basic rules (r_5^o, r_6^o), with a head of either ΔM_1^- or ΔM_1^+, with the following new ones, whose heads are adapted correspondingly to ΔM_{1b}^- or ΔM_{1b}^+:

Algorithm 3: Templatizing the Effects of FDs

procedure TEMPLATIZEEFFECTFDS($\mathcal{S}_f, \mathcal{D}$):
  $E \leftarrow \emptyset$
  for $r = H :- B. \in \mathcal{D}$ **do**
    $V, Ss \leftarrow$ RELATION(H), RELATION(B)
    for $S \in Ss$ **do**
      if $\mathcal{F}_S = \emptyset$ **then continue**
      $\Delta S_b^-, \Delta S_b^+ \leftarrow$ base deletion and insertion rules
      // strategy: conflict => deletion
      for $X \to A_k \in \mathcal{F}_S$ **do**
        $ars_1, ars_2 \leftarrow [v_1, \ldots, v_n], [\_] * n$
        for $i \in [1..n]$ **do**
          if $A_i \in X$ **then** $ars_2[i] \leftarrow v_i$
          if $A_i = A_k$ **then** $ars_2[i] \leftarrow v_k^x$
        Add to E the rule: $S_d^{\mathcal{F}}(ars_1) :- \Delta S_b^+(ars_2), S(ars_1), v_k \neq v_k^x$.
      Add to E the rules: $\Delta S^-(ars_1) :- \Delta S_b^-(ars_1)$. and $\Delta S^-(ars_1) :- S_d^{\mathcal{F}}(ars_1)$.
      // strategy: conflict => revision
      $S_{i_0}^{\mathcal{F}} \leftarrow$ FRESHNAME()
      $ars_1 \leftarrow [v_1, \ldots, v_n]$
      Add to E the rule with head $S_{i_0}^{\mathcal{F}}(ars_1)$ that calculates tuples which might need to be revised in S
      $T_{\mathcal{F}} \leftarrow$ tree form of $\mathcal{F}_S$
      while $roots(T_{\mathcal{F}}) \neq \emptyset$ **do**
        $root \leftarrow$ a node in $roots(T_{\mathcal{F}})$
        $children \leftarrow$ set of child nodes of $root$
        for $child \in children$ **do**
          $il, ir \leftarrow [index(a)$ for $a \in$ VALUE$(root)], [index(a)$ for $a \in$ VALUE$(right)]$
          $S_{i_1}^{\mathcal{F}} \leftarrow$ FRESHNAME()
          $ars_2 \leftarrow [v_i$ if $i \in il$ else $\_$ for $i \in [1..n]]$
          $ars_3 \leftarrow [\_$ if $i \in ir$ else v_i for $i \in [1..n]]$
          $ars_4 \leftarrow [v_i$ if $i \in il \cup ir$ else $\_$ for $i \in [1..n]]$
          Add to E the following rules: $S_{i_1}^{\mathcal{F}}(ars_1) : -S_{i_0}^{\mathcal{F}}(ars_1), \neg\Delta S_b^+(ars_2)$. and $S_{i_1}^{\mathcal{F}}(ars_1) : -S_{i_0}^{\mathcal{F}}(args_3), \Delta S_b^+(args_4)$.
          $S_{i_0}^{\mathcal{F}} \leftarrow S_{i_1}^{\mathcal{F}}$
        Remove $root$ from $T_{\mathcal{F}}$ and rebuild $T_{\mathcal{F}}$ in tree form
      Add the following rules to E:
        rule with head $S_{i_\#}^{\mathcal{F}}(ars_1)$ that calculates violations of PUTGET,
        $\Delta S^+(ars_1) :- \Delta S_b^+(ars_1)$. and $\Delta S^+(ars_1) :- S_{i_1}^{\mathcal{F}}(ars_1), \neg S_{i_\#}^{\mathcal{F}}(ars_1)$.
  return E

$$r_1^e \;\; \Delta M_{1b}^-(v_0, v_1, v_2) :- \neg M_2'(v_0, v_1, v_2) \;,\; M_1(v_0, v_1, v_2) \;,\; v_2 = \text{“}T\text{”}.$$
$$r_2^e \;\; \Delta M_{1b}^+(v_0, v_1, v_2) :- M_2'(v_0, v_1, v_2) \;,\; \neg M_1(v_0, v_1, v_2) \;,\; v_2 = \text{“}T\text{”}.$$

The remaining basic candidate rules prepared previously are unchanged.

To encode a strategy that resolves the conflict on the FDs of the source ($\mathcal{F}_{M_1} = \{A \to B\}$) by deletion, we generate more three rules r_{10}^o, r_{11}^o, r_{12}^o as mentioned at the end of Sect. 3. For the strategy that resolves the conflict on $\mathcal{F}_{M_1} = \{A \to B\}$ by revision, we will generate more rules as follows:

r_3^e $M_{1i_0}^{\mathcal{F}}(v_0, v_1, v_2) :- M_1(v_0, v_1, v_2), \neg M_2(v_0, v_1, v_2)$.
r_4^e $M_{1i_1}^{\mathcal{F}}(v_0, v_1, v_2) :- M_{1i_0}^{\mathcal{F}}(v_0, v_1, v_2), \neg \Delta M_{1b}^{+}(v_0, \_, \_)$.
r_5^e $M_{1i_1}^{\mathcal{F}}(v_0, v_1, v_2) :- M_{1i_0}^{\mathcal{F}}(v_0, \_, v_2), \Delta M_{1b}^{+}(v_0, v_1, \_)$.
r_6^e $M_{1i_\#}^{\mathcal{F}}(v_0, v_1, v_2) :- M_{1i_1}^{\mathcal{F}}(v_0, v_1, v_2), v_2 = \text{“}T\text{”}, \neg M_2'(v_0, v_1, v_2)$
r_7^e $\Delta M_1^{+}(v_0, v_1, v_2) :- \Delta M_{1b}^{+}(v_0, v_1, v_2)$.
r_8^e $\Delta M_1^{+}(v_0, v_1, v_2) :- \Delta M_{1i_1}^{\mathcal{F}}(v_0, v_1, v_2), \neg \Delta M_{1i_\#}^{\mathcal{F}}(v_0, v_1, v_2)$.

Rule r_3^e defines $M_{1i_0}^{\mathcal{F}}$ as keeping all tuples in the source M_1 that might need to be revised. Then, for an FD f whose *lhs* is a root of the tree form of $\mathcal{F}_{M_1}$, we prepare a pair of rules with the same head whose name specifies a new relation, for instance, $M_{1i_1}^{\mathcal{F}}$, to compute the relation revision $M_{1i_0}^{\mathcal{F}} \leftarrow_f \Delta M_{1b}^{+}$ (i.e., the results of this relation revision are kept in $M_{1i_1}^{\mathcal{F}}$). More generally, we translate the recursive definition of the relation revision (end of Sect. 2.3) to a series of pairs of NR-Datalog rules, where each pair calculates $M_{1i_j}^{\mathcal{F}} \leftarrow_f \Delta M_{1b}^{+}$ and assigns it to a new relation $M_{1i_{j+1}}^{\mathcal{F}}$ (where f is an FD in the rebuilt tree form with a root in the *lhs* of f, and $j = 0, 1, \ldots$). Rules r_3^e and r_4^e indicate a pair of revisions where ΔM_{1b}^{+} is used to revise $M_{1i_0}^{\mathcal{F}}$ into $M_{1i_1}^{\mathcal{F}}$ on FD $f \equiv A \rightarrow B$. Informally, a tuple $\langle v_0, v_1, v_2 \rangle$ is kept in $M_{1i_1}^{\mathcal{F}}$ if either (rule r_3^e - without conflict) $\langle v_0, v_1, v_2 \rangle$ is in $M_{1i_0}^{\mathcal{F}}$ while there is no tuple in ΔM_{1b}^{+} with the first attribute (A-position) value equal to v_0 or (rule r_4^e - with conflict) there are some tuples $\langle v_0, \_, v_2 \rangle$ in $M_{1i_0}^{\mathcal{F}}$ and $\langle v_0, v_1, \_ \rangle$ in ΔM_{1b}^{+} that have the same A-position value of v_0 (note that v_1 is a variable in the B-position and v_2 represents a variable not in the positions of the *lhs* or *rhs* of f). After finishing an FD f, the corresponding edge in tree form will be removed. We can remove a root of the tree form if that node is not in the *lhs* of any remaining FDs and rebuild the forest.

Rule r_6^e defines $M_{1i_\#}^{\mathcal{F}}$ as keeping all violations of PutGet. Supposing the results of the last relation revision in the previous step are in $M_{1i_1}^{\mathcal{F}}$, then $M_{1i_1}^{\mathcal{F}}$ contains tuples that have been revised with $\mathcal{F}_{M_1}$ following the tree form and should be inserted into M_1'; however, some tuples may violate PutGet [4].

The last two rules r_7^e and r_8^e describe two ways that a tuple $\langle v_0, v_1, v_2 \rangle$ would be inserted into M_1. The former requires $\langle v_0, v_1, v_2 \rangle$ to be in ΔM_{1b}^{+} as usual. The latter requires $\langle v_0, v_1, v_2 \rangle$ to be in the last revised relation $M_{1i_1}^{\mathcal{F}}$ but not in the violation relation $M_{1i_\#}^{\mathcal{F}}$. ▲

Algorithm 3 describes how we can templatize the effects of FDs in NR-Datalog. TemplatizeEffectFDs takes a set $\mathcal{S}_f$ of schemas with computed FDs and a set of atomic queries $\mathcal{D}$ as input and produces a set E consisting of addition candidate rules related to handling the effects of FDs. For each atomic rule r in $\mathcal{D}$, we can specify the view V and the source S against r as well as their given FDs in $\mathcal{S}_f$. This procedure only makes more rules about the effects of FDs if a considered source has a nonempty set of FDs in tree form. In such a case, the procedure will (1) (line 7) replace the basic candidate rules whose heads are either ΔS^{-} or ΔS^{+} with new base rules whose heads are, respectively, either ΔS_b^- or ΔS_b^+; (2–3) prepare the rules encoding the strategy that resolves conflicts caused by FDs by deletion (lines 8–15) and by revision (lines 16–33).

To prepare rules for deletions, TEMPLATIZEEFFECTFDS uses the two-step pattern: (1) defining a relation that keeps conflicting tuples due to FDs and (2) preparing rules for usual deletions and deletions that occur due to conflicts.

To prepare rules for revisions, TEMPLATIZEEFFECTFDS uses the four-step pattern: (1) defining a relation that keeps tuples in S that might need to be revised; (2) following the tree form of $\mathcal{F}_S$ from roots to leaves and preparing pairs of rules that each define a new relation expressing a recursive step of revision relations with ΔS_b^+; (3) generating another relation to calculate violations of PUTGET; and (4) preparing rules for usual insertions and insertions that occur due to conflicts.

7 Implementation

We have implemented a prototype named SYNTHBP of our proposed approach using around 8,000 lines of Python. The full source code and other artifacts are available at https://anonymous.4open.science/r/prototype0x00synthbp. To test the power of SYNTHBP, we adopted a suite of practical view update benchmarks listed in [29], totaling 32 benchmarks, out of which 16 have no FDs, 13 incorporate primary keys, and 3 utilize general FDs. SYNTHBP is capable of automatically synthesizing bidirectional programs for 31/32 benchmarks. A failure happens here because the query contains an aggregation whose view update strategies have not been carefully investigated to be templated in Datalog. It is remarked that we have not yet developed an automatic way to check the closeness between the programs synthesized by SYNTHBP and those that are manually written or generated by other systems. This has the potential to act as a focal point for our future research efforts.

8 Related Work

- *Template-Based Synthesis* Templates are commonly used to guide the search in program synthesis [2,23,25,27]. ZAATAR [2] encodes templates as SMT formulas whose solutions produce the expected program. ALPS [25] and PROSYNTH [23] search for the target program as a subset of templates. Template-based synthesizers depend greatly on the quantity and quality of templates. This paper provides a set of templates for synthesizing atomic view update programs put_as given atomic queries get_as. The provided templates encode the existing minimal-effect view update strategies and the constraints and effects imposed by FDs.
- *Synthesizing Relational Queries* Many studies have been proposed to synthesize relational queries from input–output tables [6,19,23,25,28,31,35]. SQLSYNTHESIZER [35], SQLSOL [6], SCYTHE [31] and PATSQL [28] specialize in synthesizing SQL queries, whereas ALPS [25], PROSYNTH [23] and GENSYNTH[19] target Datalog query synthesis. While ALPS and PROSYNTH are

template-guided synthesizers, GenSynth synthesizes programs without templates by introducing an evolutionary search strategy that mutates candidate programs and evaluates their fitness on examples with a Datalog interpreter. These synthesizers cannot directly and efficiently synthesize well-behaved bidirectional programs on relations and cannot work successfully with examples containing internal FDs.

- *Synthesizing Bidirectional Programs* A number of papers have addressed the synthesis problem for bidirectional programs [17,20,21,34]. Optician [17, 20,21] synthesizes bidirectional programs in the bidirectional language Boomerang [3] for textual transformations by rewriting and aligning pairs of regular expressions. Synbit [34] synthesizes bidirectional programs in the tree-oriented bidirectional language HOBit [18] by sketching the code of *put* in HOBit with some holes from the common code of *get* and filling the holes by using the properties of bidirectional programs. Neither Optician nor Synbit can deal with the synthesis on relations because of the complexity of relations and query languages.

9 Conclusion

We propose an approach to synthesizing bidirectional programs from an example on relations with FDs, emphasizing the importance of FDs in the synthesis. If we have obtained a satisfying *get* which is a set of atomic queries get_as, we can forward-propagate FDs from the source to the view. Then, with our well-design templates encoding minimal-effect view update strategies as well as constraints and effects of FDs, we can prepare a set of candidate clauses to the synthesis of the corresponding well-behaved put_a with ProSynth. We have developed a prototype of our proposed approach, named SynthBP, which is powerful enough to automatically synthesize many interesting bidirectional programs.

References

1. Abiteboul, S., Hull, R., Vianu, V.: Foundations of Databases. Addison Wesley, Boston (1995)
2. Albarghouthi, A., Koutris, P., Naik, M., Smith, C.: Constraint-based synthesis of datalog programs. In: Beck, J.C. (ed.) CP 2017. LNCS, vol. 10416, pp. 689–706. Springer, Cham (2017). https://doi.org/10.1007/978-3-319-66158-2_44
3. Bohannon, A., Foster, J.N., Pierce, B.C., Pilkiewicz, A., Schmitt, A.: Boomerang: resourceful lenses string data. SIGPLAN Not. **43**(1), 407–419 (2008)
4. Bohannon, A., Pierce, B.C., Vaughan, J.A.: Relational lenses: a language for updatable views. In: Proceedings of the Twenty-Fifth ACM SIGMOD-SIGACT-SIGART Symposium on Principles of Database Systems, PODS 2006, pp. 338–347. Association for Computing Machinery, New York, NY, USA (2006)
5. Ceri, S., Gottlob, G., Tanca, L.: What you always wanted to know about datalog (and never dared to ask). IEEE Trans. on Knowl. Data Eng. **1**(1), 146–166 (1989)
6. Cheng, L.: SqlSol: an accurate SQL query synthesizer. In: Ait-Ameur, Y., Qin, S. (eds.) ICFEM 2019. LNCS, vol. 11852, pp. 104–120. Springer, Cham (2019). https://doi.org/10.1007/978-3-030-32409-4_7

7. Czarnecki, K., Foster, J.N., Hu, Z., Lämmel, R., Schürr, A., Terwilliger, J.F.: Bidirectional transformations: a cross-discipline perspective. In: Paige, R.F. (ed.) ICMT 2009. LNCS, vol. 5563, pp. 260–283. Springer, Heidelberg (2009). https://doi.org/10.1007/978-3-642-02408-5_19
8. Feng, Y., Martins, R., Van Geffen, J., Dillig, I., Chaudhuri, S.: Component-based synthesis of table consolidation and transformation tasks from examples. In: Proceedings of the 38th ACM SIGPLAN Conference on Programming Language Design and Implementation, PLDI 2017, pp. 422–436. Association for Computing Machinery, New York, NY, USA (2017)
9. Foster, J.N., Greenwald, M.B., Moore, J.T., Pierce, B.C., Schmitt, A.: Combinators for bidirectional tree transformations: a linguistic approach to the view-update problem. ACM Trans. Program. Lang. Syst. **29**(3), 17-es (2007)
10. Gupta, A., Mumick, I.S., Subrahmanian, V.S.: Maintaining views incrementally. In: Proceedings of the 1993 ACM SIGMOD International Conference on Management of Data, SIGMOD 1993, pp. 157–166. Association for Computing Machinery, New York, NY, USA (1993)
11. Horn, R., Perera, R., Cheney, J.: Incremental relational lenses. Proc. ACM Program. Lang. **2**(ICFP) (2018)
12. Jordan, H., Scholz, B., Subotic, P.: Soufflé: On synthesis of program analyzers. In: CAV (2016)
13. Keller, A.M.: Algorithms for translating view updates to database updates for views involving selections, projections, and joins. In: Proceedings of the Fourth ACM SIGACT-SIGMOD Symposium on Principles of Database Systems, PODS 1985, pp. 154–163. Association for Computing Machinery, New York, NY, USA (1985)
14. Keller, A.M.: Choosing a view update translator by dialog at view definition time. In: Proceedings of the 12th International Conference on Very Large Data Bases, VLDB 1986, p. 467–474. Morgan Kaufmann Publishers Inc., San Francisco, CA, USA (1986)
15. Larson, J.A., Sheth, A.P.: Updating relational views using knowledge at view definition and view update time. Inf. Syst. 16(2), 145–168 (1991)
16. Le, V., Gulwani, S.: Flashextract: a framework for data extraction by examples. In: Proceedings of the 35th ACM SIGPLAN Conference on Programming Language Design and Implementation, PLDI 2014, pp. 542–553. Association for Computing Machinery, New York, NY, USA (2014)
17. Maina, S., Miltner, A., Fisher, K., Pierce, B.C., Walker, D., Zdancewic, S.: Synthesizing quotient lenses. Proc. ACM Program. Lang. **2**(ICFP) (2018)
18. Matsuda, K., Wang, M.: HOBiT: programming lenses without using lens combinators. In: Ahmed, A. (ed.) ESOP 2018. LNCS, vol. 10801, pp. 31–59. Springer, Cham (2018). https://doi.org/10.1007/978-3-319-89884-1_2
19. Mendelson, J., Naik, A., Raghothaman, M., Naik, M.: Gensynth: Synthesizing datalog programs without language bias. Proc. AAAI Conf. Artif. Intell. **35**(7), 6444–6453 (2021)
20. Miltner, A., Fisher, K., Pierce, B.C., Walker, D., Zdancewic, S.: Synthesizing bijective lenses. Proc. ACM Program. Lang. **2**(POPL), 1–30 (2017)
21. Miltner, A., Maina, S., Fisher, K., Pierce, B.C., Walker, D., Zdancewic, S.: Synthesizing symmetric lenses. Proc. ACM Program. Lang. **3**(ICFP), 1–28 (2019)
22. Papenbrock, T., et al.: Functional dependency discovery: an experimental evaluation of seven algorithms. Proc. VLDB Endow. **8**(10), 1082–1093 (2015)

23. Raghothaman, M., Mendelson, J., Zhao, D., Naik, M., Scholz, B.: Provenance-guided synthesis of datalog programs. Proc. ACM Program. Lang. **4**(POPL), 1–27 (2019)
24. Shen, Y., Chakrabarti, K., Chaudhuri, S., Ding, B., Novik, L.: Discovering queries based on example tuples. In: Proceedings of the 2014 ACM SIGMOD International Conference on Management of Data, SIGMOD 2014, pp. 493–504. Association for Computing Machinery, New York, NY, USA (2014)
25. Si, X., Lee, W., Zhang, R., Albarghouthi, A., Koutris, P., Naik, M.: Syntax-guided synthesis of datalog programs. In: Proceedings of the 2018 26th ACM Joint Meeting on European Software Engineering Conference and Symposium on the Foundations of Software Engineering, ESEC/FSE 2018, pp. 515–527. Association for Computing Machinery, New York, NY, USA (2018)
26. Solar-Lezama, A., Tancau, L., Bodik, R., Seshia, S., Saraswat, V.: Combinatorial sketching for finite programs. SIGARCH Comput. Archit. News **34**(5), 404–415 (2006)
27. Srivastava, S., Gulwani, S., Foster, J.S.: Template-based program verification and program synthesis. Int. J. Softw. Tools Technol. Transfer **15**(5), 497–518 (2012). https://doi.org/10.1007/s10009-012-0223-4
28. Takenouchi, K., Ishio, T., Okada, J., Sakata, Y.: PatSQL: efficient synthesis of SQL queries from example tables with quick inference of projected columns. Proc. VLDB Endow. **14**(11), 1937–1949 (2021)
29. Tran, V.D., Kato, H., Hu, Z.: Programmable view update strategies on relations. Proc. VLDB Endow. **13**(5), 726–739 (2020)
30. Tsushima, K., Trong, B.N., Glück, R., Hu, Z.: An efficient composition of bidirectional programs by memoization and lazy update. In: Nakano, K., Sagonas, K. (eds.) FLOPS 2020. LNCS, vol. 12073, pp. 159–178. Springer, Cham (2020). https://doi.org/10.1007/978-3-030-59025-3_10
31. Wang, C., Cheung, A., Bodik, R.: Synthesizing highly expressive SQL queries from input-output examples. SIGPLAN Not. **52**(6), 452–466 (2017)
32. Wang, Y., Shah, R., Criswell, A., Pan, R., Dillig, I.: Data migration using datalog program synthesis. Proc. VLDB Endow. **13**(7), 1006–1019 (2020)
33. Yaghmazadeh, N., Wang, X., Dillig, I.: Automated migration of hierarchical data to relational tables using programming-by-example. Proc. VLDB Endow. **11**(5), 580–593 (2018)
34. Yamaguchi, M., Matsuda, K., David, C., Wang, M.: Synbit: synthesizing bidirectional programs using unidirectional sketches. Proc. ACM Program. Lang. **5**(OOPSLA), 1–31 (2021)
35. Zhang, S., Sun, Y.: Automatically synthesizing SQL queries from input-output examples. In: 2013 28th IEEE/ACM International Conference on Automated Software Engineering (ASE), pp. 224–234 (2013)

Transforming Big-Step to Small-Step Semantics Using Interpreter Specialisation

John P. Gallagher[1,4(✉)], Manuel Hermenegildo[2,4], José Morales[2,4], and Pedro Lopez-Garcia[3,4]

[1] Roskilde University, Roskilde, Denmark
jpg@ruc.dk
[2] Universidad Politécnica de Madrid (UPM), Madrid, Spain
[3] Spanish Council for Scientific Research (CSIC), Madrid, Spain
[4] IMDEA Software Institute, Madrid, Spain
{manuel.hermenegildo,josef.morales,pedro.lopez}@imdea.org

Abstract. Natural semantics (big-step) and structural operational semantics (small-step) each have advantages, so it can be useful to produce both semantic forms for a language. Previous work has shown that big-step semantics can be transformed to small-step semantics. This is also the goal of our work, but our main contribution is to show that this can be done by specialisation of an interpreter that imposes a small-step execution on big-step transition rules. This is arguably more direct, transparent and flexible than previous methods. The paper contains two examples and further examples are available in an online repository.

Keywords: Interpreter specialisation · Operational semantics

1 Introduction

The goal of this work is to transform big-step operational semantics to small-step operational semantics. This has previously been studied [2,18,29]. The main novelty is the method, which we consider to be more direct and transparent than previous approaches. We formulate the transformation as the specialisation of a "small-step" interpreter for big-step semantic rules. Once a suitable interpreter has been written, in which the definition of a "small step" has been encoded (see Sect. 3), the transformation consists of partially evaluating it with respect to given big-step semantics. The specialised interpreter contains the small-step transition rules, with minor syntactic modification. We describe experiments using an off-the-shelf partial evaluator for logic programs [22] (Sect. 4).

Partially funded by MICINN projects PID2019-108528RB-C21 *ProCode*, TED2021-132464B-I00 *PRODIGY*, and FJC2021-047102-I, and by the Tezos foundation.

R. Glück and B. Kafle (Eds.): LOPSTR 2023, LNCS 14330, pp. 28–38, 2023.
https://doi.org/10.1007/978-3-031-45784-5_3

2 Background

Natural semantics (NS) was proposed by Kahn [21] as a proof-theoretic view of program semantics. Structural operational semantics (SOS) was developed by Plotkin [26,27]. The motivation of SOS was to define machine-like execution of programs in a syntax-directed style, omitting all unnecessary details of the machine. Both styles have their advantages, which we do not discuss here.

We use the nicknames *big-step* and *small-step* for NS and SOS respectively, as they neatly express the difference between NS and SOS. Both approaches define the behaviour of a program as runs in a transition system. The system states (or *configurations*) have the form $\langle s, \sigma \rangle$ where s is a program expression (such as a statement) and σ is a program environment (such as a store); sometimes s is omitted when it is empty or associated with a final state.

In big-step semantics, transitions are of the form $\langle s, \sigma \rangle \Longrightarrow \sigma'$, or $\langle s, \sigma \rangle \Longrightarrow s'$ depending on the language being defined, which means that s is completely evaluated in σ, terminating in final state σ' or value s'. In small-step semantics, a transition has the form $\langle s, \sigma \rangle \Rightarrow \langle s', \sigma' \rangle$, which defines a single step from s in environment σ to the *next* configuration $\langle s', \sigma' \rangle$. We may also have transitions of the form $\langle s, \sigma \rangle \Rightarrow \sigma'$ or $\langle s, \sigma \rangle \Rightarrow s'$ for the case that s terminates in one step. There is a small-step (terminating) *run* iff $(\langle s, \sigma \rangle, v)$ is in $\Rightarrow^*$, the transitive closure of $\Rightarrow$. Note that we use $\Longrightarrow$ and $\Rightarrow$ for big and small-step transitions respectively. For transition relations $\Longrightarrow$ and $\Rightarrow$ for a given language, the equivalence requirement is that $\langle s, \sigma \rangle \Longrightarrow v$ iff for some n, $\langle s, \sigma \rangle \Rightarrow^n v$, for all $\langle s, \sigma \rangle$.

Interpreter Specialisation. The idea of specialising a program with respect to partial input, known as program specialisation, partial evaluation or mixed computation, originated in the 1960s and 1970s [3,7,9,23]. Specialisation of a program interpreter with respect to an object program is related to compilation [9]. When the interpreter and the object program are written in the same language, the specialisation may be viewed as a source transformation of the object program (whereas it is in fact a transformation of the interpreter). This idea was exploited to transform programs [10,12–14,20,28], and can result in deep changes in program structure, possibly yielding superlinear speedups [20], in contrast to partial evaluation itself, which gives only linear speedups and does not fundamentally alter program structure. A transformation technique for logic programs with the similar aim of "compiling-in" non-standard semantics, *compiling control* [5], has also been shown to be realisable as interpreter specialisation [25].

The idea of transformation by interpreter specialisation is thus well known, yet its potential has not been fully realised, probably due to the fact that effective specialisation of complex interpreters is beyond the power of general purpose program specialisers and needs further research.

Summary of the Approach. Let **b** be a set of big-step rules for a language and $\langle \mathbf{s}, \sigma \rangle \Longrightarrow \mathbf{v}$ be a big-step transition derived using **b**; let **I** be an interpreter for big-step rules (written in a small-step style, see Sect. 3) and **pe** be a partial evaluator. Following the notational conventions of Jones *et al.* [19], $[\![p]\!]$ denotes the function corresponding to program p and we have the following equations.

$$\begin{aligned}\mathbf{v} &= [\![\mathbf{b}]\!]\ \langle \mathbf{s}, \sigma\rangle \\ &= [\![\mathbf{I}]\!]\ [\mathbf{b}, \langle \mathbf{s}, \sigma\rangle] \\ &= [\![\ [\![\mathbf{pe}]\!]\ [\mathbf{I}, \mathbf{b}]\ ]\!]\ \langle \mathbf{s}, \sigma\rangle\end{aligned}$$

In the first equation, $\mathbf{b}$ is itself an evaluator (indeed, a set of big-step rules is a logic program). $[\![\mathbf{I}]\!]\ [\mathbf{b}, \langle \mathbf{s}, \sigma\rangle]$ is the result of running the interpreter on $\mathbf{b}$ and $\langle \mathbf{s}, \sigma\rangle$ and the equation expresses the assumption that the interpreter yields the same result as running $\mathbf{b}$. The expression $[\![\mathbf{pe}]\!]\ [\mathbf{I}, \mathbf{b}]$ represents the result of specialising $\mathbf{I}$ with respect to the set of big-step rules $\mathbf{b}$. This yields an interpreter specific to $\mathbf{b}$ that follows the small-step style of $\mathbf{I}$, which can be applied directly to a configuration. It contains (after some minor syntactic modification) the small-step semantic rules corresponding to $\mathbf{b}$.

Horn Clause Representation of Semantics and Interpreters. Both big-step and small-step semantics are defined using rules with premises and conclusion, typically written as follows.

$$\frac{\textit{premises}}{\textit{conclusion}} \quad \text{if } \textit{condition}$$

With a suitable encoding of syntactic objects and environments as first-order terms, this is a first-order logic implication *premises* $\wedge$ *condition* $\rightarrow$ *conclusion* The conclusion is an atomic formula (a big- or small-step transition) so assuming that the premises and conditions are conjunctions, it is a Horn clause.

The close connection between transition rules and Horn clauses, and hence to the logic programming language Prolog, was noticed by Kahn and his co-workers and exploited in the Typol tool [6]. Similarly, small step transition rules, together with a rule specifying a run of small-step transitions, can also be written as Horn clauses and used to execute programs.

Interpreters for logic programs can themselves be written as logic programs, where the program being interpreted is represented in some way as a data structure in the interpreter (see [16,17] for a discussion of representations).

In the following, we use Prolog syntax and teletype font for Horn clauses.

3 A Small-Step Interpreter for Big-Step Semantics

Rule Normalisation. A big-step rule has the following form (following [24]).

$$\frac{\langle s_1, \sigma_1\rangle \Longrightarrow \sigma_1', \ldots, \langle s_n, \sigma_n\rangle \Longrightarrow \sigma_n'}{\langle s_0, \sigma_0\rangle \Longrightarrow \sigma_0'} \quad \text{if } c$$

This will be written as a Horn clause, where `E1` stands for σ_1, etc.

```
bigstep(S,E0,E01):-C,bigstep(S1,E1,E11),...,bigstep(Sn,En,En1)
```

The condition C could in general be interspersed among the other rule premises, rather than appearing on the left.

To simplify the interpreter, we assume that rules have *at most two premises*, including the conditions c. Rules can always be transformed to this normal form, possible adding extra syntax constructors. We could incorporate the normalisation in the interpreter, but we chose to automatically pre-process the rules to conform to the two-premise form. As an example, consider the following big-step inference rule taken from the call-by-value semantics of the λ-calculus, which is not in normal form.

$$\frac{\langle e_1, \rho\rangle \Longrightarrow \mathsf{clo}(x, e, \rho') \quad \langle e_2, \rho\rangle \Longrightarrow v_2 \quad \rho'[x/v_2] = \rho'' \quad \langle e, \rho''\rangle \Longrightarrow v}{\langle \mathsf{app}(e_1, e_2), \rho\rangle \Longrightarrow v}$$

After normalising, we get three rules, with new constructors $\mathsf{app1}$ and $\mathsf{app2}$.

$$\frac{\langle e_1, \rho\rangle \Longrightarrow \mathsf{clo}(x, e, \rho') \quad \langle \mathsf{app1}(x, e, \rho', e_2), \rho\rangle \Longrightarrow v}{\langle \mathsf{app}(e_1, e_2), \rho\rangle \Longrightarrow v}$$

$$\frac{\langle e_2, \rho\rangle \Longrightarrow v_2 \quad \langle \mathsf{app2}(x, e, \rho', v_2), \rho\rangle \Longrightarrow v}{\langle \mathsf{app1}(x, e, \rho', e_2), \rho\rangle \Longrightarrow v} \qquad \frac{\rho'[x/v_2] = \rho'' \quad \langle e, \rho''\rangle \Longrightarrow v}{\langle \mathsf{app2}(x, e, \rho', v_2), \rho\rangle \Longrightarrow v}$$

Structure of the Interpreter. The main interpreter loop is as follows.

```
run([A]) :- smallStep(A,As), run(As).
run([]).
```

The `run` predicate takes as argument a stack of `bigstep` goals. The height of the stack is at most one. At each iteration of the main loop, if the stack is not empty, the top of the stack `A` is taken and a small step is applied, that is, `smallStep(A,As)` is called, resulting in `As`, which is either `[]` or `[A1]`. The loop is repeated until the stack is empty.

Definition of a Small Step. We now proceed to define `smallStep`, the crucial predicate in the interpreter. Given a call `smallStep(bigstep(S,E,V),As)`, the cases of the `smallStep` procedure in Fig. 1 correspond to whether the rule with conclusion `bigstep(S,E,V)` has 0, 1 or 2 premises. For base cases 0 and 1, `smallStep` terminates immediately, returning either `[]` (for 0 premises) or `[B]` (where `B` is the single big-step premise). In the third case, the premises are `B1` and `B2`. We recursively call `smallStep` on `[B1]`, yielding `[D1]`, and then construct a new big-step call for the resulting goals `[D1,B2]`. This last step is performed by the predicate `foldStack`, which is now described.

Folding the Stack. Consider the general form of a big-step rule with 2 premises. The rule has one of the following forms.

$$\frac{\langle s'_1, \sigma_1\rangle \Longrightarrow \sigma'_1 \quad \langle s'_2, \sigma_2\rangle \Longrightarrow \sigma'_2}{\langle f(s_1, \ldots, s_k), \sigma_0\rangle \Longrightarrow \sigma'_0} \qquad \frac{\langle s'_1, \sigma_1\rangle \Longrightarrow \sigma'_1 \quad c}{\langle f(s_1, \ldots, s_k), \sigma_0\rangle \Longrightarrow \sigma'_0}$$

Small step evaluation of such a rule evaluates the first premise, applying small steps until the first premise is completely evaluated, and then continues to the second premise. A typical example is the big-step rule for statement composition.

$$\frac{\langle s_1, \sigma\rangle \Longrightarrow \sigma' \quad \langle s_2, \sigma'\rangle \Longrightarrow \sigma''}{\langle s_1\,; s_2, \sigma\rangle \Longrightarrow \sigma''}$$

```
smallStep(A,[]) :-                % rule with zero big step premises
      givenRule(_,A,Bs),
      evalConditions(Bs,[]).
smallStep(A,[B]) :-               % rule with one big step premise
      givenRule(_,A,Bs),
      evalConditions(Bs,[B]).
smallStep(A,As) :-                % rule with 2 premises
      rule(K,A,[B1,B2]),
      bigStepPred(B1),
      smallStep(B1,D1),
      foldStack(D1,B2,K,As).

foldStack([],B2,_,As) :-     % B1 terminated
      evalConditions([B2],As).
foldStack([D1],B2,K,[H]) :- % Make new big step H with [D1,B2]
      newBigStep(D1,B2,K,H).
```

Fig. 1. Definition of a small step

Evaluating $s_1\,; s_2$ in small steps, the evaluation of the first premise may take several small steps: $\langle s_1, \sigma\rangle \Rightarrow \langle s_{1,1}, \sigma_{1,1}\rangle \Rightarrow \ldots \Rightarrow \sigma'$, which we can rewrite as the first small step followed by a big step for the rest.

$$\langle s_1, \sigma\rangle \Rightarrow \langle s_{1,1}, \sigma_{1,1}\rangle, \langle s_{1,1}, \sigma_{1,1}\rangle \Longrightarrow \sigma'$$

Thus after the first small step $\langle s_1, \sigma\rangle \Rightarrow \langle s_{1,1}, \sigma_{1,1}\rangle$, the remaining premises of the rule are are $\langle s_{1,1}, \sigma_{1,1}\rangle \Longrightarrow \sigma', \langle s_2, \sigma'\rangle \Longrightarrow \sigma''$. These form an instance of the rule premise, and so we can *fold* them to yield a single big-step, namely the rule conclusion $\langle s_{1,1}\,; s_2, \sigma_{1,1}\rangle \Longrightarrow \sigma''$. Note that if we apply the rule to this configuration, we obtain the same premises again. Hence, we derive the following relation between small-step pairs of big-step calls.

$$\frac{(\langle s_1, \sigma\rangle \Longrightarrow \sigma') \Rightarrow (\langle s_{1,1}, \sigma_{1,1}\rangle \Longrightarrow \sigma')}{(\langle s_1\,; s_2, \sigma\rangle \Longrightarrow \sigma'') \Rightarrow (\langle s_{1,1}\,; s_2, \sigma_{1,1}\rangle \Longrightarrow \sigma'')}$$

The final state variables σ' and σ'' are arbitrary and can be eliminated, yielding the following recursive small-step rule for $s_1\,; s_2$.

$$\frac{\langle s_1, \sigma\rangle \Rightarrow \langle s_{1,1}, \sigma_{1,1}\rangle}{\langle s_1\,; s_2, \sigma\rangle \Rightarrow \langle s_{1,1}\,; s_2, \sigma_{1,1}\rangle}$$

Auxiliary Rules and Constructors. In the general case for 2-premise rules, the first premise $\langle s'_1, \sigma_1 \rangle \Longrightarrow \sigma'_1$ is split into a first small step and then a big step.

$$\langle s'_1, \sigma_1 \rangle \Rightarrow \langle s'_{1,1}, \sigma_{1,1} \rangle, \langle s'_{1,1}, \sigma_{1,1} \rangle \Longrightarrow \sigma'_1$$

After executing the small step, the remaining rule premises are thus

$$\langle s'_{1,1}, \sigma_{1,1} \rangle \Longrightarrow \sigma'_1, \langle s'_2, \sigma_2 \rangle \Longrightarrow \sigma'_2$$

(and similarly where the second premise is c). This is not always an instance of the original rule, and so it is not always possible to fold using the same rule, as we did with the rule for $s_1 \,;\, s_2$. In particular, the variables s'_1, σ_1 might be reused later in the premises. In such cases, we invent a new constructor, including s'_1 and/or σ_1 if needed as arguments, and construct a new auxiliary rule for the new constructor. We illustrate with an example. Consider the (normalised) rule for app shown above.

$$\frac{\langle e_1, \rho \rangle \Longrightarrow \mathsf{clo}(x, e, \rho') \quad \langle \mathtt{app1}(x, e, \rho', e_2), \rho \rangle \Longrightarrow v}{\langle \mathsf{app}(e_1, e_2), \rho \rangle \Longrightarrow v}$$

After executing a small step $\langle e_1, \rho \rangle \Rightarrow \langle e_{1,1}, \rho_{1,1} \rangle$ the remaining premises are $\langle e_{1,1}, \rho_{1,1} \rangle \Longrightarrow \mathsf{clo}(x, e, \rho') \quad \langle \mathtt{app1}(x, e, \rho', e_2), \rho \rangle \Longrightarrow v$. Note that ρ is used again later in the premises, so it is not possible to fold them into an app construct. Instead, we make a new constructor $\mathsf{app\_aux}$, and build rules as follows.

$$\frac{\langle e_1, \rho \rangle \Rightarrow \langle e_{1,1}, \rho_{1,1} \rangle}{\langle \mathsf{app}(e_1, e_2), \rho \rangle \Rightarrow \langle \mathsf{app\_aux}(e_{1,1}, e_2, \rho), \rho_{1,1} \rangle}$$

$$\frac{\langle e_{1,1}, \rho_{1,1} \rangle \Longrightarrow \mathsf{clo}(x, e, \rho'), \langle \mathtt{app1}(x, e, \rho', e_2), \rho \rangle \Longrightarrow v}{\langle \mathsf{app\_aux}(e_{1,1}, e_2, \rho), \rho_{1,1} \rangle \Longrightarrow v}$$

The second rule is an auxiliary big-step rule for $\mathsf{app\_aux}$, which is used later in the interpreter when needed. The interpreter does not store these auxiliary rules, but rather reconstructs them as needed, as this simplifies partial evaluation.

The complete interpreter, implemented in Ciao Prolog [15] along with the annotation file for the partial evaluator (LOGEN [22]), and a number of examples including the ones in the paper, are available online[1].

4 Examples

Simple Imperative Language. Fig. 2(a) shows the big-step semantics for a simple imperative language containing assignments, statement composition, if-then-else and while statements. These are already in normal form. There is a function V that evaluates expressions and conditionals in a state. Specialising our small-step interpreter (using LOGEN) with respect to these rules gives the output

[1] https://github.com/jpgallagher/Semantics4PE/tree/main/Big2Small.

$$\frac{}{\langle x := e, \sigma\rangle \Longrightarrow \sigma[x/v]} \text{ if } V(e,\sigma) = v$$

$$\frac{\langle s_1, \sigma\rangle \Longrightarrow \sigma' \quad \langle s_2, \sigma'\rangle \Longrightarrow \sigma''}{\langle s_1 \,;\, s_2, \sigma\rangle \Longrightarrow \sigma''}$$

$$\frac{}{\langle \mathsf{skip}, \sigma\rangle \Longrightarrow \sigma}$$

$$\frac{\langle s_1, \sigma\rangle \Longrightarrow \sigma'}{\langle \mathsf{if}\ (b)\ s_1\ \mathsf{else}\ s_2, \sigma\rangle \Longrightarrow \sigma'} \text{ if } V(b,\sigma) = \mathsf{true}$$

$$\frac{\langle s_2, \sigma\rangle \Longrightarrow \sigma'}{\langle \mathsf{if}\ (b)\ s_1\ \mathsf{else}\ s_2, \sigma\rangle \Longrightarrow \sigma'} \text{ if } V(b,\sigma) = \mathsf{false}$$

$$\frac{\langle \mathsf{if}\ (b)\ s; \mathsf{while}\ (b)\ s\ \mathsf{else\,skip}, \sigma\rangle \Longrightarrow \sigma'}{\langle \mathsf{while}\ (b)\ s, \sigma\rangle \Longrightarrow \sigma'}$$

(a) Big-step rules for a simple imperative language

```
smallStep__1(asg(var(D),C),A,B,[]) :-
    eval__2(C,A,E,F),
    eval__3(D,F,E,B).
smallStep__1(ifthenelse(C,D,_),A,B,[bigstep(D,E,B)]) :-
    eval__2(C,A,E,1).
smallStep__1(ifthenelse(C,_,D),A,B,[bigstep(D,E,B)]) :-
    eval__2(C,A,E,0).
smallStep__1(while(C,D),A,B,[bigstep(ifthenelse(C,seq(D,while(C,D)),skip),
     A,B)]).
smallStep__1(seq(C,D),A,B,[bigstep(D,E,B)]) :-
    smallStep__1(C,A,E,[]).
smallStep__1(seq(C,D),A,B,[bigstep(seq(F,D),E,B)]) :-
    smallStep__1(C,A,G,[bigstep(F,E,G)]).
```

(b) Small-step clauses from the specialised interpreter.

$$\frac{}{\langle \mathsf{if}\ (b)\ s_1\ \mathsf{else}\ s_2, \sigma\rangle \Rightarrow \langle s_1, \sigma'\rangle} \text{ if } V(b,\sigma) = \mathsf{true}$$

$$\frac{}{\langle \mathsf{if}\ (b)\ s_1\ \mathsf{else}\ s_2, \sigma\rangle \Rightarrow \langle s_2, \sigma'\rangle} \text{ if } V(b,\sigma) = \mathsf{false}$$

$$\frac{\langle s_1, \sigma\rangle \Rightarrow \sigma'}{\langle s_1 \,;\, s_2, \sigma\rangle \Rightarrow \langle s_2, \sigma'\rangle}$$

$$\frac{}{\langle \mathsf{while}\ (b)\ s, \sigma\rangle \Rightarrow \langle \mathsf{if}\ (b)\ s; \mathsf{while}\ (b)\ s\ \mathsf{else\,skip}, \sigma\rangle}$$

$$\frac{}{\langle x := e, \sigma\rangle \Rightarrow \sigma[x/v]} \text{ if } V(e,\sigma) = v$$

$$\frac{}{\langle \mathsf{skip}, \sigma\rangle \Rightarrow \sigma}$$

$$\frac{\langle s_1, \sigma\rangle \Rightarrow \langle s_1', \sigma'\rangle}{\langle s_1 \,;\, s_2, \sigma\rangle \Rightarrow \langle s_1' \,;\, s_2, \sigma'\rangle}$$

(c) Small-step rules from (b) rewritten in standard form.

Fig. 2. Transformation of the semantics of a simple imperative language.

shown in Fig. 2(b). The small-step rules shown in Fig. 2(c) are directly extracted (eliminating the redundant "final state" arguments as shown above). The rules are similar to textbook small-step semantics for imperative constructs.

Call-by-value semantics for λ-calculus. This example is taken from Vesely and Fisher's paper [29], and we applied normalisation to obtain 2-premise form (see the rule for $\mathsf{app}(e_1, e_2)$ shown at the start of Sect. 3). The big-step rules are shown in Fig. 3(a). The specialised clauses for `smallStep` are in Fig. 3(b) and the same rules typeset in standard notation in Fig. 3(c). The results are somewhat different from those in [29], where the authors use small-step transitions yielding values rather than configurations.

$$\frac{}{\langle \mathsf{var}(x), \rho\rangle \Longrightarrow v} \text{ if } \rho x = v \qquad \frac{\langle e_1, \rho\rangle \Longrightarrow \mathsf{clo}(x, e, \rho) \quad \langle \mathsf{a41}(e_2, x, e, \rho'), \rho\rangle \Longrightarrow v}{\langle \mathsf{app}(e_1, e_2), \rho\rangle \Longrightarrow v}$$

$$\frac{}{\langle \mathsf{val}(v), \rho\rangle \Longrightarrow v} \qquad \frac{\langle e_2, \rho\rangle \Longrightarrow v_2 \quad \langle \mathsf{a42}(x, e, \rho', v_2), \rho\rangle \Longrightarrow v}{\langle \mathsf{a41}(e_2, x, e, \rho'), \rho\rangle \Longrightarrow v}$$

$$\frac{}{\langle \mathsf{lam}(x, e), \rho\rangle \Longrightarrow \mathsf{clo}(x, e, \rho)} \qquad \frac{\rho'[x/v_2] = \rho'' \quad \langle e, \rho''\rangle \Longrightarrow v}{\langle \mathsf{a42}(x, e, \rho', v_2), \rho\rangle \Longrightarrow v}$$

(a) Big-step rules for the call-by-value λ-calculus (from [30]), after normalising

```
smallStep1(val(A),_,A,[]).
smallStep__1(var(C),A,B,[]) :-
   eval__2(A,C,B).
smallStep__1(lam(B,C),A,clo(B,C,A),[]).
smallStep__1(app4_2(C,D,E,F),A,B,[bigstep(D,A,B)]) :-
   eval__3(C,F,E,A).
smallStep__1(app(C,D),A,B,[bigstep(app4_1(D,E,F,G),A,B)]) :-
   smallStep__1(C,A,clo(E,F,G),[]).
smallStep__1(app(C,D),A,B,[bigstep(app_aux_3(F,D,A),E,B)]) :-
   smallStep__1(C,A,clo(G,H,I),[bigstep(F,E,clo(G,H,I))]).
smallStep__1(app4_1(C,D,E,F),A,B,[bigstep(app4_2(D,E,F,G),_,B)]) :-
   smallStep__1(C,A,G,[]).
smallStep__1(app4_1(C,D,E,F),A,B,[bigstep(app4_1(H,D,E,F),G,B)]) :-
   smallStep__1(C,A,I,[bigstep(H,G,I)]).
smallStep__1(app_aux_3(C,D,E),A,B,[bigstep(app4_1(D,F,G,H),E,B)]) :-
   smallStep__1(C,A,clo(F,G,H),[]).
smallStep__1(app_aux_3(C,D,E),A,B,[bigstep(app_aux_3(G,D,E),F,B)]) :-
   smallStep__1(C,A,clo(H,I,J),[bigstep(G,F,clo(H,I,J))]).
```

(b) Small-step rules taken from the specialised interpreter

$$\frac{}{\langle \mathsf{val}(v), \rho\rangle \Rightarrow v} \qquad \frac{\langle e_1, \rho\rangle \Rightarrow \langle e_3, \rho'\rangle}{\langle \mathsf{app}(e_1, e_2), \rho\rangle \Rightarrow \langle \mathsf{app}'(e_3, e_2, \rho), \rho'\rangle}$$

$$\frac{\rho\, x = v}{\langle \mathsf{var}(x), \rho\rangle \Rightarrow v} \qquad \frac{\langle e_2, \rho\rangle \Rightarrow v_2}{\langle \mathsf{a41}(e_2, x, e, \rho'), \rho\rangle \Rightarrow \langle \mathsf{a42}(x, e, \rho', v_2), \rho''\rangle}$$

$$\frac{}{\langle \mathsf{lam}(x, e), \rho\rangle \Rightarrow \mathsf{clo}(x, e, \rho)} \qquad \frac{\langle e_2, \rho\rangle \Rightarrow \langle e_3, \rho''\rangle}{\langle \mathsf{a41}(e_2, x, e, \rho'), \rho\rangle \Rightarrow \langle \mathsf{a41}(e_3, x, e, \rho'), \rho''\rangle}$$

$$\frac{\rho'[x/v_2] = \rho''}{\langle \mathsf{a42}(x, e, v_2, \rho'), \rho''\rangle \Rightarrow \langle e, \rho''\rangle} \qquad \frac{\langle e_3, \rho'\rangle \Rightarrow \mathsf{clo}(x, e, \rho'')}{\langle \mathsf{app}'(e_3, e_2, \rho), \rho'\rangle \Rightarrow \langle \mathsf{a41}(e_2, x, e, \rho''), \rho\rangle}$$

$$\frac{\langle e_1, \rho\rangle \Rightarrow \mathsf{clo}(x, e, \rho')}{\langle \mathsf{app}(e_1, e_2), \rho\rangle \Rightarrow \langle \mathsf{a41}(e_2, x, e, \rho'), \rho\rangle} \qquad \frac{\langle e_3, \rho'\rangle \Rightarrow \langle e_4, \rho''\rangle}{\langle \mathsf{app}'(e_3, e_2, \rho), \rho'\rangle \Rightarrow \langle \mathsf{app}'(e_4, e_2, \rho), \rho''\rangle}$$

(c) Small-step rules from (b) rendered in standard notation.

Fig. 3. Transformation of big-step to small-step semantics for the call-by-value λ-calculus.

5 Related Work

Vesely and Fisher [29] start from an evaluator for big-step semantics and then transform it in (ten) stages to a small-step evaluator. While our interpreter embodies some of the same transformations (for instance, continuation-passing transformation corresponds roughly to specialisation of our `run` predicate), some of their transformations are more low-level, and are subsumed by standard features of partial evaluation (for instance, argument lifting). We also exploit the uniform representation as Horn clauses and the term representation of object programs in the interpreter to avoid explicit defunctionalisation or continuations-to-terms. When comparing our results to theirs, we note (as also observed in [2]) that they choose a version of small-step transitions that yields a term rather than a configuration. Therefore our transitions are not directly comparable in terms of the number of rules and constructors in the resulting small-step semantics.

Ambal *et al.* [2] describe a transformation that also starts from a continuation-passing transformation of a big-step evaluator. The transformation steps are certified in Coq. To eliminate the continuation stack they introduce a new syntax constructor for each continuation, much as we do for the case when direct folding cannot be applied. Overall, the transformation seems similar to ours though the method differs and we are comparing the results more closely.

Huizing *et al.* [18] describe a direct transformation of big-step rules - so their approach is not explicitly based on an interpreter. Ager [1] defines a transformation from L-attributed big-step rules to abstract machines, a related problem. His is also a direct transformation of rules rather than based on an explicit evaluator. Our procedure can also handle rules that are not L-attributed (such as Kahn's big-step semantics for Mini-ML [21]).

Discussion and Future Research. We claim that interpreter specialisation gives a more direct and transparent approach. Its correctness depends on validating the interpreter and the correctness of the partial evaluator, an established and well-tested tool. We do not yet have a formal proof of correctness of the interpreter. However, our interpretive approach using Horn clauses allows execution of the original big-step rules, the interpreter and its specialisation, so we have been able to perform extensive validation showing that they all produce the same results for a given configuration. This is a practical advantage of exploiting the close relationship between semantic rules and Horn clauses, though clearly not a replacement for a formal proof of correctness. Furthermore, the definition of what is a small step can be modified; for example, evaluation of conditionals in `if` statements could be done in small steps instead of as an atomic operation by a small modification of the interpreter. We are applying the method to further cases of big-step semantics; among other challenging examples we are targeting the semantics for Clight [4].

At present we generate structural operational semantics, with transitions from configurations to configurations. Other styles that could be targeted by an interpreter are transitions that yield values rather than configurations (e.g. as used by Vesely and Fisher [29]) and reduction semantics [8]. The related problem of transforming a big-step semantics to an abstract machine seems also a feasible goal for interpreter specialisation; in this case, the interpreter would incorporate implementation details that would be inherited by the abstract machine.

We also note that our previous work on translating imperative programs to Horn clauses [11] is related to the present work. Instead of performing the specialisation $[\![\mathbf{pe}]\!]$ $[\mathbf{I}, \mathbf{b}]$, we would also provide the first component of the initial configuration $\langle \mathbf{s}, \sigma \rangle$; that is, we compute $[\![\mathbf{pe}]\!]$ $[\mathbf{I}, \mathbf{b}, \mathbf{s}]$, obtaining Horn clauses which would compute directly on the environment σ.

Acknowledgements. Discussions with Robert Glück, Bishoksan Kafle, Morten Rhiger and Mads Rosendahl are gratefully acknowledged. The paper was improved by the suggestions of the anonymous reviewers.

References

1. Ager, M.S.: From natural semantics to abstract machines. In: Etalle, S. (ed.) LOPSTR 2004. LNCS, vol. 3573, pp. 245–261. Springer, Heidelberg (2005). https://doi.org/10.1007/11506676_16
2. Ambal, G., Lenglet, S., Schmitt, A., Noûs, C.: Certified derivation of small-step from big-step skeletal semantics. In: Proceedings of PPDP 2022, pp. 11:1–11:48. ACM (2022). https://doi.org/10.1145/3551357.3551384
3. Beckman, L., Haraldson, A., Oskarsson, Ö., Sandewall, E.: A partial evaluator, and its use as a programming tool. Artif. Intell. **7**(4), 319–357 (1976). https://doi.org/10.1016/0004-3702(76)90011-4
4. Blazy, S., Leroy, X.: Mechanized semantics for the Clight subset of the C language. J. Autom. Reasoning **43**(3), 263–288 (2009). https://doi.org/10.1007/s10817-009-9148-3
5. Bruynooghe, M., De Schreye, D., Krekels, B.: Compiling control. J. Log. Program. **6**(2–3), 135–162 (1989)
6. Despeyroux, T.: Executable specification of static semantics. In: Kahn, G., MacQueen, D.B., Plotkin, G. (eds.) SDT 1984. LNCS, vol. 173, pp. 215–233. Springer, Heidelberg (1984). https://doi.org/10.1007/3-540-13346-1_11
7. Ershov, A.P.: On the partial computation principle. Inf. Process. Lett. **6**(2), 38–41 (1977). https://doi.org/10.1016/0020-0190(77)90078-3
8. Felleisen, M., Friedman, D.P.: A reduction semantics for imperative higher-order languages. In: de Bakker, J.W., Nijman, A.J., Treleaven, P.C. (eds.) PARLE 1987. LNCS, vol. 259, pp. 206–223. Springer, Heidelberg (1987). https://doi.org/10.1007/3-540-17945-3_12
9. Futamura, Y.: Partial evaluation of computation process - an approach to a compiler-compiler. Syst. Comput. Controls **2**(5), 45–50 (1971)
10. Gallagher, J.P.: Transforming logic programs by specialising interpreters. In: Proceedings of ECAI-86, pp. 109–122 (1986)
11. Gallagher, J.P., Hermenegildo, M.V., Kafle, B., Klemen, M., López-García, P., Morales, J.F.: From big-step to small-step semantics and back with interpreter specialisation. In: Proceedings of VPT/HCVS@ETAPS 2020. EPTCS, vol. 320, pp. 50–64 (2020). https://doi.org/10.4204/EPTCS.320.4
12. Giacobazzi, R., Jones, N.D., Mastroeni, I.: Obfuscation by partial evaluation of distorted interpreters. In: PEPM, pp. 63–72. ACM (2012). https://doi.org/10.1145/2103746.2103761

13. Glück, R.: On the generation of specializers. J. Funct. Program. **4**(4), 499–514 (1994). https://doi.org/10.1017/S0956796800001167
14. Glück, R., Jørgensen, J.: Generating transformers for deforestation and supercompilation. In: Le Charlier, B. (ed.) SAS 1994. LNCS, vol. 864, pp. 432–448. Springer, Heidelberg (1994). https://doi.org/10.1007/3-540-58485-4_57
15. Hermenegildo, M.V., et al.: An overview of Ciao and its design philosophy. Theor. Pract. Logic Program. **12**(1–2), 219–252 (2012). https://doi.org/10.1017/S1471068411000457
16. Hill, P.M., Gallagher, J.P.: Handbook of logic in artificial intelligence and logic programming, vol. 5, chap. Meta-Programming in Logic Programming, pp. 421–498. Oxford University Press (1998)
17. Hill, P.M., Lloyd, J.W.: Analysis of meta-programs. In: Meta-Programming in Logic Programming, pp. 23–51. MIT Press (1988)
18. Huizing, C., Koymans, R., Kuiper, R.: A small step for mankind. In: Dams, D., Hannemann, U., Steffen, M. (eds.) Concurrency, Compositionality, and Correctness. LNCS, vol. 5930, pp. 66–73. Springer, Heidelberg (2010). https://doi.org/10.1007/978-3-642-11512-7_5
19. Jones, N.D., Gomard, C., Sestoft, P.: Partial Evaluation and Automatic Software Generation. Prent. Hall (1993). https://doi.org/10.1016/j.scico.2004.03.010
20. Jones, N.D.: Transformation by interpreter specialisation. Sci. Comput. Program. **52**, 307–339 (2004). https://doi.org/10.1016/j.scico.2004.03.010
21. Kahn, G.: Natural semantics. In: Brandenburg, F.J., Vidal-Naquet, G., Wirsing, M. (eds.) STACS 1987. LNCS, vol. 247, pp. 22–39. Springer, Heidelberg (1987). https://doi.org/10.1007/BFb0039592
22. Leuschel, M., Jørgensen, J.: Efficient specialisation in Prolog using the hand-written compiler generator LOGEN. Elec. Notes Theor. Comp. Sci. 30(2) (1999). DOI: https://doi.org/10.1017/S1471068403001662
23. Lombardi, L.A.: Incremental computation: the preliminary design of a programming system which allows for incremental data assimilation in open-ended man-computer information systems. Adv. Comput. **8**, 247–333 (1967). https://doi.org/10.1016/S0065-2458(08)60698-1
24. Nielson, H.R., Nielson, F.: Semantics with applications - a formal introduction. Wiley, Wiley professional computing (1992)
25. Nys, V., De Schreye, D.: Compiling control as offline partial deduction. In: Mesnard, F., Stuckey, P.J. (eds.) LOPSTR 2018. LNCS, vol. 11408, pp. 115–131. Springer, Cham (2019). https://doi.org/10.1007/978-3-030-13838-7_7
26. Plotkin, G.D.: The origins of structural operational semantics. J. Log. Alg. Prog. **60–61**, 3–15 (2004). https://doi.org/10.1016/j.jlap.2004.03.009
27. Plotkin, G.D.: A structural approach to operational semantics. J. Log. Alg. Prog. **60–61**, 17–139 (2004)
28. Turchin, V.F.: Program transformation by supercompilation. In: Ganzinger, H., Jones, N.D. (eds.) Programs as Data Objects. LNCS, vol. 217, pp. 257–281. Springer, Heidelberg (1986). https://doi.org/10.1007/3-540-16446-4_15
29. Vesely, F., Fisher, K.: One step at a time. In: Caires, L. (ed.) ESOP 2019. LNCS, vol. 11423, pp. 205–231. Springer, Cham (2019). https://doi.org/10.1007/978-3-030-17184-1_8

Constrained Horn Clauses Satisfiability via Catamorphic Abstractions

Emanuele De Angelis[1(✉)], Fabio Fioravanti[2(✉)], Alberto Pettorossi[1,3(✉)], and Maurizio Proietti[1(✉)]

[1] IASI-CNR, Rome, Italy
{emanuele.deangelis,maurizio.proietti}@iasi.cnr.it
[2] DEc, University 'G.d'Annunzio', Chieti-Pescara, Italy
fabio.fioravanti@unich.it
[3] DICII, University of Rome 'Tor Vergata', Rome, Italy
pettorossi@info.uniroma2.it

Abstract. Catamorphisms are functions recursively defined on Algebraic Data Types (such as lists and trees), which are often used to compute suitable abstractions (such as list size and tree height) of programs that manipulate those data types. It is well known that program properties specified through catamorphisms can be proved by showing the satisfiability of suitable Constrained Horn Clauses (CHCs). We address the problem of checking the satisfiability of sets of CHCs that encode program properties, and we propose a method for transforming a given set of CHCs into an equisatisfiable one where catamorphisms are no longer present. As a consequence, clauses with catamorphisms can be handled without extending the satisfiability algorithms present in existing CHC solvers. Through an experimental evaluation on a non-trivial benchmark consisting of many list and tree processing sets of CHCs, we show that our technique is indeed effective and significantly enhances the performance of state-of-the-art CHC solvers.

1 Introduction

Catamorphisms are functions that compute abstractions over Algebraic Data Types (ADTs), such as lists or trees. The definition of a catamorphism is based on a simple recursion scheme, called a *fold* in the context of functional programming [22]. Examples of catamorphisms on lists of integers include functions that compute the length of a list, the orderedness, and the sum of its elements. Similarly, examples of catamorphisms on trees are functions that compute the size of a tree, the height of a tree, and the minimum of the integer values at its nodes.

Through catamorphisms we can specify many useful program properties such as, for instance, the one stating that the list computed by a program for sorting lists is indeed ordered, or that it has the same length of the input list. For this reason, program analysis tools based on *abstract interpretation* [6,15] and *program verifiers* [23] have implemented special purpose techniques that handle catamorphisms.

R. Glück and B. Kafle (Eds.): LOPSTR 2023, LNCS 14330, pp. 39–57, 2023.
https://doi.org/10.1007/978-3-031-45784-5_4

In recent years, it has been shown that verification problems that use catamorphisms can be reduced to satisfiability problems for Constrained Horn Clauses (CHCs) by following a general approach that is very well suited for automatic proofs [3,7,14]. A practical advantage of CHC-based verification is that it is supported by several CHC *solvers* which can be used as back-end tools [4,10,17,19].

Unfortunately, the direct translation of catamorphism-based verification problems into CHCs is not always helpful, because CHC solvers may lack mechanisms for deriving solutions by performing induction over ADTs. To overcome this difficulty, some CHC solvers have been extended with special purpose satisfiability algorithms that handle (some classes of) catamorphisms [13,17,20]. For instance, Eldarica's module for solving CHCs has been extended by allowing constraints that use the built-in *size* function counting the number of function symbols in an ADT [17].

In this paper we follow a different approach based on CHC transformation [9, 11]. Given a set P of CHCs that uses catamorphisms and includes one or more queries encoding the properties of interest, we transform P into a set P' such that: (i) P is satisfiable if and only if P' is satisfiable, and (ii) no catamorphism is present in P'. Thus, the satisfiability of P' can be verified by a CHC solver that is not extended for handling catamorphisms and performing induction over ADTs.

The main difference between the technique we present in this paper and the above cited work [9,11] is that the algorithm we present here does not need, for each predicate in the given set P of CHCs, a specification of how the catamorphisms relate to that predicate. For instance, if we want to verify that the output list S of the set of CHCs defining $quicksort(L, S)$ has the same length of the input list L, we need not state that for the auxiliary predicate $partition(X, Xs, Ys, Zs)$, partitioning the list Xs into the two lists Ys and Zs, it is the case that the length of Xs is the sum of the lengths of Ys and Zs. This property will automatically be derived by the CHC solver when it acts on the set of CHCs derived by transformation. In this sense, our technique allows the invention of suitable lemmas needed for the proof of the property of interest.

We will show through a benchmark set of list and tree processing CHCs that our transformation technique is indeed effective and is able to dramatically increase the performance of state-of-the-art CHC solvers such as Eldarica [17] (with the built-in catamorphism *size*) and Z3 with the SPACER engine [12,19].

The rest of the paper is organized as follows. In Sect. 2 we recall some preliminary notions on CHCs and catamorphisms. In Sect. 3 we show an introductory example to motivate our technique. In Sect. 4 we present our transformation algorithm and prove that it guarantees the equisatisfiability of the initial and the transformed sets of clauses. In Sect. 5 we present the implementation of our technique in the VeriCaT$_{abs}$ tool, and through an experimental evaluation, we show the beneficial effect of the transformation on the Eldarica and Z3 CHC solvers. We will consider several abstractions based on catamorphisms relative to lists and trees, such as size, minimum element, orderedness, element membership, element multiplicity, and combinations thereof. Finally, in Sect. 6, we discuss related work and we outline future research directions.

2 Basic Notions

The programs and the properties we consider in this paper are expressed as sets of constrained Horn clauses written in a many-sorted first-order language $\mathcal{L}$ with equality (=). Constraints are expressions in linear integer arithmetic (*LIA*) and boolean algebra (*Bool*). In particular, a *constraint* is a quantifier-free formula c, where the *LIA* constraints may occur as subexpressions of boolean constraints, according to the SMT approach [2]. The syntax of a constraint c is as follows:

$$c ::= d \mid B \mid \mathit{true} \mid \mathit{false} \mid {\sim}c \mid c_1 \,\&\, c_2 \mid c_1 \vee c_2 \mid c_1 \Rightarrow c_2 \mid c_1 = c_2 \mid \mathit{ite}(c, c_1, c_2) \mid t = \mathit{ite}(c, t_1, t_2)$$

$$d ::= t_1 < t_2 \mid t_1 \leq t_2 \mid t_1 = t_2 \mid t_1 \geq t_2 \mid t_1 > t_2$$

where: (i) B is a boolean variable, (ii) $\sim$, &, $\vee$, and $\Rightarrow$ denote negation, conjunction, disjunction, and implication, respectively, (iii) the ternary function *ite* denotes the if-then-else operator (in particular, $\mathit{ite}(c, c_1, c_2)$ = if c holds then c_1 else c_2), and (iv) t is a *LIA* term of the form $a_0 + a_1 X_1 + \cdots + a_n X_n$ with integer coefficients $a_0, \ldots, a_n$ and variables $X_1, ..., X_n$. The equality symbol will be used both for integers and booleans. We will allow ourselves to write the constraint $B = \mathit{true}$ as B, and the constraint $B = \mathit{false}$ as ${\sim}B$. The theory of *LIA* and boolean constraints will collectively be denoted by $\mathit{LIA} \cup \mathit{Bool}$. The integer and boolean sorts are said to be *basic sorts*. A recursively defined sort (such as the sort of lists and trees) is said to be an *algebraic data type* (ADT, for short).

An *atom* is a formula of the form $p(t_1, \ldots, t_m)$, where p is a predicate symbol not occurring in $\mathit{LIA} \cup \mathit{Bool}$, and $t_1, \ldots, t_m$ are first-order terms in $\mathcal{L}$. A *constrained Horn clause* (CHC), or simply, a *clause*, is an implication of the form $H \leftarrow c, G$. The conclusion H, called the *head*, is either an atom or *false*, and the premise, called the *body*, is the conjunction of a constraint c and a conjunction G of zero or more atoms. A clause is said to be a *query* if its head is *false*, and a *definite clause*, otherwise. Without loss of generality, at the expense of introducing suitable equalities, we assume that every atom of the body of a clause has distinct variables (of any sort) as arguments. Given an expression e, by $\mathit{vars}(e)$ we denote the set of all variables occurring in e. By $\mathit{bvars}(e)$ (or $\mathit{adt\text{-}vars}(e)$) we denote the set of variables in e whose sort is a basic sort (or an ADT sort, respectively). The *universal closure* of a formula φ is denoted by $\forall(\varphi)$.

Let $\mathbb{D}$ be the usual interpretation for the symbols of theory $\mathit{LIA} \cup \mathit{Bool}$. Given a set P of definite clauses, by $M(P)$ we denote the *least* $\mathbb{D}$-model of P [18].

The catamorphisms we consider in this paper are defined by first-order, relational recursive schemata as we now indicate. Similar definitions are introduced also in (higher-order) functional programming [16,22].

Let f be a predicate symbol with $m+n$ arguments (for $m \geq 0$ and $n \geq 0$) with sorts $\alpha_1, \ldots, \alpha_m, \beta_1, \ldots, \beta_n$, respectively. We say that f is a *functional predicate* from the sort $\alpha_1 \times \ldots \times \alpha_m$ to the sort $\beta_1 \times \ldots \times \beta_n$, with respect to a given set P

of definite clauses that define f, if $M(P) \models \forall X,Y,Z.\ f(X,Y) \wedge f(X,Z) \rightarrow Y = Z$, where X is an m-tuple of distinct variables, and Y and Z are n-tuples of distinct variables. In this case, when we write the atom $f(X, Y)$, we mean that X and Y are the tuples of the *input* and *output* variables of f, respectively. We say that f is a *total predicate* if $M(P) \models \forall X \exists Y.\ f(X, Y)$. In what follows, a 'total, functional predicate' f from a tuple α of sorts to a tuple β of sorts is said to be a 'total function' in $[\alpha \rightarrow \beta]$, and it is denoted by $f \in [\alpha \rightarrow \beta]$.

Now we introduce the notions of a list catamorphism and a binary tree catamorphism. We leave to the reader the task of introducing the definitions of similar catamorphisms for recursively defined algebraic data types that may be needed for expressing properties of interest. Let α, β, γ, and δ be (products of) basic sorts. Let $list(\beta)$ be the sort of lists with elements of sort β, and $btree(\beta)$ be the sort of binary trees with values of sort β.

Definition 1 (List and Binary Tree Catamorphisms). *A* list catamor-phism ℓ *is a total function in* $[\alpha \times list(\beta) \rightarrow \gamma]$ *defined as follows:*

$\ell(X, [\,], Y) \leftarrow \ell\_basis(X, Y).$
$\ell(X, [H|T], Y) \leftarrow f(X, T, Rf),\ \ell(X, T, R),\ \ell\_combine(X, H, R, Rf, Y).$

where: (*i*) $\ell\_basis \in [\alpha \rightarrow \gamma]$, (*ii*) $\ell\_combine \in [\alpha \times \beta \times \gamma \times \delta \rightarrow \gamma]$, *and* (*iii*) f *is itself a list catamorphism in* $[\alpha \times list(\beta) \rightarrow \delta]$. *A* binary tree catamorphism bt *is a total function in* $[\alpha \times btree(\beta) \rightarrow \gamma]$ *defined as follows:*

$bt(X, leaf, Y) \leftarrow bt\_basis(X, Y).$
$bt(X, node(L, N, R), Y) \leftarrow g(X, L, RLg),\ g(X, R, RRg),$
$\quad bt(X, L, RL),\ bt(X, R, RR),\ bt\_combine(X, N, RL, RR, RLg, RRg, Y).$

where: (*i*) $bt\_basis \in [\alpha \rightarrow \gamma]$, (*ii*) $bt\_combine \in [\alpha \times \beta \times \gamma \times \gamma \times \delta \times \delta \rightarrow \gamma]$, *and* (*iii*) g *is itself a binary tree catamorphism in* $[\alpha \times btree(\beta) \rightarrow \delta]$.

Instances of the schemas of the catamorphisms ℓ and bt of Definition 1 may lack some components, such as the parameter X of basic sort α, or the catamorphisms f or g.

3 An Introductory Example

Let us consider an introductory example consisting of a set of CHCs for doubling lists (see clauses 1–4 in Fig. 1), that is, we have that $double(Xs, Zs)$ holds iff list Zs is the concatenation of two copies of the same list Xs. The atom $eq(Xs, Ys)$ holds iff list Xs is equal to list Ys. The atom $append(Xs,\ Ys, Zs)$ holds iff list Zs is the result of concatenating list Ys to the right of list Xs.

Let us assume that we want to verify that whenever $double(Xs, Zs)$ holds, we have that for any integer X, the number of occurrences of X in Zs is an even number (it is 0 if X is not in Xs). In order to do so, we use the list catamorphim $count(X, Zs, M)$ (see clauses 5–6 in Fig. 1) that holds iff M is the number of occurrences of X in list Zs. Thus, our verification task can be expressed as query 7 in Fig. 1, whereby we derive *false* if the number of occurrences of X is odd (recall that $M = 2\,N + 1$ is a *LIA* constraint).

*** Initial set of CHCs including the catamorphism *count*.

1. $double(Xs,Zs) \leftarrow eq(Xs,Ys),\ append(Xs,Ys,Zs).$
2. $eq(Xs,Xs).$
3. $append([\,],Ys,Ys).$
4. $append([X|Xs],Ys,[X|Zs]) \leftarrow append(Xs,Ys,Zs).$
5. $count(X,[\,],N) \leftarrow N{=}0.$
6. $count(X,[H|T],N) \leftarrow N{=}ite(X{=}H, NT{+}1, NT),\ count(X, T, NT).$

*** Query.

7. $false \leftarrow M{=}2\,N{+}1,\ count(X, Zs, M),\ double(Xs, Zs).$

Fig. 1. The initial set of CHCs including the catamorphism *count* (clauses 5–6) and query 7 specifying the property of interest. The clauses for *count* are an instance of the list catamorphism schema in Definition 1, where predicate ℓ is *count*, predicate ℓ_basis is the constraint $N=0$, predicate f is absent, and predicate $\ell\_combine$ is the if-then-else constraint $N= ite(X{=}H, NT{+}1, NT)$.

Now, in contrast to previous approaches [9,11], we need *not* specify any property of *count* when it acts upon the predicates *double*, *eq*, and *append*. Thus, much less ingenuity is required on the part of the programmer for specifying program correctness. Neither Eldarica nor Z3 with the SPACER engine is able to prove the satisfiability of the set of CHCs shown in Fig. 1.

The transformation technique we propose in this paper introduces, for each predicate p occurring in the initial set of CHCs, a new predicate *newp* defined by the conjunction of a p atom and, for each ADT argument of p, a *count* atom. In our example, the new predicate definitions are clauses $D1$–$D3$ listed in Fig. 2. In particular, the body of definition $D2$ is the conjunction of $append(\underline{H},\underline{B},\underline{E})$ and of the three *count* atoms, one for each of the lists $\underline{H}$, $\underline{B}$, and $\underline{E}$.

Then, by applying variants of the fold/unfold transformation rules, we derive a new version of the initial CHCs where each predicate p has been replaced by the corresponding *newp*. Now, when the CHC solver looks for a model of the new, derived set of CHCs, it is guided by the fact that suitable constraints, inferred from the query, must relate the arguments of *newp*.

In our transformation we also introduce, for each predicate *newp*, a predicate *newp_woADTs* whose definition is obtained by removing the ADT arguments from the definition of *newp*. It is often easier to find a model for *newp_woADTs*, rather than for *newp*, because the solver need not handle ADTs at all. However, since each *newp_woADTs* is an overapproximation of *newp*, by using the clauses with the ADTs removed, one could wrongly infer unsatisfiability in cases when, on the contrary, the initial set of CHCs is satisfiable. To guarantee the equisatisfiability of the initial set of clauses with respect to the transformed set, we simply add to the body of every clause a *newp_woADTs* atom for each *newp* atom (see Theorem 1 for the correctness of this transformation). Now Z3 is able to prove the satisfiability of the derived set of CHCs that we have shown in Fig. 2.

*** New predicate definitions introduced (with underlined ADT arguments).

$D1.\ new1(A,\underline{B},C,\underline{E},F) \leftarrow count(A,\underline{B},C),\ count(A,\underline{E},F),\ double(\underline{B},\underline{E}).$

$D2.\ new2(A,\underline{B},C,\underline{E},F,\underline{H},I) \leftarrow count(A,\underline{B},C),\ count(A,\underline{E},F),\ count(A,\underline{H},I),$
$append(\underline{H},\underline{B},\underline{E}).$

$D3.\ new3(A,\underline{B},C,\underline{E},F) \leftarrow count(A,\underline{B},C),\ count(A,\underline{E},F),\ eq(\underline{E},\underline{B}).$

*** Transformed CHCs

11. $false \leftarrow C{=}2\,D{+}1,\ new1(A,E,F,G,C),\ new1\_woADTs(A,F,C).$

12. $new1(A,B,C,E,F) \leftarrow new2(A,M,K,E,F,B,C),\ new2\_woADTs(A,K,F,C),$
$new3(A,M,K,B,C),\ new3\_woADTs(A,K,C).$
13. $new2(A,B,C,B,C,[\,],G) \leftarrow G{=}0,\ count(A,B,C),\ count\_woADTs(A,C).$
14. $new2(A,B,C,[E|F],G,[E|J],K) \leftarrow G{=}ite(A{=}E,N{+}1,N),\ K{=}ite(A{=}E,P{+}1,P),$
$new2(A,B,C,F,N,J,P),\ new2\_woADTs(A,C,N,P).$
15. $new3(A,B,C,B,C) \leftarrow count(A,B,C),\ count\_woADTs(A,C).$

16. $new1\_woADTs(A,B,D) \leftarrow new2\_woADTs(A,I,D,B),\ new3\_woADTs(A,I,B).$
17. $new2\_woADTs(A,B,B,F) \leftarrow F{=}0,\ count\_woADTs(A,B).$
18. $new2\_woADTs(A,B,D,F) \leftarrow D{=}ite(A{=}I,K{+}1,K),\ F{=}ite(A{=}I,L{+}1,L),$
$new2\_woADTs(A,B,K,L).$
19. $new3\_woADTs(A,B,B) \leftarrow count\_woADTs(A,B).$
20. $count\_woADTs(A,B) \leftarrow B{=}0.$
21. $count\_woADTs(A,B) \leftarrow B{=}ite(A{=}C,D{+}1,D),\ count\_woADTs(A,D).$

Fig. 2. The predicate definitions $D1$–$D3$ (with underlined ADT arguments) introduced during the transformation, and the derived, final set of CHCs (11–21).

4 CHC Transformation via Catamorphic Abstractions

In this section we present our transformation algorithm, called $\mathcal{T}_{abs}$. The input of $\mathcal{T}_{abs}$ is: (i) a set P of definite clauses, (ii) a query Q expressing the property to be verified, and (iii) for each ADT sort, a conjunction of catamorphisms whose definitions are included in P. $\mathcal{T}_{abs}$ introduces a set of new predicates, which incorporate as extra arguments information coming from the catamorphisms, and transforms $P \cup \{Q\}$ into a new set $P' \cup \{Q'\}$ such that $P \cup \{Q\}$ is satisfiable if and only if so is $P' \cup \{Q'\}$.

The transformation is effective when the catamorphisms used in the new predicate definitions establish relations that are useful to solve the query. In particular, it is often useful to use in the new definitions catamorphisms that include the ones used in the query. For instance, in our introductory example of Sect. 3, the catamorphism used for the transformation is the predicate *count*, which is the same catamorphism used in the query. However, as we will see later, there are cases in which it is important to consider catamorphisms not present in the query. The choice of the suitable catamorphisms to use in the transformation rests upon the programmer's ingenuity, and the problem of introducing them in a fully automatic way is left for future research.

4.1 Catamorphic Abstractions and Catamorphic Abstraction Specifications

The predicates in the set P of clauses different from catamorphisms are called *program predicates* and the atoms having a program predicate are called *program atoms*. The atoms having a catamorphism predicate are called *catamorphism atoms*. Without loss of generality, we assume that no clause in P has occurrences of both program atoms and catamorphism atoms. The query Q given in input to $\mathcal{T}_{abs}$ is of the form:

$$false \leftarrow c,\ cata_1(X,T_1,Y_1),\ \ldots,\ cata_n(X,T_n,Y_n),\ p(Z).$$

where: (i) $p(Z)$ is a program atom and Z is a tuple of distinct variables; (ii) $cata_1$, ..., $cata_n$ are catamorphisms; (iii) X is a tuple of distinct variables of basic sort; (iv) $T_1,\ldots,T_n$ are ADT variables occurring in Z; and (v) $Y_1,\ldots,Y_n$ are pairwise disjoint tuples of distinct variables of basic sort not occurring in $vars(\{X,Z\})$. Without loss of generality, we assume that the $cata_i$'s over the same ADT variable are all distinct (this assumption is trivially satisfied by query 7 of Fig. 1).

For each sort τ, a *catamorphic abstraction* for the ADT sort τ is a conjunction of catamorphisms defined as follows:

$$cata_\tau(X,T,\overline{Y}) =_{def} cata_1(X,T,Y_1),\ \ldots,\ cata_n(X,T,Y_n)$$

where: (i) T is a variable of ADT sort τ; (ii) $X,Y_1,\ldots,Y_n$ are tuples of variables of basic sort; (iii) the variables in $\{X,Y_1,\ldots,Y_n\}$ are all distinct; (iv) $\overline{Y}$ is a shorthand for $Y_1,\ldots,Y_n$; and (v) the $cata_i$ predicates are all distinct.

Given a set P of clauses and the catamorphic abstractions for the ADT sorts $\tau_1,\ldots,\tau_k$, a *catamorphic abstraction specification for* P is a set of expressions, one expression for each program predicate p in P that has at least an argument of ADT sort. The expression for the predicate p is called the *catamorphic abstraction specification for* p and it is of the form:

$$p(Z) \Longrightarrow cata_{\tau_1}(X,T_1,V_1),\ldots,cata_{\tau_k}(X,T_k,V_k).$$

where: (i) Z is a tuple of distinct variables, (ii) $T_1,\ldots,T_k$ are the distinct variables in Z of (not necessarily distinct) ADT sorts $\tau_1,\ldots,\tau_k$, respectively, (iii) $V_1,\ldots,V_k$ are pairwise disjoint tuples of distinct variables of basic sort not occurring in $vars(\{X,Z\})$; and (iv) $vars(X)\cap vars(Z)=\emptyset$.

Example 1. Let us consider our introductory *double* example (see Sect. 3 and, in particular, Fig. 1) and the catamorphic abstraction for the sort *list*(*int*):

$$cata_{list(int)}(X,L,N) =_{def} count(X,L,N)$$

This abstraction determines the following catamorphic abstraction specifications for the predicates *double*, *eq*, and *append*:

$$double(Xs,Zs) \Longrightarrow count(X,Xs,N1),\ count(X,Zs,N2).$$
$$eq(Xs,Zs) \Longrightarrow count(X,Xs,N1),\ count(X,Zs,N2).$$
$$append(Xs,Ys,Zs) \Longrightarrow count(X,Xs,N1), count(X,Ys,N2), count(X,Zs,N3).$$ □

Example 2. Let us consider: (i) a set *Quicksort* of clauses for ordering lists such that the atom $quicksort(L,S)$ holds iff S is the list ordered in ascending order which is a permutation of the list L, and (ii) the following query stating the orderedness of S:

$false \leftarrow \sim BS,\ is\_asorted(S,BS),\ quicksort(L,S).$
where $is\_asorted(S,BS)$ returns $BS = true$ if S is ordered in ascending order, and $BS = false$, otherwise. The catamorphism *is_asorted* is defined as follows in term of the catamorphism *hd* returning the head of a list (if the list is empty, its head has the arbitrary value 0 which is never used elsewhere):

$is\_asorted([\,], B) \leftarrow B = true.$
$is\_asorted([H|T], B) \leftarrow B = (IsDef \Rightarrow (H \leq HdT \ \&\ BT)),$
$\quad hd(T, IsDef, HdT),\ is\_asorted(T, BT).$
$hd([\,], IsDef, Hd) \leftarrow IsDef = false,\ Hd = 0.$
$hd([H|T], IsDef, Hd) \leftarrow IsDef = true,\ Hd = H.$

Note that, with reference to Definition 1, no parameter X occurs in the list catamorphisms *is_asorted* and *hd*. Now we consider the following catamorphic abstraction for the sort *list*(*int*) (which is the sort of the variable L) made out of the conjunction of three list catamorphisms:

$cata_{list(int)}(L, BMinL, MinL, BMaxL, MaxL, BL) =_{def}$
$\quad listmin(L, BMinL, MinL),\ listmax(L, BMaxL, MaxL),\ is\_asorted(L, BL)$

where $listmin(L, BMinL, MinL)$ returns $BMinL = true$ and the minimum integer $MinL$ of L, if L is not empty, and $BMinL = false$ and an arbitrary integer $MinL$, otherwise. Analogously for *listmax*. Let us consider the atom $partition(V,L,A,B)$, which it is assumed to occur in the set *Quicksort*. We have that, given an integer V and a list L, $partition(V,L,A,B)$ partitions L into the two lists A, whose elements are not larger than V, and B, whose elements are larger than V. The catamorphic abstraction specification for *partition* is as follows:

$partition(V,L,A,B) \Longrightarrow$
$\quad listmin(L,BMinL,MinL),\ listmax(L,BMaxL,MaxL),\ is\_asorted(L,BL),$
$\quad listmin(A,BMinA,MinA),\ listmax(A,BMaxA,MaxA),\ is\_asorted(A,BA),$
$\quad listmin(B,BMinB,MinB),\ listmax(B,BMaxB,MaxB),\ is\_asorted(B,BB).$ □

4.2 Transformation Rules

The rules we use for transforming CHCs using catamorphisms are variants of the usual fold/unfold rules for CHCs (and CLP programs) [7].

A *transformation sequence from* S_0 *to* S_n is a sequence $S_0 \Rrightarrow S_1 \Rrightarrow \ldots \Rrightarrow S_n$ of sets of CHCs such that, for $i = 0, \ldots, n-1$, S_{i+1} is derived from S_i, denoted $S_i \Rrightarrow S_{i+1}$, by performing a transformation step consisting in applying one of the following rules R1–R5.

The goal of a transformation sequence constructed by Algorithm $\mathcal{T}_{abs}$ is to derive, for each program predicate p, a new predicate *newp* whose definition is given by the conjunction of an atom for p with the catamorphism atoms. *newp* has extra arguments that hold the values of the catamorphisms for the ADT arguments of p.

(R1) *Definition Rule.* Let D be a clause of the form $newp(X_1, \ldots, X_k) \leftarrow Catas, A$, where: (1) *newp* is a predicate symbol not occurring in the sequence $S_0 \Rrightarrow S_1 \Rrightarrow \ldots \Rrightarrow S_i$ constructed so far, (2) $\{X_1, \ldots, X_k\} = vars(\{Catas, A\})$, (3) *Catas* is a conjunction of catamorphism atoms, with $adt\text{-}vars(Catas) \subseteq$

adt-vars(A), and (4) A is a program atom. By *definition introduction* we add D to S_i and we get the new set $S_{i+1} = S_i \cup \{D\}$.

We denote by $Defs_j$ the set of clauses, called *definitions*, introduced by rule R1 during the construction of $S_0 \Rrightarrow S_1 \Rrightarrow \ldots \Rrightarrow S_j$.

Example 3. In our *double* example, by applying the definition rule we may introduce the following clause, whose variables of sort *list*(*int*) are B and E:

$D1$. $new1(A,B,C,E,F) \leftarrow count(A,B,C),\ count(A,E,F),\ double(B,E)$.

Thus, $S_1 = S_0 \cup \{D1\}$, where S_0 consists of clauses 1–7 of Fig. 1. □

Now, by making use of the *Unf* function (see Definition 2) and Rule R2, we introduce the unfolding rule, which consists of some unfolding steps followed by the application of the functionality property, which has been presented in previous work [11]. Recall that list and binary tree catamorphisms and, in general, all catamorphisms are assumed to be total functions (see Definition 1).

Definition 2 (*One-step Unfolding*). Let D: $H \leftarrow c, L, A, R$ be a clause, where A is an atom, and let P be a set of definite clauses with $vars(D) \cap vars(P) = \emptyset$. Let *Cls*: $\{K_1 \leftarrow c_1, B_1,\ \ldots,\ K_m \leftarrow c_m, B_m\}$, with $m \geq 0$, be the set of clauses in P, such that: for $j = 1, \ldots, m$, (*i*) there exists a most general unifier ϑ_j of A and K_j, and (*ii*) the conjunction of constraints $(c, c_j)\vartheta_j$ is satisfiable. The *one-step unfolding* produces the following set of CHCs:

$$Unf(D, A, P) = \{(H \leftarrow c, c_j, L, B_j, R)\vartheta_j \mid j = 1, \ldots, m\}.$$

In the following Rule R2 and in the sequel, *Catas* denotes a conjunction of catamorphism atoms.

(R2) *Unfolding Rule.* Let D: $newp(U) \leftarrow Catas, A$ be a definition in $S_i \cap Defs_i$, where A is a program atom, and P be the set of definite clauses in S_i. We derive a new set *UnfD* of clauses by the following three steps.

Step 1. (*One-step unfolding of program atom*) $UnfD := Unf(D, A, P)$;

Step 2. (*Unfolding of the catamorphism atoms*)

while there exists a clause E: $H \leftarrow d, L, C, R$ in *UnfD*, for some conjunctions L and R of atoms, such that C is a catamorphism atom whose argument of ADT sort is not a variable **do**

$UnfD := (UnfD \setminus \{E\}) \cup Unf(E, C, P)$;

Step 3. (*Applying Functionality on catamorphism atoms*)

while there exists a clause E: $H \leftarrow d, L, cata(X,T,Y1), cata(X,T,Y2), R$ in *UnfD*, for some catamorphism *cata* **do**

$UnfD := (UnfD - \{E\}) \cup \{H \leftarrow d, Y1{=}Y2, L, cata(X,T,Y1), R\}$;

Then, by *unfolding* D we derive $S_{i+1} = (S_i \setminus \{D\}) \cup UnfD$.

Example 4. For instance, in our *double* example, by unfolding clause $D1$ we get:

$E1$. $new1(A,B,C,E,F) \leftarrow count(A,B,C),\ count(A,E,F),\ eq(B,G),$
$append(B,G,E)$.

Thus, $S_2 = S_0 \cup \{E1\}$. □

By the following *catamorphism addition rule* we use the catamorphic abstraction specifications and we add catamorphism atoms to the bodies of the clauses.

(R3) *Catamorphism Addition Rule.* Let C: $H \leftarrow c, Catas^C, A_1, \ldots, A_m$ be a clause in S_i, where H is either *false* or a program atom and $A_1, \ldots, A_m$ are program atoms. Let E be the clause derived from C as follows:
for $k = 1, \ldots, m$ **do**

- consider program atom A_k; let $Catas^C_k$ be the conjunction of every catamorphism atom F in $Catas^C$ such that $adt\text{-}vars(A_k) \cap adt\text{-}vars(F) \neq \emptyset$;
- let $A_k \Longrightarrow cata_1(X, T_1, Y_1), \ldots, cata_n(X, T_n, Y_n)$ be a catamorphic abstraction specification for the predicate of A_k, where the variables in $Y_1, \ldots, Y_n$ do not occur in C, and the conjunction $cata_1(X, T_1, Y_1), \ldots, cata_n(X, T_n, Y_n)$ can be split into two subconjunctions B_1 and B_2 such that: (i) a variant $B_1\vartheta$ of B_1, for a substitution ϑ acting on $vars(B_1)$, is a subconjunction of $Catas^C_k$, and (ii) for every catamorphism atom $cata_j(X, T_j, Y_j)$ in $B_2\vartheta$, there is no catamorphism atom in $Catas^C_k$ of the form $cata_j(V, T_j, W)$ (i.e., there is no catamorphism atom with the same predicate acting on the same ADT variable T_j)
  then add the conjunction $B_2\vartheta$ to the body of C.

Then, by catamorphism addition, we get $S_{i+1} = (S_i \setminus \{C\}) \cup \{E\}$.

Example 5. In our *double* example, by applying the catamorphism addition rule to clause $E1$, we add the catamorphism $count(A,H,I)$ and we get:

$E2.\ new1(A,B,C,E,F) \leftarrow count(A,B,C),\ count(A,E,F),\ count(A,H,I),$
$\quad eq(B,H),\ append(B,H,E).$

Thus, we get the new set of clauses $S_3 = S_0 \cup \{E2\}$. □

The *folding rule* allows us to replace a conjunction of a program atom and one or more catamorphisms by a single atom, whose predicate has been introduced in a previous application of the Definition Rule.

(R4) *Folding Rule.* Let C: $H \leftarrow c, Catas^C, A_1, \ldots, A_m$ be a clause in S_i, where either H is *false* or C has been obtained by the unfolding rule, possibly followed by catamorphism addition rule. For $k = 1, \ldots, m$,

- let $Catas^C_k$ be the conjunction of every catamorphism atom F in $Catas^C$ such that $adt\text{-}vars(A_k) \cap adt\text{-}vars(F) \neq \emptyset$;
- let D_k: $H_k \leftarrow Catas^D_k, A_k$ be a clause in $Defs_i$ (modulo variable renaming) such that $Catas^C_k$ is a subconjunction of $Catas^D_k$.

Then, by *folding* C *using* $D_1, \ldots, D_m$, we derive clause E: $H \leftarrow c, H_1, \ldots, H_m$, and we get $S_{i+1} = (S_i \setminus \{C\}) \cup \{E\}$.

Example 6. In order to fold clause $E2$, we introduce two new definitions $D2$ and $D3$, one for each program atom occurring in the body of that clause (see Fig. 2) and, by folding clause $E2$ using $D2$ and $D3$, we get:

$E3.\ new1(A,B,C,E,F) \leftarrow new2(A,M,K,E,F,B,C),\ new3(A,M,K,B,C).$

Also, query 7 (see Fig. 1) can be folded using definition $D1$, and we get:

$E4.\ false \leftarrow C = 2\,D+1,\ new1(A,E,F,G,C).$

Thus, $S_4 = (S_0 \backslash \{7\}) \cup \{E3, E4, D2, D3\}$. Then, the transformation will continue by looking for the clauses relative to the newly introduced predicates $new2$ (see Definition $D2$) and $new3$ (see Definition $D3$). □

The following Rule R5 is a new transformation rule that allows the introduction of new predicates by erasing ADT arguments from existing predicates, and the addition of atoms with these new predicates to the body of a clause.

(R5) *Erasure Addition Rule.* Let A be the atom $p(t_1, \ldots, t_k, u_1, \ldots, u_m)$, where $t_1, \ldots, t_k$ have (possibly distinct) basic sorts and $u_1, \ldots, u_m$ have (possibly distinct) ADT sorts. We define the *ADT-erasure* of A, denoted $\chi(A)$, to be the atom $\chi(p)(t_1, \ldots, t_k)$, where $\chi(p)$ is a new predicate symbol. Let C: $H \leftarrow c, A_1, \ldots, A_n$ be a clause in S_i. By *erasure addition* we derive the two new clauses:

$\chi_1(C)$: $H \leftarrow c, A_1, \chi(A_1), \ldots, A_n, \chi(A_n)$ and
$\chi_2(C)$: $\chi(H) \leftarrow c, \chi(A_1), \ldots, \chi(A_n)$

Then, $S_{i+1} = \{\chi_1(C) \mid C \in S_i\} \cup$
$\{\chi_2(C) \mid C$ is a clause in S_i whose head is not *false*$\}$.

Example 7. Let us consider clause $E3$ of Example 6. Then, let us consider that:

$$\begin{aligned}
\chi(new1(A,B,C,E,F)) &= new1_woADTs(A,C,F),\\
\chi(new2(A,M,K,E,F,B,C)) &= new2_woADTs(A,K,F,C),\\
\chi(new3(A,M,K,B,C)) &= new3_woADTs(A,K,C).
\end{aligned}$$

Thus, from clause $E3$, by erasure addition we get clauses 12 and 16 of Fig. 2. □

The following theorem is a consequence of well-known results for CHC transformations [7] (see, for instance, a recent survey [7] and the original papers cited therein).

Theorem 1 (Correctness of the Rules). *Let* $S_0 \Rightarrow S_1 \Rightarrow \ldots \Rightarrow S_n$ *be a transformation sequence using rules* R1–R5. *Then,* S_0 *is satisfiable if and only if* S_n *is satisfiable.*

Proof. (Sketch) The rules we use for transforming CHCs are variants of the usual fold/unfold rules for CHCs and CLP programs [7]. In particular, Rule R3 allows us to derive a new clause E by adding to the body of clause C in S_i one or more catamorphism atoms of the form $cata_j(X, T_j, Y_j)$, where the variables in the tuple Y_j do not occur in C. To simplify the proof, let us regard *false* as a program atom. Hence, every set of clauses has a least $\mathbb{D}$-model and it is satisfiable iff that model does not contain *false*. The assumption that catamorphisms are total functions enforces that $M(S_i) \models \forall X, T_j\ \exists Y_j.\ cata_j(X, T_j, Y_j)$, and thus the body of C is equivalent in $M(S_i)$ to the body of E. Furthermore, $cata_j$ does not depend on the predicate of H, which is a program atom, and thus no new dependence of the predicate of H on itself is introduced. Thus, $M(S_i) = M((S_i \setminus \{C\}) \cup \{E\})$ and therefore the two sets of clauses S_i and $(S_i \setminus \{C\}) \cup \{E\}$ are equisatisfiable.

The correctness of Rule R5 follows from the fact that each predicate $\chi(p)$ is an overapproximation of p, that is, $M(S_i \cup \chi_2(S_i)) \models \forall X_1, \ldots, X_k, Y_1, \ldots, Y_m.\ p(X_1, \ldots, X_k, Y_1, \ldots, Y_m) \rightarrow \chi(p)(X_1, \ldots, X_k)$, where $\chi_2(S_i) = \{\chi_2(C) \mid C$ is a clause in S_i whose head is not *false*$\}$. Thus, the body of a clause C that has an occurrence of $p(t_1, \ldots, t_k, u_1, \ldots, u_m)$ is equivalent in $M(S_i \cup \chi_2(S_i))$ to the body of the clause $\chi_1(C)$ obtained by adding $\chi(p)(t_1, \ldots, t_k)$. This addition does not introduce any new dependence of the head of C on itself and, by an argument similar to the one used for the correctness of Rule R3, satisfiability is not affected. □

4.3 The Transformation Algorithm $\mathcal{T}_{abs}$

The set of new definitions needed by the transformation algorithm $\mathcal{T}_{abs}$ is not given in advance. In general, that set depends on: (i) the given query, (ii) the given catamorphic abstraction, and (iii) the auxiliary catamorphisms occurring in the definitions of the catamorphisms used in the query and in the abstraction. We will compute the set of new definitions needed by algorithm $\mathcal{T}_{abs}$ as the least fixpoint of an operator $\tau_{P\cup\{Q\},\alpha}$, where: (i) P is a set of CHC clauses, (ii) Q is a query, and (iii) α is a given catamorphic abstraction specification. $\tau_{P\cup\{Q\},\alpha}$ transforms a set Δ of definitions into a new set Δ' of definitions.

A set Δ of definitions is called *monovariant* if, for each program predicate p, there is at most one definition in Δ having an occurrence of p in its body.

Definition 3. *Let D_1: $newp1(U_1) \leftarrow B_1$ and D_2: $newp2(U_2) \leftarrow B_2$ be two definitions. We say that D_2 is an* extension *of D_1, written $D_1 \sqsubseteq D_2$, if B_1 is a subconjunction of B_2. Let Δ_1 and Δ_2 be two sets of definitions. We say that Δ_2 is an* extension *of Δ_1, written $\Delta_1 \sqsubseteq \Delta_2$, if for each D_1 in Δ_1 there exists D_2 in Δ_2 such that $D_1 \sqsubseteq D_2$.*

Given a set *Cls* of clauses and a set Δ of definitions, the *Define* function (see Fig. 3) derives a set Δ' of definitions that can be used for folding all clauses in *Cls*. If Δ is monovariant, then also Δ' is monovariant. In particular, due to the (Add) case, Δ' contains a definition for each program predicate occurring in the body of the clauses in *Cls*. Due to the (Extend) case, $\Delta \sqsubseteq \Delta'$. The *Unfold* and *AddCata* functions (see Fig. 3) apply the unfolding and catamorphism addition rules, respectively, to sets of clauses.

Now, we define the operator $\tau_{P\cup\{Q\},\alpha}$ as follows:

$$\tau_{P\cup\{Q\},\alpha}(\Delta) = \begin{cases} \mathit{Define}(\mathit{AddCata}(Q), \emptyset) & \text{if } \Delta = \emptyset \\ \mathit{Define}(\mathit{AddCata}(\mathit{Unfold}(\Delta, P), \alpha), \Delta) & \text{otherwise} \end{cases}$$

If Δ is empty, $\tau_{P\cup\{Q\},\alpha}$ introduces by the *Define* function (see (Add) case), a new definition for each program predicate occurring in query Q, after adding suitable catamorphisms. If Δ is not empty, $\tau_{P\cup\{Q\},\alpha}(\Delta)$ is an extension of Δ obtained by first unfolding all clauses in Δ, then applying the catamorphism addition rule, and finally, applying the *Define* function.

The *AddCata* function guarantees that there is a bound on the number of catamorphisms that can occur in a definition. Since, as already mentioned,

Given a set *Cls* of clauses and a monovariant set Δ of definitions, *Define*(Cls, Δ) returns a monovariant set Δ' of new definitions computed as follows.

$\Delta' := \Delta$;
for each clause $H \leftarrow c, G$ in *Cls*, where G contains at least one ADT variable **do**
  for each program atom A in G **do**
    $Catas_A = \{F \mid F$ is a catamorphism atom in G and $adt\text{-}vars(F) \subseteq adt\text{-}vars(A)\}$;
    if there is a clause D: $newp(U) \leftarrow B, A$ in Δ', for any conjunction B of catamorphism atoms **then**
      if $Catas_A$ is *not* a subconjunction of B **then** // (**Extend**)
      introduce definition $ExtD$: $extp(V) \leftarrow A, B'$, where: (i) *extp* is a new predicate symbol, (ii) $V = vars(\{B', A\})$, and (iii) B' is the conjunction of the distinct catamorphism atoms occurring either in B or in $Catas_A$;
      $\Delta' := (\Delta' \setminus \{D\}) \cup \{ExtD\}$;
    else // (**Add**)
    introduce definition $NewD$: $newp(V) \leftarrow A, Catas_A$, where: (i) *newp* is a new predicate symbol, and (ii) $V = vars(\{A, Catas_A\})$;
    $\Delta' := \Delta' \cup \{NewD\}$;

Given a set $\Delta = \{D_1, \ldots, D_n\}$ of definitions and a set P of definite clauses, $Unfold(\Delta, P) = \bigcup_{i=1}^{n} UnfD_i$, where $UnfD_i$ is the set of clauses derived by unfolding D_i.

Given a set $Cls = \{C_1, \ldots, C_n\}$ of clauses and a catamorphic abstraction specification α, $AddCata(Cls, \alpha) = \{E_i \mid E_i$ is derived from C_i by catamorphism addition using $\alpha\}$.

Given a set $Cls = \{C_1, \ldots, C_n\}$ of clauses and a monovariant set Δ of definitions, $Fold(Cls, \Delta) = \{E_i \mid E_i$ is derived from C_i by folding C_i using the definitions in $\Delta\}$.

Given a set $Cls = \{C_1, \ldots, C_n\}$ of clauses, $AddErasure(Cls) = \{\chi_1(C) \mid C \in Cls\} \cup \{\chi_2(C) \mid C$ is a clause in *Cls* whose head is not *false*$\}$.

Fig. 3. The *Define*, *Unfold*, *AddCata*, *Fold*, and *AddErasure* functions. When introducing these functions we assume that, for each clause C in *Cls* and each catamorphism atom *Cata* in the body of C, there is a program atom A in the body of C such that $adt\text{-}vars(Cata) \subseteq adt\text{-}vars(A)$. If A is absent for a catamorphism atom *Cata* having ADT variable X of sort τ, we can always add an atom $true_\tau(X)$ that is recursively defined and holds for every X of sort τ.

$\tau_{P\cup\{Q\},\alpha}$ is monotonic with respect to $\sqsubseteq$, its least fixpoint $\tau_{fix} = lfp(\tau_{P\cup\{Q\},\alpha})$ is equal to $\tau^n_{P\cup\{Q\},\alpha}(\emptyset)$, for some finite number n of iterations. By construction, τ_{fix} is monovariant. Then, starting from a set P of CHC clauses, by using the set τ_{fix} of definitions, the transformation algorithm $\mathcal{T}_{abs}$ first applies the *Unfold* function, and then the *AddCata* function, and finally, the *AddErasure* function that uses the erasure addition rule R5. Thus, $\mathcal{T}_{abs}$ can formally be written as follows:

$$\mathcal{T}_{abs}(P \cup \{Q\}, \alpha) = AddErasure\big(Fold(AddCata\big(Unfold(\tau_{fix}, P), \alpha\big), \tau_{fix})\big)$$

The termination of $\mathcal{T}_{abs}$ follows immediately from the fact that the least fixpoint τ_{fix} is computed in a finite number of steps. Thus, by the correctness of the transformation rules (see Theorem 1), we get the following result.

Theorem 2 (Total Correctness of Algorithm $\mathcal{T}_{abs}$). *$\mathcal{T}_{abs}$ terminates for any set P of definite clauses, query Q, and catamorphic abstraction specification α. Also, $P \cup \{Q\}$ is satisfiable if and only if $\mathcal{T}_{abs}(P \cup \{Q\}, \alpha)$ is satisfiable.*

Finally, we would like to comment on the fact that our transformation algorithm $\mathcal{T}_{abs}$ introduces a monovariant set of definitions. Other definition introduction policies could have been applied. In particular, one could introduce more than one definition for each program predicate, thus producing a *polyvariant* set of definitions. The choice between monovariant and polyvariant definitions has been subject to ample discussion in the literature [7] and both have advantages and disadvantages. Our techniques is adequate in our benchmark, as we will show in the next section. However, we leave a more accurate experimental evaluation to future work.

5 Implementation and Experimental Evaluation

We have implemented algorithm $\mathcal{T}_{abs}$ in a tool, called VeriCaT$_{abs}$, based on VeriMAP [8], which is a system for transforming CHCs. In order to check satisfiability of sets of CHCs (before and after their transformation) we have used the following two solvers: (i) Eldarica (v. 2.0.9) [17], and (ii) Z3 (v. 4.12.2) [12] with the SPACER engine [19] and the *global guidance* option [21].

Our benchmark consists of 150 sets of CHCs that encode properties of various sorting algorithms (such as bubblesort, heapsort, insertionsort, mergesort, quicksort, selectionsort, and treesort), and simple list and tree manipulation algorithms (such as reversing lists, constructing permutations, deleting copies of elements, manipulating binary search trees). Properties of those algorithms are expressed via the following catamorphisms: (i–iv) $size(L, S)$, $listmin(L, Min)$, $listmax(L, Max)$, and $sum(L, Sum)$ computing, respectively, the size S of list L, the minimum Min, the maximum Max, and the sum Sum of the elements of list L, (v) $is\_asorted(L, BL)$ returning $BL = true$ iff list L is ordered in ascending order, (vi) $allpos(L, B)$ returning $B = true$ iff list L is made out of all positive elements, (vii) $member(X, L, B)$ returning $B = true$ iff X is an element of the list L, and (viii) $count(X, L, N)$, which holds iff N is the number (≥ 0) of occurrences of X in the list L. For some properties, we have used more than one catamorphism at a time and, in particular, we have used the conjunction of *member* and *count*, and also the conjunction of *listmin*, *listmax*, and *is_asorted*.

A property holds if and only if its CHC encoding via a query Q is satisfiable, and a verification task consists in using a CHC solver to check satisfiability of Q. Thus, when a property holds, the solver should return *sat* and the property is said to be a *sat* property. Analogously, when a property does not hold, the solver should return *unsat* and the property is said to be an *unsat* property. In our benchmark, for each verification task of a *sat* property, we have considered a companion task whose CHCs have been modified so that the associated property is *unsat*. In particular, we have 75 *sat* properties and 75 *unsat* properties.

We have performed our experiments on an Intel(R) Xeon(R) Gold 6238R CPU 2.20 GHz with 221 GB RAM under CentOS with a time limit of 300 s per verification task. The results of our experiments are reported in Table 1. Our benchmark and tool are available at https://fmlab.unich.it/vericatabs.

Table 1. Problems solved by Eldarica (Eld) and SPACER (Z3) before (-Src) and after (-Transf) transformation. Times are expressed in seconds.

Program	Properties		Eld-Src		Eld-Transf		Z3-Src		Z3-Transf		Transf
	sat	*unsat*	*sat*	*unsat*	*sat*	*unsat*	*sat*	*unsat*	*sat*	*unsat*	Time
			E_1	E_2	E_3	E_4	Z_1	Z_2	Z_3	Z_4	T
List Deletion	7	7	0	7	3	5	0	7	7	7	8.51
List Permutation	5	5	1	5	5	3	0	5	5	5	5.87
Reverse	6	6	1	6	4	6	0	6	6	6	6.94
Reverse w/Accum.	6	6	0	6	5	6	0	6	5	6	6.96
Bubblesort	6	6	1	6	6	6	0	6	6	6	7.26
Heapsort	6	6	0	6	1	3	0	6	6	6	8.01
Insertionsort	6	6	1	6	6	6	0	6	6	6	6.96
Mergesort	7	7	0	7	1	7	0	7	7	7	8.79
Quicksort	8	8	0	5	2	5	0	8	6	8	9.94
Selectionsort	6	6	1	6	4	6	0	6	5	6	7.08
Treesort	6	6	0	5	2	6	0	6	5	6	7.26
Binary Search Tree	6	6	0	4	0	0	0	6	6	6	10.14
Total	75	75	5	69	39	59	0	75	70	75	93.72

Table 1 shows that, for each verification task, the transformation of the CHCs allows a significant improvement of the performance of the Eldarica solver and an even more significant improvement of the Z3 solver.

In particular, before CHC transformation, Z3 did not prove any of the 75 *sat* properties of our benchmark. After CHC transformation, Z3 proved 70 of them to be *sat* (see columns Z_1 and Z_3 of Table 1). Z3 almost always took less than 1 s to prove those 70 *sat* properties after transformation, and only six of them required a few more seconds. For the remaining five *sat* properties, Z3 exceeded the timeout. The time cost of this improvement is very limited. Indeed, most CHC transformations take well below 1 s and only two of them take a little more than 1 s (see column T where each entry is the sum of the times taken for the verification tasks of each row).

Out of 75 *sat* properties, Eldarica proved 5 *sat* properties (all relative to list size) before transformation and 39 *sat* properties (relative also to catamorphisms different from list size) after transformation (see columns E_1 and E_3). However, one property that was proved *sat* before transformation, was not proved after transformation. This is the only example where the built-in *size* function of Eldarica has been more effective than our transformation-based approach.

The 75 *unsat* properties were proved to be *unsat* by Z3 before transformation and also after transformation (see columns Z_2 and Z_4). In almost all examples, the proofs before transformation took well-below 1 s and after transformation took a shorter time. For the 75 *unsat* properties of our benchmark, Eldarica proved 69 of them to be *unsat* before transformation, and only 59 of them after transformation (see columns E_2 and E_4). This is the only case where we experienced a degradation of performance after transformation. This degradation may be related to the fact that in some cases the time taken by Eldarica (even before transformation) is close to the timeout.

In summary, our experimental evaluation shows that VeriCaT$_{abs}$ with Z3 as a back-end solver outperforms the other CHC solving tools we have considered. Indeed, our tool shows much higher effectiveness than the others when verifying *sat* properties, while retains the excellent performance of Z3 for *unsat* properties.

6 Conclusions and Related Work

It is well known that the proof of many program properties can be reduced to a proof of satisfiability of sets of CHCs [3,7,14]. In order to make it easier to automatically prove satisfiability, whenever a program is made out of many functions, possibly recursively defined and depending on each other, it is commonly suggested to provide properties also for the auxiliary functions that may occur in the program. Those extra properties basically play the role of lemmas, which often make the proof of a property of interest much easier.

We have focused our study on the automatic proof of properties of programs that compute over ADTs, when these properties can be defined using catamorphisms. In a previous paper [9], we have proposed an algorithm for dealing with a multiplicity of properties of the various program functions to be proved at the same time. In this paper, we have investigated an approach, whereby the auxiliary properties need not be explicitly defined, but it is enough to indicate the catamorphisms involved in their specifications. This leaves to the CHC solver the burden of discovering the suitable auxiliary properties needed for the proof of the property of interest. Thus, this simpler requirement avoids the task of providing a full specification for the auxiliary functions occurring in the program. However, in principle, the proofs of the properties may become harder for the CHC solver. Our experimental evaluation shows that this is not the case if we follow a transformation-based approach. Indeed, the results presented in this paper support the following two-step approach: (1) use algorithm $\mathcal{T}_{abs}$ proposed here to derive a new, transformed set of CHCs from the given initial set of CHCs that translate the program together with its property of interest, and then (2) use the Z3 solver with *global guidance* [21] on the derived set.

We have shown that our approach is a valid alternative to the development of algorithms for extending CHC solvers with special purpose mechanisms that handle ADTs. In fact, recently proposed approaches extend CHC solvers to the case of CHCs over ADTs through the use of various mechanisms such as: (i) the combination with inductive theorem proving [24], (ii) the lemma generation based on syntax-guided synthesis, (iii) the invariant discovery based on finite tree automata [20], and (iv) the use of suitable abstractions on CHCs with recursively defined function symbols [13].

One key feature of our algorithm $\mathcal{T}_{abs}$ is that it is sound and complete with respect to satisfiability, that is, the transformed set of CHCs is satisfiable if and only if so is the initial one. In this respect, our results here improve over previous work [11], where algorithm $\mathcal{T}_{cata}$ only preserves soundness, that is, if the transformed set of CHCs is satisfiable, then so is the initial one, while if the transformed set is unsatisfiable, nothing can be inferred for the initial one.

In our experiments, we have also realized the usefulness of having more catamorphisms acting together when performing a specific verification. For instance, in the case of the quicksort program, when using the catamorphism *is_asorted* alone, Z3 is unable to show (within the timeout) sortedness of the output list, while when using also the catamorphisms *listmin* and *listmax*, after transformation Z3 proved sortedness in less than 2 s. We leave it for future work to automatically derive the catamorphisms that are useful for showing the property of interest, even if they are not strictly necessary for specifying that property.

Our approach is very much related to *abstract interpretation* [6], which is a methodology for checking properties by interpreting the program as computing on an abstract domain. Catamorphisms can be seen as specific abstraction functions. Abstract interpretation techniques have been studied also in the field of logic programming. In particular, the CiaoPP preprocessor [15] implements abstract interpretation techniques that use *type-based norms*, which are a special kind of integer-valued catamorphisms. These techniques have important applications in *termination analysis* [5] and *resource analysis* [1].

Usually, abstract interpretation is the basis for sound analysis techniques by computing an (over-)approximation of the concrete semantics of a program, and hence these techniques may find counterexamples to the properties of interest that hold in the abstract semantics but that are not feasible in the concrete semantics. As already mentioned, our transformation guarantees the equisatisfiability of the initial and the transformed CHCs, and hence all counterexamples found are feasible in the initial CHCs.

Our transformation-based approach is, to a large extent, agnostic with respect to the theory of constraints used in the CHCs. Thus, it can easily be extended to theories different from *LIA* and *Bool* used in this paper to other theories such as linear real/rational arithmetic or bit-vectors, as far as they are supported by the CHC solver. This is a potential advantage with respect to those abstract interpretation techniques that require the design of an ad-hoc abstract domain for each specific program analysis.

Acknowledgements. We thank Arie Gurfinkel for helpful suggestions on the use of the Z3/SPACER solver. The authors are members of the INdAM Research Group GNCS.

References

1. Albert, E., Genaim, S., Gutiérrez, R., Martin-Martin, E.: A transformational approach to resource analysis with typed-norms inference. Theory Pract. Log. Program. **20**(3), 310–357 (2020)
2. Barrett, C.W., Sebastiani, R., Seshia, S.A., Tinelli, C.: Satisfiability modulo theories. In: Handbook of Satisfiability, volume 185 of Frontiers in Artificial Intelligence and Applications, pp. 825–885. IOS Press (2009)

3. Bjørner, N., Gurfinkel, A., McMillan, K., Rybalchenko, A.: Horn clause solvers for program verification. In: Beklemishev, L.D., Blass, A., Dershowitz, N., Finkbeiner, B., Schulte, W. (eds.) Fields of Logic and Computation II. LNCS, vol. 9300, pp. 24–51. Springer, Cham (2015). https://doi.org/10.1007/978-3-319-23534-9_2
4. Blicha, M., Fedyukovich, G., Hyvärinen, A.E.J., Sharygina, N.: Transition power abstractions for deep counterexample detection. In: TACAS 2022, Part I. LNCS, vol. 13243, pp. 524–542. Springer, Cham (2022). https://doi.org/10.1007/978-3-030-99524-9_29
5. Bruynooghe, M., Codish, M., Gallagher, J.P., Genaim, S., Vanhoof, W.: Termination analysis of logic programs through combination of type-based norms. ACM Trans. Program. Lang. Syst. **29**(2), 10-es (2007)
6. Cousot, P., Cousot, R.: Abstract interpretation: a unified lattice model for static analysis of programs by construction of approximation of fixpoints. In: 4th Symposium on Principles of Programming Languages, POPL 1977, pp. 238–252. ACM (1977)
7. De Angelis, E., Fioravanti, F., Gallagher, J.P., Hermenegildo, M.V., Pettorossi, A., Proietti, M.: Analysis and transformation of constrained Horn clauses for program verification. Theory Pract. Log. Program. **22**(6), 974–1042 (2022)
8. De Angelis, E., Fioravanti, F., Pettorossi, A., Proietti, M.: VeriMAP: a tool for verifying programs through transformations. In: Ábrahám, E., Havelund, K. (eds.) TACAS 2014. LNCS, vol. 8413, pp. 568–574. Springer, Heidelberg (2014). https://doi.org/10.1007/978-3-642-54862-8_47
9. De Angelis, E., Fioravanti, F., Pettorossi, A., Proietti, M.: Multiple query satisfiability of constrained Horn clauses. In: Hanus, M., Inclezan, D. (eds.) PADL 2023. LNCS, vol. 13880, pp. 125–143. Springer, Cham (2023). https://doi.org/10.1007/978-3-031-24841-2_9
10. De Angelis, E., Govind V. K., H.: CHC-COMP 2022: competition report. In: Proceedings of the 9th Workshop on Horn Clauses for Verification and Synthesis and 10th International Workshop on Verification and Program Transformation, EPTCS 373, pp. 44–62. Open Publishing Association (2022)
11. De Angelis, E., Proietti, M., Fioravanti, F., Pettorossi, A.: Verifying catamorphism-based contracts using constrained Horn clauses. Theory Pract. Log. Program. **22**(4), 555–572 (2022)
12. de Moura, L., Bjørner, N.: Z3: an efficient SMT solver. In: Ramakrishnan, C.R., Rehof, J. (eds.) TACAS 2008. LNCS, vol. 4963, pp. 337–340. Springer, Heidelberg (2008). https://doi.org/10.1007/978-3-540-78800-3_24
13. Hari Govind, V.K., Shoham, S., Gurfinkel, A.: Solving constrained Horn clauses modulo algebraic data types and recursive functions. In: Proceedings of the ACM on Programming Languages, POPL 2022, vol. 6, pp. 1–29 (2022)
14. Gurfinkel, A.: Program verification with constrained Horn clauses (invited paper). In: Shoham, S., Vizel, Y. (eds.) CAV 2022. LNCS, vol. 13371, pp. 19–29. Springer, Cham (2022). https://doi.org/10.1007/978-3-031-13185-1_2
15. Hermenegildo, M.V., Puebla, G., Bueno, F., López-García, P.: Integrated program debugging, verification, and optimization using abstract interpretation (and the Ciao system preprocessor). Sci. Comput. Program. **58**(1–2), 115–140 (2005)
16. Hinze, R., Wu, N., Gibbons, J.: Unifying structured recursion schemes. In: International Conference on Functional Programming, ICFP 2013, pp. 209–220. ACM (2013)
17. Hojjat, H., Rümmer, P.: The ELDARICA Horn solver. In: Formal Methods in Computer Aided Design, FMCAD 2018, pp. 1–7. IEEE (2018)

18. Jaffar, J., Maher, M.: Constraint logic programming: a survey. J. Log. Program. **19**(20), 503–581 (1994)
19. Komuravelli, A., Gurfinkel, A., Chaki, S.: SMT-based model checking for recursive programs. Formal Methods Syst. Des. **48**(3), 175–205 (2016)
20. Kostyukov, Y., Mordvinov, D., Fedyukovich, G.: Beyond the elementary representations of program invariants over algebraic data types. In: Conference on Programming Language Design and Implementation, PLDI 2021, pp. 451–465. ACM (2021)
21. Vediramana Krishnan, H.G., Chen, Y., Shoham, S., Gurfinkel, A.: Global guidance for local generalization in model checking. In: Lahiri, S.K., Wang, C. (eds.) CAV 2020, Part II. LNCS, vol. 12225, pp. 101–125. Springer, Cham (2020). https://doi.org/10.1007/978-3-030-53291-8_7
22. Meijer, E., Fokkinga, M., Paterson, R.: Functional programming with bananas, lenses, envelopes and barbed wire. In: Hughes, J. (ed.) FPCA 1991. LNCS, vol. 523, pp. 124–144. Springer, Heidelberg (1991). https://doi.org/10.1007/3540543961_7
23. Suter, P., Köksal, A.S., Kuncak, V.: Satisfiability modulo recursive programs. In: Yahav, E. (ed.) SAS 2011. LNCS, vol. 6887, pp. 298–315. Springer, Heidelberg (2011). https://doi.org/10.1007/978-3-642-23702-7_23
24. Unno, H., Torii, S., Sakamoto, H.: Automating induction for solving Horn clauses. In: Majumdar, R., Kunčak, V. (eds.) CAV 2017, Part II. LNCS, vol. 10427, pp. 571–591. Springer, Cham (2017). https://doi.org/10.1007/978-3-319-63390-9_30

Static Analysis and Type Systems

A Reusable Machine-Calculus for Automated Resource Analyses

Hector Suzanne(✉) and Emmanuel Chailloux

Sorbonne Université – CNRS, LIP6, Paris, France
{hector.suzanne,emmanuel.chailloux}@lip6.fr

Abstract. We introduce an automated resource analysis technique is introduced, targeting a Call-By-Push-Value abstract machine, with memory prediction as a practical goal. The machine has a polymorphic and linear type system enhanced with a first-order logical fragment, which encodes both low-level operational semantics of resource manipulations and high-level synthesis of algorithmic complexity.

Resource analysis must involve a diversity of static analysis, for escape, aliasing, algorithmic invariants, and more. Knowing this, we implement the *Automated Amortized Resource Analysis* framework (AARA) from scratch in our generic system. In this setting, access to resources is a state-passing effect which produces a compile-time approximation of runtime resource usage.

We implemented type inference constraint generation for our calculus, accompanied with an elaboration of bounds for iterators on algebraic datatypes, for minimal ML-style programming languages with Call-by-Value and Call-By-Push-Value semantics. The closed-formed bounds are derived as multivariate polynomials over the integers. This now serves as a base for the development of an experimental toolkit for automated memory analysis of functional languages.

Keywords: Type Theory · Static Analysis · Memory Consumption · Amortized analysis · Call-by-Push-Value

1 Introduction

Typed functional programming offers some structural safety out-of-the-box, but correctness of systems also depends on quantitative, material concerns: memory consumption must remain within bounds, latency and energy cost must be low, etc. This highlights the need for general-purpose resource analysis tools for typed functional languages. But functional languages in the style of ML or Haskell pose specific challenges for resource predictions. First, dynamic allocations is an inherent problem, since the size of the allocated data cannot be fully determined statically. Second, prevalent use of garbage collectors and reference counting in

This work has been partially performed at the IRILL center for Free Software Research and Innovation in Paris, France.

R. Glück and B. Kafle (Eds.): LOPSTR 2023, LNCS 14330, pp. 61–79, 2023.
https://doi.org/10.1007/978-3-031-45784-5_5

those languages means de-allocation points are implicit. Lastly, closures (and high-order programming in general) purposefully hide the amount of resources and state of data they close over.

Amortized complexity [16] has been used to extend functional type systems with resource analyses, notably in Hoffmann's *Automated Amortized Resource Analysis (AARA)* [4]. But extending both the precision and generality of current methods puts a large burden on formalisms and implementations. In this paper, we develop a three-step approach to improve this situation:

1. We extend a Call-by-Push-Value abstract machine typed with intuitionistic linear logic introduced by Curien et al. Programs are decomposed as interaction between values and stacks, whose types can involve *parameters* variables, which denotes quantities of resources and number of combinatorial patterns in data. These parameters are guarded by first-order constraints. Call-by-Push-Value semantics strictly partition types into data-types and computation-types, and use *closures* and *thunks* to mediate between them.
2. Then, we devise a Call-By-Push-Value effects, which reflects at type-level the logical requirements inputs and outputs states of programs: execution go well for all states ($\forall$) with enough resources, and returns some arbitrary state ($\exists$) with some allocated resources.
3. Finally, our implementation extracts a global constraint on resource usage from the type of the rewritten program. Those final constraints are expressed in first-order arithmetic, and can be exported or solved automatically using our heuristic mimicking AARA reasoning. Solvers restricted to intuitionistic logic can elaborate resource expression back into the program.

Users can annotate higher-order code with domain-specific constraints which partially specify runtime behavior. This allows for verification of high-order programs through annotations in the general case, which is, to our knowledge, novel in implementations of AARA. Using our system, resources analyses can be decomposed into independent phases: a program is compiled into the machine according to its CBPV semantics, it is then automatically rewritten with our effect and typechecked. Finally, the domain-specific constraints obtained by type-checking are solved using arithmetic solvers. Note that this last step does not involve the original programs or the semantics of the programming language, as opposed to previous work.

Producing resources bounds has many non-trivial requirements: one must unravel memory aliasing, lifetime of allocations, algorithmic complexity and invariants, etc. When all those analyses interact, it becomes beneficial to use a formalism that puts them all on equal footings, as opposed to one dedicated uniquely to resource analyses. In our experiments, combinations of those analyses are easier implement and verify thanks to factorization, effect system, and core inference procedure.

Plan. Section 2 is dedicated to the wider context of amortized static analysis, the AARA method, and its recent formalizations in linear, Call-By-Push-Value

λ-calculus. This ends with a more detailed summary of our technical setup implementing AARA. In Sect. 3, we introduce our generic abstract machine adopting those advances, and follow with its type system in Sect. 4. We then explain how to encode resource analyses for high-level languages as a Call-By-Push-Value effect in our model in Sect. 5. We discuss our implementation and automation of analyses for functional languages in Sect. 6, and describe perspectives for further research in the conclusion Sect. 7.

2 Context and *State of the Art*

We begin by fixing some important notions regarding *amortized algorithm analysis* [16], reviewing the AARA framework, and presenting its most recent instantiations. Amortized algorithm analysis is a method for determining the complexity of some operations on a data structure. Instead of merely accumulating costs, it represent programs and their resources together as a closed system, and characterizes cost as the minimum of total resource allowing the execution to proceed. We then present with the *Automated Amortized Resource Analysis* framework and its recent advances using *Call-By-Push-Value.* Once those concepts are set up, we end the section with our setup for recovering AARA in a generic Call-By-Push-Value system.

2.1 Amortized Analysis

Amortized analysis is an ubiquitous tool for the analysis of algorithms over the entire lifetime of some structure, introduced by Tarjan [16] to determine asymptotic costs, but it applies just as well to quantitative prediction. Foreseeing the rest of the paper, we will represent programs by abstract machines and follow the nomenclature of previous works [1]. States of the abstract machine are *commands* $c \in \mathbf{C}$, and are made up of a *value* $V \in \mathbf{V}$ and an *continuation stack* $S \in \mathbf{S}$ with syntax $c = \langle V \parallel S \rangle$. Semantics are given by deterministic, small-step reduction which will be assumed to terminate throughout the paper. The execution of a program is therefore a finite sequence of commands $c = (c_i)_{i \leq n}$.

Costs. A *cost metric* is a function $m : \mathbf{C} \times \mathbf{C} \to \mathbb{Z}$ giving a cost for a transition $c \to c'$. When $m(c, c') \geq 0$ we call the cost a *debit*, and when $m(c, c') < 0$ we call it a *credit.* Those credits do not occur for some costs models like time and energy, which cannot be recouped. Models with credits, like memory or currency, require credits and follow an extra condition, mimicking absence of bankruptcy: all intermediate costs $\sum_{j \leq i} m_j$ must be positive. Figuratively, this means that memory cannot be freed before having been allocated, that currency cannot be spent from an empty account, etc.

For a sequence of deterministic reductions $(c_i)_{i \leq n}$, we write $m_i = m(c_i, c_{i+1})$ the cost of a reduction step, and $m(c)$ the total cost of the reduction sequence. This total cost is the maximum of costs that can be reached at an intermediate state, that is $m(c) = \max_{i \leq n} \sum_{j \leq i} m_j$.

Potential. This formalism for costs can be reformulated as a matter of *transfer of resources*, an idea originally put forward by Tarjan [16]. Assume given a fixed, sufficiently high amount of resources P to run a program (pick any $P \geq m(c)$). Each intermediate command c_i has a positive amount of *allocated* resources $q_i = \sum_{j \leq i} m_j$, and a positive amount of *free* resources $p_i = P - q_i$. At the beginning of execution, we have $p_0 = P$ and $q_0 = 0$, and as reduction progresses, we have the two inductive relations $p_i = p_{i+1} + m_i$ and $q_i + m_i = q_{i+1}$. Therefore, $p_i + q_i = p_0 + q_0 = P$ is an invariant of execution: resources are neither created nor lost, but preserved.

Predicting Amortized Costs. The "potential" point of view frames the problem of cost analysis as one of invariant search: given $V \in \mathbf{V}$, find some function $f : \mathbf{S} \to \mathbb{N}$ such that $f(S) \geq m(\langle V \parallel S \rangle)$. Specifically, for each type for environment, we define numerical invariants called *parameters* (size, length, height, etc.) which gives a function $\varphi : \mathbf{S} \to \mathbb{N}^k$ taking each environment to its numerical invariant, and call φ a *parameterization* of S. Many such parameterizations exists for the same datum. For example, a tree might be parameterized by its size, its depth and width, or more complex combinatorial data. Then given a parameterization φ of the runtime data, the amortized complexity of V is a function $P_V : \mathbb{N}^k \to \mathbb{N}$ such that $P_V(\varphi(S)) \geq m(\langle V \parallel S \rangle)$.

2.2 Automated Amortized Resource Analysis and *RAML*

Hoffmann's *Automated Amortized Resource Analysis* (introduced in [4], see [6] for a retrospective) is a type-theoretic framework for resource usage inference in functional languages. We give here a short introduction to AARA for non-recuperable costs. Nevertheless, both AARA and our methods support them.

In Hoffmann's work, costs are represented by pairs $p = (p_{\max}, p_{\text{out}})$ with $p_{\max} \geq p_{\text{out}}$, which means "evaluation has a maximal cost of $p_{\max}$ of which p_{out} are still allocated at the end". They are endowed with sequencing written additively. Judgements $\Gamma \vdash^{p}_{p'} e : T$ means that if p resources are free before evaluating e, then p' are available afterward.

Parameters in AARA are linear combinations of specialized parameters called *indices*, which directly represent the number of some pattern in a structure; For example, the base indices of a list l are the binomial coefficients $\binom{len(l)}{k}$ with constant k, which count the number of non-contiguous sublists of l with length k. The weights with which indices are combined are subject to a linear-programming optimization to derive bounds on $p_{\max}$ and p_{out}. AARA doesn't use a linear type system. Instead, source programs must be *syntactically affine*: every variable is used at most once, and explicitly duplicated, which splits its weights.

We show the rule for pairs below, exhibits an important property of AARA typing: it encodes operational semantics of the specific source language within its typing rules. Below for example, the cost k_{pair} is payed from $p + k_{\text{pair}}$, then e is evaluated, then e', yielding the sequence of potentials $(p+k_{\text{pair}}) \to p \to p' \to p''$.

$$\frac{\Gamma \vdash^{p}_{p'} e : A \qquad \Gamma \vdash^{p'}_{p''} e' : B}{\Gamma \vdash^{p+k_{\text{pair}}}_{p''} (e, e') : A \times B}$$

Instances of AARA cover different complexity classes [7], some aspects of garbage collection [12] for pure functional programming, and some aspects of imperative programming with mutable arrays [9]. Hoffmann et al. have implemented AARA in *Resource-Aware ML* [5] (RAML), a type system for a purely-functional subset of OCaml that infers memory bounds, and supports reasoning the number of nodes in algebraic datatypes, iteration on lists, deeply-nested pattern matching, and limited form of closures. On those programs, RAML can infer costs for a class of algorithms of polynomial complexity. The key point allowing RAML to precisely bound memory usage of OCaml programs is its compile-time representation of heap pointers, allowing it to be aware of memory aliasing. RAML support high-order programming, if high-order arguments do not change during successive calls to the high-order function that uses them. Our continuation-passing, defunctionalized system allows for such changes to be represented as modification to the argument's evaluation context, with can in theory be tracked using the same tools as data structures.

2.3 dℓPCF and λ_{amor}

On the other end of the spectrum, type systems inspired from program logics can prove complex properties, even for non-terminating programs. Dal Lago & Gaboardi's dℓPCF [2,3] is a type system for the λ-calculus with integers and fixpoints (PCF for short), with a highly-parametric, linear, and dependent type system. It is relatively complete up to a solver for arithmetic. This can encode, for example, the number of execution steps of programs in the Krivine machine in the presence of fixpoints, but finding closed forms of this number of steps is undecidable. This highlights the impossibility of typing the costs of fixpoint in the general case.

Originally, dℓPCF could only bound accumulative costs, but subsequent work by Rajani, Gaboardi, Garg & Hoffmann [15] have recovered amortization within this setting. The resulting system, λ_{amor}, is a family of program logics, parameterized by a first-order theory describing resources. Changing this theory tunes the resulting system to be close to the syntax-directed, inferable, and amortized costs of AARA, or the recursion logic of dℓPCF. Resources and costs are represented using two primitive type constructors. Computation incurring costs are typed $\mathbb{M}_I A$ (with I the cost), and implement a cost-accumulating monad. The type of values of type A holding potential is $[I]A$, and implements the dual potential-spending comonad. This system uses Levy's *Call-By-Push-Value* [8] formalism for encoding effectful λ-calculi, with two apparent limitation: first, it uses two different reductions: one for cost-free expression, and second that performs resource interaction on normal forms of the previous one. Second, the finer semantics of Call-by-Push-Value are only used in λ_{amor} to analyse programs with coarser Call-by-Value semantics.

2.4 Abstract Interpretation for Resource Analysis

While the current work focuses on type-based resource analysis and extension to finer program semantics, other resource analysis techniques have been created. We note the *CioaPP* system for resource analysis [10], based on *abstract interpretation.* This techniques approximates the semantics of values using *abstract domains.* For example, and integer could be abstracted by an union of interval, to which the integer is guaranteed to belong. Multiple languages are supported through compilation to *Horn clauses* in the style of logic programming: programs are represented by predicated $C(\overrightarrow{x})$ linking their source and semantics, defined by relation to other predicates in clauses $C_1'(\overrightarrow{x}) \wedge \cdots \wedge C_2'(\overrightarrow{x}) \Rightarrow C(\overrightarrow{x})$, in which the $\overrightarrow{x}$ are all quantified universally. Abstract domains for $\overrightarrow{x}$ can then be directly built using the clauses, and a purpose-built *fixpoint operator* for each domain that abstract iteration. *Cioa/PP* can be used to derive polynomial, exponential and logarithmic complexities, and verify that programs manipulate resources according to quantitative bounds over all inputs or a restricted domain. Implementations exists for many monotone resource metrics, such as time, energy and *gas* (execution fees for smart contracts on blockchains) [13]. To our knowledge, recuperable resources aren't supported.

2.5 Our Technical Setup

Decomposing AARA into a Call-By-Push-Value effect allows for a simplified embedding of languages and programming paradigms: Call-By-Push-Value programs explicitly define their evaluation order and allow for mixed-style evaluation. We exploit this in the next section. Furthermore, this allows embedding AARA's index languages into a mainstream, general-purpose type system (sequent-style System-F) and simplifies formalization. We'll describe our type system and how to encode resource analyses in Sects. 4 and 5. As a consequence of those two changes, the vast literature of typechecking and type inference then becomes directly applicable, which we discuss in Sect. 6.

3 The ILL-Calculus

We now introduce the *polarized **ILL**-calculus*, an abstract machine calculus due to Curien, Fiore & Munch-Maccagnoni [1,11], which we extend with algebraic datatypes, fixpoints, and explicit sharing. The name is a nod to its type-level semantics which are exactly *polarized **I**ntuitionnistic **L**inear **L**ogic.* At runtime, it is exactly a continuation-passing abstract machine for the *Call-By-Push-Value* λ-calculus. This technical setup allows for a state-passing effects, and an encoding resource manipulations at type-level. The core of the machine is taken as-is from [1], and we introduce the following additions for our purposes: explicit sharing of variables; polymorphism; fixpoints; and a notation for thunks and closures.

3.1 Generalities

At the term level, the **ILL**-machine is an abstract machine, whose terms are described in "**Terms (linear)**", Fig. 1. The first line defines *commands* c, which are a pair $\langle V \parallel S\rangle$ of a value V and a stack S. Both parts are tagged with a *polarity*: $+$ for data and $-$ for computations. When a value and a stack interact in a command, we call V *left side* and S *right side.*

Below commands in the figure, values and stacks are defined in matching pairs of same polarity. Some values are built inductively from constructors $V = K(\overrightarrow{V})$ and interact with pattern matching stacks with many branches $S = \mu(K(\overrightarrow{x}).c \mid \dots)$. Dually, some stack defined inductively and terminated with a *continuation variable*, giving $S = K_1(\overrightarrow{V_1}) \cdot K_2(\overrightarrow{V_2}) \cdot \dots \cdot \alpha$, and interact with pattern-matching values $V = \mu((K(\overrightarrow{x}) \cdot \alpha).c \mid \dots)$. The continuation variable α stands for a yet-unspecified stack, and value variables x stand for yet-unspecified values. This implements *continuation passing*: instead of *returning* a value, programs *jump to the current continuation* by passing it to a stack.

3.2 Linear Fragment

The **ILL** machine works with *linear substitutions* unless stated otherwise. In this subsection, the machine encodes linear computations, which preserve resources held by values *by definition.* We now describe each pair of compatible values and stack which use linear substitution. For each following **(bold label)**, please refer to the corresponding definition in **Terms** and reduction in **Reduction**.

***(let-value)* and *(let-stack)*.** The machine manipulates values and stacks with binders: the stack $\mu^+x.c$ captures the data on the other side, and jumps to c with x bound, which can be understood as "`let` $x = \dots$ `in` c". Dually, the term $\mu^-\alpha.c$ captures the evaluation context on the other side of the command in α and jumps to c. Those are the two reductions in **Reduction**, Fig. 1.

(data). Algebraic type constructors are defined as in functional languages *à la* OCaml or Haskell. They have value-constructors K to build values with the familiar syntax $K(\overrightarrow{V})$. Data structures then are consumed by *pattern-matching* stacks: for example, a type with two constructors $K_1(-)$, and $K_2(-,-)$ matches with a stack $\mu(K_1(x_1).c_1 \mid K_2(x_2, y_2).c_2)$. Those two reduce together by branching and binding variables:

$$\langle K_1(V_1) \parallel \mu(K_1(x_1).c_1 \mid K_2(x_2, y_2).c_2)\rangle \to c_1[V_1/x_1].$$

(computation). The same way datatypes has values build inductively from constructors $K(\overrightarrow{V})$, computation types have *stacks* defined inductively from constructors $K(\overrightarrow{V}) \cdot S$. Functions are the prototypal example: the function $A \multimap B$ has a constructor $\lambda(V) \cdot (S)$ which carries an argument of type A and a continuation stack consuming A B. Then, the λ-calculus call $f(V)$ corresponds to the command $\langle f \parallel \lambda(V) \cdot S\rangle$, where S is the outer context of the call (hidden in λ-calculus). The body of f is a pattern-matching value: we write $f = \mu(\lambda(x) \cdot \alpha).c$,

Terms (linear)

$$c ::= \langle V^+ \parallel S^+\rangle^+ \mid \langle V^- \parallel S^-\rangle^- \quad \textit{(cut)}$$

$$\begin{array}{rllll}
 & \textit{(var)} & \textit{(let-val)} & \textit{(data)} & \textit{(closure)} \\
V^+ ::= & x^+ & / & K(\overrightarrow{V^+}) & \Downarrow(V^-) \\
S^+ ::= & \alpha^+ & \mu x^+.c & \mu\left(\overrightarrow{K(\overrightarrow{x^+}).c}\right) & \mu\Downarrow(x^-).c \\
 & \textit{(var)} & \textit{(let-stk)} & \textit{(computation)} & \textit{(thunk)} \\
V^- ::= & x^- & \mu\alpha^-.c & \mu\left(\overrightarrow{(K(\overrightarrow{x^+})\cdot\alpha^-).c}\right) & \mu(\Uparrow\cdot\alpha^+).c \\
S^- ::= & \alpha^- & / & K(\overrightarrow{V^+})\cdot S^- & \Uparrow\cdot S^+
\end{array}$$

Terms (non-linear)

$$c ::= \langle V^+ \parallel \mu\mathbf{del}.c\rangle \mid \langle V^+ \parallel \mu\mathbf{dup}(x,y).c\rangle \quad \textit{(structure)}$$

$$\begin{array}{rll}
 & \textit{(sharing)} & \textit{(fixpoint)} \\
V^+ ::= & \mu(!\cdot\alpha^-).c & \mu(\mathbf{fix}\cdot\alpha^-).\langle\mathbf{self} \parallel S^+\rangle \\
S^+ ::= & !\cdot S^- & \mathbf{fix}\cdot S^-
\end{array}$$

Reductions

$$\begin{array}{rrcll}
\textit{(let-stack)} & \langle\ \mu^+\alpha.c & \parallel & S\ \rangle & \to c[S/\alpha] \\
\textit{(let-value)} & \langle\ V & \parallel & \mu^-x.c\ \rangle & \to c[V/x] \\
\textit{(weakening)} & \langle\ V & \parallel & \mu\mathbf{del}.c\ \rangle & \to c \\
\textit{(contraction)} & \langle\ V & \parallel & \mu\mathbf{dup}(x,y).c\ \rangle & \to c[V/x, V/y] \\
\textit{(closure)} & \langle\ \Downarrow(V) & \parallel & \mu\Downarrow(x).c\ \rangle & \to c[V/x] \\
\textit{(thunk)} & \langle\ \mu(\Uparrow\cdot\alpha).c & \parallel & \Uparrow\cdot S\ \rangle & \to c[S/\alpha] \\
\textit{(datatypes)} & \langle\ K_j(\vec{V}) & \parallel & \mu\left(\overrightarrow{K_i(\vec{x_i}).c_i}\right)\ \rangle & \to c_j[\vec{V}/\vec{x_j}] \\
\textit{(computations)} & \langle\ \mu\left(\overrightarrow{(K_i(\vec{x_i})\cdot\alpha_i).c_i}\right) & \parallel & K_j(\vec{V})\cdot S\ \rangle & \to c_j[\vec{V}/\vec{x_j}, S/\alpha_j] \\
\textit{(sharing)} & \langle\ \mu(!\cdot\alpha).c & \parallel & !\cdot S\ \rangle & \to c[S/\alpha] \\
\textit{(fixpoint)} & \langle\ \mu(\mathbf{fix}\cdot\alpha).\langle\mathbf{self} \parallel S\rangle & \parallel & \mathbf{fix}\cdot S'\ \rangle & \\
 & & & & \to \langle\mu(\mathbf{fix}\cdot\beta)\langle\mathbf{self} \parallel S[\beta/\alpha]\rangle \parallel S\rangle[S'/\alpha]
\end{array}$$

Fig. 1. **ILL**-machine: term-level syntax

in which x binds the argument and α binds the continuation. They interact by reducing as:

$$\langle \mu(\lambda(x) \cdot \alpha).c \parallel \lambda(V) \cdot S \rangle \to c[V/x, S/\alpha].$$

Types with many stack constructors implement computation with many different calls, each call sharing the same environment (think, in OOP, of an object with multiple methods, all sharing the same instance variables).

(thunks $\Uparrow$) and (closures $\Downarrow$). Closures and thunks implement local control flow, by delaying calls to computations and generation of data. Thunks $\mu(\Uparrow \cdot \alpha).c$ are commands c blocked from reducing, with free stack variable α. When evaluated together with a stack $\Uparrow \cdot S$, they bind S to α, and jump to c. Formally, they reduces as $\langle \mu(\Uparrow \cdot \alpha^+).c \parallel \Uparrow \cdot S^+ \rangle \to c[S^+/\alpha^+]$. The commands $c[S/\alpha]$ immediately evaluates the thunk, and eventually its return value will interact with S. Closures go the other way around, and delay launching computation. This allows, for example, to store a function within a data structure. They are the symmetric of thunks: a closed computation $\Downarrow(V^-)$ is opened with a blocked context $\mu\Downarrow(x^-).c$, which captures V^- as x^- and launches c, which sets up a new evaluation context for it.

3.3 Call-By-Value Semantics

The canonical encoding of linear call-by-value functions $A \multimap B$ into Call-By-Push-Value translates them as $\Downarrow(A \multimap \Uparrow B)$. At the term-level, the linear function $\lambda x.e$ becomes a closure $\Downarrow$ over a function $\mu(\lambda(x) \cdot \alpha)$, which defines a thunk $\mu(\Uparrow \cdot \beta)$, which evaluates e. We write $[\![-]\!]$ the Call-By-Push-Value embedding of a call-by-value term or type. Putting it all together, we have:

$$[\![A \multimap B]\!] = \Downarrow [\![A]\!] \multimap \Uparrow [\![B]\!]$$

$$[\![\lambda x.e]\!] = \Downarrow \mu(\lambda(x) \cdot \alpha).\langle \mu(\Uparrow \cdot \beta).\langle [\![e]\!] \parallel \beta \rangle \parallel \alpha \rangle$$

The main point of interest of those semantics of CBV in CBPV is that they are extendable with effects, which are implemented as systematic rewriting of thunks and closures. Those rewritings can be sequenced to refine effects. In the last sections, we combine an effect of type-level tracking of quantities and one for state-passing to recover AARA.

3.4 Non-linear Fragment

In order to encode non-linear programs, including recursion, and track them at type-level, we introduce variations to closures that encode shared values and recursive values.

(sharing). Shareable data is encoded as *shareable commands* $\mu(! \cdot \alpha).c$, whichare shared as-is then pass data to a stack $! \cdot S$. Linearity is enforced at the type level by making them have a distinct type, and asking that all value-variables bound in shared commands also have a shareable type. In order to track non-linear substitutions, sharing is explicitly implemented as stack matching shared values. The stack μ**del**.c implements weakening by silently ignoring the value it matches on, and μ**dup**$(x, y).c$ implements contraction by binding two copies x and y of the shared value.

(fixpoint). Finally, recursive computations are encoded as *fixpoints*. They are also subject to weakening and contraction, which enables the usual recursion schemes of λ-calculus to be encoded into **ILL**. Formally, the stack constructor **fix** $\cdot\, S$ opens a fixpoint closure, expands its definition in its body once, and feeds the resulting computation to S. On the other side, fixpoints have syntax $\mu(\mathbf{fix} \cdot \alpha).\langle \mathbf{self} \parallel S\rangle$, where **self** is a hole to be filled with the recursive value, and S captures the self-referent closure once filled-it and returns the defined recursive computation to α. The reduction substitutes the entire fixpoint into **self**, which copies S. This is made formal in the associated rule in **Reduction**, Fig. 1. Note the α-conversion in this rule, which protects one of the copies of S from unwanted substitution.

4 Type System

The end game of the type system is to derive a first-order constraint C over relevant quantities of a program, from which we then derive a bound. We call those quantities *parameters*. They represent amount of liquid resources, or combinatorial information on data and computation. In this paper, we focus on parameterizing data, for brevity.

It is capital that computations operate on data of arbitrary parameters. For example, fixpoints will call themselves with arguments of varying sizes to encode iteration. This means polymorphism over size *must* be accounted for. We solve this issue by bundling quantified parameters within constructors.

4.1 Generalities

At the type level, **ILL** is polarized *intuitionistic linear sequent calculus*. Its syntax is described in **Types** and **Parameters**, Fig. 2. The types A, B, C of values and stack can have two base sorts $\mathcal{T} \in \{+, -\}$ reproducing their polarity. We also have parameters n, p, q, with sorts in $\mathcal{P}$ which includes the integers $\mathbb{N}$. Types can depend on parameters: they have sorts $\overrightarrow{\mathcal{P}} \to \mathcal{T}$. Finally, type constructors are polymorphic over types and parameters: they have sort $\overrightarrow{\mathcal{T}} \to \overrightarrow{\mathcal{P}} \to \mathcal{T}$. For example, lists can have heterogeneous parameters for each element: a list $[a_0; a_1; \ldots; a_n]$ which each a_i of type $A(i)$ has type $\mathtt{List}(A, n)$, with the arguments having type $A(n-1)$ for the head, then $A(n-2)$, all the way to $A(0)$. The associated type constructor is $\mathtt{List} : (\mathbb{N} \to +) \to \mathbb{N} \to +$.

Primitives and Parameters. The usual connectives of instuitionistic linear logic are definable as type constructors: $\otimes$ and $\mathbb{1}$ ("pattern matching pairs" and "unit type"), $\oplus$ and $\mathbb{0}$ ("sums" and "empty type"), $\&$ and $\top$ ("lazy pairs" and "top"), and $\multimap$ ("linear functions"). Thunks and closures are given their own types: closures over a computation A^- have the positive type $\Downarrow A^-$, and thunks returning some data typed A^+ have negative type $\Uparrow A^+$. We also take as given the integers $(\mathbb{N}, 0, 1, +, \times)$ for parameterization. Those can be extended to any first-order signature.

Judgements. Judgements are sequents $\Theta; C; \Gamma \vdash \Delta$, which represent a typed interface: inputs are denoted by value variables $\Gamma = (\overrightarrow{x : A})$, and output by one stack variable $\Delta = (\alpha : A)$. The parameters of this interface are $\Theta = (\overrightarrow{p : \mathcal{P}})$ and are guarded by a first-order constraint C. The parameters in Θ are bound in C, Γ and Δ, and denote free quantities than be tuned within limits given by C. Given this, the three judgements, for values V, stacks S and commands c are:

Syntax	*Sequent*	*Given* $\boldsymbol{\Theta}$ *such that* $\boldsymbol{C}$*, we have ...*
Values	$\Theta; C; \Gamma \vdash V : A$	*a value* $\boldsymbol{V}$ *of type* $\boldsymbol{A}$ *in context* $\boldsymbol{\Gamma}$
Stacks	$\Theta; C; \Gamma \mid S : A \vdash \Delta$	*a stack* $\boldsymbol{S}$ *of type* $\boldsymbol{A}$ *in context* $\boldsymbol{\Gamma}, \boldsymbol{\Delta}$
Commands	$c : (\Theta; C; \Gamma \vdash \Delta)$	*a valid command* $\mathbf{c}$ *under context* $\boldsymbol{\Gamma}, \boldsymbol{\Delta}$

The central rules of the type system are shown in "**Example rules**" Fig. 2. Commands are built in the (cut) rule by matching a value and stack on their type and taking a conjunction of their constraints. Rules (μL) and (μR) are for binders. For example, (μR) turns a command c with a free variable $x : A$ into a stack $\mu x.c : A$ which interacts with values of type A by substituting them for x.

4.2 Datatypes with Parameters

Building up the logical constraint for resources and algorithmic invariants is done by accumulating generic information about constructors of values and stack. To present how this machinery works, we encode a very simple constraint: *a list is always one element longer than its tail.* The corresponding type definition for lists, and resulting rules are shown in **Example type definition**, Fig. 2. Lists have type $\texttt{List}(A, n)$ with a type parameter $n : \mathbb{N}$ denoting size. The definition of the `Cons` constructor is reproduced below.

| Cons **of** A(m)$\otimes$`List`(A,m) **where** $(m : \mathbb{N})$ **with** $n = m + 1$

The definition states that lists $\texttt{List}(A, n)$ have a head of type $A(m)$ and a tail of type $\texttt{List}(A, m)$. The type of list elements is $A : \mathbb{N} \to +$, which allows each element to be given a distinct parameterization according to its position. For example, $\texttt{List}(\texttt{List}(\mathbb{N}, -), n)$ is a type of lists of lists of integer of decreasing lengths: the first list has size 10, the next one 9, etc. Formally, the parameter m is

Types

$$\mathcal{T} ::= + \mid - \mid \mathcal{P} \mid \mathcal{P} \to \mathcal{T}$$
$$A ::= p \mid T_{\mathrm{cons}}(\overrightarrow{A}) \mid \Downarrow A \mid \Uparrow A \mid !A \mid \textbf{Fix } A$$
$$A ::= \mathbb{1} \mid A \otimes A \mid \mathbb{0} \mid A \oplus A \mid \top \mid A \& A \mid A \multimap A \mid \exists \Theta[C].C \mid \forall \Theta[C].A \quad \textit{(definable)}$$

Parameters

$$\mathcal{P} ::= \mathbb{N} \mid \ldots$$
$$p ::= 0 \mid 1 \mid p + q \mid \ldots$$
$$C ::= \mathbb{T} \mid \mathcal{R}(\overrightarrow{p}) \mid p = p \mid C \wedge C \mid C \Rightarrow C \mid \exists \overrightarrow{p}.C \mid \forall \overrightarrow{p}.C$$

Example type definition: lists

```
data List(A:ℕ → +, n:ℕ) =
  | Cons of A(m) ⊗ List(A,m) where (m:ℕ) with n = m+1
  | Nil with n = 0 . (*no 'where' clause for Nil*)
```

Example type definition: state token

```
data ST(p,q : ℕ) =
| init where q = 0
| debit_k  of ST(p',q') with p',q' : ℕ    where p' + k = p ∧ q + k = q'
| credit_k of ST(p',q') with p',q' : ℕ    where p + k = p' ∧ q' + k = q
| slack    of ST(p',q') with p',q',k : ℕ  where p' + k = p ∧ q + k = q'
```

Example rules: identity and lists

$$\frac{c : (\Theta; C; \Gamma \vdash \alpha : A^-)}{\Theta; C; \Gamma \vdash \mu^- \alpha.c : A^-}\ (\mu\mathrm{L}) \qquad \frac{c : (\Theta; C; \Gamma, x : A^+ \vdash \Delta)}{\Theta; C; \Gamma \mid \mu^+ x.c : A^+ \vdash \Delta}\ (\mu\mathrm{R})$$

$$\frac{\Theta; C; \Gamma \vdash V : A^{\pm} \qquad \Theta'; C'; \Gamma' \mid S : A^{\pm} \vdash \Delta}{\langle t \parallel e \rangle^{\pm} : (\Theta, \Theta'; C \wedge C'; \Gamma, \Gamma' \vdash \Delta)}\ (\mathrm{cut})$$

$$\frac{\Theta_1; C_1; \Gamma_1 \vdash V_1 : A(m) \qquad \Theta_2; C_2; \Gamma_2 \vdash V_2 : \mathtt{List}(A, m)}{\Theta_1, \Theta_2; C; \Gamma_1, \Gamma_2 \vdash \mathtt{Cons}(V_1, V_2) : \mathtt{List}(A, n)}\ (\mathtt{ConsR})$$
$$C = \exists m.(n = m + 1) \wedge C_1 \wedge C_2$$

$$\frac{c_1 : (\Theta; C_1; \Gamma \vdash \Delta) \qquad c_2 : (\Theta, m : \mathbb{N}; C_2; \Gamma, x : A(m), y : \mathtt{List}(A, m) \vdash \Delta)}{\Theta; C; \Gamma \mid \mu(\ \mathtt{Nil}().c_1 \mid \mathtt{Cons}(x, y).c_2\ ) : \mathtt{List}(A, n) \vdash \Delta}$$
$$C = ((n = 0) \Rightarrow C_1) \wedge (\forall m.(n = m + 1) \Rightarrow C_2) \quad (\mathtt{ListL})$$

Fig. 2. ILL-machine: type system and examples

introduced in the **where** clause, and is guarded by the first-order constraint $n = m+1$ in the **with** clause. This is to be understood as "**where** m is fresh integer parameter **with** $n = m + 1$". When constructing a list $\texttt{List}(A, n)$ with the rule ($\texttt{Cons}$R), m is added to Θ and the constraint $n = m+1$ is added. Symmetrically, when pattern matching on a list $\texttt{List}(A, n)$ with the rule ($\texttt{List}$L), the branch of the pattern matching for `Cons` must be well-typed for any m such that $n = m+1$, which yields a constraint $\forall m.(n = m + 1) \Rightarrow C'$ in which $n = m + 1$ is assumed.

4.3 Implementing Polymorphism

Once some parameterization of data is chosen, we want parameters-aware data and computations. Recall that when introducing constructors, some parameters Θ satisfying some constraint C are introduced existentially, and when this constructor is matched on, they are introduced universally. This allows us to encode polymorphism over parameters as types with only one constructor. We define existential quantification over parameters Θ such that C with the $\exists\Theta[C].A$ datatype as follows:

data $\exists\Theta[C]$.A $=$ $\texttt{Pack}_{\Theta;C}$ **of** A(Θ) **where** Θ **with** C

Introducing $\texttt{Pack}_{\Theta;C}(V)$ produces the constraint $\exists\Theta.C$, and when pattern-matching on it, C is assumed to hold for some unknown Θ, giving a constraint $\forall\Theta.C \Rightarrow C''$. Universal quantification goes the other way around, binding some constraint existentially in stacks, and universally in values. Compile-time information Θ, C about a continuation stack $S : A^-(\Theta)$ is witnessed by the stack constructor $\texttt{Spec}_{\Theta;C} \cdot S$. On the value side, $\mu(\texttt{Spec}_{\Theta;C} \cdot \alpha).c$ requires that C in the command c, and generates $\forall\Theta.C \Rightarrow C'$.

Closures over universally quantified computations take any input such that some constraint holds. Likewise, thunks over existential quantification type delayed computations with (yet undetermined) parameters. For example, a thunk which returns a pair of lists whose total length is 10 can be typed as $\Uparrow\exists(n, m : \mathbb{N})[n + m = 10].\ \texttt{List}(A, n) \otimes \texttt{List}(A, m)$.

4.4 An Example of Encoding: *append*

A minimal, non-trivial example of parameter polymorphism is the `append` function on lists. We implement it in two phases. First, we implement `rev_append`, which flips the first lists and appends it to the second. Then, we define `append` with two calls to `rev_append`. This decomposition shows the function of parameter polymorphism, as both call to `rev_append` occur on lists of different sizes. Figure 3 lists the original ML code for both functions and the compiled version of `rev_append`. We omit giving the translation of `append`, since it is straightforward once given `rev_append`.

`rev_append` is defined as a fixpoint. The first line in the definition binds a self-reference to f and binds a continuation α to which it returns the function. In c_1, when the function is called for lists l_1 of size n and l_2 of size m, the execution context built by the caller instantiates the sizes with $\forall_{(n,m)}$ which

```
let rec rev_append l1 l2 = match l1 with [] -> l2
    | h::t -> rev_append t (h::l2)
let append l1 l2 = rev_append (rev_append l1 []) l2
```

$$\begin{aligned}
&\texttt{rev_append} : \textbf{Fix}\, \forall n, m, A.\ \mathtt{L}(A, n) \multimap \mathtt{L}(A, m) \multimap \Uparrow\mathtt{L}(A, n+m) \\
&\quad = \mu(\textbf{fix} \cdot \alpha).\langle \textbf{self} \parallel \mu f.c_1 \rangle \\
&\quad c_1 = \langle \mu(\forall_{(n,m)} \cdot l_1 \cdot l_2 \cdot \Uparrow \cdot \beta).c_2 \parallel \alpha \rangle \\
&\quad c_2 = \langle l_1 \parallel \mu(\ \mathtt{Nil}_{(n=0)}.\langle l_2 \parallel \beta \rangle \mid \mathtt{Cons}_{(\exists n'.n=n'+1)}(h, t).c_3\ ) \rangle \\
&\quad c_3 = \langle f \parallel \textbf{fix} \cdot \forall_{(n', m+1)} \cdot t \cdot \mathtt{Cons}_{(m+1)}(h, l_2) \cdot \Uparrow \cdot \beta \rangle
\end{aligned}$$

Fig. 3. BILL Source code of the `rev_append` function

the callee matches on. Then, in c_2, we pattern-match on l_1, which introduces $\exists n'.n = n' + 1$ (resp. $n = 0$) if the list has a head (resp. is empty). In this last case, the function recurses on itself in c_3. This recursive call is done with an execution context $\forall_{(n',m+1)} \cdot S$, in which the new values for n and m are instantiated.

4.5 Soundness

Reduction preserves parameterizations in the following sense:

Theorem 1. *If $c : (\Theta; C; \Gamma \vdash \Delta)$ reduces as $c \to c'$, and $c' : (\Theta'; C'; \Gamma' \vdash \Delta')$, then $\Theta' \subset \Theta$, $\Gamma' \subset \Gamma$, $\Delta = \Delta'$, and for every instantiation of Θ, $C \Rightarrow C'$.*

The proof is done by induction over typed reduction of commands, after proving the standard Barendregt properties (which can be done following [11]). We only have space to briefly summarize the salient point. First, we prove the statement for $\langle \mu\alpha.c \parallel S \rangle$ and $\langle V \parallel \mu x.c \rangle$. Then, the only significant cases are $\langle \mathtt{Pack}_{\Theta;C}(V) \parallel \mu\mathtt{Pack}_{\Theta;C}(x).c \rangle$ and its dual with $\mathtt{Spec}$. The $\mathtt{Pack}$ command reduce to $c[V/x]$ and generates the constraint $(\exists\Theta.C) \wedge (\forall\Theta.C \Rightarrow C')$ with C' the constraint for c. This immediately implies $C \wedge C'$, which is also constraint generated by $\langle V \parallel \mu x.c \rangle$, and therefore $c[V/x]$. The case of $\mathtt{Spec}$ is purely identical.

5 Embedding AARA as an Effect

In Sect. 3, we refined the CBPV embedding of CBV functions to polymorphic closures and thunks. This allowed to track parameters as control flow switches in and out of programs. To recover AARA, we merely need to specialize this translation to track sizes and resources.

5.1 An Effect for Parameters

With our setup, we can translate CBV programs to **ILL**-machine that associates a constraint C on their free parameters Θ. This is implemented by refining closures and thunks. Closures $\Downarrow A$ are replaced by *closures over quantified computations* $\Downarrow\forall\Theta[C].A(\Theta)$, that is, computations that take *any* arguments with parameters Θ satisfying C. On the other side, thunks $\Uparrow B$ are replaced with $\Uparrow\exists\Theta'[C'].B(\Theta')$, which returns data parameterized by Θ' such that C'. With this effect, the call-by-value linear function $A \multimap B$ is translated to a parameter-aware version that accept *all* ($\forall$) inputs with the right parameters and return *some* ($\exists$) output with its own parameters. For example, the function `append` on lists has a length-aware type (here in long form, to show the implicit $\exists$ binder):

$$\Downarrow\forall n, m.\ \texttt{List}(A, n) \multimap \texttt{List}(A, m) \multimap \Uparrow\exists k[k = m + n].\ \texttt{List}(A, k)$$

5.2 Polymorphic State-Passing Effect

We extend the translation of call-by-value functions with another effect: state passing. Closures now accept a token $\mathrm{ST}(p, q)$ with p free resources and q allocated resources, and thunks return a token $\mathrm{ST}(p', q')$. Closures $\Downarrow\forall\Theta[C].(-)$ become $\Downarrow\forall\Theta[C].\mathrm{ST}(p, q) \multimap (-)$, in which C guards the resources p and q. This means closures take in *any* state whose resources satisfy C. Likewise, thunks becomes $\Uparrow\exists\Theta[C'].\mathrm{ST}(p', q') \otimes (-)$, and return resources p' and q' specified by C'.

This can lift the hidden inner behavior of `append` at type-level. Relying on linear typing, the effects detect that the progressive deallocations of the intermediate reversed list compensate for the progressive allocation of the final result (under an ideal garbage collector). When typed with state-passing below, the tokens' types shows that only n nodes are allocated *simultaneously* for the call.

$$\begin{aligned}\Downarrow\forall n, m, p, q.\ \mathrm{ST}(p + n * k_{\texttt{Cons}}, q) \multimap \texttt{List}(A, n) \multimap \texttt{List}(A, m)\\ \multimap \Uparrow\exists k[k = m + n].\ \mathrm{ST}(p, q + n * k_{\texttt{Cons}}) \otimes \texttt{List}(A, k)\end{aligned}$$

5.3 Token Encoding

To implement this translation without specific primitives, we define a state token capable of representing the operations of *debit* (spending resources), *credit* (recovering resources), and *slack* (aligning costs upwards) at type-level. We define a type constructor ST with two resource parameters, that implements those operations, in **Example type definition: state token**, Fig. 2.

The token begins its life as `init`, which has type $\mathrm{ST}(p, 0)$. Debiting k_0 resources from a token $s : \mathrm{ST}(p + k_0, q)$ is done by using the constructor $\texttt{debit}_{k_0}(s)$ which creates a new token of type $ST(p, q{+}k_0)$. The `credit` constructor implements the opposite operation. For slack, the amount of resources being wasted k is left free. At call site, k is introduced existentially in the constraint, and left to be specified later at the whims of the constraint solver. Lower values of k lead to better bounds, but must remain high enough to run all branches.

5.4 Potential in Shared Values

AARA usually stores potential within shared values as opposed to a centralized token. We take a somewhat different approach to sharing: we want shared values $!A(\Theta)$ to specify how much potential their instances commonly occupy, and store those resources in the token. To do so, we define below a type $!_\varphi A(\Theta)$ which represent shared copies with potential. Building the value requires a token with $\varphi(\Theta)$ free resources and allocates them; Extracting the underlying $!A(\Theta)$ from $!_\varphi A(\Theta)$ frees $\varphi(\Theta)$ resources. This is definable without any primitive in the **ILL**-machine, together with resource-aware contraction and weakening, which fully reproduce AARA potential.

$$!_\varphi A(\Theta) = \Downarrow\forall p, q.\, \mathrm{ST}(p, q + \varphi(\Theta)) \multimap \Uparrow \mathrm{ST}(p + \varphi(n), q) \otimes\, !\Uparrow A(\Theta).$$

6 Implementation for ML-Like Languages

We have implemented a prototype[1] of the **ILL**-machine, together with type inference and constraint generation using the HM(X) technique [14]. HM(X) (*Hindley-Milner extended with X*), is a generic constraint-based type inference procedure extending Hindley-Milner with user-definable sorts, types and predicates. Our extension of covers arbitrary first-order signatures for parameters, and features a generic constraint simplifier. It then can export simplified constraints to the *Coq* theorem prover for verification by hand, or to the *MiniZinc*[2] optimization suite to for full cost inference with minized slack. This yields complexity bounds as a multivariate polynomial. Our heuristic for elaborating polynomial parameter expressions from a first-order constraint works as following:

1. Take as input a first-order constraint over the integers. Its syntax is generated by $(\forall, \exists, \wedge, \Rightarrow, =, \leq)$
2. Skolemize all existential variables: $\exists y.C$ generates a fresh multivariate polynomial $p(\overrightarrow{x})$ over the variables $\overrightarrow{x}$ in scope, and reduces to $C[p(\overrightarrow{x})/y]$. Those polynomial p are formal sums of monomials with coefficients $\overrightarrow{\alpha}$, which are all held in a global context for the polynomials.
3. Assume all implications are of the form $(p(\overrightarrow{x}) = e[\overrightarrow{x}]) \Rightarrow C$, and substitute p for e in C
4. Put the constraint under prenex form. We have arrived at a constraint $C = \forall\overrightarrow{x}.\bigwedge_i(e_i[\overrightarrow{x}, \overrightarrow{\alpha}] = e'_i[\overrightarrow{x}, \overrightarrow{\alpha}])$. Reinterpret the constraint as a system of polynomial equations with variables $\overrightarrow{x}$ and unknown coefficients $\overrightarrow{\alpha}$.
5. Finally, instantiate and optimize $\overrightarrow{\alpha}$ under this final system of equations. The metric for the optimization is the sum of the leading non-zero coefficients of the complexity being computed.

Our preliminary experiments indicate that when manually annotating datatypes definitions with their RAML parameterization, the tight algorithmic complexities derivable for list iterators can be recovered in **BILL**. We are currently

[1] https://gitlab.lip6.fr/suzanneh/autobill.
[2] https://www.minizinc.org.

exploring ways to extend parameterization to tree-shaped datatypes, as well as the potential precision gains that can be obtained by parameterizing to Call-By-Push-Value evaluation contexts.

The direct translation from ML-style languages to **ILL**-with-token is factored in the implementation. User-facing languages are be translated to a Call-By-Push-Value λ-calculus the canonical way, and then compiled into **ILL** through a CPS-translation and explicit duplication of shared variables. Later passes implement the Call-By-Push-Value effects described in this paper, to-and-from **ILL**. High-level languages can be analyzed more easily, as they only need to be translated to a Call-By-Push-Value λ-calculus with credit/debit primitives.

Limitations. Higher-order functions are a pain-point for AARA analyses, as getting correct bounds require lifting constraints out of high-order arguments. Depending on the theory modeling parameters, this can be quite tricky. Our implementation compares favorably to RAML in this regard, as it supports native constraints annotations on high-order arguments. Fixpoints are also a thorny issue. This has two mitigations: (1) require user-provided annotations for fixpoint invariants, or (2) reproduce RAML's constraints on iteration: (mutually) recursive functions which define folds and traversals through nested pattern-matching and accumulation. In our experiments, we found our system to be amenable to a third approach: general purpose iterators can be defined with manual annotations using fixpoints, and then used without annotations.

7 Conclusion

Extending the static type discipline of functional languages for resource analysis is a tantalizing prospect. But understanding the operational properties of programs means recovering a diverse swath of information like memory aliasing, algorithmic invariants, and sharing of data outside their scope of definition.

To create a fine-grained, generic, extendable base for AARA, we extended the **ILL** Call-By-Push-Value calculus developed by Curien at al. [1,11] with fixpoints, polymorphism and native first-order constraints. We combined this with a decomposition of λ-calculi in a Call-By-Push-Value machine, which explicits control flow. With this, expressions are a combination of closures requiring some properties to hold on their inputs, and thunks which witness some properties of their output. Instantiating our generic system to represent a finite amount of resources within the program's state, well-typedness stipulates that this finite amount is sufficient to cover all allocations and liberations. It recovers the core of the AARA [6] method for resource analysis from first principles, from a generic Call-By-Push-Value intermediate representation for static analysis.

Perspectives. Our implementation covers the target machine, the constraint-aware type system, and a heuristic to solve constraints over multivariate polynomial. Current work focuses on implementing program-wide analysis *à la* RAML.

This requires automatically annotating the constraints associated to each constructor in datatype definitions to encode a particular flavor of AARA analyses. We also aim to support shared regions, reusing the parameterized type system to generate constraints on region lifetimes.

References

1. Curien, P.L., Fiore, M., Munch-Maccagnoni, G.: A theory of effects and resources: adjunction models and polarised calculi. In: Proceedings of the ACM on Programming Languages (POPL) (2016). https://doi.org/10.1145/2837614.2837652
2. Dal Lago, U., Gaboardi, M.: Linear dependent types and relative completeness. In: 2011 IEEE 26th Annual Symposium on Logic in Computer Science (2011). https://doi.org/10.1109/LICS.2011.22
3. Dal lago, U., Petit, B.: The geometry of types. ACM SIGPLAN Notices (POPL) (2013). https://doi.org/10.1145/2480359.2429090
4. Hoffmann, J.: Types with potential: polynomial resource bounds via automatic amortized analysis, Ph. D. thesis, Ludwig-Maximilians-Universität München, Berlin (2011). https://doi.org/10.5282/edoc.13955
5. Hoffmann, J., Das, A., Weng, S.C.: Towards automatic resource bound analysis for OCaml. In: Proceedings of the ACM on Programming Languages (POPL) (2017). https://doi.org/10.1145/3009837.3009842
6. Hoffmann, J., Jost, S.: Two decades of automatic amortized resource analysis. Mathematical Structures in Computer Science, pp. 1–31 (2022). https://doi.org/10.1017/S0960129521000487
7. Kahn, D.M., Hoffmann, J.: Exponential automatic amortized resource analysis. In: FoSSaCS 2020. LNCS, vol. 12077, pp. 359–380. Springer, Cham (2020). https://doi.org/10.1007/978-3-030-45231-5_19
8. Levy, P.B.: Call-By-Push-Value. Springer, Dordrecht (2003). https://doi.org/10.1007/978-94-007-0954-6
9. Lichtman, B., Hoffmann, J.: Arrays and references in resource aware ML. In: Miller, D. (ed.) International Conference on Formal Structures for Computation and Deduction (FSCD) (2017). https://doi.org/10.4230/LIPIcs.FSCD.2017.26
10. Lopez-Garcia, P., Darmawan, L., Klemen, M., Liqat, U., Bueno, F., Hermenegildo, M.V.: Interval-based resource usage verification by translation into Horn clauses and an application to energy consumption. Theory Pract. Logic Program. **18**(2), 167–223 (2018). https://doi.org/10.1017/S1471068418000042
11. Munch-Maccagnoni, G.: Note on curry's style for linear call-by-push-value. Tech. Rep. (2017). https://hal.inria.fr/hal-01528857
12. Niu, Y., Hoffmann, J.: Automatic space bound analysis for functional programs with Garbage collection. In: LPAR-22. 22nd International Conference on Logic for Programming, Artificial Intelligence and Reasoning, pp. 543–521. https://doi.org/10.29007/xkwx
13. Pérez, V., Klemen, M., López-García, P., Morales, J.F., Hermenegildo, M.: Cost analysis of smart contracts via parametric resource analysis. In: Pichardie, D., Sighireanu, M. (eds.) Static Analysis. SAS 2020. LNCS, vol. 12389. Springer, Cham (2020). https://doi.org/10.1007/978-3-030-65474-0_2
14. Pottier, F., Rémy, D.: The essence of ML type inference. In: Pierce, Benjamin C (ed.) Advanced Topics in Types and Programming Languages, pp. 389–489. The MIT Press (2005)

15. Rajani, V., Gaboardi, M., Garg, D., Hoffmann, J.: A unifying type-theory for higher-order (amortized) cost analysis. Proceed. ACM Programm. Lang. (POPL) (2021). https://doi.org/10.1145/3434308
16. Tarjan, R.E.: Amortized computational complexity. SIAM J. Algebr. Discret. Methods (1985). https://doi.org/10.1137/0606031

A Rule-Based Approach for Designing and Composing Abstract Domains

Daniel Jurjo[1,3(✉)], José Morales[1,3], Pedro Lopez-Garcia[2,3], and Manuel Hermenegildo[1,3]

[1] Universidad Politécnica de Madrid (UPM), Madrid, Spain
[2] Spanish Council for Scientific Research (CSIC), Madrid, Spain
[3] IMDEA Software Institute, Madrid, Spain
{daniel.jurjo,josef.morales,pedro.lopez,manuel.hermenegildo}@imdea.org

Abstract. Abstract interpretation allows constructing sound static analysis tools by safely approximating program semantics. Frameworks for abstract interpretation typically provide an implementation of a specialized iteration strategy to compute an abstract fixpoint, as well as a number of abstract domains in order to approximate different program properties. However, the design and implementation of additional domains, as well as their combinations, is eventually necessary to successfully prove arbitrary program properties. We propose a rule-based methodology for rapid design and prototyping of new domains and combining existing ones, with a focus on the analysis of logic programs. We provide several examples for domains combining numerical properties and data types and apply them to proving complex program properties.

Keywords: Abstract Domain Development · Abstract Domain Combination · Abstract Interpretation · Static Analysis · Logic Programming · Prolog

1 Introduction

The technique of Abstract Interpretation [10] allows constructing sound program analysis tools which can extract properties of a program by safely approximating its semantics. Abstract interpretation proved practical and effective in the context of (Constraint) Logic Programming ((C)LP) [17,25,26,32,33,39,40], which was one of its first application areas [18], and the techniques developed in this context have also been applied to the analysis and verification of other programming languages by using semantic translation into (Constraint) Horn Clauses (CHCs) [13,19,28]. *Frameworks* for abstract interpretation (such as PLAI/CiaoPP [20] or Astrée [12]) provide efficient implementations of algorithms for computing abstract fixpoints as well as several abstract domains,

Partially funded by MICINN projects PID2019-108528RB-C21 *ProCode*, TED2021-132464B-I00 *PRODIGY*, and FJC2021-047102-I, and by the Tezos foundation. We also thank the anonymous reviewers for their very useful feedback.

R. Glück and B. Kafle (Eds.): LOPSTR 2023, LNCS 14330, pp. 80–98, 2023.
https://doi.org/10.1007/978-3-031-45784-5_6

which approximate different program properties. Moreover, due to undecidability [7,10], loss of precision is inevitable, which makes the design (and implementation) of more domains, as well as their combinations, eventually necessary to successfully prove arbitrary program properties. In order to facilitate this task, we propose a rule-based approach for the design and rapid prototyping of new domains, as well as composing and combining existing ones. Our techniques are partially inspired in logic-based languages for implementing constraint domains [14]. We provide several examples for domains combining numerical properties and data types, and apply them to proving complex properties of Prolog programs.

Related Work. The challenges of designing sound, precise, and efficient analyses have made static analysis designers search for ways to simplify these tasks, and logic programming-related technologies such as Datalog (see, e.g., [4,8,41]) have in fact become quite popular recently in this context. However, these approaches are quite different from the abstract interpretation *framework*-based approaches that we address herein, where significant parts of the analysis (such as abstracting execution paths) are taken care of by the framework. In addition, the lack of data structures makes the Datalog approach less natural for defining domains in our context. Some more general, Datalog-derived languages have been proposed that are more specifically oriented to the implementation of analyses, such as FLIX [27], a form of Datalog with lattices, which has been used to define several types of analyses for imperative programs, and other work generalizes Datalog with constraints (see again [13]). However, these approaches do not provide *per se* a specific formalism for defining the abstract domains as in our work. Another promising approach to performing static analysis of complex programs involving algebraic data types is [1], which introduces a transformation technique to convert programs to deal only with basic data types (integers, booleans) that can be handled with other CHC solvers. This method can analyze CHC programs with data types and infer properties like sortedness, but the approach is very different from ours (which works directly on the original program using abstract interpretation). A previous rule-based approach to defining abstract domains was proposed in [30], using Constraint Handling Rules (CHR) [14] but this work only handled conjunctions of constraints in a simple dependency domain, and did not address other fundamental operations such as the *least upper bound*, nor the application for combining domains. Finally, rewriting systems have also been used to prove the correctness of abstract unifications [5].

2 Preliminaries

Lattices. A *partial order* on a set X is a binary relation $\sqsubseteq$ that is reflexive, transitive and anti-symmetric. The *least upper bound* (*lub*) or *join* of two elements of a set $a, b \in X$, denoted by $a \sqcup b$ is the smallest element in X greater than both of them ($a \sqsubseteq a \sqcup b \wedge b \sqsubseteq a \sqcup b$). If it exists, it is unique. Similarly, the *greatest lower bound* (*glb*) or *meet* is defined as the greatest element less than both. A partially ordered set or *poset* is a pair $(X, \sqsubseteq)$ where X is a set and $\sqsubseteq$ is a partial order relation on X. X is a *lattice* if $(X, \sqsubseteq)$ is a poset and for every two elements of X there exist a meet and a join. A lattice is *complete* if every subset $S \subseteq X$ has both a supremum and an infimum (which are unique). The maximum element of a complete lattice is called *top* and the minimum *bottom* (denoted by $\top$ and $\bot$ resp.).

Abstract Interpretation. The standard, collecting semantics of a program can be described in terms of a *concrete domain* that contains sets of execution states, e.g., in the case of Logic Programming it typically consists of sets of variable substitutions that may occur at run time. The main idea behind abstract interpretation is to interpret the program over a special, abstract domain whose elements are finite representations of possibly infinite sets of actual substitutions in the concrete domain. We denote the concrete domain as D and the abstract domain as D_α. We denote the functions that relate sets of concrete substitutions with abstract substitutions as the *abstraction* function $\alpha : D \to D_\alpha$ and the *concretization* function $\gamma : D_\alpha \to D$. The concrete domain is typically a complete lattice with the set inclusion order which induces an ordering relation in the abstract domain that we represent by $\sqsubseteq$. Under this relation the abstract domain is usually a complete lattice and $(D, \alpha, D_\alpha, \gamma)$ is a Galois insertion/connection [10].

The Top-Down Algorithm. *Top-down* analyses build an *analysis graph* starting from a series of program *entry points*. This approach was first used in analyzers such as MA3 and Ms [40], and matured in the PLAI analyzer [32,33], now also referred to as the *top-down algorithm* or *solver*, using an optimized fixpoint algorithm. It was later applied to the analysis of CLP/CHCs [17] and imperative programs [13,19,28,29], and used in analyzers such as GAIA [26], the CLP($\mathcal{R}$) analyzer [25], or Goblint [37,38]. The graph inferred by PLAI is a finite, abstract object whose concretization approximates the (possibly infinite) set of (possibly infinite) maximal AND-trees of the concrete semantics. The PLAI approach separates the abstraction of the structure of the concrete trees (the paths through the program) from the abstraction of the *substitutions* at the nodes in those concrete trees (the program states in those paths). The first abstraction (T_α) is typically built-in, as an abstract domain of *analysis graphs*. The framework is *parametric* on a second abstract domain, D_α, whose elements appear as labels in the nodes of the analysis graph. We refer to such nodes with tuples $\langle p(V_1, \ldots, V_n), \lambda^c, \lambda^s \rangle$, where p is a predicate in the program under analysis, and λ^c, λ^s (both elements of D_α), are respectively, the abstract call and success substitutions over the variables $V_1, \ldots, V_n$. Such tuples represent the set of (concrete) call and success substitutions of the nodes in the concrete AND-trees. A more detailed recent discussion can be found in [13]. Many other PLAI extensions have been proposed, such as incremental and modular versions [15,16,22,35].

Example 1. Figure 1 (from [16]) shows a possible analysis graph (center) for a set of CHCs (left) that encode the computation of the parity of a binary message using the exclusive or, denoted `xor`. E.g., the parity of message `[1,0,1]` is `0`.

We consider an abstract domain (right) with the following abstract values: $\perp$ s.t. $\gamma(\perp) = \emptyset$, `z` (zero) s.t. $\gamma(\texttt{z}) = \{0\}$, `o` (one) s.t. $\gamma(\texttt{o}) = \{1\}$, `b` (bit) s.t. $\gamma(\texttt{b}) = \{0, 1\}$, and $\top$ such that $\gamma(\top)$ is the set of all concrete values. Consider an initial abstract goal $G_\alpha = \langle$ `main(Msg,P)`, (`Msg/`$\top$, `P/`$\top$) $\rangle$, representing that the arguments of `main` can be bound to any concrete value (see node `A` in the figure). Node `B` = ($\langle$ `par(Msg,X,P)`, (`Msg/`$\top$, `X/z`, `P/`$\top$), (`Msg/`$\top$, `X/z`, `P/b`) $\rangle$) captures the fact that `par` may be called with `X` bound to 0 in $\gamma(\texttt{z})$ and, if such a call succeeds, the third argument `P` will be bound to any value in $\gamma(\texttt{b}) = \{0, 1\}$. Note that node `C` captures the fact that, after this call, there are other calls to `par` where `X/b`. Edges in the graph capture calls and paths. For example, two such edges exist from node `B`, denoting that `par` may call `xor` (edge from `B` to `D`) or `par` itself with a different call description (edge from `B` to `C`).

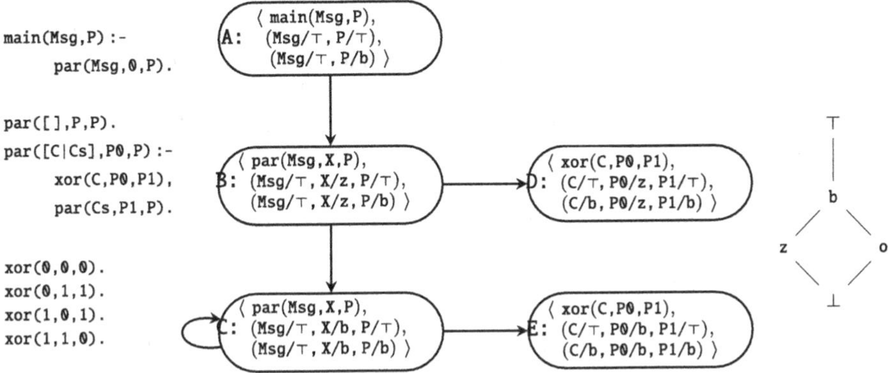

Fig. 1. A set of CHCs for computing parity (left) and a possible analysis graph (right).

As mentioned before, the abstract interpretation-based algorithms that we are considering are *parametric on the data-related abstract domain*, i.e., they are independent of the data abstractions used. Each such abstract domain is then defined by providing (we follow the description in [15,22]): a number of basic lattice operations ($\sqsubseteq, \sqcap, \sqcup$ and, optionally, the widening ∇ operator); the abstract semantics of the primitive constraints (representing the *built-ins*, or basic operations of the source language) via *abstract transfer functions* (f^α); and the following additional instrumental operations over abstract substitutions:

- `Aproj`(λ, Vs): restricts the abstract substitution λ to the set of variables Vs.
- `Aextend`$(A_{k,n}, \lambda^c, \lambda^s)$: propagates the abstract success substitution λ^s, defined over the variables of the n-th literal of clause k ($A_{k,n}$), to λ^c, which is defined over all the variables of clause k (which contains $A_{k,n}$ in its body).
- `Acall`(A, λ, A_k): performs the *abstract call*, i.e., the unification (conjunction) of a literal call $\langle A, \lambda\rangle$ with the head A_k of a clause k defining the predicate of A. The result is a substitution in terms of the variables of clause k.

- `Aproceed`(A_k, λ_k^s, A): performs the *abstract proceed*, i.e., the reverse operation of `Acall`. It unifies the head of clause k (A_k) and the abstract substitution at the end of clause k (λ_k^s) with the original call A to produce the success substitution over the variables of A.
- `Ageneralize`$(\lambda, \{\lambda^1, \ldots, \lambda^k\})$: joins λ with the set of abstract substitutions $\{\lambda^1, \ldots, \lambda^k\}$, all over the same variables. The result is an abstract substitution greater than or equal to λ. It either returns λ, when no generalization is needed; performs the least upper bound ($\sqcup$); or performs the widening (∇) of λ together with $\{\lambda^1, \ldots, \lambda^k\}$, depending on termination, precision, and performance needs.

Note that this general approach and operations are not specific to logic programs, applying in general to a set of blocks that call each other, possibly recursively.

Combining Abstract Domains. The idea of combining abstract domains to gain precision is already present in [11], showing that precision can be gained by removing redundancies and introducing new basic operations. Let E be a concrete domain and $(E, \alpha_i, D_i, \gamma_i)$, $i \in \{1, \ldots, n\}$ Galois insertions. The *direct product domain* is a quadruple $(E, \alpha_x, D_x, \gamma_x)$ where $D_x = D_1 \times \cdots \times D_n$, $\gamma_x : D_x \to E$ such that $\gamma_x((d_1, \ldots, d_n)) = \gamma_1(d_1) \sqcap_E \cdots \sqcap_E \gamma_n(d_n)$ and $\alpha_x : E \to D_x$ where $\alpha_x(e) = (\alpha_1(e), \ldots, \alpha_n(e))$. However the direct product domain is *not* a Galois insertion, as shown in [9]. Consider a direct product $(E, \alpha_x, D_x, \gamma_x)$ and the relation $\equiv \subseteq D_x \times D_x$ defined by $d \equiv d' \Leftrightarrow \gamma_x(d) = \gamma_x(d')$. The *reduced product domain* is a quadruple $(E, \alpha_\equiv, D_\equiv, \gamma_\equiv)$ where $\alpha_\equiv : E \to D_\equiv$ such that $\alpha_\equiv(e) = [\alpha_x(e)]_\equiv$ and $\gamma_\equiv : D_\equiv \to E$ such that $\gamma_\equiv([d]_\equiv) = \gamma_x(d)$. Let $\mu : E \to E$ be a concrete function and $\mu_i : D_i \to D_i$, for $i \in \{1, \ldots, n\}$, its approximation via γ_i. The *reduced product function*, $\mu_\equiv : D_\equiv \to D_\equiv$ is defined by $\mu_\equiv([d]_\equiv) = [(\mu_1(d_1)), \ldots, \mu_n(d_n)]_\equiv$ where $(d_1, \ldots, d_n) = \sqcap_{D_x}[d]_\equiv$. In [9] a practical approach to such domain combinations is presented, which simplifies proofs and domain implementation reuse. It also shows that it is possible in practice to benefit from such combinations, obtaining a high degree of precision. Many domain combinations are used in the context of logic programs: groundness and sharing, modes and types, sharing and freeness, etc.

3 The Approach

Using Property Literals/Constraints. The `CiaoPP` *framework* includes, in addition to the PLAI analysis algorithm, an assertion language [6,21,34] that is used for multiple purposes, including reporting static analysis results to the user. These results are expressed as assertions which contain conjunctions of literals of special predicates that are labeled as *properties*, which we also refer sometimes as *constraints*. An example of such a conjunction is "`ground(X), Y > 0`," where `ground/1` and `>/2` are examples of properties/constraints. This allows representing the analysis information inferred by the different domains available in the system syntactically as terms, independently of the internal representations used by the domains. Often, the same properties are reused to

Algorithm 1. AND-rewriting algorithm

```
function AND-REWRITING(Store, Context, R^)
    R ← ApplicableRule(Store, Context, R^)
    if R = false then
        return Store
    else
        (RmEls, NewEls) ← ApplyRule(R, Store, Context)
        Store' ← (Store \ RmEls) ∪ NewEls
        return AND-REWRITING(Store', Context, R^)
```

represent anaysis results from domains that infer similar types of information. Also, every abstract domain defines operations for translating from the internal representation of abstract elements into these properties, which thus constitute in practice a *common language among domains.* A first key component of our approach is to make use of such properties while defining the domain operations.

Abstract-Domain Rules. A second component of our approach is a specialized language, which we call Abstract-Domain Rules (ADRs), aimed at easing the process of defining domain operations. It consists of *AND*- and *OR*-rules with the following syntax:

$$AND\text{-rules}: \; l_1, \ldots, l_n \mid g_1, \ldots, g_l \Rightarrow r_1, \ldots, r_m \; \# \, label \quad (1)$$

$$OR\text{-rules}: \; l_1 \; ; \; l_2 \mid g_1, \ldots, g_l \Rightarrow r_1, \ldots, r_m \; \# \, label \quad (2)$$

where $l_1, \ldots, l_n$, $r_1, \ldots, r_m$ are elements of a set of properties $\mathcal{L}$ and each $g_1, \ldots, g_l$ is an element of $\mathcal{C}_1, \ldots, \mathcal{C}_s$, which are also sets of properties. The elements $l_1, \ldots, l_n$ constitute the *left side* of the rule; $r_1, \ldots, r_m$ the *right side*; and $g_1, \ldots, g_l$ the *guards*. Intuitively, rules operate on a "store," which contains a subset of properties from $\mathcal{L}$, while checking the contents of s stores containing properties respectively from $\mathcal{C}_1, \ldots, \mathcal{C}_s$ (the "context"). Since the language is parameterized by the sets of properties being used, we will use $AND(\mathcal{L}, (\mathcal{C}_1, \ldots, \mathcal{C}_s))$ (resp. $OR(\mathcal{L}, (\mathcal{C}_1, \ldots, \mathcal{C}_s))$) to refer to the language of *AND*-rules (resp. *OR*-rules) where the left and right sides are elements of $\mathcal{L}$ and the guards are elements of $\mathcal{C}_1, \ldots, \mathcal{C}_s$.

We say that an *abstract substitution* λ is in *extended form* iff for each program variable $x \in vars(\lambda)$ there is a unique element of λ which captures all the information related to x. The extended form is frequently used in non-relational domains (although usually elements for which there is no information may be not shown).

Example 2. Consider a program with variables $\{\mathtt{X}, \mathtt{Y}, \mathtt{Z}\}$.

- The abstract substitution $\{\mathtt{X}/i(1,2), \mathtt{Y}/i(0,1), \mathtt{Z}/i(-\infty,\infty)\}$ of the non-relational domain of intervals is in extended form (as usual for this domain).
- The abstract substitutions of the `bit` domain in Fig. 1 are in extended form.

- The set representation (`[[X, Y], [Z]]`) of the sharing property [23,31] is not in extended form, but it can be transformed into a (more verbose) extended form `[sh(X, [Y]), sh(Y, [X]), sh(Z, [])]`, where the property `sh(A, ShSet)` expresses that all the variables in `ShSet` share with `A`.

Let $\mathcal{L}, \mathcal{C}_1, \ldots, \mathcal{C}_n$ be lattices and *Context* an element of $\mathcal{P}(\mathcal{C}_1) \times \cdots \times \mathcal{P}(\mathcal{C}_n)$ where $\mathcal{P}(S)$ denotes the powerset of S. We also assume that abstract substitutions are in *extended form* representation.

AND Semantics. Let $\mathcal{R}^\wedge \subseteq AND(\mathcal{L}, (\mathcal{C}_1, \ldots, \mathcal{C}_n))$ and $Store \subseteq \mathcal{L}$. The operational meaning of applying the set of rules $\mathcal{R}^\wedge$ over store *Store* in context *Context* is given by function AND-REWRITING(*Store*, *Context*, $\mathcal{R}^\wedge$) defined in Algorithm 1. Function ApplicableRule(*Store*, *Context*, $\mathcal{R}^\wedge$) (Line 2), returns a rule $R \in \mathcal{R}^\wedge$ of the form *Left* | *Guard* ⇒ *Right* such that *Left* unifies with elements *RmEls* in *Store* with *unifier* θ, and *Guard* holds in *Context*, if such a rule exists, otherwise it returns `false`. Then, function ApplyRule(R, *Store*, *Context*) (Line 6) returns the pair (*RmEls*, *NewEls*), where *NewEls* are the elements in $(Right)\theta$, i.e., the instance of the right hand side of the unifying rule. Finally, a new store *Store'* is created by taking out *RmEls* from, and adding *NewEls* to *Store*, and the process is continued.

Example 3. Consider the sets $Store = \{\mathtt{leq(X,+\infty)},\ \mathtt{leq(Y,+\infty)},\ \mathtt{leq(Z,+\infty)}\}$, $Context = \{\mathtt{X} \le \mathtt{Y}+\mathtt{Z},\ \mathtt{Y} \le \mathtt{Z}+3,\ \mathtt{Z}=0\}$ and $\mathcal{R}^\wedge = \{$

$$\mathtt{leq(A,+\infty)} \mid \mathtt{A} = Val \Rightarrow \mathtt{leq}(\mathtt{A}, Val)\ \#\ eq,$$
$$\mathtt{leq(A,+\infty)},\ \mathtt{leq}(\mathtt{B}, Val1) \mid \mathtt{A} \le \mathtt{B} + Val2 \Rightarrow$$
$$\mathtt{leq}(\mathtt{A}, Val1 + Val2),\ \mathtt{leq}(\mathtt{B}, Val1)\ \#\ addVInt,$$
$$\mathtt{leq(A,+\infty)},\ \mathtt{leq}(\mathtt{B}, Val1),\ \mathtt{leq}(\mathtt{C}, Val2) \mid \mathtt{A} \le \mathtt{B} + \mathtt{C} \Rightarrow$$
$$\mathtt{leq}(\mathtt{A}, Val1 + Val2),\ \mathtt{leq}(\mathtt{B}, Val1),\ \mathtt{leq}(\mathtt{C}, Val2)\ \#\ addVarVar\ \}$$

Then, Algorithm 1 (AND-rewriting) proceeds as follows:

- In Line 2, function ApplicableRule(*Store*, *Context*, $\mathcal{R}^\wedge$) returns in R the rule with *eq* label (if no rule were applicable it would return `false`).
- ApplyRule(R, *Store*, *Context*) returns the pair $(\{\mathtt{leq(Z,+\infty)}\},\ \{\mathtt{leq(Z,0)}\})$.
- The new store is (Line 7) $Store' = (\{\mathtt{leq(X,+\infty)}, \mathtt{leq(Y,+\infty)}, \mathtt{leq(Z,+\infty)}\} \setminus \{\mathtt{leq(Z,\infty)}\}) \cup \{\mathtt{leq(Z,0)}\} = \{\mathtt{leq(X,\infty)},\ \mathtt{leq(Y,+\infty)},\ \mathtt{leq(Z,0)}\}$.
- The recursive call in Line 8 selects the *addVInt* rule and applies it, obtaining $Store' = \{\mathtt{leq(X,+\infty)},\ \mathtt{leq(Y,3)},\ \mathtt{leq(Z,0)}\}$.
- The next recursive call in Line 8 selects the *addVarVar* rule, whose application obtains $Store' = \{\mathtt{leq(X,3)},\ \mathtt{leq(Y,3)},\ \mathtt{leq(Z,0)}\}$.
- Finally, since there is no applicable rule in the next recursive call, R is assigned `false` (Line 2) and the process finishes, returning the current store.

OR Semantics. Let $\mathcal{R}^\vee \subseteq OR(\mathcal{L}, (\mathcal{C}_1, \ldots, \mathcal{C}_n))$ and $Store_i \subseteq \mathcal{L}$, $1 \le i \le m$. The operational meaning of applying the set of rules $\mathcal{R}^\vee$ over the set of m stores $\{Store_1, \ldots, Store_m\}$ in context *Context* is given by function OR-REWRITING($\{Store_1, \ldots, Store_m\}$, *Context*, $\mathcal{R}^\vee$), defined in Algorithm 2.

Algorithm 2. OR-rewriting algorithm

1: **function** OR-REWRITING($Stores, Context, \mathcal{R}^{\vee}$)
2: **if** $|Stores| > 1$ **then**
3: $(Store_1, Store_2) \leftarrow$ takeTwo($Stores$)
4: $Store \leftarrow$ OR-REWRITING-PAIR($Store_1, Store_2, Context, \mathcal{R}^{\vee}$)
5: $Stores' \leftarrow (Stores \setminus \{Store_1, Store_2\}) \cup \{Store\}$
6: **return** OR-REWRITING($Stores', Context, \mathcal{R}^{\vee}$)
7: **else**
8: **return** $Stores$
9: **function** OR-REWRITING-PAIR($Store_1, Store_2, Context, \mathcal{R}^{\vee}$)
10: $(St_1, St_2, RewSt) \leftarrow$ APPLY-OR-RULES($Store_1, Store_2, Context, \mathcal{R}^{\vee}, \emptyset$)
11: **if** $St_1 = St_2$ **then**
12: **return** $St_1 \cup RewSt$
13: **else**
14: $Ints \leftarrow St_1 \cap St_2$
15: $Diffs \leftarrow (St_1 \setminus Ints) \cup (St_2 \setminus Ints)$
16: $TopInfo \leftarrow$ sendToTop($Diffs$)
17: **return** $RewSt \cup Ints \cup TopInfo$
18: **function** APPLY-OR-RULES($Store_1, Store_2, Context, \mathcal{R}^{\vee}, AccStore$)
19: $R \leftarrow$ ApplicableRule($Store_1, Store_2, Context, \mathcal{R}^{\vee}$)
20: **if** $Store_1 = Store_2 \vee R =$ **false** **then**
21: **return** $(Store_1, Store_2, AccStore)$
22: **else**
23: $(MSt_1, MSt_2, RElems) \leftarrow$ ApplyRule($R, Store_1, Store_2, Context$)
24: $St_1 \leftarrow Store_1 \setminus MSt_1$
25: $St_2 \leftarrow Store_2 \setminus MSt_2$
26: $AccSt \leftarrow AccStore \cup RElems$
27: **return** APPLY-OR-RULES($St_1, St_2, Context, \mathcal{R}^{\vee}, AccSt$)

Example 4. Consider the sets $Store_1 = \{\texttt{leq}(\texttt{X},\texttt{Y}),\ \texttt{leq}(\texttt{Y},+\infty),\ \texttt{leq}(\texttt{Z},\texttt{X})\}$, $Store_2 = \{\texttt{leq}(\texttt{X},3),\ \texttt{leq}(\texttt{Y},+\infty),\ \texttt{leq}(\texttt{Z},\texttt{Y})\}$, $Context = \{\texttt{Y} >= 3\}$, and $\mathcal{R}^{\vee} = \{$

$$\texttt{leq}(\texttt{A}, Val1)\ ;\ \texttt{leq}(\texttt{A}, Val2) \mid Val1 \geq Val2 \Rightarrow \texttt{leq}(\texttt{A}, Val1)\ \#\ grval,$$
$$\texttt{leq}(\texttt{A}, Val1)\ ;\ \texttt{leq}(\texttt{A}, Val1) \Rightarrow \texttt{leq}(\texttt{A}, Val1)\ \#\ identical\ \}$$

Then, OR-REWRITING($\{Store_1, Store_2\}, Context, \mathcal{R}^{\vee}$) proceeds as follows:

- The condition in Line 2 holds, so that, after selecting the two stores (Line 3), the call to OR-REWRITING-PAIR (Line 4) calls function APPLY-OR-RULES in turn (Line 10), which selects the rule with label *grval* (Line 19).[1]
- The condition in Line 20 does not hold, so the rule is applied (Line 23) obtaining: $MSt_1 = \{\texttt{leq}(\texttt{X},\texttt{Y})\}$, $MSt_2 = \{\texttt{leq}(\texttt{X},3)\}$, and $RElems = \{\texttt{leq}(\texttt{X},\texttt{Y})\}$.

[1] In this context, functions ApplicableRule and ApplyRule are similar to the ones defined for *AND*-rules, but the left hand side of the *OR*-rules is unified with two stores.

- The stores are updated (Lines 24–26), obtaining $St_1 = \{\texttt{leq(Y,}+\infty\texttt{)}, \texttt{leq(Z,X)}\}$, $St_2 = \{\texttt{leq(Y,}+\infty\texttt{)}, \texttt{leq(Z,Y)}\}$, and $AccSt = \{\texttt{leq(X,Y)}\}$.
- The recursive call to APPLY-OR-RULES is performed (Line 27). In this new invocation, the rule with label *identical* is selected (Line 19), and since condition in Line 20 does not hold either, such a rule is applied (Line 23).
- The stores are updated (Lines 24–26), obtaining: $St_1 = \{\texttt{leq(Z,X)}\}$, $St_2 = \{\texttt{leq(Z,Y)}\}$, and $AccSt = \{\texttt{leq(X,Y)}, \texttt{leq(Y,}+\infty\texttt{)}\}$.
- A new recursive invocation of APPLY-OR-RULES is performed (Line 27). Now, the condition in Line 20 does not hold because there is no applicable rule ($R =$ `false` in Line 19), so that the APPLY-OR-RULES "loop" finishes in Line 21, returning control to Line 10 with result $St_1 = \{\texttt{leq(Z,X)}\}$, $St_2 = \{\texttt{leq(Z,Y)}\}$, and $RewSt = \{\texttt{leq(X,Y)}, \texttt{leq(Y,}+\infty\texttt{)}\}$.
- Now, the updates in Lines 14–16 obtain: $Ints = \emptyset$, $Diffs = \{\texttt{leq(Z,X)}, \texttt{leq(Z,Y)}\}$, and $TopInfo = \{\texttt{leq(Z,}+\infty\texttt{)}\}$. Note that function sendToTop assigns the `top` ($\top$) value (of the corresponding lattice) to the variables corresponding to the elements in the set *Diffs*: only variable Z in this case, the one on the left hand side of `leq(_,_)`.
- The call to OR-REWRITING-PAIR in Line 4 finishes, returning store $Store = \{\texttt{leq(X,Y)}, \texttt{leq(Y,}+\infty\texttt{)}, \texttt{leq(Z,}+\infty\texttt{)}\}$, and the recursive call in Line 6 also finishes, returning $\{Store\}$ (since condition in line 2 does not hold and such a result is returned in Line 8).

Connecting Rule-Based Domains to PLAI. We now sketch how the previously defined *AND*-rules and *OR*-rules are connected to the abstract domain operations introduced in Sect. 2. Let $D_1, \ldots, D_m$ be a collection of m abstract domains with lattices $\mathcal{L}_1, \ldots, \mathcal{L}_m$ and $\lambda = (\lambda_1, \ldots, \lambda_m)$ an abstract substitution of the combined analysis with abstract domains $D_1, \ldots, D_m$, where each λ_i is an abstract substitution of domain D_i, i.e., $\lambda_i \subseteq \mathcal{L}_i$. We want to perform a rewriting over a collection of domains $D_1, \ldots, D_l$, for some l s.t. $l \leq m$. For each i in $\{1, \ldots, l\}$, let we define $RC_i = (D_1, \ldots, D_{i-1}, D_{i+1}, \ldots, D_m)$, $\mathcal{R}_i^{\wedge} \subseteq AND(D_i, RC_i)$ and $\mathcal{R}_i^{\vee} \subseteq OR(D_i, RC_i)$. Then, the application of the collection of sets of *AND*-rules $\mathcal{R}_1^{\wedge}, \ldots, \mathcal{R}_l^{\wedge}$ over λ (i.e., applying $\mathcal{R}_i^{\wedge}$ over each λ_i in the corresponding context) is a fixpoint computation, defined in Algorithm 3. Termination of this computation is in principle the responsibility of the rule writer, i.e., the rules provided should be confluent. It would be interesting to introduce heuristics for ensuring termination, but this is beyond of the scope of this paper, and for simplicity we assume that the algorithm always terminates. Note that a limit on the number of iterations can always be set up in practice to ensure termination or to improve performance, possibly at the prize of accuracy loss (but of course always ensuring the correctness of the results).

Note that the rules may have different objectives. We may just be interested in combining some existing domains. In this case each domain has its own predefined operations and the objective of the rules is only to propagate the information in the abstract substitutions among domains in order to improve precision. We may instead want the rules to define a collection of domains $D_1, \ldots, D_l$ exploiting the information inferred by domains $D_{l+1}, \ldots, D_m$. In this case the

Algorithm 3. AND-rewriting fixpoint

function AND-FIXP(λ, $\langle \mathcal{R}_1^\wedge, \ldots, \mathcal{R}_l^\wedge \rangle$)
    $(\lambda_1, \ldots, \lambda_m) \leftarrow \lambda$
    for $i \in \{1, \ldots, l\}$ **do**
        $Context_i \leftarrow (\lambda_1, \ldots, \lambda_{i-1}, \lambda_{i+1}, \ldots, \lambda_m)$
        $\lambda_i^{rew} \leftarrow$ AND-REWRITING(λ_i, $Context_i$, $\mathcal{R}_i^\wedge$)
    $\lambda^{rew} \leftarrow (\lambda_1^{rew}, \ldots, \lambda_l^{rew}, \lambda_{l+1}, \ldots, \lambda_m)$
    if areEqual(λ, λ^{rew}) **then**
        return λ^{rew}
    else
        return AND-FIXP(λ^{rew}, $\langle \mathcal{R}_1^\wedge, \ldots, \mathcal{R}_l^\wedge \rangle$)

rules will implement general domain operations (usually reduced to set operations and unifications) and the information will be mainly gathered from the information obtained by the domains $D_{l+1}, \ldots, D_m$, after the given operation.

Finally, given a domain operation (for example `Aproj`), we denote the corresponding operation for domain D_i as `Aproj`$_i$. Now the operations for rule-based domains are:

- `Aproj`(λ, Vs) = (`Aproj`$_1$(λ_1, Vs), …,`Aproj`$_m$(λ_m, Vs)).
- `Aextend`($A_{k,n}, \lambda^c, \lambda^s$) = AND-FIXP($\lambda^{ext}$, $\langle \mathcal{R}_1^\wedge, \ldots, \mathcal{R}_l^\wedge \rangle$) where $\lambda^{ext} = (\lambda_1^{ext}, \ldots, \lambda_m^{ext})$ and λ_j^{ext} =`Aextend`$_j$($A_{k,n}, \lambda^c{}_j, \lambda^s{}_j$) for $j \in \{1, \ldots, m\}$.
- `Acall`(A, λ, A_k) = AND-FIXP(λ^{call}, $\langle \mathcal{R}_1^\wedge, \ldots, \mathcal{R}_l^\wedge \rangle$) where $\lambda^{call} = (\lambda_1^{call}, \ldots, \lambda_m^{call})$, λ_j^{call} =`Acall`$_j$(A, λ_j, A_k) for $j \in \{1, \ldots, m\}$.
- `Aproceed`(A_k, λ_k^s, A) = AND-FIXP(λ^{pri}, $\langle \mathcal{R}_1^\wedge, \ldots, \mathcal{R}_l^\wedge \rangle$) where $\lambda^{pri} = (\lambda_1^{pri}, \ldots, \lambda_m^{pri})$, λ_j^{pri} =`Aproceed`$_j$(A_k, λ_{kj}^s, A) for $j \in \{1, \ldots, m\}$.
- `Ageneralize`($\lambda, \{\lambda^1, \ldots, \lambda^k\}$) = AND-FIXP($\lambda^{gen}$, $\langle \mathcal{R}_1^\wedge, \ldots, \mathcal{R}_l^\wedge \rangle$) where $\lambda = (\lambda_1, \ldots, \lambda_m)$, $\lambda^{gen} = (\lambda_1^{gen}, \ldots, \lambda_m^{gen})$, and:
  - If we are defining domains $D_1, \ldots, D_l$, then, for $j \in \{l+1, \ldots, m\}$, λ_j^{gen} = `Ageneralize`$_j$($\lambda_j, \{\lambda_j^1, \ldots, \lambda_j^k\}$), and for $j \in \{1, \ldots, l\}$, λ_j^{gen} = OR-REWRITING$\lambda_j^{tmp}, (\lambda_1^{tmp}, \ldots, \lambda_{j-1}^{tmp}, \lambda_{j+1}^{tmp}, \ldots, \lambda_m^{tmp}), \mathcal{R}_j^\vee$, where $\lambda_t^{tmp} = \{\lambda_t\} \cup \{\lambda_t^1, \ldots, \lambda_t^k\}$ for $t \in \{1, \ldots, l\}$, and $\lambda_t^{tmp} = \lambda_t^{gen}$ for $t \in \{l+1, \ldots, m\}$.
  - If we are combining domains $D_1, \ldots, D_m$, then, for $j \in \{1, \ldots, m\}$, λ_j^{gen} = `Ageneralize`$_j$($\lambda_j, \{\lambda_j^1, \ldots, \lambda_j^k\}$).

When referring to some operation of a domain D_j with $j \in \{1, \ldots, l\}$ (for example `Aproj`$_j$), if there is no given definition, a default one (`Aproj`$_{def}$) is used. These default operations (marked as $_{def}$) are defined as follows:

- `Aproj`$_{def}$($ASub$, $Vars$) = $\{elem \in ASub \mid \exists v \in$ varset($elem$) $s.t.\ v \in Vars\}$.
- `Aextend`$_{def}$(A, $ASub1$, $ASub2$) = $ASub1 \cup ASub2$.
- `Acall`$_{def}$($A, ASub, A_k$) = `Aproj`$_{def}$($ASub_k$, varset(A_k)) where $ASub_k$ is $ASub$ after the unification of A and A_k.

– $\mathtt{Aproceed}_{def}(A_k, \lambda_k^s, A) = \lambda^{pri}$ where λ^{pri} is λ_k^{pri} after the unification of A_k with A and $\lambda_k^{pri} = \mathtt{Aproj}_{def}(\lambda_k^s, \mathsf{varset}(A_k))$.

The *built-ins* are abstracted in each of the domains $D_1, \ldots, D_n$ and then captured in the combined abstract substitution with the application of the corresponding *AND*-rules. It is possible to define the abstraction predicates of given built-ins if needed.

A Motivating Example: the Bit Domain. We return to the domain of Example 1. We will use here the following abstract values (for a given variable X) for additional readability: $\mathtt{X}/zero$, $\mathtt{X}/one$, $\mathtt{X}/bit$, $\mathtt{X}/\top$, and $\mathtt{X}/\bot$. In order to correctly capture this, our analysis should meet the following conditions, encoded in the rules of Fig. 2: **(i)** If a unification $\mathtt{X} = 0$ is encountered, then X should be abstracted to $\mathtt{X}/zero$; this behaviour is captured by Rule 3 (labeled abs_{zero}); **(ii)** if a unification $\mathtt{X} = 1$ is encountered, then X should be abstracted to $\mathtt{X}/one$, as is captured by Rule 4 (labeled abs_{one}); **(iii)** if a variable has been abstracted to *bot* and also to any other element of the lattice, then it has to be kept as *bot*, captured by Rule 5 (labeled glb_1); **(iv)** if a variable has been abstracted to $\top$ and to any other element of the lattice then it must be kept as the other non-top element, captured by Rule 6 (labeled glb_2); **(v)** if a variable X has been abstracted to $\mathtt{X}/zero$, and to $\mathtt{X}/one$, then it has to be abstracted to $\mathtt{X}/\bot$, captured by Rule 7 (labeled glb_3); **(vi)** if a variable X has been abstracted to $\mathtt{X}/\bot$ and to $\mathtt{X}/zero$ then it has to be kept as $\mathtt{X}/zero$, captured by Rule 8 (labeled glb_4); **(vii)** if a variable X has been abstracted to $\mathtt{X}/bit$ and to $\mathtt{X}/one$ then it has to be kept as $\mathtt{X}/one$, captured by Rule 9 (labeled glb_5).

In a similar fashion we need to describe the behaviour of the *lub* or *join* of a pair of abstract substitutions. We do it as follows: **(i)** if a variable X has been abstracted to $\mathtt{X}/zero$ in one sustitution and to $\mathtt{X}/one$ in other, then the join is $\mathtt{X}/bit$, captured by Rule 10 (labeled lub_1); **(ii)** if a variable X has been abstracted to $\mathtt{X}/\bot$ in one sustitution and to anything else in the other, then the *lub* is the latter, captured by Rule 11 (labeled lub_2); **(iii)** if a variable X has been abstracted to $\mathtt{X}/\top$ in one sustitution and to anything else in the other, then the *lub* is $\mathtt{X}/\top$, this is captured by Rule 12 (labeled lub_3); **(iv)** if a variable X has been abstracted to the same value in both substitutions then the *lub* is such a value, captured by Rule 13 (labeled lub_4). To also keep track of the structures that variables are bound to we will use the **depth-k** domain, presented in [36] and discussed in [24]. So the rules presented in Fig. 2 are subsets of $AND(Bit, Depth\text{-}k)$ and $OR(Bit, Depth\text{-}k)$ respectively.

Example 5. Consider the very simple Prolog program with two clauses: `is_a_bit(A) :- A=0.` and `is_a_bit(A) :- A=1.`, and the set of *AND*- and *OR*-rules in Fig. 2 ($\mathcal{R}_{bit}^{\wedge}$ and $\mathcal{R}_{bit}^{\vee}$ resp.). Figure 3 shows the analysis flow of the first clause for the combination of the **bit** and **depth-3** domains. The analysis starts with a top entry ASub1= $(\{\mathtt{X}/\top\}, \{\mathtt{X{=}U}\})$ for a call `is_a_bit(X)`, where X is abstracted to $\top$ in the **bit** domain and unified to a fresh free variable U in the **depth-3** domain (which means that no information about the

$$\mathtt{X}/\top \mid \mathtt{X} = 0 \Rightarrow \mathtt{X}/zero \,\#\, abs_{zero} \quad (3)$$
$$\mathtt{X}/\top \mid \mathtt{X} = 1 \Rightarrow \mathtt{X}/one \,\#\, abs_{one} \quad (4)$$
$$\mathtt{X}/\bot\,, \mathtt{X}/\mathtt{Y} \Rightarrow \mathtt{X}/\bot \,\#\, glb_1 \quad (5)$$
$$\mathtt{X}/\top\,, \mathtt{X}/\mathtt{Y} \Rightarrow \mathtt{X}/\mathtt{Y} \,\#\, glb_2 \quad (6)$$
$$\mathtt{X}/one\,, \mathtt{X}/zero \Rightarrow \mathtt{X}/\bot \,\#\, glb_3 \quad (7)$$
$$\mathtt{X}/bit\,, \mathtt{X}/zero \Rightarrow \mathtt{X}/zero \,\#\, glb_4 \quad (8)$$
$$\mathtt{X}/bit\,, \mathtt{X}/one \Rightarrow \mathtt{X}/one \,\#\, glb_5 \quad (9)$$
$$\mathtt{X}/one\,;\, \mathtt{X}/zero \Rightarrow \mathtt{X}/bit \,\#\, lub_1 \quad (10)$$
$$\mathtt{X}/\bot\,;\, \mathtt{X}/\mathtt{Y} \Rightarrow \mathtt{X}/\mathtt{Y} \,\#\, lub_2 \quad (11)$$
$$\mathtt{X}/\top\,;\, \mathtt{X}/\mathtt{Y} \Rightarrow \mathtt{X}/\top \,\#\, lub_3 \quad (12)$$
$$\mathtt{X}/\mathtt{Y}\,;\, \mathtt{X}/\mathtt{Y} \Rightarrow \mathtt{X}/\mathtt{Y} \,\#\, lub_4 \quad (13)$$

Fig. 2. Sets of *AND*-rules and *OR*-rules capturing the behaviour of the `bit` domain.

structure of `X` is given). Since we are carrying a substitution with information about just one variable, projecting over that variable results in the same abstract substitution. The execution of `Acall` performs the renaming of `X` to `A`. Since no rule is applicable after such renaming, the analysis proceeds, and when the *built-in* `A=0` is processed, the available domain operations are performed. Domain `depth`-3 has specific operation definitions, while `bit` has none,[2] so nothing is done for the latter domain. In contrast, an updated abstract substitution $\{\mathtt{A} = 0\}$ is obtained for the former, `depth`-3. Now, the execution of AND-FIXP($\{\mathtt{A}/\top\}, \{\mathtt{A} = 0\}, \mathcal{R}^{\wedge}_{bit}$), which applies Rule 3, results in `ASub4`=($\{\mathtt{A}/zero\}, \{\mathtt{A} = 0\}$). `Aproceed` perfoms a back unification (renaming in this case), obtaining `ASub5`= ($\{\mathtt{X}/zero\}, \{\mathtt{X} = 0\}$). Finally, `Aextend` extends the abstract substitution before the `Aproceed` operation (`ASub1`) with `ASub5`. Since there is no specific $\mathtt{Aextend}_{\mathtt{bit}}$ operation for the `bit` domain, the default $\mathtt{Aextend}_{\mathtt{def}}$ is used, obtaining the abstract substitution $\{\mathtt{X}/zero, \mathtt{X}/\top\}$ for such a domain. The application of the corresponding, specific `Aextend` operation for the `depth`-3 domain ($\mathtt{Aextend}_{\mathtt{depth\text{-}3}}$) obtains $\{\mathtt{X} = 0\}$. Now, the AND-FIXP operation applies Rule 6 to obtain a (combined) abstract success substution: AND-FIXP($\{\mathtt{X}/\top, \mathtt{X}/zero\}, \{\mathtt{X} = 0\}, \mathcal{R}^{\wedge}_{bit}$)= ($\{\mathtt{X}/zero, \{\mathtt{X} = 0\}$). Similarly, the anaysis of the second clause, `is_a_bit(A) :- A=1.`, obtains the abstract substitution ($\{\mathtt{X}/one, \{\mathtt{X} = 1\}$). Now, the global analysis applies the `Ageneralize` operation to the abstract substitutions resulting from the analysis of the two clauses, by calling `Ageneralize`(($\{\mathtt{X}/one, \{\mathtt{X} = 1\}), \{(\{\mathtt{X}/zero\}, \{\mathtt{X} = 0\})\}$), which, for the *bit* domain, calls OR-REWRITING($\{\{\mathtt{X}/one\}, \{\mathtt{X}/zero\}\}, \{\{\mathtt{X} = 1\}, \{\mathtt{X} = 0\}\}$) in turn, obtaining $\{\mathtt{X}/bit\}$, due to the application of Rule 10. For the `depth`−3 domain, `Ageneralize` applies $\mathtt{Ageneralize}_{\mathtt{depth\text{-}3}}$ to abstract substituions $\{\mathtt{X} = 1\}$ and $\{\mathtt{X} = 0\}$, obtaining $\{\mathtt{X} = \mathtt{V}\}$, where `V` is a fresh free variable. The analysis finishes with the execution of AND-FIXP(($\{\mathtt{X}/bit\}, \{\mathtt{X} = \mathtt{V}\}), \mathcal{R}^{\wedge}_{bit}$), which performs the AND-rewriting on the resulting abstract generalization for the combined domain, obtaining the success abstract substitution ($\{\mathtt{X}/bit\}, \{\mathtt{X} = \mathtt{V}\}$) for the initial call `is_a_bit(X)`.

[2] As mentioned before, it is possible to give concrete operations for some built-ins, but in this case we let the rules deal with unifications.

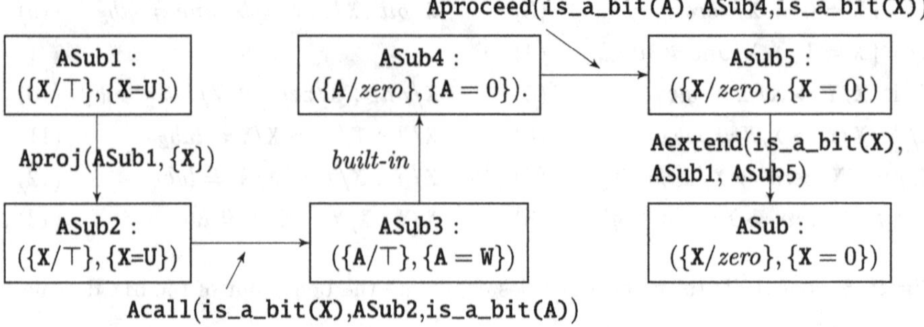

Fig. 3. Analysis flow for the clause `is_a_bit(A):-A=0.` with `Bit` domain.

4 Inferring Program Properties Using Rule-Based Combined Domains

We now show how the technique presented in the previous section can be used to define abstract domains for non-trivial properties. Concretely, we present a rule-based domain to infer sortedness. As an aid in defining this domain, consider the classical implementation in Prolog of the *quick sort* algorithm in Fig. 4. Given a query `qsort(A, B)` we aim at inferring that `B` is a sorted list. To do so we first need to consider the lattice over which to abstract the sortedness property. Let that lattice be $\{\top, sorted, unsorted, \bot\}$ where $\top$ captures that is it unknown whether the element is sorted or not, and $\bot$ that some error has been found. The structure of the lattice is given by the order relation such that $\top$ is greater or equal than every other element, $\bot$ is smaller or equal than every other element, and *sorted* and *unsorted* cannot be compared. Now we start defining rules about the behaviour that we expect from our domain. Clearly, given an empty list we can abstract that element as sorted (which we represent as `L`/*sorted*); this property is captured by Rule 28 (labeled *absEmpty*) in Fig. 7. We can also define rules to capture the expected behaviour of the *glb*, taking into account the order that we introduced before: if a variable has been abstracted to *sorted* and also to *unsorted* the *glb* is $\bot$; if the variable has been abstracted to $\top$ and to any other element, then the latter is the *glb*; finally, if it has been abstracted to $\bot$ and to something else the result is $\bot$. These behaviors are captured by Rules 33, 34, and 35 respectively. If a list `L` is known to be sorted, and `L=[H|T]`, then clearly `T` must be sorted, which is represented by Rule 32. Conversely, if we know that `T` is a sorted list, and `H` is smaller or equal than any element in `T` then we can infer that `L` is sorted. To this end, it is clear the need to introduce (in Figs. 5 and 6) two new abstract domains, `inf` and `sup`, which abstract the property of an element `X` being lower or equal (resp., greater or equal) than any element in a given list `L`. This is represented by property `inf(L,X)` (resp. `sup(L,X)`). With the help of the new `inf` domain, we can now represent the previous inference reasoning with Rule 30. In these domains we not only need to capture the unifications occurring during the pro-

```
qsort([], []).
qsort([X|L], R) :-
    partition(L, X, L1, L2),
    qsort(L2, R2), qsort(L1, R1), append(R1, [X|R2], R).

partition([], _, [], []).
partition([E|R], C, Left, [E|Right1]) :- E >= C, partition(R, C, Left, Right1).
partition([E|R], C, [E|Left1], Right) :- E < C, partition(R, C, Left1, Right).

append([],Z, Z).
append([H|T], S, [H|Z]) :- append(T, S, Z).
```

Fig. 4. A classical implementation of *quick sort* in Prolog (using append/3).

$$\mathtt{inf}(\mathtt{L},\top) \mid \mathtt{L=[]} \Rightarrow \mathtt{inf}(\mathtt{L},\infty)\ \#\ \textit{empty} \tag{14}$$

$$\mathtt{inf}(\mathtt{L},\mathtt{X}) \mid \mathtt{L=[H|T]} \Rightarrow \mathtt{inf}(\mathtt{L},\mathtt{X}), \mathtt{inf}(\mathtt{T},\mathtt{X})\ \#\ \textit{prop1} \tag{15}$$

$$\mathtt{inf}(\mathtt{T},\mathtt{X}) \mid \mathtt{L=[H|T]}, \mathtt{X} \leq \mathtt{H} \Rightarrow \mathtt{inf}(\mathtt{L},\mathtt{X}), \mathtt{inf}(\mathtt{T},\mathtt{X})\ \#\ \textit{prop2} \tag{16}$$

$$\mathtt{inf}(\mathtt{T},\mathtt{X}) \mid \mathtt{L=[H|T]}, \mathtt{H} \leq \mathtt{X} \Rightarrow \mathtt{inf}(\mathtt{L},\mathtt{H}), \mathtt{inf}(\mathtt{T},\mathtt{X})\ \#\ \textit{prop3} \tag{17}$$

$$\mathtt{inf}(\mathtt{L1},\mathtt{X}) \mid \mathtt{L1=L2} \Rightarrow \mathtt{inf}(\mathtt{L1},\mathtt{X}), \mathtt{inf}(\mathtt{L2},\mathtt{X})\ \#\ \textit{unif} \tag{18}$$

$$\mathtt{inf}(\mathtt{L},\mathtt{X}) \mid \mathtt{Y} \leq \mathtt{X} \Rightarrow \mathtt{inf}(\mathtt{L},\mathtt{Y})\ \#\ \textit{reduce} \tag{19}$$

$$\mathtt{inf}(\mathtt{L},\mathtt{X}); \mathtt{inf}(\mathtt{L},\mathtt{Y}) \mid \mathtt{X} \leq \mathtt{Y} \Rightarrow \mathtt{inf}(\mathtt{L},X)\ \#\ \textit{lub} \tag{20}$$

Fig. 5. Sets of *AND*-rules (14–19) and *OR*-rules (20) for the inf domain.

gram execution/analysis but also the arithmetic properties involved. To this end, we use CiaoPP's polyCLPQ, a polyhedra domain based on [2]. The sets of *AND*- and *OR*-rules for the inf and sup domains are in fact subsets of *AND*(inf, (depth-k,polyCLPQ)) and *OR*(inf, (depth-k,polyCLPQ)), shown in Fig. 5, and *AND*(sup, (depth-k,polyCLPQ)) and *OR*(sup, (depth-k,polyCLPQ)), shown in Fig. 6, respectively. The sets of *AND*- and *OR*-rules for the sort domain that are presented in Fig. 7 are subsets of *AND*(sort, (inf, depth-k, polyCLPQ)) and *OR*(sort, (inf, depth-k, polyCLPQ)) respectively. However the previously defined rules may not be enough to infer sortedness. With the domains inf and sup the analysis after partition(L, X, L1, L2) in the qsort algorithm in Fig. 4 would have inferred that sup(L1, X) and inf(L2, X) (the complete analysis of the partition/4 predicate with the inf domain can be found in [24] but even assuming that after the qsort(L2, R2), qsort(L1, R1) recursive calls R2/*sorted* and R1/*sorted* are inferred, we would not be able to propagate that the element [X|R2] is a sorted list; nor that X is greater than all elements in R1, which would be key to obtain the sortedness of R. What we are missing is the fact that, given a query qsort(A, B), A is a permutation of B. And that if an element X satisfies inf(A, X), then clearly inf(B, X). To deal with this we introduce a new abstract domain, mset, to abstract properties between multisets of the lists in the program. This domain is discussed in [24]. The abstraction is represented by the property mset(A $=$ B) capturing that B is a permutation of A and mset(A $=$ B+C) meaning that the multiset A is a permutation of the union of the multisets B and C.

$$\texttt{sup(L,}\top\texttt{)} \mid \texttt{L=[]} \Rightarrow \texttt{sup(L,}-\infty\texttt{)} \; \# \; \textit{empty} \tag{21}$$

$$\texttt{sup(L,X)} \mid \texttt{L=[H|T]} \Rightarrow \texttt{sup(L,X), sup(T,X)} \; \# \; \textit{prop1} \tag{22}$$

$$\texttt{sup(T,X)} \mid \texttt{L=[H|T]}, \texttt{H} \leq \texttt{X} \Rightarrow \texttt{sup(L,X), sup(T,X)} \; \# \; \textit{prop2} \tag{23}$$

$$\texttt{sup(T,X)} \mid \texttt{L=[H|T]}, \texttt{X} \leq \texttt{H} \Rightarrow \texttt{sup(L,H), sup(T,X)} \; \# \; \textit{prop3} \tag{24}$$

$$\texttt{sup(L1,X)} \mid \texttt{L1=L2} \Rightarrow \texttt{sup(L1,X), sup(L2,X)} \; \# \; \textit{unif} \tag{25}$$

$$\texttt{sup(L,X)} \mid \texttt{X} \leq \texttt{Y} \Rightarrow \texttt{sup(L,Y)} \; \# \; \textit{reduce} \tag{26}$$

$$\texttt{sup(L,X); sup(L,Y)} \mid \texttt{X} \leq \texttt{Y} \Rightarrow \texttt{sup(L,}X\texttt{)} \; \# \; \textit{lub} \tag{27}$$

Fig. 6. Sets of *AND*-rules (21–26) and *OR*-rules (27) for the sup domain.

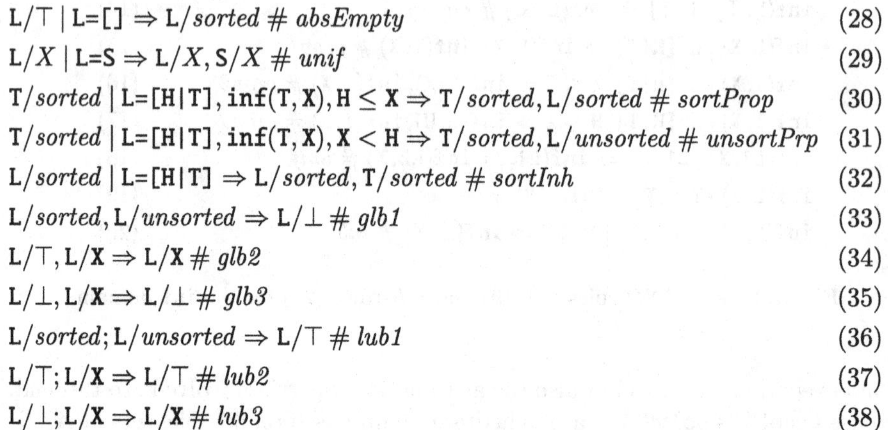

$$\texttt{L}/\top \mid \texttt{L=[]} \Rightarrow \texttt{L}/\textit{sorted} \; \# \; \textit{absEmpty} \tag{28}$$

$$\texttt{L}/X \mid \texttt{L=S} \Rightarrow \texttt{L}/X, \texttt{S}/X \; \# \; \textit{unif} \tag{29}$$

$$\texttt{T}/\textit{sorted} \mid \texttt{L=[H|T]}, \texttt{inf(T,X)}, \texttt{H} \leq \texttt{X} \Rightarrow \texttt{T}/\textit{sorted}, \texttt{L}/\textit{sorted} \; \# \; \textit{sortProp} \tag{30}$$

$$\texttt{T}/\textit{sorted} \mid \texttt{L=[H|T]}, \texttt{inf(T,X)}, \texttt{X} < \texttt{H} \Rightarrow \texttt{T}/\textit{sorted}, \texttt{L}/\textit{unsorted} \; \# \; \textit{unsortPrp} \tag{31}$$

$$\texttt{L}/\textit{sorted} \mid \texttt{L=[H|T]} \Rightarrow \texttt{L}/\textit{sorted}, \texttt{T}/\textit{sorted} \; \# \; \textit{sortInh} \tag{32}$$

$$\texttt{L}/\textit{sorted}, \texttt{L}/\textit{unsorted} \Rightarrow \texttt{L}/\bot \; \# \; \textit{glb1} \tag{33}$$

$$\texttt{L}/\top, \texttt{L/X} \Rightarrow \texttt{L/X} \; \# \; \textit{glb2} \tag{34}$$

$$\texttt{L}/\bot, \texttt{L/X} \Rightarrow \texttt{L}/\bot \; \# \; \textit{glb3} \tag{35}$$

$$\texttt{L}/\textit{sorted}; \texttt{L}/\textit{unsorted} \Rightarrow \texttt{L}/\top \; \# \; \textit{lub1} \tag{36}$$

$$\texttt{L}/\top; \texttt{L/X} \Rightarrow \texttt{L}/\top \; \# \; \textit{lub2} \tag{37}$$

$$\texttt{L}/\bot; \texttt{L/X} \Rightarrow \texttt{L/X} \; \# \; \textit{lub3} \tag{38}$$

Fig. 7. Sets of *AND*-rules (28–35) and *OR*-rules (36–38) for the sort domain.

Consider the goal append(R1, S, R) together with the information inferred on call ({R1/*sorted*, R2/*sorted*}, {A=[X|L],S=[X|R2]}, {}, {inf(L2,X), inf(R2,X)}, {sup(L1,X), sup(R1,X)}, {mset(L = L1+L2), mset(L1 = R1), mset(L2 = R2)}). In the first case we get the unifications: C_1 = ({R1 = [],S = Z}, {R1/*sorted*, S/*sorted*, Z/*sorted*}, {inf(S,X)}, {sup(R1,X)}) after applying Rules *absEmpty* 28 and *unif* 29. In the second case we have the entry: C_2 = ({R1 = [H|L],Z = [H|T]}, {R1/*sorted*, S/*sorted*}, {inf(S,X)}, {sup(R1,X)}). However, after append(X, Y, Z) we have to apply the *lub* and we get: ({}, {R1/*sorted*, S/*sorted*}, {{inf(S,X)}, {sup(R1,X)}}) which is not proving that R is sorted. This is because if Z is sorted and inf(Z,X) (which is inferred in the recursive call) since R=[H|Z], what we need for R to be sorted is that H≤X holds. polyCLPQ is not able to prove that, but it can be enhanced to use sup by adding a purely combinatorial rule:

$$\texttt{true} \mid \texttt{sup(L,X)}, \texttt{L=[H|T]} \Rightarrow \texttt{H} \leq \texttt{X} \; \# \; \textit{combinePoly} \tag{39}$$

Note that this rule is enhancing the precision of a previously defined domain in CiaoPP, by exploiting properties that have been defined using rules. In this sense a number of other rules could be introduced to enhance the precision of `polyCLPQ` as for example `true` | `L`/*sorted*, `L=[H|T]`, `inf(T,X)` $\Rightarrow$ `H` $\leq$ `X`, which exploits both the sortedness and the `inf` property to get better abstractions for `polyCLPQ`. Now, with this new information, we can infer that, since `H`$\leq$`X`, then `inf(Z,H)`. With this, since `Z` is sorted and `R = [H|Z]`, then `R` is sorted and `inf(R,H)`, and therefore we infer that the second argument of `qsort/2` is sorted. Thus, we have shown how the rule language presented in Sect. 3 can be used to define a number of new domains complementing each other and enhancing the precision of some predefined domains as `polyCLPQ`. Moreover they are powerful enough to prove that given a query `qsort(A, B)` of the *quicksort* implementation presented in Fig. 4, `B` is a sorted list and a permutation of `A`. `CiaoPP` outputs the analysis result as the following assertion:

```
:- true pred qsort(A,B)
    : ( asub([s(A,top),s(B,top)]),
        ↪ asub(([inf(A,top),inf(B,top)],[sup(A,top),sup(B,top)])), true,
        ↪ true )
    => ( asub([s(A,top),s(B,sorted)]),
        ↪ asub(([inf(A,top),inf(B,top)],[sup(A,top),sup(B,top)])),
        ↪ mset([A=B]), true ).
```

The complete program-point analysis information for the analysis, as produced by `CiaoPP`, can be found in [24].

Variable Scope. It is important to point out that we have to take into account the fact that the scope of the variable `X` that we carry around in the abstract substitutions goes beyond the argument and local variables of `append/3`. In order not to lose precision, the domain projection operation must preserve the relation between program variables and `X` in the form of *"existential"* variables. That is, to capture that "there exists a variable that holds a given property" (for example the `inf` property). This kind of issues are common when trying to capture properties of data structures, and they are more involved when combining domains, since a projection for one domain must be aware of the relevant variables for the others. In our current implementation, we rely for simplicity on syntactic transformations that include "extra" arguments to the required predicates (see the call to `append/4` in [24], similar to *cell morphing* proposed in [3]. We are working on fixing this limitation and extending the combination framework to share the information about "existential" variables among the combined domains without syntactic transformations nor losses of precision.

5 Conclusions

We have presented a rule-based methodology for rapid design and prototyping of new domains, as well as for combining existing ones. We have demonstrated the power of our approach by showing how several domains and their combinations can be defined with reduced effort. We have also shown how these techniques can be used to develop domains for interesting properties, using list *sortedness* (a property not supported by the previously existing CiaoPP domains) as an example. We have also shown how our prototype implementation infers this property for the classical Prolog implementation of the quick sort algorithm. From our experience using this implementation, the proposed approach seems promising for prototyping and experimenting with new domains, adding domain combinations, and enhancing precision for particular programs, without the need for a deep understanding of the analysis framework internals. Our current implementation is focused on the feasibility and usefulness of the approach, and lacks many possible optimizations. However, given the promising results so far, we plan to optimize the implementation and to use it to define new domains, exploring the trade-offs between rule-based and native, hand-tuned domains. Other avenues for future work are exploring the use of rules both as an input language for *abstract domain compilation* and as a specification language for debugging or verifying properties of hand-written domains.

References

1. de Angelis, E., Proietti, M., Fioravanti, F., Pettorossi, A.: Verifying catamorphism-based contracts using constrained horn clauses. Theory Pract. Logic Program. **22**(4), 555–572 (2022). https://doi.org/10.1017/S1471068422000175
2. Benoy, F., King, A., Mesnard, F.: Programming pearl: computing convex hulls with a linear solver. TPLP **5**, 259–271 (2005). https://doi.org/10.1017/S1471068404002261
3. Braine, J., Gonnord, L., Monniaux, D.: Data abstraction: a general framework to handle program verification of data structures. In: Drăgoi, C., Mukherjee, S., Namjoshi, K. (eds.) SAS 2021. LNCS, vol. 12913, pp. 215–235. Springer, Cham (2021). https://doi.org/10.1007/978-3-030-88806-0_11
4. Bravenboer, M., Smaragdakis, Y.: Strictly declarative specification of sophisticated points-to analyses. SIGPLAN Not. **44**(10), 243–262 (2009). https://doi.org/10.1145/1639949.1640108
5. Bruynooghe, M., Codish, M.: Freeness, sharing, linearity and correctness — all at once. In: Cousot, P., Falaschi, M., Filé, G., Rauzy, A. (eds.) WSA 1993. LNCS, vol. 724, pp. 153–164. Springer, Heidelberg (1993). https://doi.org/10.1007/3-540-57264-3_37
6. Bueno, F., Cabeza, D., Hermenegildo, M., Puebla, G.: Global analysis of standard Prolog programs. In: Nielson, H.R. (ed.) ESOP 1996. LNCS, vol. 1058, pp. 108–124. Springer, Heidelberg (1996). https://doi.org/10.1007/3-540-61055-3_32
7. Campion, M., Preda, M.D., Giacobazzi, R.: Partial (in)completeness in abstract interpretation: limiting the imprecision in program analysis. Proc. ACM Program. Lang. **6**(POPL), 1–31 (2022). https://doi.org/10.1145/3498721
8. Ceri, S., Gottlob, G., Tanca, L.: What you always wanted to know about datalog (and never dared to ask). IEEE TKDE **1**(1), 146–166 (1989). https://doi.org/10.1109/69.43410
9. Codish, M., Mulkers, A., Bruynooghe, M., García de la Banda, M., Hermenegildo, M.: Improving abstract interpretations by combining domains. ACM TOPLAS **17**(1), 28–44 (1995)

10. Cousot, P., Cousot, R.: Abstract interpretation: a unified lattice model for static analysis of programs by construction or approximation of fixpoints. In: ACM Symposium on Principles of Programming Languages (POPL 1977), pp. 238–252. ACM Press (1977). https://doi.org/10.1145/512950.512973
11. Cousot, P., Cousot, R.: Systematic design of program analysis frameworks. In: POPL 1979, pp. 269–282. ACM (1979)
12. Cousot, P., et al.: The ASTREÉ analyzer. In: Sagiv, M. (ed.) ESOP 2005. LNCS, vol. 3444, pp. 21–30. Springer, Heidelberg (2005). https://doi.org/10.1007/978-3-540-31987-0_3
13. De Angelis, E., Fioravanti, F., Gallagher, J.P., Hermenegildo, M.V., Pettorossi, A., Proietti, M.: Analysis and transformation of constrained horn clauses for program verification. TPLP **22**(6), 974–1042 (2021)
14. Frühwirth, T.: Theory and practice of constraint handling rules. JLP Spec. Issue CLP **37**(1–3) (1998)
15. Garcia-Contreras, I., Morales, J.F., Hermenegildo, M.V.: Incremental and modular context-sensitive analysis. TPLP **21**(2), 196–243 (2021)
16. Garcia-Contreras, I., Morales, J.F., Hermenegildo, M.V.: Incremental analysis of logic programs with assertions and open predicates. In: Gabbrielli, M. (ed.) LOPSTR 2019. LNCS, vol. 12042, pp. 36–56. Springer, Cham (2020). https://doi.org/10.1007/978-3-030-45260-5_3
17. García de la Banda, M., Hermenegildo, M.V., Bruynooghe, M., Dumortier, V., Janssens, G., Simoens, W.: Global analysis of constraint logic programs. ACM Trans. Program. Lang. Syst. **18**(5), 564–615 (1996)
18. Giacobazzi, R., Ranzato, F.: History of abstract interpretation. IEEE Ann. Hist. Comput. **44**(2), 33–43 (2022). https://doi.org/10.1109/MAHC.2021.3133136
19. Henriksen, K.S., Gallagher, J.P.: Abstract interpretation of PIC programs through logic programming. In: SCAM 2006, pp. 184–196. IEEE Computer Society (2006). https://doi.org/10.1109/SCAM.2006.1
20. Hermenegildo, M., Puebla, G., Bueno, F., Garcia, P.L.: Integrated program debugging, verification, and optimization using abstract interpretation (and the ciao system preprocessor). Sci. Comput. Program. **58**(1–2), 115–140 (2005)
21. Hermenegildo, M.V., Puebla, G., Bueno, F.: Using global analysis, partial specifications, and an extensible assertion language for program validation and debugging. In: Apt, K.R., Marek, V.W., Truszczynski, M., Warren, D.S. (eds.) The Logic Programming Paradigm: a 25-Year Perspective, pp. 161–192. Springer, Heidelberg (1999). https://doi.org/10.1007/978-3-642-60085-2_7
22. Hermenegildo, M.V., Puebla, G., Marriott, K., Stuckey, P.: Incremental analysis of constraint logic programs. ACM TOPLAS **22**(2), 187–223 (2000). https://doi.org/10.1145/349214.349216
23. Jacobs, D., Langen, A.: Accurate and efficient approximation of variable aliasing in logic programs. In: North American Conference on Logic Programming (1989)
24. Jurjo, D., Morales, J.F., Lopez-Garcia, P., Hermenegildo, M.: A methodology for designing and composing abstract domains using rewriting rules. Technical report, CLIP-1/2023.0, CLIP Lab, UPM and IMDEA Software Institute (2023). https://cliplab.org/papers/jurjo-domcons-tr.pdf
25. Kelly, A., Marriott, K., Søndergaard, H., Stuckey, P.: A practical object-oriented analysis engine for CLP. Softw. Pract. Exp. **28**(2), 188–224 (1998)
26. Le Charlier, B., Van Hentenryck, P.: Experimental evaluation of a generic abstract interpretation algorithm for prolog. ACM TOPLAS **16**(1), 35–101 (1994)
27. Madsen, M., Yee, M., Lhoták, O.: From datalog to FLIX: a declarative language for fixed points on lattices. In: PLDI, pp. 194–208. ACM (2016)

28. Méndez-Lojo, M., Navas, J., Hermenegildo, M.V.: A flexible, (C)LP-based approach to the analysis of object-oriented programs. In: King, A. (ed.) LOPSTR 2007. LNCS, vol. 4915, pp. 154–168. Springer, Heidelberg (2008). https://doi.org/10.1007/978-3-540-78769-3_11
29. Méndez-Lojo, M., Navas, J., Hermenegildo, M.V.: An efficient, parametric fixpoint algorithm for analysis of java bytecode. In: ETAPS Workshop on Bytecode Semantics, Verification, Analysis and Transformation (BYTECODE 2007) (2007)
30. Mesnard, F., Neumerkel, U.: CHR for Protoyping Abstract Interpretation (1997, unpublished note). http://lim.univ-reunion.fr/staff/fred/Publications/00-MesnardN.pdf
31. Muthukumar, K., Hermenegildo, M.: Determination of variable dependence information at compile-time through abstract interpretation. In: NACLP 1989, pp. 166–189. MIT Press (1989)
32. Muthukumar, K., Hermenegildo, M.: Deriving a fixpoint computation algorithm for top-down abstract interpretation of logic programs. Technical report ACT-DC-153-90, Microelectronics and Computer Technology Corporation (MCC) (1990). http://cliplab.org/papers/mcctr-fixpt.pdf
33. Muthukumar, K., Hermenegildo, M.: Compile-time derivation of variable dependency using abstract interpretation. JLP **13**(2/3), 315–347 (1992)
34. Puebla, G., Bueno, F., Hermenegildo, M.: An assertion language for constraint logic programs. In: Deransart, P., Hermenegildo, M.V., Małuszynski, J. (eds.) Analysis and Visualization Tools for Constraint Programming. LNCS, vol. 1870, pp. 23–61. Springer, Heidelberg (2000). https://doi.org/10.1007/10722311_2
35. Puebla, G., Hermenegildo, M.: Optimized algorithms for incremental analysis of logic programs. In: Cousot, R., Schmidt, D.A. (eds.) SAS 1996. LNCS, vol. 1145, pp. 270–284. Springer, Heidelberg (1996). https://doi.org/10.1007/3-540-61739-6_47
36. Sato, T., Tamaki, H.: Enumeration of success patterns in logic programs. In: Diaz, J. (ed.) ICALP 1983. LNCS, vol. 154, pp. 640–652. Springer, Heidelberg (1983). https://doi.org/10.1007/BFb0036944
37. Seidl, H., Vogler, R.: Three improvements to the top-down solver. Math. Struct. Comput. Sci. **31**(9), 1090–1134 (2021). https://doi.org/10.1017/S0960129521000499
38. Tilscher, S., Stade, Y., Schwarz, M., Vogler, R., Seidl, H.: The top-down solver-an exercise in A^2I. In: Arceri, V., Cortesi, A., Ferrara, P., Olliaro, M. (eds.) Challenges of Software Verification. Intelligent Systems Reference Library, vol. 238, pp. 157–179. Springer, Singapore (2023). https://doi.org/10.1007/978-981-19-9601-6_9
39. Van Roy, P., Despain, A.M.: The benefits of global dataflow analysis for an optimizing prolog compiler. In: North American Conference on Logic Programming, pp. 501–515. MIT Press (1990)
40. Warren, R., Hermenegildo, M., Debray, S.K.: On the practicality of global flow analysis of logic programs. In: JICSLP, pp. 684–699. MIT Press (1988)
41. Whaley, J., Lam, M.S.: Cloning-based context-sensitive pointer alias analysis using binary decision diagrams. In: PLDI, pp. 131–144. ACM (2004)

A Logical Interpretation of Asynchronous Multiparty Compatibility

Marco Carbone[1(✉)], Sonia Marin[2], and Carsten Schürmann[1]

[1] Computer Science Department, IT University of Copenhagen, Copenhagen, Denmark
{maca,carsten}@itu.dk

[2] School of Computer Science, University of Birmingham, Birmingham, UK
s.marin@bham.ac.uk

Abstract. Session types specify the protocols that communicating processes must follow in a concurrent system. When composing two or more processes, a session typing system must check whether such processes are *compatible*, i.e., that all sent messages are eventually received and no deadlock ever occurs. After the propositions-as-types paradigm, relating session types to linear logic, previous work has shown that *duality*, in the binary case, and more generally *coherence*, in the multiparty case, are sufficient syntactic conditions to guarantee compatibility for two or more processes, yet do not characterise all compatible set of processes.

In this work, we generalise duality/coherence to a notion of *forwarder compatibility*. Forwarders are specified as a restricted family of proofs in linear logic, therefore defining a specific set of processes that can act as middleware by transfering messages without using them. As such, they can guide a network of processes to execute asynchronously. Our main result establishes forwarder compatibility as a sufficient and necessary condition to fully capture all well-typed multiparty compatible processes.

Keywords: Linear Logic · Session Types · Process Compatibility

1 Introduction

Session types [16] are type annotations that ascribe protocols to processes in a concurrent system and determine how they communicate. *Binary session types* found a logical justification in *linear logic*, identified by Caires and Pfenning [3,4] and later by Wadler [27], which establishes the following correspondences: session types *as* linear logic propositions, processes *as* proofs, reductions in the operational semantics *as* cut reductions in linear logic, and duality *as* a notion of compatibility ensuring that two processes communication pattern match.

In binary session types, a sufficient condition for two protocols to be *compatible* in a synchronous execution is that their type annotations are dual: a send action of one party must match a corresponding receive action of the other party,

R. Glück and B. Kafle (Eds.): LOPSTR 2023, LNCS 14330, pp. 99–117, 2023.
https://doi.org/10.1007/978-3-031-45784-5_7

and vice versa. Because of asynchronous interleavings, however, there are protocols that are compatible but not dual. The situation is even more complex for *multiparty session types* [17], which generalise binary session types for protocols with more than two participants. A central observation is that compatibility of sessions requires a property stronger than duality, ensuring that all messages sent by any participating party will eventually be collected by another. Deniélou and Yoshida [11] proposed the semantic notion of *multiparty compatibility*. The concept has then found many successful applications in the literature [11,12,21]. Yet, the question whether this notion "would be applicable to extend other theoretical foundations such as the correspondence with linear logic to multiparty communications" has not been answered since their original work.

As a first step in defining a logical correspondent to multiparty compatibility, Carbone et al. [5,8] extended Wadler's embedding of binary session types into classical linear logic (CLL) to the multiparty setting by generalising logical duality to the notion of *coherence* [17]. Coherence is also a sufficient compatibility condition: coherent processes are multiparty compatible, which ensures that their execution never leads to a communication error. Coherence is characterised proof-theoretically, and each coherence proof corresponds precisely to a multiparty protocol specification (*global type*), and in fact, coherence proofs correspond to a definable subset of the processes typable in linear logic, so-called *arbiters* [5]. In retrospect, the concept of coherence has sharpened our proof-theoretic understanding of how to characterise compatibility, but coherence, similarly to duality, cannot capture completely the notion of multiparty compatibility, i.e., there are compatible processes that are not coherent.

In this paper, we show that coherence (hence also duality) can be generalised to a notion of *forwarder compatibility*. Forwarders are processes that transfer messages between endpoints according to a protocol specification. Forwarders are more general than arbiters (every arbiter corresponds to a forwarder, not vice versa) but still can be used to guide the communication of multiple processes and guarantee they *communicate safely*. Our main result (Theorem 14) is that forwarders fully capture multiparty compatibility, which let us answer Deniélou and Yoshida's original question positively. In this work, we show that *i) any possible interleaving of a set of multiparty compatible processes can be encoded as a forwarder, and, conversely, ii) if a possible execution of a set of processes can be described by a forwarder, then such processes are indeed multiparty compatible.*

Forwarders are processes that dispatch messages: their behaviour can be seen as a specification, similarly to global types in multiparty session types. They capture the message flow by preventing messages from being *duplicated*, as superfluous messages would not be accounted for, and by preventing messages from being *lost*, otherwise a process might get stuck, awaiting a message. However, when data-dependencies permit, forwarders can choose to receive messages from different endpoints and forward such messages at a later point, or decide to buffer a certain number of messages. Eventually, they simply re-transmit messages after receiving them, *without* computing with them. Intuitively, this captures an interleaving of the communications between the given endpoints. Forwarders can be used to explain communication patterns as they occur in practice, including message routing, proxy services, and runtime monitors for message flows [19]. This paper shows that forwarders, as they capture multiparty compatibility, can supersede duality or coherence for composing processes. We achieve this logically: we generalise the linear logic cut rule with a new rule called MCutF which allows us to compose two or more processes (proofs) using a forwarder instead of duality [4] or coherence [5]. Our second main result is that MCutF can be eliminated by reductions that correspond to asynchronous process communications.

Contributions. The key contributions of this paper include: a definition of *multiparty compatibility* for classical linear logic (Sect. 3); a logical characterisation of *forwarders* that corresponds to multiparty compatibility (Sect. 4); and a composition mechanism (MCutF) for processes *with asynchronous communication* that uses forwarders and guarantees lack of communication errors (Sect. 5). Additionally, Sect. 2 provides some background on types, processes, typing using linear logic, Sect. 6 discusses related work, and concluding remarks and future work are in Sect. 7.

All details, including proofs, can be found in our extended version [6].

2 CP and Classical Linear Logic

In this section, we give an introduction to Wadler's proposition-as-sessions approach [27], which comprises our variant of the CP language (Classical Processes) and its interpretation as sequent proofs in classical linear logic (CLL).

Types. Participants in a communication network are connected via endpoints acting as sockets where processes can write/read messages. Each endpoint is used according to its given session type describing how each endpoint must act.

Following the propositions-as-types approach, *types*, taken to be propositions (formulas) of CLL, denote the way an endpoint (a channel end) must be used at runtime. Their formal syntax is given by the following grammar:

$$\text{Types} \quad A ::= \quad a \mid a^{\perp} \mid \mathbf{1} \mid \perp \mid A \otimes A \mid A \parr A \mid A \oplus A \mid A \,\&\, A \mid\, !A \mid\, ?A \qquad (1)$$

Atoms a and negated atoms $a^{\perp}$ are basic dual types. Types $\mathbf{1}$ and $\perp$ denote an endpoint that must close with a last synchronisation. Type $A \otimes B$ is assigned to an endpoint that outputs a message of type A and then is used as B, and similarly, an endpoint of type $A \parr B$, receives a message of type A and continues as B. In a branching choice, $A \oplus B$ is the type of an endpoint that may select to go left or right and continues as A or B, respectively, and $A \,\&\, B$ is the type of an endpoint that offers two choices (left or right) and then, based on such choice, continues as A or B. Finally, $!A$ types an endpoint offering an unbounded number of copies of a service of type A, while $?A$ types an endpoint of a client invoking some replicated/unbounded service with behaviour A.

Duality. Operators can be grouped in pairs of duals that reflect the input-output duality. Consequently, standard duality $(\cdot)^{\perp}$ on types is inductively defined as:

$$(a^{\perp})^{\perp} = a \qquad \mathbf{1}^{\perp} = \perp \qquad (A \otimes B)^{\perp} = A^{\perp} \parr B^{\perp} \quad (A \oplus B)^{\perp} = A^{\perp} \,\&\, B^{\perp} \quad (!A)^{\perp} = ?A^{\perp}$$

In the remainder, for any binary operators $\oslash, \odot \in \{\otimes, \parr, \oplus, \&\}$, we sometimes write $A \oslash B \odot C$ to mean $A \oslash (B \odot C)$.

Example 1 (Two-buyer protocol [17]*).* Two buyers intend to buy a book jointly from a seller. They are connecting through endpoints b_1, b_2 and s, respectively. The first buyer sends the title of the book to the seller, who, in turn, sends a quote to both buyers. Then, the first buyer decides how much she wishes to contribute and informs the second buyer, who either pays the rest or cancels by informing the seller. If the decision is to buy the book, the second buyer provides the seller with an address for shipping the book.

It is possible to type the first buyer's behaviour as $b_1 : \mathbf{name} \otimes \mathbf{cost}^\perp \parr \mathbf{cost} \otimes \mathbf{1}$ indicating that buyer b_1 first sends (expressed by $\otimes$) a value of type **name** (the book title), then receives (expressed by $\parr$) a value of type $\mathbf{cost}^\perp$ (the price of the book), then sends a value of type **cost** (the amount of money she wishes to contribute), and finally terminates. The behaviour of buyer b_2 and seller s can similarly be specified by session types, respectively $b_2 : \mathbf{cost}^\perp \parr \mathbf{cost}^\perp \parr ((\mathbf{addr} \otimes \mathbf{1}) \oplus \mathbf{1})$ and $s : \mathbf{name}^\perp \parr \mathbf{cost} \otimes \mathbf{cost} \otimes ((\mathbf{addr} \parr \perp) \& \perp)$.

Processes. As a language for *processes* we use a variant of the π-calculus [22] with specific communication primitives as standard for session calculi. Moreover, given that our theory is based on the proposition-as-sessions correspondence with CLL, we adopt a syntax akin to that of Wadler's CP [27]. For space reasons, we report the syntax of processes together with typing: each process can be found on the left-hand side of the turnstyle $\vdash$ in the conclusion of each rule in Fig. 1. We briefly comment each process term. A link $x \leftrightarrow y$ is a binary forwarder, i.e., a process that forwards any communication between endpoints x and y. This yields a sort of equality relation on names: it says that endpoints x and y are equivalent, and communicating something over x is like communicating it over y. Note that we use endpoints instead of channels [26]. The terms $x().P$ and $x[]$ handle synchronisation (no message passing); $x().P$ can be seen as an empty input on x, while $x[]$ terminates the execution of the process. The term $x[y \triangleright P].Q$ denotes a process that creates a fresh name y (hence a new session), spawns a new process P, and then continues as Q. The intuition behind this communication operation is that P uses y as an interface for dealing with the continuation of the dual primitive (denoted by term $x(y).R$, for some R). Note that output messages are always fresh, as for the internal π-calculus [23], hence the output term $x[y \triangleright P].Q$ is a compact version of the π-calculus term $(\nu y)\, \overline{x}y.(P \,|\, Q)$. Branching computations are handled by $x.\mathsf{case}(P, Q)$, $x[\mathsf{inl}].P$ and $x[\mathsf{inr}].P$. The former denotes a process offering two options (external choice) from which some other process can make a selection with $x[\mathsf{inl}].P$ or $x[\mathsf{inr}].P$ (internal choice). Finally, $!x(y).P$ denotes a persistently available service that can be invoked by $?x[z].Q$ which will spawn a new session to be handled by a copy of process P.

Example 2 (Two-buyers, continued). For some contionuations P_i, Q_j, R_k, we provide possible implementations for the processes from the 2-buyer example, as

$$\begin{aligned} P_s &= s(book).\ s[price \triangleright P_1].\ s[price \triangleright P_2].\ s.\mathsf{case}(s(addr).P_3, P_4), \\ P_{b_1} &= b_1[book \triangleright Q_1].\ b_1(price).\ b_1[contr \triangleright Q_2].Q_3, \text{ and} \\ P_{b_2} &= b_2(price).\ b_2(contr).\ b_2[\mathsf{inl}].b_2[addr \triangleright R_1].R_2 \end{aligned}$$

Note that the order in which the two buyers receive the price is not relevant.

$$\frac{}{x \leftrightarrow y \vdash x : \boldsymbol{a}^\perp, y : \boldsymbol{a}}\ \text{Ax} \qquad \frac{}{x[] \vdash x : \mathbf{1}}\ \mathbf{1} \qquad \frac{P \vdash \Delta}{x().P \vdash \Delta, x : \bot}\ \bot$$

$$\frac{P \vdash \Delta_1, y : A_1 \quad Q \vdash \Delta_2, x : A_2}{x[y \triangleright P].Q \vdash \Delta_1, \Delta_2, x : A_1 \otimes A_2}\ \otimes \qquad \frac{P \vdash \Delta, y : A_1, x : A_2}{x(y).P \vdash \Delta, x : A_1 \parr A_2}\ \parr$$

$$\frac{P \vdash \Delta, x : A_1}{x[\mathsf{inl}].P \vdash \Delta, x : A_1 \oplus A_2}\ \oplus_1 \qquad \frac{P \vdash \Delta, x : A_2}{x[\mathsf{inr}].P \vdash \Delta, x : A_1 \oplus A_2}\ \oplus_2$$

$$\frac{P \vdash \Delta, x : A_1 \quad Q \vdash \Delta, x : A_2}{x.\mathsf{case}(P, Q) \vdash \Delta, x : A_1 \,\&\, A_2}\ \& \qquad \frac{P \vdash\ ?\Delta, y : A}{!x(y).P \vdash\ ?\Delta, x : !A}\ !$$

$$\frac{P \vdash \Delta, y : A}{?x[y].P \vdash \Delta, x : ?A}\ ? \qquad \frac{P \vdash \Delta}{P \vdash \Delta, x : ?A}\ \text{W} \qquad \frac{P \vdash \Delta, y : ?A, z : ?A}{P\{x/y, x/z\} \vdash \Delta, x : ?A}\ \text{C}$$

Fig. 1. Sequent Calculus for CP and Classical Linear Logic

CP-Typing. Wadler [27] defined *Classical Processes* (CP) and showed that CLL proofs define a subset of well-behaved processes, satisfying deadlock freedom and session fidelity. Judgements are defined as $P \vdash \Delta$ with Δ a set of named types

$$\Delta ::= \ \varnothing \mid x : A, \Delta$$

We interpret a judgement $P \vdash x_1 : A_1, \ldots, x_n : A_n$ as "P communicates on each endpoint x_i according to the protocol specified by A_i." System CP is given on Fig. 1. It can be extended with a structural rule for defining composition of processes which corresponds to the CUT rule from CLL:

$$\frac{P \vdash \Delta_1, x : A \quad Q \vdash \Delta_2, y : A^\perp}{(\nu xy)\,(P \mid Q) \vdash \Delta_1, \Delta_2}\ \text{Cut}$$

The process constructor corresponding to this rule is the *restriction* (νxy) which connects the two endpoints x and y. In CLL, this rule is admissible, i.e., cut-free derivations of the premises can be combined into a derivation of the conclusion with no occurrence of the CUT rule. This can then be extended into a constructive procedure, called *cut-elimination*, transforming a proof with cuts inductively into a cut-free proof. The strength of the proposition-as-type correspondence stems from the fact that it carries on to the proof level, since the cut-elimination steps correspond to computation in the form of reductions between processes [4,27]. In a multiparty setting, duality can be generalised and compatibility can be expressed as *coherence* [5].

However, not all compatible processes have dual types, as we can see in the following example.

Example 3 (Multiplicative criss-cross). Consider the two endpoints x and y willing to communicate with the following protocol – called a *criss-cross*: they both send a message to each other, and then the messages are received, according to the types $x : \mathbf{name} \otimes \mathbf{cost} ⅋ \mathbf{1}$ and $y : \mathbf{cost}^\perp \otimes \mathbf{name}^\perp ⅋ \perp$. Such protocol leads to no error (assuming asynchrony), still the two types above are not dual.

3 Multiparty Compatibility

Multiparty compatibility [11,12,21] allows for the composition of *multiple* processes while guaranteeing they will not get stuck or reach an error. It is a semantic notion that uses session types as an abstraction of process behaviours and simulates their execution. If no error occurs during any such simulation then the composition is considered compatible.

Extended Types and Queues. In order to define multiparty compatibility in the CLL setting, we extend the type syntax with annotations making explicit where messages should be forwarded from and to, similarly to local types $!\mathsf{p}.T$ and $?\mathsf{p}.T$ [10] expressing an output and an input to and from role p respectively. The meaning of each operator and the definition of duality remain as in CP.

$$\text{Local types} \qquad B, C ::= \; a \mid a^\perp \mid \mathbf{1}^{\tilde{u}} \mid \perp^u \mid (A \otimes^{\tilde{u}} B) \mid (A ⅋^u B) \\ \mid\, !^{\tilde{u}} B \mid ?^u B \mid (B \oplus^u C) \mid (B \,\&^{\tilde{u}}\, C)$$

Annotations are either single endpoints x or a set of endpoints $u_1, \ldots, u_n$, which we write as $\tilde{u}$ when its size is irrelevant. The left-hand side A of $\otimes$ and ⅋ is a type as defined in (1) hence not annotated (but becomes dynamically so when needed). Units demonstrate some *gathering* behaviour which explains the need to annotate $\mathbf{1}$ with a non-empty list of distinct names. On the contrary, additives and exponential implement broadcasting: both & and ! are annotated with a non-empty list of distinct names.

After annotated types, to give a semantics to types, we introduce queues as

$$\Psi ::= \; \epsilon \mid A \cdot \Psi \mid * \cdot \Psi \mid \mathcal{L} \cdot \Psi \mid \mathcal{R} \cdot \Psi \mid \mathcal{Q} \cdot \Psi$$

Intuitively, a queue (FIFO) is an ordered list of messages. A message can be a proposition A, a session termination $*$, a choice $\mathcal{L}$ or $\mathcal{R}$, or an exponential $\mathcal{Q}$. Every ordered pair of endpoints can be construed as having an associated queue. Hence, we formally define a *queue environment* σ as a mapping from ordered pairs of endpoints to queues: $\sigma : (x, y) \mapsto \Psi$. In the sequel, σ_ϵ denotes the queue environment with empty queues, while $\sigma[(x, y) \mapsto \Psi]$ denotes a new environment where the entry for (x, y) has been updated to Ψ. Finally, we define the type-context semantics for an annotated environment, i.e., an environment Δ where each formula is annotated (we abuse notation and overload the category Δ).

Definition 4 (Type-Context Semantics). *We define* $\xrightarrow{\alpha}$ *as the minimum relation of the form* $\Delta \bullet \sigma \xrightarrow{\alpha} \Delta' \bullet \sigma'$ *satisfying the following rules:*

$$
\begin{aligned}
\Delta, x : \bot^{y} \bullet \sigma[(x,y) \mapsto \Psi] &\xrightarrow{x \bot y} \Delta \bullet \sigma[(x,y) \mapsto \Psi \cdot *] \\
x : \mathbf{1}^{\tilde{y}} \bullet \; \sigma_\epsilon[\{(y_i,x) \mapsto *\}_i] &\xrightarrow{\tilde{y}\mathbf{1}x} \varnothing \bullet \sigma_\epsilon \\
x : a^\bot, y : a \bullet \sigma_\epsilon &\xrightarrow{x \leftrightarrow y} \varnothing \bullet \sigma_\epsilon \\
\Delta, x : A \mathbin{⅋^{y}} B \bullet \sigma[(x,y) \mapsto \Psi] &\xrightarrow{x ⅋ y} \Delta, x : B \bullet \sigma[(x,y) \mapsto \Psi \cdot A] \\
\Delta, x : A \otimes^{\tilde{y}} B \bullet \sigma[\{(y_i,x) \mapsto A_i \cdot \Psi_i\}_i] &\xrightarrow{\tilde{y} \otimes x[A, \{A_i\}_i]} \Delta, x : B \bullet \sigma[\{(y_i,x) \mapsto \Psi_i\}_i] \\
\Delta, x : B \mathbin{\&^{\tilde{y}}} C \bullet \sigma[\{(x,y_i) \mapsto \Psi_i\}_i] &\xrightarrow{x \&_{\mathcal{L}} \tilde{y}} \Delta, x : B \bullet \sigma[\{(x,y_i) \mapsto \Psi_i \cdot \mathcal{L}\}_i] \\
\Delta, x : B \mathbin{\&^{\tilde{y}}} C \bullet \sigma[\{(x,y_i) \mapsto \Psi_i\}_i] &\xrightarrow{x \&_{\mathcal{R}} \tilde{y}} \Delta, x : C \bullet \sigma[\{(x,y_i) \mapsto \Psi_i \cdot \mathcal{R}\}_i] \\
\Delta, x : B \oplus^{y} C \bullet \sigma[(y,x) \mapsto \mathcal{L} \cdot \Psi] &\xrightarrow{y \oplus_{\mathcal{L}} x} \Delta, x : B \bullet \sigma[(y,x) \mapsto \Psi] \\
\Delta, x : B \oplus^{y} C \bullet \sigma[(y,x) \mapsto \mathcal{R} \cdot \Psi] &\xrightarrow{y \oplus_{\mathcal{R}} x} \Delta, x : C \bullet \sigma[(y,x) \mapsto \Psi] \\
\{y_i : ?B_i\}_i, x : !^{\tilde{y}} C \bullet \sigma_\epsilon &\xrightarrow{x ! \tilde{y}} \{y_i : ?B_i\}_i, x : C \bullet \sigma_\epsilon[\{(x,y_i) \mapsto \mathcal{Q}\}_i] \\
\Delta, x : ?^{\tilde{y}} B \bullet \sigma[(y,x) \mapsto \mathcal{Q} \cdot \Psi] &\xrightarrow{y ? x} \Delta, x : B \bullet \sigma[(y,x) \mapsto \Psi]
\end{aligned}
$$

where α *ranges over labels denoting the type of action performed by the semantics, e.g.,* $\tilde{y}\mathbf{1}x$ *signals an interaction from* $\tilde{y}$ *to* x *of type* $\mathbf{1}$*. Formally,*

$$
\begin{aligned}
\alpha ::= \;& x \bot y \mid \tilde{y}\mathbf{1}x \mid x \leftrightarrow y \mid x ⅋ y \mid \tilde{y} \otimes x[A, \{A_i\}_i] \\
& \mid x \&_{\mathcal{L}} \tilde{y} \mid x \&_{\mathcal{R}} \tilde{y} \mid y \oplus_{\mathcal{L}} x \mid y \oplus_{\mathcal{R}} x \mid x ! \tilde{y} \mid y ? x
\end{aligned}
$$

Intuitively, $\Delta \bullet \sigma \xrightarrow{\alpha} \Delta' \bullet \sigma'$ says that the environment Δ under the current queue environment σ performs α and becomes Δ' with updated queues σ'. The rules thus capture an asynchronous semantics for typing contexts.

Example 5. Assume we wish to compose three CP proofs through endpoints $\Delta = b_2 : \mathbf{cost}^\bot ⅋ B, b_1 : \mathbf{cost}^\bot ⅋ \mathbf{cost} \otimes \mathbf{1}, s : \mathbf{cost} \otimes C$. In order to obtain an execution of Δ, we first dualise and *choose* a way to annotate Δ as, e.g., $\Delta^\bot = b_2 : \mathbf{cost} \otimes^{b_1} B^\bot, b_1 : \mathbf{cost} \otimes^{s} \mathbf{cost}^\bot ⅋^{b_2} \bot^{s}, s : \mathbf{cost}^\bot ⅋^{b_2} C^\bot$. Then, from $\Delta^\bot \bullet \sigma_\epsilon$ we may obtain the execution

$$
\begin{aligned}
&\xrightarrow{s ⅋ b_1} b_2 : \mathbf{cost} \otimes^{b_1} B^\bot, b_1 : \mathbf{cost} \otimes^{s} \mathbf{cost}^\bot ⅋^{b_1} \bot^{s}, s : C \bullet \; \sigma_\epsilon[(s, b_1) \mapsto \mathbf{cost}^\bot] \\
&\xrightarrow{s \otimes b_1 [\mathbf{cost}, \mathbf{cost}^\bot]} b_2 : A \otimes^{b_2} B^\bot, b_1 : \mathbf{cost}^\bot ⅋^{b_1} \bot^{s}, s : C \; \bullet \; \sigma_\epsilon \\
&\xrightarrow{b_1 ⅋ b_2} b_2 : \mathbf{cost} \otimes^{b_1} B^\bot, b_1 : \bot^{s}, s : C \; \bullet \; \sigma_\epsilon[(b_1, b_2) \mapsto \mathbf{cost}^\bot] \\
&\xrightarrow{b_1 \otimes b_2 [\mathbf{cost}, \mathbf{cost}^\bot]} b_2 : B^\bot, b_1 : \bot^{s}, s : C \; \bullet \; \sigma_\epsilon
\end{aligned}
$$

Note the general rule for the multiplicative connectors $\otimes$ and $\parr$. In their multiparty interpretation [5], they implement a gathering communication, where many $A_i \otimes B_i$ can communicate with a single $A \parr B$. As a consequence, the A_i's are enqueued to a single endpoint which will consume such messages. The effect of a gathering communication with such connectives is to spawn a new session with the environment $\{A_i\}_i$ shown in the label. Ideally, we could have enriched the semantics to work on different contexts running in parallel, where $\{A_i\}_i$ would be added to. However, since the semantics is used to define compatibility, we just observe the label. Units also have a similar gathering behaviour. On the other hand, additives and exponentials model broadcasting.

Using the relation on contexts above, we can define when a set of endpoints successfully progresses without reaching an error. This can be formalised by the concept of live path. In the sequel, let $\alpha_1, \ldots, \alpha_n$ ($\tilde{\alpha}$ for short) be a *path* for some annotated Δ whenever there exist $\Delta_1, \sigma_1, \ldots \Delta_n, \sigma_n$ such that $\Delta \bullet \sigma_\epsilon \xrightarrow{\alpha_1} \Delta_1 \bullet \sigma_1 \ldots \xrightarrow{\alpha_n} \Delta_n \bullet \sigma_n$. This path is *maximal* if there is no $\Delta_{n+1}, \sigma_{n+1}$ and α_{n+1} such that $\Delta_n \bullet \sigma_n \xrightarrow{\alpha_{n+1}} \Delta_{n+1} \bullet \sigma_{n+1}$.

Definition 6 (Live Path). *A path $\tilde{\alpha}$ for an environment $\Delta \bullet \sigma$ is* live *if $\Delta \bullet \sigma \xrightarrow{\alpha_1} \ldots \xrightarrow{\alpha_n} \varnothing \bullet \sigma_\epsilon$.*

Intuitively, a maximal path is live whenever we can consume all send/receive operations specified in the type context and all queues are empty, i.e., an error is never reached. With this notion, we are ready to define multiparty compatibility.

Definition 7 (Multiparty Compatibility). *Environment $\Delta \bullet \sigma$ is* executable *if all maximal paths $\alpha_1, \ldots, \alpha_n$ for Δ are live and such that $\alpha_i = \tilde{y} \otimes x[A, \{A_i\}_i]$ implies $x : A^\perp, \{y_i : A_i^\perp\}_i$ is multiparty compatible for some annotation.*
A context $\Delta \neq \varnothing$ is multiparty compatible *if there exists an annotation such that $\Delta^\perp \bullet \sigma_\epsilon$ is executable.*

Multiparty compatibility states that *for a certain annotation* all maximal paths are live, i.e., no error ever occurs. This inductive definition is well-founded since propositions get smaller at each reduction.

Relationship to Previous Definitions. The original definition of compatibility given by Deniélou and Yoshida [11] was for communicating automata. Instead, Definition 4 is an adaptation of the *typing environment reduction* (Definition 4.3, [12]) with a little twist: in order not to overload notation, we are defining it on the dual of formulas. For example, similarly to [12], a process with endpoint x of type $A \otimes^y B$ stores something of type A in the queue from x to y. In our notation, we dualise the type of x to $A^\perp \parr^y B^\perp$ but keep the same behaviour, i.e., storing something of type $A^\perp$ in the queue from x to y. Moreover, for the sake of simplicity, we are using a single queue environment σ as a function from pairs of endpoints to a FIFO, while [12] attaches labelled queues to each endpoint of the typing context: the two approaches are equivalent. Finally, our definition, being an adaptation to CLL, uses different language constructs. In particular, we do not combine value passing and branching, and $\otimes$ and $\parr$ spawn new sessions (hence the well-founded recursive definition).

Properties of Multiparty Compatibility. As a consequence of multiparty compatibility, we can formalise the lack of errors with the following:

Proposition 8 (No Error). *Let Δ be multiparty compatible and $\alpha_1, \ldots, \alpha_n$ be a maximal path for an annotated $\Delta^{\perp}$ such that $\Delta^{\perp} \bullet \sigma_{\epsilon} \xrightarrow{\alpha_1} \Delta_1 \bullet \sigma_1 \ldots \xrightarrow{\alpha_n} \varnothing \bullet \sigma_{\epsilon}$. Then, for $i < n$,*

1. (a) *$\sigma_i(x, y) = * \cdot \Psi$ implies that $\alpha_n = x\tilde{z}\mathbf{1}y$;*
   (b) *$\sigma_i(x, y) = A \cdot \Psi$ implies that there exists $k > i$ such that $\alpha_k = x\tilde{z} \otimes y[A, \{A_i\}_i]$;*
   (c) *$\sigma_i(x, y) = \mathcal{L} \cdot \Psi$ implies that there exists $k > i$ such that $\alpha_k = x \oplus_{\mathcal{L}} y$;*
   (d) *$\sigma_i(x, y) = \mathcal{R} \cdot \Psi$ implies that there exists $k > i$ such that $\alpha_k = x \oplus_{\mathcal{R}} y$;*
   (e) *$\sigma_i(x, y) = \mathcal{Q} \cdot \Psi$ implies that there exists $k > i$ such that $\alpha_k = x \,?\, y$;*
2. (a) *$\Delta_i = \Delta'_i, x : \mathbf{1}^{\tilde{y}}$, then $\alpha_n = \tilde{y}\mathbf{1}x$;*
   (b) *$\Delta_i = \Delta'_i, x : A \otimes^{\tilde{y}} B$, then there exists $k > i$ such that $\alpha_k = \tilde{y} \otimes x[\{A_i\}_i]$;*
   (c) *$\Delta_i = \Delta'_i, x : B \oplus^{y} C$, then there exists $k > i$ such that $\alpha_k = y \oplus_{\mathcal{L}} x$ or $\alpha_k = y \oplus_{\mathcal{R}} x$;*
   (d) *$\Delta_i = \Delta'_i, x : ?^{y}B$, then there exists $k > i$ such that $\alpha_k = y \,?\, x$.*

Conditions in (1) state that every message that has been enqueued is eventually consumed, while conditions in (2) state that every input instruction is eventually executed. As CLL has no infinite behaviour, fairness conditions are not needed.

Are Annotations Important? A careful reader may be wondering why the definitions of type-context semantics and multiparty compatibility are not given for annotation-free contexts. Unfortunately, doing so would make multiparty compatibility too strong as it would allow for messages to be sent to different endpoints in *different paths*. As an example, $\Delta = b_2 : \mathbf{cost}^{\perp} \parr B, b_1 : \mathbf{cost}^{\perp} \parr \mathbf{cost} \otimes \mathbf{1}, s : \mathbf{cost} \otimes C$ can get stuck if s communicates with b_2 first, violating property (2b) in Proposition 8. Note that previous definitions of multiparty compatibility [12,21] indeed also use annotations.

4 Asynchronous Forwarders

Forwarders form a subclass of processes that are typable in classical linear logic. To identify them, we must add further information in the standard CP contexts.

Contexts. What we need is to be able to enforce the main features that characterise a forwarder, namely i) anything received must be forwarded, ii) anything that is going to be sent must be something that has been previously received, and iii) the order of messages between any two points must be preserved. In order to enforce these requirements, we add more information to the standard CP judgement. For example, let us consider the input process $x(y).P$. In CP, the typing environment for such process must be such that endpoint x has type $A \parr B$ such that P is typed in a context containing $y : A, x : B$. However, this does not make explicit that y is actually a message that has been received and, as such, should not be used by P for further communications but forwarded over some other channel. In order to remember this when we type the subprocess P, we insert $y : A$ into a queue that belongs to endpoint x where we put all the types of messages received over it. Namely, when typing P, the context will contain $[\![\Psi]\!][^{u}y : A]x : B$ meaning that x has type B and y type A in P, but moreover that $y : A$ has been received over x (it is in x's queue) and also that it is intended to be forwarded to endpoint u. In this setting, Ψ contains the types of messages that have been previously received over x. The forwarders behave asynchronously. They can input arbitrarily many messages, which are enqueued at the arrival point, without blocking the possibility of producing an output from the same endpoint. This behaviour is captured by the notion of queues of *boxed* messages, i.e. messages that are in-transit.

$$[\![\Psi]\!] ::= \varnothing \mid [^{u}*][\![\Psi]\!] \mid [^{u}y : A][\![\Psi]\!] \mid [^{u}\mathcal{Q}][\![\Psi]\!] \mid [^{u}\mathcal{L}][\![\Psi]\!] \mid [^{u}\mathcal{R}][\![\Psi]\!]$$

A queue element $[^{u}x : A]$ expresses that x of type A has been received and will need to later be forwarded to endpoint u. Similarly, $[^{u}*]$ indicates that a received request for closing a session must be forwarded to u. $[^{u}\mathcal{L}]$ (or $[^{u}\mathcal{R}]$) and $[^{u}\mathcal{Q}]$ indicate that a received branching request and server invocation, respectively, must be forwarded.

The order of messages needing to be forwarded to *independent* endpoints is irrelevant. Hence, we consider queue $[\![\Psi_1]\!][^{x}\ldots][^{y}\ldots][\![\Psi_2]\!]$ equivalent to queue $[\![\Psi_1]\!][^{y}\ldots][^{x}\ldots][\![\Psi_2]\!]$ whenever $x \neq y$. For a given endpoint x however the order of two messages $[^{x}\ldots][^{x}\ldots]$ is crucial and must be maintained throughout the forwarding. This follows the idea of having a queue for every ordered pair of endpoints in the type-context semantics in Definition 4. By attaching a queue to each endpoint we get a typing context

$$\Gamma ::= \varnothing \mid \Gamma, [\![\Psi]\!]x : B \mid \Gamma, [\![\Psi]\!]x : \cdot$$

The element $[\![\Psi]\!]x : B$ of a context Γ indicates that the messages in $[\![\Psi]\!]$ have been received at endpoint x. The special case $[\![\Psi]\!]x : \cdot$ is denoting the situation when endpoint x no longer needs to be used for communication, but still has a non-empty queue of messages to forward.

When forwarding to many endpoints, we use $[^{\tilde{u}}\mathcal{X}]$ to denote $[^{u_1}\mathcal{X}]\ldots[^{u_n}\mathcal{X}]$, with $\tilde{u} = u_1, \ldots, u_n$. We also assume the implicit rewriting $[^{\varnothing}\mathcal{X}][\![\Psi]\!] \equiv [\![\Psi]\!]$.

Judgements and Rules. Judgement $P \Vdash \Gamma$ types the forwarder P connecting the endpoints in Γ. The rules for $\bot$, $⅋$, & and ! enforce asynchronous forwarding by adding elements to queues which are later dequeued by the corresponding rules for **1**, $\otimes$, $\oplus$ or ?. The rules are reported in Fig. 2.

Rule Ax is identical to the one of CP. Rules **1** and $\bot$ forward a request to close a session. Rule $\bot$ receives the request on endpoint x and enqueues it as $[^{u}*]$ if it needs to forward it to u. Note that in the premiss of $\bot$ the endpoint is terminated pending the remaining messages in the corresponding queue being dispatched.

$$\frac{}{x \leftrightarrow y \Vdash x : \boldsymbol{a}^{\perp}, y : \boldsymbol{a}}\ \mathrm{Ax} \qquad \frac{P \Vdash \Gamma, \llbracket \Psi \rrbracket [{}^{u}*]x : \cdot}{x().P \Vdash \Gamma, \llbracket \Psi \rrbracket x : \perp^{u}}\ \perp \qquad \frac{}{x[] \Vdash \{[{}^{x}*]u_i : \cdot\}_i, x : \mathbf{1}^{\tilde{u}}}\ \mathbf{1}$$

$$\frac{P \Vdash \Gamma, \llbracket \Psi \rrbracket [{}^{u}y : A]x : B}{x(y).P \Vdash \Gamma, \llbracket \Psi \rrbracket x : A \parr^{u} B}\ \parr \qquad \frac{P \Vdash \{y_i : A_i\}_i, y : A \quad Q \Vdash \Gamma, \{\llbracket \Psi_i \rrbracket u_i : A_i\}_i, \llbracket \Psi \rrbracket x : B}{x[y \triangleright P].Q \Vdash \Gamma, \{[{}^{x}y_i : A_i]\llbracket \Psi_i \rrbracket u_i : C_i\}_i, \llbracket \Psi \rrbracket x : A \otimes^{\tilde{u}} B}\ \otimes$$

$$\frac{P \Vdash \Gamma, \llbracket \Psi \rrbracket [{}^{\tilde{u}}\mathcal{L}]x : B \quad Q \Vdash \Gamma, \llbracket \Psi \rrbracket [{}^{\tilde{u}}\mathcal{R}]x : C}{x.\mathsf{case}(P, Q) \Vdash \Gamma, \llbracket \Psi \rrbracket x : B \mathbin{\&}^{\tilde{u}} C}\ \&$$

$$\frac{P \Vdash \Gamma, \llbracket \Psi_z \rrbracket z : D, \llbracket \Psi_x \rrbracket x : B}{x[\mathsf{inl}].P \Vdash \Gamma, [{}^{x}\mathcal{L}]\llbracket \Psi_z \rrbracket z : D, \llbracket \Psi_x \rrbracket x : B \oplus^{z} C}\ \oplus_l \qquad \frac{P \Vdash \Gamma, \llbracket \Psi_z \rrbracket z : D, \llbracket \Psi_x \rrbracket x : C}{x[\mathsf{inr}].P \Vdash \Gamma, [{}^{x}\mathcal{R}]\llbracket \Psi_z \rrbracket z : D, \llbracket \Psi_x \rrbracket x : B \oplus^{z} C}\ \oplus_r$$

$$\frac{P \Vdash \{u_i : ?B_i\}_i, [{}^{\tilde{u}}\mathcal{Q}]y : C}{!x(y).P \Vdash \{u_i : ?B_i\}_i, x : !^{\tilde{u}}C}\ ! \qquad \frac{P \Vdash \Gamma, \llbracket \Psi_z \rrbracket z : C, \llbracket \Psi_x \rrbracket y : B}{?x[y].P \Vdash \Gamma, [{}^{x}\mathcal{Q}]\llbracket \Psi_z \rrbracket z : C, \llbracket \Psi_x \rrbracket x : ?^{z}B}\ ?$$

Fig. 2. Proof System for Forwarders – in rules $\mathbf{1}$, $\otimes$, & and !, we ask that $\tilde{u} \neq \varnothing$

Eventually all endpoints but one will be terminated in the same manner. Rule **1** will then be applicable. Note that $x().P$ and $x[]$ behave as gathering, where several terminated endpoints connect to the last active one typed with a **1**. Rules $\otimes$ and $\parr$ forward a message. Rule $\parr$ receives $y : A$ and enqueues it as $[{}^{u}y : A]$ to be forwarded to endpoint u. Dually, rule $\otimes$ sends the messages at the top of the queues of endpoints u_i's, meaning that several messages are sent at the same time. Messages will be picked from queues belonging to distinct endpoints, as a consequence, the left premiss of the $\otimes$-rule spawns a new forwarder (the gathered messages). In the case of additives and exponentials, the behaviour is *broadcasting*, i.e., an external choice $[{}^{u}\mathcal{L}]$ or $[{}^{u}\mathcal{R}]$, or a server opening $[{}^{u}\mathcal{Q}]$, resp., is received and can be used several (at least one) times to guide internal choices or server requests, resp., later on. Note how annotations put constraints on how proofs are constructed, e.g., annotating $x : A \parr B$ with u makes sure that the application of a $\parr$-rule for this formula will be followed by a $\otimes$-rule application on u later in the proof.

Example 9 (Two-buyers, continued). The forwarder process dispatching messages between the two buyers and the seller could be implemented as:

$$b_1'(book).\ s'[book \triangleright T_1].\ s'(price).\ s'(price).\ b_1'[price \triangleright T_2].\ b_2'[price \triangleright T_3].$$
$$b_1'(contr).\ b_2'[contr \triangleright T_4].b_2'.\mathsf{case}(s'[\mathsf{inl}].\ b_2'(addr).\ s[addr \triangleright T_5].\ T_6, T_7)$$

for some continuations T_i's. It captures the message flows between the different endpoints. Namely, it receive a name from b_1, forward it to s, and then proceed to receiving the price from s, forward it to b_1 and b_2, and so on.

The following example illustrates the need to support buffering, and reordering in order to capture the message flows between several processes.

Example 10 (Multiplicative criss-cross, continued). We can write a forwarder typable in the context $x : \mathbf{name}^{\perp} \parr \mathbf{cost}^{\perp} \otimes \perp, y : \mathbf{cost} \parr \mathbf{name} \otimes \mathbf{1}$ formed by the duals of the types in Example 3, i.e., a process that first receives on both x and y and then forwards the received messages over to y and x, respectively. $P := x(u).y(v).y[u' \triangleright u \leftrightarrow u'].x[v' \triangleright v' \leftrightarrow v].x().y[]$ is one of the forwarders that can prove the compatibility of the types involved in the criss-cross protocol, as illustrated by the derivation below.

$$\dfrac{\dfrac{\dfrac{\dfrac{F_1 := u \leftrightarrow u'}{\Vdash u : \mathbf{name}^\perp, u' : \mathbf{name}}\,\mathrm{Ax} \quad \dfrac{\dfrac{F_2 := v' \leftrightarrow v}{\Vdash v' : \mathbf{cost}^\perp, v : \mathbf{cost}}\,\mathrm{Ax} \quad \dfrac{\dfrac{F_3 := x().y[]}{y[] \Vdash [^y *]x : \cdot, y : \mathbf{1}}\,\mathbf{1}}{F_3 \Vdash x : \bot^y, y : \mathbf{1}^x}\,\bot}{x[v' \triangleright F_2].F_3 \Vdash x : \mathbf{cost}^\perp \otimes^y \bot^y, [^x v : \mathbf{cost}]y : \mathbf{1}^x}\,\otimes}{y[u' \triangleright F_1].x[v' \triangleright F_2].F_3 \Vdash [^y u : \mathbf{name}^\perp]x : \mathbf{cost}^\perp \otimes^y \bot^y, [^x v : \mathbf{cost}]y : \mathbf{name} \otimes^x \mathbf{1}^x}\,\otimes}{y(v).y[u' \triangleright F_1].x[v' \triangleright F_2].F_3 \Vdash [^y u : \mathbf{name}^\perp]x : \mathbf{cost}^\perp \otimes^y \bot^y, y : \mathbf{cost} \parr^x \mathbf{name} \otimes^x \mathbf{1}^x}\,\parr}{P \Vdash x : \mathbf{name}^\perp \parr^y \mathbf{cost}^\perp \otimes^y \bot^y, y : \mathbf{cost} \parr^x \mathbf{name} \otimes^x \mathbf{1}^x}\,\parr$$

Properties of Forwarders. We write $\llcorner B \lrcorner$ for the formula obtained from any B by removing all the annotations. We state that every forwarder is also a CP process, the embedding $\llcorner \cdot \lrcorner$ being extended to contexts and queues as:

$$\llcorner \llbracket \Psi \rrbracket x : B, \Gamma \lrcorner = \llcorner \llbracket \Psi \rrbracket \lrcorner, x : \llcorner B \lrcorner, \llcorner \Gamma \lrcorner \qquad \llcorner \llbracket \Psi \rrbracket x : \cdot, \Gamma \lrcorner = \llcorner \llbracket \Psi \rrbracket \lrcorner, \llcorner \Gamma \lrcorner$$

$$\llcorner [^u y : A] \llbracket \Psi \rrbracket \lrcorner = y : A, \llcorner \llbracket \Psi \rrbracket \lrcorner \qquad \llcorner [^u \mathcal{X}] \llbracket \Psi \rrbracket \lrcorner = \llcorner [^u *] \llbracket \Psi \rrbracket \lrcorner = \llcorner \llbracket \Psi \rrbracket \lrcorner$$

where $\mathcal{X} \in \{\mathcal{L}, \mathcal{R}, \mathcal{Q}\}$

Proposition 11. *Any forwarder is typable in CP, i.e., if $P \Vdash \Gamma$, then $P \vdash \llcorner \Gamma \lrcorner$.*

Moreover, forwarders enjoy an invertibility property, i.e., in each rule if the conclusion is correct then so are the premisses. In CLL, the rules $\otimes$ or $\oplus$ are not invertible because of the choice involved either in splitting the context in the conclusion of $\otimes$ into the two premisses or the choice of either disjuncts for $\oplus$. In our case on the other hand, the annotations put extra syntactic constraints on what can be derived and hence are restricting these choices to a unique one and as a result the rules are invertible. This is formalised by the following.

Proposition 12. *All the forwarder rules are invertible, that is, for any rule if there exists a forwarder F such that $F \Vdash \Gamma$, the conclusion of the rule, there is a forwarder $F_i \Vdash \Gamma_i$, for each of its premisses, $i = 1$ or 2.*

Relation to Multiparty Compatibility. Forwarders relate to transitions in the type-context semantics introduced in the previous section. In order to formalise this, we first give a translation from type-contexts into forwarder contexts:

- $\mathsf{tr}(\varnothing \bullet \sigma_\epsilon) := \varnothing$;
- $\mathsf{tr}(\Delta, x : B \bullet \sigma\,[(y_i,x) \mapsto \Psi_i]_i) := \llbracket^{y_1} \Psi_1 \rrbracket \ldots \llbracket^{y_n} \Psi_n \rrbracket x : B, \mathsf{tr}(\Delta \bullet \sigma)$
for a type environment $\Delta = \{y_i : B_i\}_i$ and a queue environment σ mapping the endpoints y_i.

We use the notation $\llbracket^u \Psi \rrbracket$ to indicate that all brackets in $\llbracket \Psi \rrbracket$ are labelled by u.

Lemma 13. *Let $\Delta \bullet \sigma$ be a type-context and $\Gamma = \mathsf{tr}(\Delta \bullet \sigma)$.*

1. *if there exists α and $\Delta' \bullet \sigma'$ such that $\Delta \bullet \sigma \xrightarrow{\alpha} \Delta' \bullet \sigma'$ then there exists a rule in Fig. 2 such that Γ is an instance of its conclusion and $\Gamma' = \mathsf{tr}(\Delta' \bullet \sigma')$ is an instance of (one of) the premiss(es);*
2. *otherwise, either $\Delta = \varnothing$ and $\sigma = \sigma_\epsilon$ or there is no forwarder F such that $F \Vdash \Gamma$.*

We can conclude this section by stating that forwarders characterise multiparty compatibility for CP processes (processes that are well-typed in CLL).

Theorem 14. *Δ is multiparty compatible iff there exists a forwarder F such that $F \Vdash \Delta^\perp$ where each connective in $\Delta^\perp$ is annotated.*

Proof (Sketch). From left to right, we need to prove more generally that if $\Delta \bullet \sigma$ is executable, then there exists a forwarder F such that $F \Vdash \mathsf{tr}(\Delta \bullet \sigma)$, by induction on the size of Δ, defined as the sum of the formula sizes in Δ. From right to left can be proven by contrapositive, using Lemma 13 and Proposition 12. See [6] for the full proof.

5 Composing Processes with Asynchronous Forwarders

In this section, we show how to use forwarders to correctly compose CP processes.

Multiparty Process Composition. We start by focusing on the rule CUT, as seen in Sect. 2n which corresponds to parallel composition of processes. The implicit side condition that this rule uses is *duality*, i.e., we can compose two processes if endpoints x and y carry dual types.

Carbone et al. [5] introduced the concept of *coherence*, denoted by $\vDash$, which generalises duality to many endpoints, allowing for an extended cut-rule that composes many processes in parallel

$$\frac{\{R_i \vdash \Sigma_i, x_i : A_i\}_{i \le n} \quad G \vDash \{x_i : A_i\}_{i \le n}}{(\nu \tilde{x} : G)\,(R_1 \mid \ \ldots \ \mid R_n) \vdash \{\Sigma_i\}_{i \le n}}\ \text{MCUT}$$

The judgement $G \vDash \{x_i : A_i\}_{i \le n}$ intuitively says that the $x_i : A_i$'s are compatible and the execution of the R_i will proceed with no error. G is a process term and corresponds to a global type. A MCUT elimination theorem analogous to the one of CP can be obtained.

Here, we replace coherence with an asynchronous forwarder Q, yielding rule

$$\frac{\{R_i \vdash \Sigma_i, x_i : A_i\}_{i \le n} \quad Q \Vdash \{x_i : A_i^\perp\}_{i \le n}}{(\nu \tilde{x} : Q)\,(R_1 \mid \ \ldots \ \mid R_n) \vdash \{\Sigma_i\}_{i \le n}}\ \text{MCUTF}$$

Asynchronous forwarders are more general than coherence: every coherence proof can be transformed into an *arbiter* process [5], which is indeed a forwarder, while there are judgements that are not coherent but are provable in our forwarders (see Example 10). In the MCUTF rule, the role of the forwarder is to be a middleware that decides whom to forward messages to. This means that when a process R_i sends a message, it must be stored by the forwarder, who will later forward it to the correct receiver. Our goal is to show that MCUTF is admissible (and hence we can eliminate it from any correct proof). For this purpose, we need to extend the rule to also account for messages in transit, temporarily held by the forwarder. Making use of forwarders queues and some extra premisses, we define MCUTQ as

$$\frac{\{P_j \vdash \Delta_j, y_j : A_j\}_{j \leq m} \quad \{R_i \vdash \Sigma_i, x_i : B_i\}_{i \leq n} \quad Q \Vdash \{[\![\Psi_i]\!]x_i : B_i^\perp\}_{i \leq n}, \{[\![\Psi_i]\!]x_i : \cdot\}_{n < i \leq p}}{(\boldsymbol{\nu}\tilde{x} : Q[\tilde{y} \lhd P_1, \ldots, P_m])\,(R_1 \mid \ldots \mid R_n) \vdash \{\Delta_j\}_{j \leq m}, \{\Sigma_i\}_{i \leq n}}$$

There are three kinds of process terms: P_j's, R_i's and Q. Processes R_i's are the ones communicating. Q is the forwarder who certifies compatibility, i.e., determine, at run time, who talks to whom. Finally, processes P_i's must be linked to messages in the forwarder queues. Such processes stem from the way $\otimes$ and $⅋$ work in linear logic as will become clearer when discussing the reduction steps that lead to cut-admissibility. It imposes a side condition on the rule, namely that

$$\bigcup_{i \leq p} \Psi_i \setminus \{\mathcal{L}, \mathcal{R}, \mathcal{Q}, *\} = \left\{y_j : A_j^\perp\right\}_{j \leq m}$$

We need to introduce a new term syntax for this new structural rule: in the process $(\boldsymbol{\nu}\tilde{x} : Q[\tilde{y} \lhd P_1, \ldots, P_m])\,(R_1 \mid \ldots \mid R_n)$, the list $P_1, \ldots, P_m$ denotes those messages (processes) in transit that are going to form a new session after the communication has taken place. In the remainder we (slightly abusively) abbreviate both $\{P_1, \ldots, P_m\}$ and $(R_1 \mid \ldots \mid R_n)$ as $\tilde{P}$ and $\tilde{R}$ respectively.

Semantics and MCUTF**-Admissibility.** We now formally show that MCUTF is admissible, yielding a semantics for our extended CP (with MCUTF) in a proposition-as-types fashion. We illustrate the procedure on the multiplicative fragment (see [6] for all cases). In the sequel, we use the following abbreviations $\Gamma = \{[\![\Psi_i]\!]x_i : B_i^\perp\}_{i \leq n}, \{[\![\Psi_i]\!]x_i : \cdot\}_{n < i \leq p}$ and $\Gamma{-}k = \Gamma \setminus \{[\![\Psi_k]\!]x_k : B_k^\perp\}$.

Also, we omit (indicated as "...") the premises of the MCUTQ that do not play a role in the reduction at hand, and assume that they are always the same as above, that is, $\{P_j \vdash \Delta_j, y_j : A_j\}_{j \leq m}$ and $\{R_i \vdash \Sigma_i, x_i : B_i\}_{i \leq n}$.

Send Message ($\otimes$). This is the case when a process intends to send a message, which corresponds to a $\otimes$ rule. As a consequence, the forwarder has to be ready to receive and store the message (to forward it later):

$$\dfrac{\dfrac{P \vdash \Delta, y : A \quad R \vdash \Sigma, x : B}{x[y \rhd P].R \vdash \Delta, \Sigma, x : A \otimes B}\otimes \qquad \ldots \qquad \dfrac{Q \Vdash [\![\Psi]\!][^{x_k}y : A^\perp]x : B^\perp, \Gamma}{x(y).Q \Vdash [\![\Psi]\!]x : A^\perp ⅋^{x_k} B^\perp, \Gamma}⅋}{(\boldsymbol{\nu}x\tilde{x} : x(y).Q[\tilde{y} \lhd \tilde{P}])\,(x[y \rhd P].R \mid \tilde{R}) \vdash \Delta, \Sigma, \{\Delta_j\}_{j \leq m}, \{\Sigma_i\}_{i \leq n}}\text{MCUTQ}$$

The process on the left is ready to send the message to the forwarder. By the annotation on the forwarder, it follows that the message will have to be forwarded to endpoint x_k, at a later stage. Observe that the nature of $\otimes$ is what introduces processes such as P to the rule: the idea is that when the forwarder will finalise the communication (by sending to a process R' owning endpoint x_k) process P will be composed with R'. For now, we obtain the reductum:

$$\dfrac{P \vdash \Delta, y : A \quad R \vdash \Sigma, x : B \qquad \ldots \qquad Q \Vdash [\![\Psi]\!][^{x_k} y : A^{\perp}]x : B^{\perp}, \Gamma}{(\nu x\tilde{x} : Q[y, \tilde{y} \lhd P, \tilde{P}])\,(R \mid \tilde{R}) \vdash \Delta, \Sigma, \{\Delta_j\}_{j \leq m}, \{\Sigma_i\}_{i \leq n}}\ \text{MCutQ}$$

Receive Message ($\parr$). At a later point, the forwarder will be able to complete the forwarding operation by connecting with a process ready to receive:

$$\dfrac{\dfrac{R \vdash \Sigma, y : A, x : B}{x(y).R \vdash \Sigma, x : A \parr B}\,\parr \quad \begin{array}{c} P \vdash \Delta, z : A^{\perp} \\ \end{array} \quad \begin{array}{c} \ldots \\ \dfrac{S \Vdash z : A, y : A^{\perp} \quad Q \Vdash [\![\Psi_x]\!]x : B^{\perp}, \Gamma}{x[y \rhd S].Q \Vdash [\![\Psi_x]\!]x : A^{\perp} \otimes^{x_k} B^{\perp}, [^{x} z : A][\![\Psi_k]\!]x_k : B_k^{\perp}, \Gamma - k}\,\otimes \end{array}}{(\nu x\tilde{x} : x[y \rhd S].Q[z, \tilde{y} \lhd P, \tilde{P}])\,(x(y).R \mid \tilde{R}) \vdash \Delta, \Sigma, \{\Delta_j\}_{j \leq m}, \{\Sigma_i\}_{i \leq n}}$$

This relies on process P with endpoint z of type $A^{\perp}$, endpoint x_k in the forwarder with a boxed endpoint z with type A, and process $x(y).R$ ready to receive.

After reduction, we obtain the following:

$$\dfrac{(\nu yz : S)\,(R \mid P) \vdash \Sigma, \Delta, x : B \qquad \ldots \qquad Q \Vdash [\![\Psi_x]\!]x : B^{\perp}, \Gamma}{(\nu x\tilde{x} : Q[\tilde{y} \lhd \tilde{P}])\,((\nu yz : S)\,(R \mid P) \mid \tilde{R}) \vdash \Delta, \Sigma, \{\Delta_j\}_{j \leq m}, \{\Sigma_i\}_{i \leq n}}\ \text{MCutQ}$$

Where the left premiss is obtained as follows:

$$\dfrac{R \vdash \Sigma, y : A, x : B \quad P \vdash \Delta, z : A^{\perp} \quad S \Vdash z : A, y : A^{\perp}}{(\nu yz : S)\,(R \mid P) \vdash \Sigma, \Delta, x : B}\ \text{MCutQ}$$

meaning that now the message (namely process P) has finally been delivered and it can be directly linked to R with a new (but smaller) MCutQ.

These reductions (full set in [6]) let us prove the key lemma of this section.

Lemma 15 (MCutQ Admissibility). *If* $\{P_j \vdash \Delta_j, y_j : A_j\}_{j \leq m}$ *and* $\{R_i \vdash \Sigma_i, x_i : B_i\}_{i \leq n}$ *and* $Q \Vdash \{[\![\Psi_i]\!]x_i : B_i^{\perp}\}_{i \leq n}, \{[\![\Psi_i]\!]x_i : \cdot\}_{n < i \leq p}$ *there exists a process* $S \vdash \{\Delta_j\}_{j \leq m}, \{\Sigma_i\}_{i \leq n}$ *such that* $(\nu\tilde{x} : Q[\tilde{y} \lhd \tilde{P}])\,\tilde{R} \Rightarrow^* S$.

Proof (Sketch). By lexicographic induction on (i) the sum of sizes of the B_i's and (ii) the sum of sizes of the R_i's. Some of the key cases have been detailed above; the others, as well as the base cases, can be found in the appendix of [6]. The commutative cases are straightforward and only need to consider the possible last rule applied to a premiss of the form $R_i \vdash \Sigma_i, x_i : B_i$.

We can finally conclude with the following theorem as a special case.

Theorem 16 (MCutF Admissibility). *If* $\{R_i \vdash \Sigma_i, x_i : A_i\}_{i \leq n}$ *and* $Q \Vdash \{x_i : A_i^{\perp}\}_{i \leq n}$ *then there exists a process* $S \vdash \{\Sigma_i\}_{i \leq n}$ *such that* $(\nu\tilde{x} : Q)\,(R_1 \mid \ldots \mid R_n) \Rightarrow^* S$.

6 Related Work

Our work takes [5] as a starting point. We set out to explore if coherence could be broken down into more elementary logical rules which led us to introduce forwarders, that turned out to provide a more general notion. An earlier version of this work [7] proposed synchronous forwarders: the restriction of forwarders with only buffers of size one. In that case, we show that we can always construct a coherence proof from a synchronous forwarder. However, synchronous forwarders fail to capture all the possible interleaving of an arbiter. The lack of global types in our work is strongly related to the work by Scalas and Yoshida [24], where compatibility and other properties are abstract away from the type system.

Caires and Perez [3] also study multiparty session types in the context of intuitionistic linear logic by translating global types to processes, called *mediums*. Their work does not start from a logical account of global types (their global types are just syntactic terms). But, as previous work [5], they do generate arbiters as linear logic proofs, which are special instances of forwarders. In a more recent work, van den Heuvel and Pérez [15] use *routers* in order to provide a decentralised analysis of multiparty protocols. Routers act as point-to-point forwarders but their types, called *relative types*, carry extra information on causality of events that are not local. In this work, we generalise both to characterise exactly which processes can justify the compatibility of a set of processes.

Another logical interpretation of multiparty compatibility is proposed by Horne [18]. Which uses the additional expressivity of BV, a generalisation of CLL with a non-commutative sequential operator but only a fragment expressible in the sequent calculus, unlike their previous work which relied on the full strength of deep inference [9]. It also allows one to consider compatible processes beyond duality but only for simply typed processes, which cannot spawn other processes. The main advantage of this approach is the fact that annotations are not needed.

Sangiorgi [23], probably the first to treat forwarders for the π-calculus, uses binary forwarders, i.e., processes that only forward between two channels, equivalent to our $x \leftrightarrow y$. In Caires and Pfenning [4], forwarders *à la Sangiorgi* were introduced as processes to be typed by the axiom rule in linear logic and we follow this tradition. Van den Heuvel and Perez [14] have recently developed a version of linear logic that encompasses both classical and intuitionistic logic, presenting a unified view on binary forwarders in both logics.

Barbanera and Dezani [2] study multiparty session types as *gateways* working as link forwarding communications between two multiparty sessions. Such mechanism reminds us of our forwarder composition: indeed, their related work mentions that gateways could be modelled by a "connection-cut".

Recent works [13,19] propose a variant of linear logic that models *identity providers*, monitors are similar to forwarders but restricted to binary sessions. They are asynchronous, i.e., allow for unbounded buffering of messages before forwarding. Our forwarders can be seen as a generalisation to multiparty.

7 Conclusions and Future Work

Forwarders are a logical characterisation of multiparty compatibility and they can safely replace coherence for composing any compatible processes. Below, we discuss some aspects of forwarders and identify possible extensions.

Improving Multiparty Compatibility? Multiparty compatibility concerns the error-free composition of processes by enqueueing/dequeueing messages into and from pair-wise distinct FIFO queues. We do not aim to improve multiparty compatibility, unlike, e.g., [12]. Rather, we assume a standard definition of it and give a logical characterisation, in the spirit of the approach started in [4]. The novelty is them to derive from the logical characterisation.

Are Forwarders Centralised? Following the approach taken for arbiters [5] and mediums [3], forwarders provide an orchestration of the message flows between the composed processes. To step to a fully decentralised setting would require to redefine rule MCut such that i) queues are no longer embedded in forwarders and ii) annotations in the forwarders are transferred to the composed processes. The correctness of these two steps follows from Theorem 14, since the type-context semantics in Definition 4 is indeed fully decentralised. Note that a similar decentralisation approach is also done for coherence in [5].

Process Language. Our process language is based on Wadler's CP [27], without polymorphic communications. We conjecture that forwarders can be extended to polymorphic types $\exists X.A$ and $\forall X.A$. We plan to consider a further extension to support recursion, inspired by Toninho et al. [25]. It would require an extended notion of compatibility dealing with infinite paths as done by Ghilezan et al. [12].

Variants of Linear Logic. Our theory is based on Classical LL for two main reasons. Coherence is indeed defined by Carbone et al. [5] in terms of CLL hence our results can be traced back to theirs. An early version of forwarders based on Intuitionistic Linear Logic (ILL) required many more rules, penalising the presentation. Nevertheless, our results should be adaptable to ILL. A different approach could be to include non-commutative operators which could encode our FIFO queues, e.g., non-commutative subexponentials by Kanovich et al. [20].

Beyond Linear Logic. Another interesting avenue would be to understand how the queueing mechanism of forwarders can be treated within a graphical proof system such as the one by Acclavio et al. [1]. Indeed, they observed that queues of length greater than 3 could not be expressed as linear logic formulas and thusdesigned a proof system that is based on general graphs.

Variants of Coherence. Our results show that forwarders generalise coherence proofs. Indeed, coherence would correspond to the notion of *synchronous forwarders*, the restriction of forwarders with only buffers of size one [7]. As a follow-up, we would like to investigate, whether other syntactic restrictions of forwarders also induce interesting generalised notions of coherence, and, as a consequence, generalisations of global types.

References

1. Acclavio, M., Horne, R., Mauw, S., Straßburger, L.: A graphical proof theory of logical time. In: Proceedings of 7th International Conference on Formal Structures for Computation and Deduction. LIPIcs, vol. 228 (2022)
2. Barbanera, F., Dezani-Ciancaglini, M.: Open multiparty sessions. In: Proceedings of 12th Interaction and Concurrency Experience. EPTCS, vol. 304 (2019)
3. Caires, L., Pérez, J.A.: Multiparty session types within a canonical binary theory, and beyond. In: Albert, E., Lanese, I. (eds.) FORTE 2016. LNCS, vol. 9688, pp. 74–95. Springer, Cham (2016). https://doi.org/10.1007/978-3-319-39570-8_6
4. Caires, L., Pfenning, F.: Session types as intuitionistic linear propositions. In: Gastin, P., Laroussinie, F. (eds.) CONCUR 2010. LNCS, vol. 6269, pp. 222–236. Springer, Heidelberg (2010). https://doi.org/10.1007/978-3-642-15375-4_16
5. Carbone, M., Lindley, S., Montesi, F., Schürmann, C., Wadler, P.: Coherence generalises duality: a logical explanation of multiparty session types. In: Proceedings of 27th International Conference on Concurrency Theory. LIPIcs, vol. 59 (2016)
6. Carbone, M., Marin, S., Schürmann, C.: A logical interpretation of asynchronous multiparty compatibility. CoRR abs/2305.16240 (2023)
7. Carbone, M., Marin, S., Schürmann, C.: Synchronous forwarders. CoRR abs/2102.04731 (2021)
8. Carbone, M., Montesi, F., Schürmann, C., Yoshida, N.: Multiparty session types as coherence proofs. In: Proceedings of 26th International Conference on Concurrency Theory. LIPIcs, vol. 42 (2015)
9. Ciobanu, G., Horne, R.: Behavioural analysis of sessions using the calculus of structures. In: Mazzara, M., Voronkov, A. (eds.) PSI 2015. LNCS, vol. 9609, pp. 91–106. Springer, Cham (2016). https://doi.org/10.1007/978-3-319-41579-6_8
10. Coppo, M., Dezani-Ciancaglini, M., Yoshida, N., Padovani, L.: Global progress for dynamically interleaved multiparty sessions. MSCS **760** (2015)
11. Deniélou, P.-M., Yoshida, N.: Multiparty compatibility in communicating automata: characterisation and synthesis of global session types. In: Fomin, F.V., Freivalds, R., Kwiatkowska, M., Peleg, D. (eds.) ICALP 2013. LNCS, vol. 7966, pp. 174–186. Springer, Heidelberg (2013). https://doi.org/10.1007/978-3-642-39212-2_18
12. Ghilezan, S., Pantovic, J., Prokic, I., Scalas, A., Yoshida, N.: Precise subtyping for asynchronous multiparty sessions. In: Proceedings of 48th ACM Symposium on Principles of Programming Languages, vol. 5 (2021)
13. Gommerstadt, H., Jia, L., Pfenning, F.: Session-typed concurrent contracts. In: Ahmed, A. (ed.) ESOP 2018. LNCS, vol. 10801, pp. 771–798. Springer, Cham (2018). https://doi.org/10.1007/978-3-319-89884-1_27
14. van den Heuvel, B., Pérez, J.A.: Session type systems based on linear logic: classical versus intuitionistic. In: Proceedings of the 12th International Workshop on Programming Language Approaches to Concurrency and Communication-cEntric Software. EPTCS, vol. 314 (2020)
15. van den Heuvel, B., Pérez, J.A.: A decentralized analysis of multiparty protocols. Sci. Comput. Program. **222**, 102840 (2022)
16. Honda, K., Vasconcelos, V.T., Kubo, M.: Language primitives and type discipline for structured communication-based programming. In: Hankin, C. (ed.) ESOP 1998. LNCS, vol. 1381, pp. 122–138. Springer, Heidelberg (1998). https://doi.org/10.1007/BFb0053567

17. Honda, K., Yoshida, N., Carbone, M.: Multiparty asynchronous session types. J. ACM **63**(1), 1–67 (2016)
18. Horne, R.J.: Session subtyping and multiparty compatibility using circular sequents. In: Proceedings of 31st International Conference on Concurrency Theory. LIPIcs, vol. 171 (2020)
19. Jia, L., Gommerstadt, H., Pfenning, F.: Monitors and blame assignment for higher-order session types. In: Proceedings of 43rd ACM Symposium on Principles of Programming Languages (2016)
20. Kanovich, M., Kuznetsov, S., Nigam, V., Scedrov, A.: A logical framework with commutative and non-commutative subexponentials. In: Galmiche, D., Schulz, S., Sebastiani, R. (eds.) IJCAR 2018. LNCS (LNAI), vol. 10900, pp. 228–245. Springer, Cham (2018). https://doi.org/10.1007/978-3-319-94205-6_16
21. Lange, J., Yoshida, N.: Verifying asynchronous interactions via communicating session automata. In: Dillig, I., Tasiran, S. (eds.) CAV 2019. LNCS, vol. 11561, pp. 97–117. Springer, Cham (2019). https://doi.org/10.1007/978-3-030-25540-4_6
22. Milner, R., Parrow, J., Walker, D.: A calculus of mobile processes, I and II. Inf. Comput. **100**(1), 1–40 (1992)
23. Sangiorgi, D.: π-calculus, internal mobility, and agent-passing calculi. Theor. Comput. Sci. **167**(1–2), 235–274 (1996)
24. Scalas, A., Yoshida, N.: Less is more: multiparty session types revisited. In: Proceedings of 46th ACM Symposium on Principles of Programming Languages, vol. 3 (2019)
25. Toninho, B., Caires, L., Pfenning, F.: Corecursion and non-divergence in session-typed processes. In: Maffei, M., Tuosto, E. (eds.) TGC 2014. LNCS, vol. 8902, pp. 159–175. Springer, Heidelberg (2014). https://doi.org/10.1007/978-3-662-45917-1_11
26. Vasconcelos, V.T.: Fundamentals of session types. Inf. Comput. **217**, 52–70 (2012)
27. Wadler, P.: Propositions as sessions. J. Funct. Program. **24**(2–3), 384–418 (2014)

Relational Solver for JAVA Generics Type System

Peter Lozov[1], Dmitry Kosarev[1], Dmitry Ivanov[2], and Dmitry Boulytchev[1(✉)]

[1] Saint-Petersburg State University, Universitetskaya emb., 7-9, 199034 St. Petersburg, Russia
dboulytchev@math.spbu.ru
[2] Huawei, St. Petersburg, Russia

Abstract. We present a solver for Java generics type system implemented using relational verifier-to-solver approach. The solver finds solutions for a system of subtyping inequations with free variables and thus can be used to determine a concrete type satisfying a set of constraints. The context of this work is symbolic execution for testing and verification of JAVA programs.

Keywords: JAVA generics · relational programming · relational solvers

1 Introduction

JAVA [1] is one of the most popular high-level programming languages with millions of developers worldwide [2] and thousands of applications written in, including critical ones. There is no surprise that methods, approaches and tools for verification and testing of JAVA code is an active research topic with applicable results. One of the most prominent and ambitious method for software testing which allows to discover some errors invisible for other methods is *symbolic execution* [10].

Our experience shows that a precise JAVA generics type solver is a crucial part of symbolic execution engine. In SBST-2022 competition [15] on automated test generation our symbolic engine UTBotJava [3] failed to generate tests for several use cases where generic parameters influenced symbolic execution process, and several generics-related issues are still unresolved[1].

In this paper we consider the problem of solving a system of subtyping inequations for JAVA generic types with free variables. Using relational programming techniques and verifier-to-solver approach we come up with a simple and declarative albeit not very efficient solver; then we apply a number of problem-specific optimizations for boosting the performance, which gives us a solver with

[1] https://github.com/UnitTestBot/UTBotJava/issues/730, https://github.com/UnitTestBot/UTBotJava/issues/1994, https://github.com/UnitTestBot/UTBotJava/issues/924.

R. Glück and B. Kafle (Eds.): LOPSTR 2023, LNCS 14330, pp. 118–128, 2023.
https://doi.org/10.1007/978-3-031-45784-5_8

a promising efficiency. As subtyping relation in JAVA with the presence of generics is known to be undecidable [14] the solver can not be total; however due to the completeness of relational search [23] it ultimately finds all existing solutions. We do not claim our current result to be an ultimate achievement; however is demonstrates pretty well the advantages and caveats of relational programming approach we investigate.

We sincerely appreciate all valuable comments and suggestions made by the reviewers which helped us to improve the quality of the manuscript and discover a few directions for future research.

2 Relational Programming, Verifiers, and Solvers

Relational programming [12] is an approach based on the idea of describing programs as relations. It can be considered as a branch of logic programming in which the use of all non-relational constructs (side-effects, extra-logical features) is discouraged. In a narrow sense relational programming amounts to writing programs in MINIKANREN—a specifically designed for this purpose embedded DSL. Initially developed for SCHEME/RACKET MINIKANREN later was ported for dozens of host languages[2]. We, specifically, use a strongly-typed MINIKANREN implementation for OCAML [19], called OCANREN [17]. MINIKANREN uses the same theory of Horn clauses as PROLOG but with a different concrete syntax with explicit unification, conjunction, disjunction and fresh variable introduction, and employs a different *interleaving* search strategy [16], which is known to be complete [23]. Besides unification with occurs-check, enabled by default, MINIKANREN can be equipped with other basic constraints like disequality constraint [11], finite-domain constraints [6], or constructs of nominal logic [8].

In the context of our work the most valuable property of MINIKANREN is its capability of expressing *reverse computations*. It is well-known [4,5] that some complicated programs can be constructed as a result of inversion of some other, much simpler, programs. The relational nature of MINIKANREN makes inverse computations particularly easy, which opens a way for relational synthesis [7, 9,18]. More specifically, we use the capability of MINIKANREN to turn *verifiers* into *solvers*.

It is rather a matter of common knowledge that verifying a solution is, as a rule, much easier than finding one. The idea of using relational programming is based on the observation that a solver for a certain search problem can be considered as an inversion of a verifier for the same problem [20]. Thus, to solve some problem one just needs (in principle) to implement a relational verifier for this problem, which is a routine task in the vast majority of cases. We demonstrate this approach by the following very simple but observable example.

The following relational program in MINIKANREN implements an addition of two natural numbers in Peano encoding[3] (see Fig. 1a). It takes *three* arguments

---

[2] http://minikanren.org/#implementations.

[3] It is a convention in MINIKANREN programming to superscript relational definitions with "^{o}".

```
let rec add° x y z = ocanren {
  x ≡ 0 ∧ z ≡ y ∨
  fresh x', z' in
    x ≡ S x' ∧
    z ≡ S z' ∧
    add° x' y z'
}
```

(a) Relational addition

```
let rec add x y =
  match x with
  | 0    → y
  | S x' → S (add x' y)
```

(b) Functional addition

Fig. 1. Relational vs. functional addition implementation

x, y, and z, and performs a case analysis on the first one using unification "$\equiv$". When x is zero, then y is unified with z. Otherwise, there is some x' which is one less than x. We recursively calculate the sum of x' and y, setting its value to z', and then unify z with z' plus one. Thus, add^o implements the relation $\{(x, y, z) \in \mathbb{N}^3 \mid x + y = z\}$. This relation can be "inspected" by using specific primitive "$\mathbf{run}_{\bar{\alpha}}$ $\{Q\}$", where Q—some relational expression (*query*), $\bar{\alpha}$—a list of fresh *query* variables. **run** initiates a search which finds all substitutions for query variables which make the query to succeed, and return them in a form of a lazy stream. For example, $\mathbf{run}_{\alpha}$ {**add**^{o} `(S O)` `(S (S O))` α} will return a single substitution $[\alpha \mapsto$ S (S (S O))], thus calculating a sum of S O (one) and S (S O) (two). However, at the same time the very same relational program can be used to decompose a number in all possible summands: $\mathbf{run}_{\alpha\beta}$ {**add**^{o} α β `(S (S (S O)))`} will do the job, decomposing S (S (S O)) into all summands and binding them to α and β respectively. Thus, a single relational definition can be run in various "directions", solving various search problems.

Finally, in many cases it is easier to obtain relational specification from functional one. For example, relational addition can be easily converted from more conventional functional code (see Fig. 1b). For our task we use a tool, called NOCANREN, to perform *typed relational conversion* [21], for which its static and dynamic correctness was proven formally. Thus, our solution is a mixture of a hand-written and converted relational code and, in fact, a few different solvers.

3 Java Generics

Here we briefly describe the relevant subpart of JAVA type system. All information in this section is directly derived from the Java Language Specification [13]. We also refrain from reiterating on the non-generic part of JAVA type system assuming the reader's familiarity with the concepts of reference types, arrays, classes, interfaces, and inheritance.

The subsystem we are dealing with contains generic class/interface types $C\,\langle\mathscr{T}^*\rangle$, array types $\mathscr{T}$ `[]`, type variables $\alpha^{\mathscr{T}}_{\mathscr{T}_\perp}$, intersection types $\bigcap \mathscr{T}$ and **null** type. Here $\mathscr{T}$ denotes a type, $\mathscr{T}_\perp$—an optional type. Type variables are bounded in the sense that they always have a certain *upper bound*. This upper bound can be either specified explicitly or assumed to be `java.lang.Object`. In addition to the upper bound a type variable can be equipped with a *lower bound.* The lower bound can only be derived implicitly as a result of *capture conversion* (see below). We denote the upper bound of a variable by superscript and lower—by subscript.

Generic class (or interface) is a class/interface which is equipped with a number of type parameters. In generic class declaration these parameters can only be type variables with specified upper bounds. Additionally a number of *direct supertypes* (notation: "$\prec$") can be specified for a generic class/interface:

$$C\left\langle \alpha_1^{U_1}\ldots\alpha_k^{U_k}\right\rangle \prec S_1\left\langle T_1^1\ldots T_{n_1}^1\right\rangle\ldots S_m\left\langle T_1^m\ldots T_{n_m}^m\right\rangle$$

Here C is the class/interface being declared, $\alpha_i^{U_i}$—its generic parameters with upper bounds, S_i—its direct supertypes, among which only one type can be a class type, T_l^j—type parameters for direct supertypes, which may contain the occurrences of α_i; note: neither of T_l^j can be an intersection type.

Type variables in scopes of their declarations behave like regular types; the scope of a type variable is determined by the position of its introduction (either generic class/interface or generic method). It is unclear what is the scope of type variables introduced implicitly as a result of capture conversion, but this might be irrelevant to the problem we are dealing with.

Intersection types can not be declared explicitly; the only positions in which they can be specified are upper bounds of type parameters in generic class/interface declarations. However intersection types can be derived as a result of capture conversion.

Null type is an artificial transparent type with no explicit representation. It is assumed to be a subtype for every other reference type.

Besides regular types generic classes can be applied to *wildcard types.* A wildcard is an anonymous type variable (notation: "?") equipped, as a regular type variable, with upper bound and optional lower bound neither of which can be of intersection type. If no upper bound is specified explicitly then `java.lang.Object` is implicitly assumed. It is important that wildcards can not be used to parameterize direct supertypes in generic class/interface declarations. Array types can not be directly parameterized by wildcards.

To establish the subtyping relation (denotation: "$\prec\!\!\prec$") between types parameterized by wildcards two additional notions are introduces.

The first one is *contains* relation "$\supseteq$":

$$
\begin{aligned}
&?^T \supseteq ?^S && ,T \lessdot\!\!\lessdot S\\
&?^T \supseteq ?\\
&?_T \supseteq ?_S && ,S \lessdot\!\!\lessdot T\\
&?_T \supseteq ?\\
&?_T \supseteq ?^{\texttt{java.lang.Object}}\\
&T \supseteq T\\
&T \supseteq ?^T\\
&T \supseteq ?_T
\end{aligned}
$$

This relation in essence is a routine check that a collection of types designated by the "right" type is contained in a collection of types designated by the "left" one.

The second is *capture conversion.* Informally, capture conversion replaces a *nameless* wildcard type argument by a freshly introduced *named* type variable, thus "capturing" some concrete (but statically unknown) type in a certain context. The motivation for introducing capture conversion is as follows: let us have some value of a wildcard-parameterized type, say, some collection of type $Collection\ \langle ?\rangle$. Without capture conversion we would be incapable of dealing with individual elements of this collection (since a wildcard is not a type, but rather a way to to describe a certain parameterization). From a type-theoretic standpoint wildcards introduce a certain form of *existential* types with capture conversion serving as a limited form of opening construct [22]. The detailed theory and the discussion of properties for the wildcard-related fragment of Java Generics type system can be found in [24].

Capture conversion is defined as follows. Let $C\ \langle T_1 \dots T_k\rangle$ be a generic class/interface type where some of T_i are wildcards. Let $\beta_i^{U_i}$ be the i-th type parameter of C's declaration. Then capture conversion of $C\ \langle T_1 \dots T_K\rangle$ is the type $C\ \langle \lfloor T_1\rfloor \dots \lfloor T_k\rfloor\rangle$ where the transformation "$\lfloor\bullet\rfloor$" is defined as follows:

$$
\lfloor T_i\rfloor = \begin{cases}
\alpha_{\textbf{null}}^{U_i[\beta_j \leftarrow \lfloor T_j\rfloor]} & \text{if } T_i = ?\ \ (\alpha \text{ is a fresh type variable})\\
\alpha_{\textbf{null}}^{B\cap U_i[\beta_j \leftarrow \lfloor T_j\rfloor]} & \text{if } T_i = ?^B\ (\alpha \text{ is a fresh type variable})\\
\alpha_{B}^{U_i[\beta_j \leftarrow \lfloor T_j\rfloor]} & \text{if } T_i = ?_B\ (\alpha \text{ is a fresh type variable})\\
T_i & \text{otherwise}
\end{cases}
$$

Here "$[\bullet \leftarrow \bullet]$" denotes a (simultaneous) substitution of type variables with some types. Note, in capture conversion type parameters of the class under conversion are substituted with the results of the conversion in all bounds.

The subtyping relation "$\lessdot\!\!\lessdot$", which is the principle notion for the problem we are dealing with, is defined as a reflexive-transitive closure of the direct supertype relation "$\prec$". We already described one case of direct supertyping, the others are as follows:

$$
\begin{array}{rll}
I \prec \texttt{java.lang.Object} & , (I \text{ is an interface with no direct superinterface}) \\
C\,\langle T_1 \dots T_k\rangle \prec C\,\langle S_1 \dots S_k\rangle & , \forall i\,.\,S_i \supseteq T_i \\
C\,\langle T_1 \dots T_k\rangle \prec S & , C\,\langle\lfloor T_1\rfloor \dots \lfloor T_k\rfloor\rangle \prec S \\
\bigcap T_i \prec T_i & \\
\alpha^{\bigcap T_i} \prec T_i & \\
T \prec \alpha_T & \\
\textbf{null} \prec T & \\
T\texttt{[]} \prec S\texttt{[]} & , T \prec S \\
\texttt{java.lang.Object[]} \prec \texttt{java.lang.Object} & \\
\texttt{java.lang.Object[]} \prec \texttt{java.lang.Cloneabe} & \\
\texttt{java.lang.Object[]} \prec \texttt{java.io.Serializable} &
\end{array}
$$

Note: the notions "$\supseteq$", "$\prec$", and "$\prec\!\!\prec$" are defined mutually recursive: "$\prec\!\!\prec$" is used to define "$\supseteq$", which is used to define "$\prec$", which, in turn, is the basic relation to define "$\prec\!\!\prec$".

4 Relational Subtyping Solver

The approach of verifier-to-solver conversion relies on the implementation of functional verifier for the problem in question. In our case such verifier should test if two given ground types are in the subtyping relation. This, in particular, requires implementation of capture conversion, "contains" relation, and direct subtyping verifier. Then a reflexive-transitive closure of the latter has to be implemented. The functional verifier is then converted into relational form which by construction delivers a subtyping solver for non-ground types with free variables.

A simple observation, however, makes its obvious that it is in fact much easier to implement reflexive-transitive closure directly in relational language. Indeed, given relation R its reflexive-transitive R^* closure can be expressed by just

$$R^*\,(x,\,y) = R\,(x,\,y) \vee x \equiv y \vee \exists\, z\,.\,R\,(x,\,z) \wedge R^*\,(z,\,y) \qquad (\star)$$

which can be easily directly encoded in OCANREN. However, from the implementation standpoint the application of this technique imposes a certain problem since "$\prec$" and "$\prec\!\!\prec$" are mutually recursive, and we expect "$\prec$" to be obtained as a result of relational conversion of functional implementation.

Functional verifier is implemented in OCAML in a straightforward manner: we encode types as data structures of certain types and give a direct implementation for all components of subtyping relation except the transitive closure. All these definitions are "wrapped" in a functor (an OCAML module parameterized by a module) which takes *class table* as a parameter. The class table contains the definitions of relevant set of classes with their direct supertyping encoding, description of their type parameters, etc. The concrete contents of the class table is supplied by the symbolic execution engine.

To build a mixture of relationally-converted code and relational implementation of transitive closure we use open recursion: the functional implementation of direct supertyping relation "$\prec$" is parameterized by subtyping relation "$\prec\!\!\prec$". In functional implementation the knot is tied not by transitive closure of "$\prec$" but by "$\prec$" itself:

```
let rec (≺≺) ta tb = ta ≺ tb
and (≺) ta tb    = Verify.(≺) (≺≺) ta tb
```

Here "Verify" is a module acquired by an instantiation of the verifier for a simple hand-written testing class table. Thus, functional verifier can only check the subtyping of types no more then two "steps" away from each other.

The next step is applying relational conversion for this functional verifier. For technical reasons this requires a mild "massaging" of initial OCAML implementation: arrays (more efficient in functional world) have to be replaced with lists, and some changes have to be made in order to compensate for the incompleteness of current relational conversion implementation. After the relational conversion and the parameterization of verifier functor with a class table a proper recursive knot is tied by a transitive closure of "$\prec$", which completes the construction of the solver. While functional verifier can only work for ground types and return a boolean value, its relational counterpart searches for all substitution for free variables in incomplete types is order to make them subtype each other.

Our first evaluation discovered the fact that the solver was unsound—it established the subtyping relation for two arbitrary types. This finding constitutes a drastic contradiction with the theory which predicts that the solver has to be correct by construction. The careful analysis, however, discovered that functional verifier was unsound as well! The reason was very simple: let us have two arbitrary types A and B. To establish, for example, that $A \prec\!\!\prec B$, take a type variable α_A^B with upper bound B and lower bound A. Then, by definition

$$A \prec\!\!\prec \alpha_A^B \wedge \alpha_A^B \prec\!\!\prec B \Rightarrow A \prec\!\!\prec B$$

In the JLS there were no explicit requirement for lower/upper bounds of type variables to respect the subtyping relation, thus this requirement was not encoded in the verifier. Another finding of the evaluation was that, contrary to the expectation, the direct supertyping relation is actually reflexive (in full accordance with the JLS).

After fixing the unsoundness we found that the performance of the solver was very low: it took seconds to come up with the first solution even for small hard-written class tables. After a careful analysis we come up with the following optimizations.

First, we changed the representation of class/interface identifiers. In functional verifier all identifiers were represented by integer numbers which, under relational conversion, were tuned into natural numbers in Peano form (essentially, lists). At the same time as no transformation are performed on identifiers (besides equality checks) this representation is excessive. We manually reverted the identifiers representation to integers.

Then, we optimized the search in class tables. Functional verifier sometimes needs to find a declaration of a class/interface by identifier, or find a superclass/superinterface for a class given this class identifier, etc. Under relational conversion all these procedures take form of disjunctions of the length proportional to the size of the class table. However, when some of the involved identifiers are ground the search can be optimized: we can query a precompiled optimized map-like structure of the class table to filter out only relevant information and synthesize the residual disjunction at the runtime. We call this optimization *dynamic class table specialization*.

Finally, we optimize the evaluation of transitive closure based on the groundness analysis of the arguments. For example, if we need to find a certain x such that $R^*(x, y)$ where y is *ground*, then the following (equivalent to ($\star$)) procedure of finding transitive closure is found to be more efficient:

$$R^*(x, y) = R(x, y) \vee x \equiv y \vee \exists z \,.\, R(z, y) \wedge R^*(x, z)$$

So, in our implementation the groundness analysis (performed on the fly) chooses one of a few versions of transitive closure calculations. We call this optimization *dynamic transitive closure evaluation*.

With all of these optimizations enabled our solver finally can demonstrate a reasonable performance. We present the results of the evaluation in the next section[4].

5 Evaluation

We evaluated our solver for a class table containing more than 40000 classes exported by the symbolic execution engine using nine benchmark queries of various shapes. By the specifics of using the solver as a part of symbolic execution engine we switched off the capture conversion. The motivation is simple: the symbolic execution engine is interested only in such types instances of which can be created at runtime. Thus, capture conversion can only be applied in a *forward* direction which eliminated wildcards. With capture conversion enabled in the relational solver it could also be applied in reverse direction, introducing superfluous wildcards which could not be utilized properly.

[4] Source code is available online: https://github.com/Lozov-Petr/JGS/tree/LOPSTR-2023.

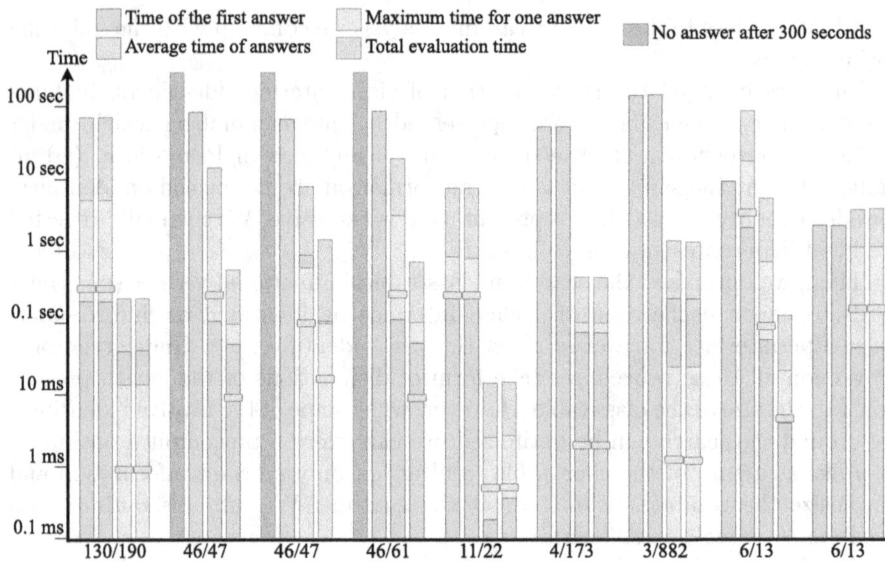

Fig. 2. Evaluation results

The results are presented in Fig. 2 in the form of a bar chart. Here the groups of four bars correspond to different benchmarks, each bar in the group corresponds to a one of four versions of the solver (left-to-right): with no optimizations, with dynamic transitive closure evaluation only, with dynamic class table specialization only, and with both optimizations enabled.

The benchmark queries are as follows:

1. $\alpha \prec\!\prec$ `java.util.List<Object>`
2. $\alpha \prec\!\prec$ `java.util.RandomAccess` $\wedge$
   $\alpha \prec\!\prec$ `java.util.AbstractCollection<Object>`
3. $\alpha \prec\!\prec$ `java.util.AbstractCollection<Object>` $\wedge$
   $\alpha \prec\!\prec$ `java.util.RandomAccess`
4. $\alpha \prec\!\prec$ `java.util.AbstractCollection<Object>` $\wedge$
   $\alpha \prec\!\prec$ `java.util.RandomAccess` $\wedge$
   $\alpha \prec\!\prec$ `java.util.List<Object>`
5. `javax.management.AttributeList` $\prec\!\prec \alpha$
6. `javax.management.AttributeList` $\prec\!\prec \alpha \wedge$
   `kotlinx.collections.PersistentVector<Object>` $\prec\!\prec \alpha$
7. `kotlinx.collections.PersistentVector<Object>` $\prec\!\prec \alpha \wedge$
   `javax.management.AttributeList` $\prec\!\prec \alpha \wedge$
   `com.google.common.collect.ImmutableSortedSet<Object>` $\prec\!\prec \alpha$
8. `kotlinx.collections.PersistentVector<Object>` $\prec\!\prec \alpha \wedge$
   $\alpha \prec\!\prec$ `java.util.List<Object>`
9. $\alpha \prec\!\prec$ `java.util.List<Object>` $\wedge$
   `kotlinx.collections.PersistentVector<Object>` $\prec\!\prec \alpha$

For each query we evaluated two quantitative measures: the overall number of answers (shown as a numerator under corresponding benchmark) and the number of unique answers (shown as a denominator). Also we evaluated four time measures: the time of calculating the first answer (this time includes the time spent on the pre-calculations required by dynamic table specialization), the maximal time for one answer (not including the first answer time), the average time taken over all answers, and the total evaluation time. We also limited the evaluation time to 300 s; in a few cases we either received only a part of the answers (in this case, only the time for calculating the first answer is indicated), or we did not receive a single answer (in this case, the red column is shown in the bar chart). All measurements are presented in a logarithmic scale.

As we can see from the results, dynamic transitive closure in some cases improves the performance by an order of magnitude (if there is an upper bound among the second and subsequent inequations), dynamic specialization of the table always improves the result by an order of magnitude, but the best performance is achieved when using both optimizations. It is also noteworthy that the performance of the solver depends on the order of inequations in the query (the benchmarks 3 and 4, 8 and 9 differ only in this aspect). Also, it can be noted that solving the inequations with lower bounds delivers a large number of duplicate answers.

We can conclude that the optimized version of the solver shows promising performance results, but the problems of performance dependance on the order of bounds and the presence of duplicates require further research.

6 Conclusion

We presented here the JAVA generics type solver implemented using relational verifier-to-solver conversion technique. Our work showcases all major steps, properties, and caveats of the approach we advocate. The solver demonstrates a promising performance and we consider integrating it into a production-level symbolic execution engine as a main task of our future work.

References

1. Java programming language page. https://www.oracle.com/java/
2. Tiobe index. https://www.tiobe.com/tiobe-index/
3. Unittestbot java. https://github.com/UnitTestBot/UTBotJava
4. Abramov, S., Glück, R.: Combining semantics with non-standard interpreter hierarchies. In: Kapoor, S., Prasad, S. (eds.) FSTTCS 2000. LNCS, vol. 1974, pp. 201–213. Springer, Heidelberg (2000). https://doi.org/10.1007/3-540-44450-5_16
5. Abramov, S., Glück, R.: From standard to non-standard semantics by semantics modifiers. Int. J. Found. Comput. Sci. **12**(02), 171–211 (2001). https://doi.org/10.1142/S0129054101000448
6. Alvis, C.E., Willcock, J.J., Carter, K.M., Byrd, W.E., Friedman, D.P.: cKanren: minikanren with constraints. In: Proceedings of the 2011 Annual Workshop on Scheme and Functional Programming. Scheme 2011 (2011)

7. Byrd, W.E., Ballantyne, M., Rosenblatt, G., Might, M.: A unified approach to solving seven programming problems (functional pearl). Proc. ACM Program. Lang. 8:1–8:26 (2017)
8. Byrd, W.E., Friedman, D.P.: α kanren a fresh name in nominal logic programming. In: Scheme and Functional Programming (2007)
9. Byrd, W.E., Holk, E., Friedman, D.P.: Minikanren, live and untagged: quine generation via relational interpreters (programming pearl). In: Proceedings of the Annual Workshop on Scheme and Functional Programming, Scheme 2012, pp. 8–29. Association for Computing Machinery, New York (2012). https://doi.org/10.1145/2661103.2661105
10. Cadar, C., Sen, K.: Symbolic execution for software testing: three decades later. Commun. ACM **56**(2), 82–90 (2013). https://doi.org/10.1145/2408776.2408795
11. Comon, H.: Disunification: a survey. In: Computational Logic – Essays in Honor of Alan Robinson, pp. 322–359 (1991)
12. Friedman, D.P., Byrd, W.E., Kiselyov, O., Hemann, J.: The Reasoned Schemer, 2nd edn. The MIT Press, Cambridge (2005). https://doi.org/10.7551/mitpress/5801.001.0001
13. Gosling, J., Joy, B., Bracha, G.S.G., Buckley, A., Smith, D., Bierman, G.: The Java Language Specification; Java SE 20 Edition (2023). https://docs.oracle.com/javase/specs/jls/se20/jls20.pdf
14. Grigore, R.: Java generics are turing complete. SIGPLAN Not. **52**(1), 73–85 (2017). https://doi.org/10.1145/3093333.3009871
15. Ivanov, D., et al.: UTBot java at the SBST2022 tool competition. In: 2022 IEEE/ACM 15th International Workshop on Search-Based Software Testing (SBST), pp. 39–40 (2022). https://doi.org/10.1145/3526072.3527529
16. Kiselyov, O., Shan, C.C., Friedman, D.P., Sabry, A.: Backtracking, interleaving, and terminating monad transformers: (functional pearl). In: Proceedings of the Tenth ACM SIGPLAN International Conference on Functional Programming, ICFP 2005, pp. 192–203. Association for Computing Machinery, New York (2005). https://doi.org/10.1145/1086365.1086390
17. Kosarev, D., Boulytchev, D.: Typed embedding of a relational language in OCaml, pp. 1–22 (2016). https://doi.org/10.4204/EPTCS.285.1
18. Kosarev, D., Lozov, P., Boulytchev, D.: Relational synthesis for pattern matching. In: Oliveira, B.C.S. (ed.) APLAS 2020. LNCS, vol. 12470, pp. 293–310. Springer, Cham (2020). https://doi.org/10.1007/978-3-030-64437-6_15
19. Leroy, X., Doligez, D., Alain Frisch, J.G., Rémy, D., Vouillon, J.: The ocaml system, release 5.0 (2022)
20. Lozov, P., Verbitskaia, E., Boulytchev, D.: Relational interpreters for search problems. In: miniKanren and Relational Programming Workshop (2019)
21. Lozov, P., Vyatkin, A., Boulytchev, D.: Typed relational conversion. In: Wang, M., Owens, S. (eds.) TFP 2017. LNCS, vol. 10788, pp. 39–58. Springer, Cham (2018). https://doi.org/10.1007/978-3-319-89719-6_3
22. Pierce, B.C.: Types and Programming Languages. MIT Press, Cambridge (2002). http://ropas.snu.ac.kr/~kwang/520/pierce_book.pdf
23. Rozplokhas, D., Vyatkin, A., Boulytchev, D.: Certified semantics for relational programming. In: Oliveira, B.C.S. (ed.) APLAS 2020. LNCS, vol. 12470, pp. 167–185. Springer, Cham (2020). https://doi.org/10.1007/978-3-030-64437-6_9
24. Torgersen, M., Ernst, E., Hansen, C.: Wild fj. In: Proceedings of FOOL 12, the Twelth International Workshop on Foundations of Object-Oriented Languages; Conference date: 15 January 2005 (2005)

Unification and Substitution in (C)LP

Predicate Anti-unification in (Constraint) Logic Programming

Gonzague Yernaux(✉) and Wim Vanhoof

University of Namur, Namur, Belgium
gonzague.yernaux@unamur.be

Abstract. The concept of anti-unification refers to the process of determining the most specific generalization (msg) of two or more input program objects. In the domain of logic programming, anti-unification has primarily been investigated for computing msgs of tree-like program structures such as terms, atoms, and goals (the latter typically seen as ordered sequences).

In this work, we study the anti-unification of whole predicate definitions. We provide a definition of a predicate generalization that allows to characterize the problem of finding the most specific generalization of two predicates as a (computationally hard) search problem. The complexity stems from the fact that a correspondence needs to be constructed between (1) some of the arguments of each of the predicates, (2) some of the clauses in each of the predicate's definitions, and (3) some of the body atoms in each pair of associated clauses. We propose a working algorithm that simultaneously computes these correspondences in a greedy manner. While our algorithm does not necessarily compute the most specific generalization, we conjecture that it allows to compute, in general, a sufficiently good generalization in an acceptable time.

Keywords: Anti-unification · Generalization · Approximation Algorithm

1 Introduction

Anti-unification, the dual operation of unification, is the process of computing so-called *most specific generalizations*. Such generalizations are defined as common templates for sets of code artifacts that harbor as much common structure as possible. Since its first formal introduction by Plotkin [10], anti-unification has become a fundamental ingredient in, for example, Inductive Logic Programming (ILP) where new, general rules are learned from specific facts [9] or in program transformation techniques such as supercompilation or partial deduction, where generalizing program terms is a necessary ingredient to control the unfolding process and thus to guarantee termination [3,14].

Other applications in which anti-unification plays a role include bug detection, program repair, and even code compression [2]. Our own work on (semantic)

R. Glück and B. Kafle (Eds.): LOPSTR 2023, LNCS 14330, pp. 131–149, 2023.
https://doi.org/10.1007/978-3-031-45784-5_9

clone detection in logic programming [19], which is the direct motivation for the current work, also relies on the availability of a anti-unification operator capable of computing generalizations at the predicate level. Semantic clone detection [12] is a powerful tool given its direct applications in program comprehension [11,15], plagiarism detection [22], malware detection [21] and finding vulnerabilities in binaries [8]. Computing a (most specific) generalization of two code fragments allows not only to compare the degree of similarity of the fragments, it also allows to steer the search process that may be involved in clone detection. As an example, the idea of using anti-unification to detect Erlang code clones is the focus of [7]. The approach exploits the abstract syntax trees of Erlang functions to detect duplication: to this effect, each function's tree is compared– through anti-unification– with templates belonging to known classes of clones.

Computing the most specific generalization of tree-like syntactical structures such as terms and atoms is widely understood and can easily be done in linear time by a straightforward recursive algorithm [10,14]. However, when considering more liberal structures (such as *sets* of atoms), the problem becomes NP-hard necessitating the need for abstractions, such as the k-swap stability abstraction that we have developed in previous work [18].

In the present work we consider the generalization of complete predicate definitions. Defining and computing the best – typically most specific – such generalization is a non-trivial problem that, to the best of our knowledge, has not received much attention in the literature. As we will show, searching for the most specific predicate generalization involves searching for a mapping between the clauses of both predicates such that a pairwise generalization of the corresponding clauses gives the best result. However, when the clause bodies are considered to be sets of atoms, a similar mapping needs to be considered between the individual literals of the corresponding clause bodies. To add yet another difficulty, the constructed generalization must be coherent, in the sense that in the resulting clauses each argument consistently generalizes a single argument in both of the generalized predicates, possibly different in each of both definitions.

Although the search of anti-unification processes operating at the level of predicates is thus in itself a rather novel quest, a few researchers did address similar or related problems. In [4], subsumption, i.e. the historical ancestor of anti-unification described in [10], is used to quantify the syntactic "closeness" of logic clauses and even entire ILP programs. Another orthogonal approach to our own that is worth mentioning is that of [6], where so-called *higher-order* anti-unification, allowing for generalization of functor and predicate names, is used to mimic analogical thinking in an ILP or, more broadly, a machine learning context. Meanwhile in the works of Schmid et al., the generalization of couples of functions is intended to be used as a blueprint of the functions' algorithmic core, in an effort to enhance machine learning processes [13]. While not far away from our own intent when anti-unifying predicates, this idea was only mentioned by Schmid and her team, and to this date no published work actually delivered the envisioned recipe.

The remainder of the paper is organized as follows. In Sect. 2 we provide some basic definitions involving the generalization of terms and goals and we define the quality function that should be optimized in order to compute the most specific generalization. Next, in Sect. 3, we provide a workable definition of what constitutes a common generalization of two predicate definitions and we discuss where the additional complexity in computing such generalizations stems from. In Sect. 4 we develop an algorithm allowing to compute an approximate solution using greedy search. The main highlight of our algorithm is that it computes the above-mentioned interdependent mappings between the clauses, arguments, and body atoms in one go. While the resulting algorithm does not necessarily compute the *most specific* generalization and while its performance needs to be established on real examples, we feel that it provides an elegant solution that allows to compute, in general, a sufficiently good generalization in an acceptable time. We end with some concluding remarks in Sect. 5.

2 Preliminaries

A CLP program is traditionally defined [5] over a CLP context, which is a 5-tuple $\langle X, \mathcal{V}, \mathcal{F}, \mathcal{L}, \mathcal{Q}\rangle$, where X is a non-empty set of constant values, $\mathcal{V}$ is a set of (uppercase) variable names, $\mathcal{F}$ a set of function names, $\mathcal{L}$ is a set of constraint predicates over X and $\mathcal{Q}$ a set of predicate symbols. The sets $X, \mathcal{V}, \mathcal{F}, \mathcal{L}$ and $\mathcal{Q}$ are all supposed to be disjoint sets. Symbols from $\mathcal{F}$, $\mathcal{L}$, and $\mathcal{Q}$ have an associated arity and as usual we write f/n to represent a symbol f having arity n. Given a CLP context $\mathcal{C} = \langle X, \mathcal{V}, \mathcal{F}, \mathcal{L}, \mathcal{Q}\rangle$, we can define the set of terms over $\mathcal{C}$ as $\mathcal{T_C} = X \cup \mathcal{V} \cup \{f(t_1, t_2, ..., t_n) | f/n \in \mathcal{F} \text{ where } \forall i \in 1..n : t_i \in \mathcal{T_C}\}$. Likewise, the set of constraints over $\mathcal{C}$ is defined as $\mathcal{C_C} = \{L(t_1, t_2, ..., t_n) \mid L/n \in \mathcal{L} \text{ and } \forall i \in 1..n : t_i \in \mathcal{T_C}\}$ and the set of atoms as $\mathcal{A_C} = \{p(t_1, \ldots, t_n) \mid p/n \in \mathcal{Q} \text{ and } \forall i : t_i \in \mathcal{T_C}\}$. A goal $G \subseteq (\mathcal{C_C} \cup \mathcal{A_C})$ is a set of atoms and/or constraints. We will use the notion of a *literal* to refer to either a constraint or an atom. A program is then defined as a set of constraint Horn clause definitions where each clause definition is of the form $p(t_1, \ldots, t_n) \leftarrow G$ where $p(t_1, \ldots, t_n)$ is an atom called the head of the clause with $t_1, \ldots, t_n$ terms, and G a goal called the body of the clause. For a predicate symbol p/n, we use $def(p/n)$ to denote the definition of p/n in the program at hand, i.e. the set of clauses having a head atom using p as predicate symbol and harboring n arguments. We might refer to a predicate p/n simply as p, provided that its arity n is obvious or irrelevant. Terms, literals, goals, clauses and predicates will sometimes be referred to as *program objects*.

In what follows we will often consider the CLP context to be implicit and talk simply about two CLP programs and the predicates and clauses defined therein. As for semantics we consider the purely declarative CLP paradigm exposed in [5].

As usual, a substitution is a mapping from variables to terms. For any mapping σ, $dom(\sigma)$ represents its domain. For a program object e (be it a term, a literal, a goal, a clause or a predicate) and a substitution σ, $e\sigma$ represents the result of simultaneously replacing in e those variables V that are in $dom(\sigma)$ by $\sigma(V)$. A fresh renaming of some program object e is a variant of e where all variables have been renamed to new, previously unused variables.

Given the notion of a substitution, we can define common generalizations.

Definition 1. *Given three terms (or three literals) g_1, g_2 and g, we say that g is a* common generalization *of g_1 and g_2 if $\exists \sigma_1, \sigma_2$, two substitutions verifying $g\sigma_1 = g_1 \wedge g\sigma_2 = g_2$.*

The definition above is sufficient for terms and literals, which are tree structures. To extend it to clause bodies we need to introduce a partial order. The definition is taken from our earlier work [18].

Definition 2. *Let G and G' be goals. We say that G is* more general than *(or, equivalently, is a generalization of) G', denoted $G \preceq G'$, if and only if there exists a substitution σ such that $G\sigma \subseteq G'$.*

Hence, a goal is more general than another goal if the former is a subset of the latter modulo a substitution. While our notion of generalization is simple and purely of syntactic nature, it is in line with what one could consider to be a generalization at the semantic level, since generalizing a goal corresponds to removing computational units (terms, constraints or atoms) and introducing new variables.

In the following example as well as in the remainder of the paper, we write terms and constraints in infix style when possible.

Example 1. The goals $\{X = Y + Z\}, \{V = 6 + W, q(3)\}, \{K = 6 + (2 * L)\}$ and $\{q(A)\}$ are all generalizations of $\{D = 6 + (2 * 5), q(3)\}$.

Also note that our relation $\preceq$ resembles the θ-subsumption relation of [10]. However, the latter is concerned with *sequences* of atoms rather than sets and is therefore more adapted to situations where the underlying semantics are not fully declarative. We now define *common generalizations* of goals as follows.

Definition 3. *For two goals G_1 and G_2, we say that any goal G such that $G \preceq G_1$ and $G \preceq G_2$ is a* common generalization *of G_1 and G_2.*

The process of computing common generalizations is usually called *anti-unification* [2]. However, given two program objects, one is typically interested in the *most specific* common generalizations, which definition depends on the context. For instance, larger common generalizations (in number of generalized elements) are often considered to be more interesting than shorter ones. This is at least the approach taken by Plotkin [10]. But other criteria than size alone can interfere in what is expected of "better" common generalizations: for example, the level of injectivity of the substitution (or renaming) σ involved in Definition 2 [18]. To keep our approach generic in that regard we will use the notion of *quality* to quantify the interest of a given generalization.

Definition 4. *Given a set of program objects E of the same nature that one wants to generalize, we define a quality function ω^E as a function that associates a real value $\omega^E(e)$ to each possible program object e of the same nature.*

The definition of a quality function ω^E is generic in the sense that there is no constraint on the exact criterion to be measured as "quality" of a generalization, except being a function of real values. A value $\omega^E(e)$ can thus simply represent the size of e – counting, e.g. the number of literals or the number of (distinct or not) terms that appear in e – or it can be more sophisticated and reflect the size of the object relative to the objects it is supposed to generalize (the set E) or any other optimization criterion that makes sense for the application at hand. In the following, whenever the set E is obvious or irrelevant, we will omit it from the notation and we will simply talk about a quality function ω.

Definition 5. *For a given quality function ω, we say that a common generalization g of two program objects e_1 and e_2 is an ω-*maximal generalization (ωmg) for e_1 and e_2 *iff no other common generalization g' is such that $\omega(g') > \omega(g)$.*

A rather straightforward and intuitive quality function can be based on the notion of a *norm* [1] which is a function $|.| : \mathcal{T} \mapsto \mathbb{N}$ that associates a natural number to any term, basically representing the term's size.

Definition 6. *Given $|.|$ a norm on terms, let $\tau_{|.|}$ denote the quality function* derived from the norm *defined such that*

- *for a term t we have $\tau_{|.|}(t) = |t|$;*
- *for the empty literal true we have $\tau_{|.|}(true) = 0$;*
- *for a non-empty literal $L \equiv p(t_1, \ldots, t_n)$ we have $\tau_{|.|}(L) = 1 + \sum_{i=1}^{n} \tau_{|.|}(t_i)$;*
- *for a goal $G \equiv \{L_1, \ldots, L_n\}$ we have $\tau_{|.|}(G) = \sum_{i=1}^{n} \tau_{|.|}(L_i)$;*
- *for a clause $c \equiv L \leftarrow G$ we have $\tau_{|.|}(c) = \tau_{|.|}(L) + \tau_{|.|}(G)$;*
- *for a predicate p/n we have $\tau_{|.|}(p) = \sum_{c \in def(p/n)} \tau_{|.|}(c)$.*

In the case of a literal L, the 1+ appearing in the formula for computing $\tau(L)$ is a way to ensure later that a generalization containing any (non-empty) literal is of higher quality that a generalization containing none. This is useful to ensure that norms returning a value of zero on given terms still encourage larger generalizations in number of atoms. The quality function from Definition 6 can be instantiated on a norm capturing the number of functors in an expression (often called the *termsize* norm).

Example 2. Let us consider the termsize norm $|.|_s$ defined for a term t as equal to the cardinality of the multiset of functors appearing in t. Given this norm, we have $\tau_{|.|_s}(f(g(X,h),h)) = \#\{f/2, g/2, h/1, h/1\} = 4$. Likewise, we have that $\tau_{|.|_s}(app([X|Xs], Y, [X|Zs]) \leftarrow \{app(Xs, Y, Zs)\}) = 1 + \#\{[|], [|]\} + 1 = 4$.

As we will use this quality function based on the termsize norm in the remainder of the paper, we will simply refer to it by τ without mentioning the underlying norm.

3 Predicate Anti-unification

The notion of a generalization can rather easily be extended to the level of clauses, as shown by the following definition.

Definition 7. *A clause* $c \equiv p(t_1, \ldots, t_n) \leftarrow G$ *is a generalization of a clause* $c' \equiv q(u_1, \ldots, u_m) \leftarrow G'$, *denoted* $c \preceq c'$, *if and only if* $n \leq m$ *and there exists a substitution* σ *and an injection* $\alpha : 1..n \mapsto 1..m$ *such that* $G\sigma \subseteq G'$, *and* $\forall i \in 1..n : t_i\sigma = u_{\alpha(i)}$. *We call* α *the* involved argument mapping *of the generalization.*

The definition states that for a clause c to be the generalization of another clause c', the body of c must be a generalization of the body of c' (first condition). Moreover, the n arguments of c must be a generalized version of n corresponding arguments in c' (second condition), possibly appearing in another order than they do in the generalized clause c'. The two conditions in the definition ensure that one and the same substitution is used both for matching the clauses' heads and their bodies.

Example 3. Consider the clauses $c_1 \equiv q(Y_1, Y_2, 5+Y_2) \leftarrow Y_1 > Y_2, Z = 5 + Y_2$ and $c_2 \equiv r(V_1, 5 + V_1) \leftarrow W = 5 + V_1$. The clause $c \equiv p(X_1, X_2) \leftarrow A = X_2$ is a common generalization of c_1 and c_2.

The definition is fine as long as we consider isolated clauses. When generalizing multiple clauses belonging to a single predicate, it is important that the individual clause generalizations are all in line with the involved argument mapping α. Another mapping, identified by γ and called a *clause mapping*, determines which couples of clauses are generalized with one another in the generalization.

Definition 8. *Let* p/n *and* q/m *be predicates. We say that* p/n *is a generalization of* q/m, *denoted* $p \preceq q$, *if and only if* $n \leq m$ *and* $|def(p)| \leq |def(q)|$ *and there exists*

1. *an injective mapping* $\alpha : 1..n \mapsto 1..m$, *and*
2. *an injective mapping* $\gamma : def(p) \mapsto def(q)$,

such that $\forall c \in dom(\gamma)$ *it holds that* $c \preceq \gamma(c)$ *with involved argument mapping* α.

The definition above states that a predicate is a generalization of another if each clause of the generalization can be mapped on a clause in the generalized predicate by means of a substitution, provided that all of clause generalizations share the same argument mapping α.

While the definition of a predicate generalization is elegant, it is immediately clear that computing a common predicate generalization will not be that straightforward. Let p/n and q/m be the predicates one wants to generalize (ideally such that the resulting generalization is maximal with respect to the chosen quality function). We can then define what constitutes a common predicate generalization with respect to the two underlying mappings:

Definition 9. *Consider predicates p/n and q/m and let α and γ be, respectively, an argument mapping and a clause mapping between p and q. Then a* common generalization of p and q with respect to α and γ *is a predicate comprised of the set of clauses $g = \{g_{(c,c')} \mid (c,c') \in \gamma\}$ where $g_{(c,c')} \preceq c$ with involved argument mapping α_1, $g_{(c,c')} \preceq c'$ with involved argument mapping α_2, and $\forall i \in dom(\alpha_1)$: $\alpha(\alpha_1(i)) = \alpha_2(i)$.*

Example 4. Let us consider the two following predicates, $take/3$, which extracts the E first elements of a list, and $negsum/3$, which succeeds if its third argument is the negative sum of the I first elements of the list in its first argument.

$take(0, Xs, [])$.
$take(E, [], [])$.
$take(E, [X|Xs], [X|Ys]) \leftarrow E > 0, E_1 = E - 1, take(E_1, Xs, Ys)$.

$negsum(Vs, 0, 0)$.
$negsum([], I, 0)$.
$negsum([V|Vs], I, U) \leftarrow I > 0, I_1 = I - 1, negsum(Vs, I_1, U_1), U = U_1 - V$.

The predicate $g/2$ such that $def(g) = \{g(0, A)., g(A, []).\}$ is a relatively trivial common generalization of the two predicates, mapping the first and second clauses of $take$ onto the first and second clauses of $negsum$ respectively, and such that $\alpha = \{(1, 2), (3, 1)\}$. A presumably better generalization, one that better exhibits the common functionality of the two predicates is the following:

$g(0, Ws, Null)$.
$g(C, [], Null)$.
$g(C, [W|Ws], R) \leftarrow C > 0, C_1 = C - 1, g(C_1, Ws, R)$.

This corresponds to a predicate that decrements a counter as it crawls through a list, and performs recursively on each encountered element of the list. It can, indeed, be seen as the functionality that is shared by both $take$ and $negsum$.

Note that a clause mapping γ and argument mapping α do not by themselves determine a unique generalization but rather a set of possible generalizations (since different generalizations compatible with α might exist for a given clause pair c and c'). Formally, if we use $m_\tau(c, c', \alpha)$ to represent the τ-maximal generalization compatible with α of clauses c and c', then computing the τ-maximal *predicate* generalization can be seen as the problem of finding α and γ such that $\sum_{(c,c')\in\gamma} \tau(m_\tau(c, c', \alpha))$ is maximal. By the above definition, the τ-maximal generalization of two predicates p and q is a generalization whose τ-value, *computed over the definition of the predicate as a whole*, is maximal among all possible generalizations of p and q. While in our approach this is the generalization we would ultimately like to compute, other definitions (resulting in somewhat different search or optimization problems) might be of interest as well. We briefly return to this point in the discussion at the end of the paper.

4 Computing Common Generalizations

Computing a τ-maximal predicate generalization is clearly a computationally hard problem. In fact, even computing a τ-maximal common generalization of two clause bodies is a computationally hard problem in itself due to goals being sets of literals [18]. In what follows, we will devise a method that does not necessarily compute a τ-maximal predicate generalization, but that arguably computes a sufficiently good (τ-wise) approximation of the τ-maximal generalization.

4.1 Terms and Literals

Terms and literals being ordered tree structures, it is easy to define an anti-unification operator that computes, in a time linear in the number of nested subterms, the τ-maximal generalization of two terms, respectively literals [10, 14]. The operator is based on a *variabilization function* that introduces, when necessary, fresh variable names.

Definition 10. *Let $V \subset \mathcal{V}$ denote a set of variables. A function $\Phi_V : \mathcal{T}^2 \mapsto \mathcal{V} \cup X$ is called a* variabilization function *if, for any $(t_1, t_2) \in \mathcal{T}^2$ it holds that if $\Phi_V(t_1, t_2) = v$, then*

1. *$v \notin V$;*
2. *$\nexists (t_1', t_2') \in \mathcal{T}^2 : (t_1', t_2') \neq (t_1, t_2) \wedge \Phi_V(t_1', t_2') = v$;*
3. *$v \in X \Leftrightarrow t_1 = t_2 \in X$ and in that case, $v = t_1 = t_2$.*

Note that a variabilization function Φ_V introduces a new variable (not present in V) for any couple of terms, except when the terms are the same constant. It can thus be seen as a way to introduce new variable names when going through the process of anti-unifying two program objects. In what follows, we will consider V to be the set of variables appearing in the structures to generalize so that all variables in the generalization are fresh variables, and abbreviate the function to Φ. The following is an example of a typical term (and literal) anti-unification operator based on the process of variabilization. In the remainder of the paper, we consider it as our working anti-unification tool for the quality function τ and the norm of Example 2.

Definition 11. *Given some variabilization function Φ defined over some numeric CLP context, let $\bowtie$ denote the function such that for any two terms or two literals $t = \hat{t}(t_1, \ldots, t_n)$ and $u = \hat{u}(u_1, \ldots, u_m)$ it holds that*

$$\bowtie(t, u) = \begin{cases} true & \text{if } \hat{t}, \hat{u} \in \mathcal{P} \cup \mathcal{L} \wedge \hat{t}/n \neq \hat{u}/m \\ \hat{t}(\bowtie(t_1, u_1), \ldots, \bowtie(t_n, u_n)) & \text{if } \hat{t} = \hat{u} \wedge n = m \wedge t, u \notin \mathcal{V} \\ \Phi(t, u) & \text{otherwise} \end{cases}$$

It is easy to see that computing $\bowtie(t, u)$ can be done in a time that is proportional to the minimal termsize of both arguments, that is a time proportional to $\mathcal{O}(\min\{|t|, |u|\})$.

Example 5. Let us consider the predicates *take* and *negsum* from Example 4. Several applications of $\bowtie$ on pairs of terms or literals are depicted in Table 1.

Table 1. Example results for $\bowtie$.

t	u	$\bowtie(t,u)$	$\tau(\bowtie(t,u))$
$[X\|Xs]$	$[]$	$\Phi([X\|Xs],[])$	0
$[X\|Xs]$	$[V\|Vs]$	$[\Phi(X,V)\|\Phi(Xs,Vs)]$	1
$E_1 = E - 1$	$U = U_1 - V$	$\Phi(E_1,U) = \Phi(E,U_1) - \Phi(1,V)$	2
$E_1 = E - 1$	$I_1 = I - 1$	$\Phi(E_1,I_1) = \Phi(E,I) - 1$	3

For two literals L and L', the output of their anti-unification through $\bowtie$ is only valuable if both L and L' are based on the same predicate symbol. Note that this prevents recursive calls to be part of a generalization when the two clauses are part of predicates that have different names. To overcome this, we suppose in the rest of the paper that recursive calls are replaced with a special literal λ that will at least allow the recursion to be explicitly part of the generalization. Note that the call's arguments are not taken into account when generalizing two recursive calls. This makes sense as such a generalization should take the argument mapping α into account. We will return to this point later in the discussion.

4.2 Predicates

When the mappings α and γ need to be computed from scratch, it is easy to see that the combinations of potential mappings to consider is exponential in the number of clauses and arguments, especially when partial mappings (i.e. mappings that concern only a subset of arguments and/or clauses) are allowed. Now, for a fixed argument mapping, computing a clause mapping giving rise to an ωmg boils down to the resolution of an instance of the classical assignment problem, which can be solved by existing Maximum Weight Matching algorithms, for which polynomial routines exist [17]. The same is true the other way round, i.e. when computing an argument mapping for a given clause mapping.

However, the mappings γ and α are not independent. Considering a clause mapping without taking an argument mapping into account makes little sense, as the different clause generalizations (resulting from the mapping γ) could map the arguments differently, making them incompatible and impossible to combine into a single predicate generalization. On the other hand, a wrongly chosen argument mapping can result in clauses being generalized in a sub-optimal way due to the fact that better generalizations exist that are incompatible with the chosen argument mapping.

Based on these observations, we develop an algorithm that does not necessarily compute the *maximal* generalization of two predicates, but a sufficiently good approximation (τ-wise). The algorithm constructs the argument- and clause mappings at the same time, basically implementing a greedy search algorithm that tries to maximize the τ-value of the resulting generalization as a whole, including the generalization of the clause bodies.

Let p and q denote the predicates we wish to generalize. Let N represent their maximal arity and, likewise, K the maximal number of clauses to be found in either definition. A basic ingredient of our algorithm is knowledge (basically, the τ-value) of the result of generalizing individual items, be it arguments or body atoms. To represent these individual τ-values, we will use two weight matrices. First, a square matrix H of dimension $(N \times K)^2$ representing the τ-value resulting from anti-unifying each argument term occurring in the definition of p with each argument term occurring in the definition of q. The matrix has thus as many rows (and columns) as the maximal number of argument terms $(N \times K)$ that could occur in p and/or q. In H, any coordinate $i \in 1..N \times K$ can be decomposed as $i = c \times N + d$ with c and d natural numbers and $0 \leq d < N$) such that c represents a clause and d an argument position (in zero-based numbering). For ease of notation, we define $cl(i) = c$ and $al(i) = d$ when i can be decomposed as per the above formula. The entries of H are then computed as follows: for a position (i, j), we have $H[i, j] = \tau(\bowtie (t, t'))$, where t represents the $al(i)$th argument from the $cl(i)$th clause of p (if it exists) and, likewise, t' represents the $al(j)$th argument of the $cl(j)$th clause of q (if it exists). If either of those arguments does not exist, then $H[i, j] = -\infty$.

Secondly and in a similar manner, if M represents the maximum number of body literals found in the clauses of p and q then a square matrix B of dimension $(M \times K)^2$ represents the τ-value resulting from anti-unifying the individual body literals from p with those of q. For a value $0 \leq i < M \times K$, we will use $bl(i)$ to represent the value l where $(0 \leq l < K)$ such that $i = c \times K + l$. As such, $B[i, j] = \tau(\bowtie (L, L'))$ where L represents the $bl(i)$th literal from the $cl(i)$th clause of predicate p and L' represents the $bl(j)$th literal from the $cl(j)$th clause of q. Again, if either of those literals does not exist, $B[i, j] = -\infty$.

Example 6. Let us once more consider the predicates of Example 4. The corresponding matrices H and B (restricted to the submatrix that does not contain exclusively $-\infty$ values) are displayed in Fig. 1. For clarity we have added to each line and column the terms and literals that are concerned by it, when these exist. The literals λ represent the recursive calls.

Constructing a generalization boils down to selecting a set of positions S_H from H and a set of positions S_B from B in such a way that the chosen positions correctly represent an argument mapping, a clause mapping, and a generalization of the corresponding clause bodies. When a position (i, j) is selected in one of the matrices, it implies that the clause mapping γ being constructed associates the $cl(i)$th clause of p with the $cl(j)$th clause of q. Therefore, after selecting (i, j), we need to exclude from further selection those positions that concern only one of $cl(i)$ and $cl(j)$, in either matrix. In what follows we use the notation $(i, j)_W$ to refer to the position (i, j) in the matrix W (where W can be one of H or B). The set of all positions to be considered in H is noted $P_H = \{(i, j)_H | i, j \in 1..N \times K \wedge H[i, j] \neq -\infty\}$ and, likewise, the set of all the positions of interest in B is noted $P_B = \{(i, j)_B | i, j \in 1..M \times K \wedge B[i, j] \neq -\infty\}$. We will use P_W to refer to the set of positions of a matrix W, with W being either H or B and

	$\boldsymbol{Vs}$	**0**	**0**	[]	$\boldsymbol{I}$	**0**	$[\boldsymbol{V}\vert\boldsymbol{Vs}]$	$\boldsymbol{I}$	$\boldsymbol{U}$
0	0	**1**	1	0	0	1	0	0	0
$\boldsymbol{Xs}$	**0**	0	0	0	0	0	0	0	0
[]	0	0	**0**	1	0	0	0	0	0
$\boldsymbol{E}$	0	0	0	0	**0**	0	0	0	0
[]	0	0	0	**1**	0	0	0	0	0
[]	0	0	0	1	0	**0**	0	0	0
$\boldsymbol{E}$	0	0	0	0	0	0	0	**0**	0
$[\boldsymbol{X}\vert\boldsymbol{Xs}]$	0	0	0	0	0	0	$\underline{1}$	0	0
$[\boldsymbol{X}\vert\boldsymbol{Ys}]$	0	0	0	0	0	0	1	0	**0**

	$\boldsymbol{I > 0}$	$\boldsymbol{I_1 = I - 1}$	$\boldsymbol{\lambda}$	$\boldsymbol{U = U_1 - V}$
$\boldsymbol{E > 0}$	**2**	0	0	0
$\boldsymbol{E_1 = E - 1}$	0	**3**	0	2
$\boldsymbol{\lambda}$	0	0	**1**	0

Fig. 1. The matrix H (top) and the submatrix $B[9-11, 9-12]$ of interest (bottom)

simply P for $P_H \cup P_B$. We will use $(i,j)_W$ or sometimes simply (i,j) to denote a position from either P_H or P_B.

Definition 12. *Let $(i,j) \in P$ be a position. Its* cl-exclusion zone *is defined as $R_{cl}(i,j) = \{(h,l)_W \in P | (cl(h) = cl(i) \oplus cl(l) = cl(j))\}$, where $\oplus$ is the traditional "exclusive or" operator.*

Intuitively, the cl-exclusion zone represents the constraint that a clause from p can only be mapped upon a single clause from q (and vice versa). Indeed, as soon as a pair of clauses is "fixed" by selecting a position (i,j) (whether that represents a generalization of two argument terms or two body literals), no other position can be selected that would generalize a term or a literal from either $cl(i)$ or $cl(j)$ with a term or literal from a third clause.

In addition, when selecting a position $(i,j)_H$ in the matrix H, representing as such the generalization of two argument terms, it furthermore implies that the argument mapping α under construction maps the argument position $al(i)$ to $al(j)$, thereby excluding from further selection those matrix elements that would map either of these argument positions to a third argument position, even in other clauses. Formally this is captured in the following notion.

Definition 13. *The* al-exclusion zone *of a cell position $(i,j)_H \in P_H$ is defined as $R_{al}(i,j) = \{(h,l)_H \in P_H | (al(h) = al(i) \oplus al(l) = al(j))\}$.*

With respect to the matrix B on the other hand, there is a similar but less stringent constraint. Indeed, a literal from p cannot be mapped onto more than one literal from q (or vice-versa). However, literals at the same position in different clauses of p do not necessarily need to be mapped to literals occupying the same positions in clauses defining q (and vice-versa). This is formalized by the notion of *bl-exclusion zone*:

Definition 14. *The* bl-exclusion zone *of a position $(i,j)_B$ is defined as* $R_{bl}(i,j) = \{(h,l)_B \in P_B | cl(h) = cl(i) \wedge cl(l) = cl(j) \wedge (bl(h) = bl(i) \oplus bl(l) = bl(j))\}$.

Example 7. Let us consider the selection of a specific position, namely $(8,7)_H$, in the matrices shown in Fig. 1. This position corresponds to the mapping of the second argument of the last clause in the *take* predicate onto the first argument of the last clause in *negsum*. The exclusion zones associated with $(8,7)_H$ can be visualized as the cells highlighted in the figure. Specifically, these exclusion zones consist of cells involving one of the aforementioned clauses but not the other ($R_{cl}(8,7)$), as well as cells that map an argument in second position in *take* or in first position in *negsum* with other positions ($R_{al}(8,7)$). Candidate positions in P_B that are part of $R_{cl}(8,7)$ are not showed in the figure, since the concerned literals do not exist; the cells in question thus contain $-\infty$ which is ignored in our selection process. In other words, the only positively valued submatrix $B[9-11, 9-12]$ being restricted to the literals populating the third clauses of each predicate, it is not part of the exclusion zones of $(8,7)_H$.

A generalization under construction being a set S of positions in P, we can now define the set of positions in P that are still compatible with S.

Definition 15. *The* compatible zone *of a set of positions $S \subseteq P$ is defined as* $A(S) = A_H(S) \cup A_B(S)$ *where*

$$A_H(S) = P_H \setminus \bigcup_{(i,j)\in S}(R_{cl}(i,j) \cup R_{al}(i,j))$$
$$A_B(S) = P_B \setminus \bigcup_{(i,j)\in S}(R_{cl}(i,j) \cup R_{bl}(i,j))$$

At any point of our search process, all the selected positions should be compatible with one another.

Definition 16. *A set $S \subseteq P$ is said to be a* valid selection *if and only if* $\forall (i,j)_W \in S : (S \setminus \{(i,j)_W\}) \subseteq A(\{(i,j)_W\})$.

Note that the maximal size of a valid selection is $(N+M) \times K$, corresponding to the assignment of each argument and literal of p to an argument, resp. literal of q (provided that these argument and literal couples exist, i.e. yield a anti-unification weight different from $-\infty$).

To develop an algorithm, we will rely on the fact that a valid selection can be built by iteratively selecting new compatible cells.

Proposition 1. *Let S be a valid selection, and let $(i,j)_W \in A(S)$ be a cell position. Then, $S \cup (i,j)_W$ is a valid selection.*

From any valid selection, one can retrieve the underlying mappings as follows.

Definition 17. *Let S be a valid selection. The* induced argument mapping $\alpha(S)$ *is defined as $\alpha(S) = \{(a,a')|\exists(i,j)_H \in S : al(i) = a \wedge al(j) = a'\}$. The induced clause mapping is defined as $\gamma(S) = \{(c,c')|\exists(i,j)_W \in S : c$ is the clause appearing in $cl(i)$th position in $def(p)$ and c' in $cl(j)$th position in $def(q)\}$.*

Now our purpose is to find a valid selection of positions in the matrix respecting the constraints above while harboring a promising weight, according to the following straightforward definition of weight of a selection.

Definition 18. *Given a set S of positions in the matrices H and B, we define the* weight of S *as* $w(S) = \sum_{(i,j)_W \in S} W[i,j]$.

Note that, in practice, the matrices H and B will presumably be sparse, as many pairs of terms or literals are expected to have different outermost functors or predicate symbols and hence will yield an anti-unification weight equal to zero. Based on this observation, we propose an algorithm for computing a set S of compatible positions in H and B. The algorithm, depicted as Algorithm 1 basically performs greedy search (selecting the highest-weight positions first), but performs backtracking when there are multiple positions having the same maximal weight.

In the algorithm, *Comp* represents the set of positions compatible with the current selection S and having maximal weight. The helper function *max* is defined on $A(S)$ as follows: $max(A(S)) = \{(i,j)_W \in A(S) \mid \forall (h,l)_{W'} \in A(S) : W[i,j] \geq W'[h,l]\}$. Note that the positions retained in *Comp* can be part of H as well as B. Also note that, initially, when $S = \{\}$, $A(S)$ contains all positions of H and B with weight other than $-\infty$. Further down the algorithm, $Comp_d$ is used to denote the positions in *Comp* that are compatible with all other positions in *Comp*. These positions can all at once be added to S, thanks to the fact that they will in any case not be excluded by later iterations – a consequence of Proposition 1. If some of the positions having maximal weight were not added to S by the previous operation, they are individually added to the previous version of S and pushed onto the stack Q for further exploration as an alternative solution. The algorithm also prunes the search when all remaining weights are equal, including the special case when all remaining weights are zero-valued.

Example 8. Let us consider how Algorithm 1 could perform on the predicates *take*/3 and *negsum*/3 from earlier examples, with the relevant parts of matrices H and B depicted in Fig. 1. During the first round of the algorithm, only one position is of maximal weight, namely $(10,10)_B$ of weight 3, which is added to the (initially empty) selection under construction S. In the second round of the algorithm, there are two positions of maximal weight, namely $(9,9)_B$ and $(10,12)_B$ of weight 2. However, the latter position belonging to $R_{bl}(10,10)$, it is not part of $A(S)$ and thus excluded from selection. Consequently, the other position being the only remaining point of weight 2, it is added to S. During a third iteration, the positions of maximal weight are those having a weight of 1. Only one of these positions, namely $(11,11)_B$, is compatible with all the available 1-valued cell positions, and can thus once more be added to S. However, the other positions are also tentatively added to (the old version of S) and each resulting set of positions is pushed onto the stack as an alternative for further exploration. The search continues, however, with the current version of S having now the positions $(10,10)_B$, $(9,9)_B$, and $(11,11)_B$. Note that this selection constrains the underlying clause mapping γ in such a way that the third clause from *take*/3 is

Algorithm 1

$S \leftarrow \{\}, S_{max} \leftarrow \{\}, Q \leftarrow []$
$push(Q, S)$
while $Q \neq []$ **do**
  $S \leftarrow pop(Q), S_0 \leftarrow S$
  $Comp \leftarrow max(A(S))$
  $Comp_d \leftarrow \{(i,j)_W \in Comp : A(\{(i,j)_W\}) \supset Comp\}$
  for all $(i,j)_W \in Comp_d$ **do**
    $S \leftarrow S \cup \{(i,j)_W\}$
  for all $(i,j)_W \in Comp \setminus Comp_d$ **do**
    $push(Q, S_0 \cup \{(i,j)_W\})$
    if $\#\{W(i,j) | (i,j)_W \in A(S)\} = 1$ **then**
      break out of the **for** loop
  if $w(S) > w(S_{max})$ **then**
    $S_{max} \leftarrow S$
  if $S \neq S_0$ **then**
    $push(Q, S)$
return S_{max}

associated with the third clause of *negsum*/3 but imposes no other constraints (yet).

The positions of maximal weight are still those of weight 1, but none of them is available without excluding others (in other words, $Comp_d$ is empty). So each of the remaining 1-weighted positions is tentatively added to S and pushed on the stack for further exploration. The last of these variants, say $S \cup (8,7)_H$, is popped from the stack and the algorithm continues with this alternative. Note that this choice constraints the underlying argument mapping α by associating the second argument of *take*/3 to the first argument of *negsum*/3. The underlying clause mapping γ remains unchanged, as the associated argument terms belong, each, to the third clause of their respective definition. The selection of $(8,7)_H$ eliminates a number of 1-weighted positions from those that were available earlier, namely $\{(9,7)_H, (6,4)_H, (3,4)_H\} \subset R_{al}(8,7)$. Suppose the algorithm chooses $(1,2)_H$ (by again pushing all alternatives on the stack and popping the last one) to continue. This implies associating the first clause of *take* to the first clause of *negsum*, and the first argument of *take* to the second argument of *negsum*. This excludes $(1,3)_H \in R_{al}(1,2)$ as well as $(1,6)_H \in R_{cl}(1,2) \cap R_{al}(1,2)$ among the remaining 1-valued cells. The only cell left of positive weight is the cell at position $(5,4)_H$. Incorporating it in S, the clause mapping $\gamma(S)$ now maps the second clauses on the predicates together. Finally, since no more available cells are of non-zero weight, remaining 0-valued positions are selected in $A(S)$ without allowing new backtracking, eventually yielding $S = S_{max}$ being the set of positions of the cells that are shown in bold in the matrices from Fig. 1, with total weight $w(S) = 9$. Backtracking on earlier versions of S is then activated, but no better solution in terms of total weight is found, so that S is the final selection of the algorithm. The resulting generalization maps the arguments according to their role in the predicates: the lists to be browsed (Xs and Vs), the number of elements to be considered (E and I), and the result (Ys and U). The generalization thus takes the following form:

$$g(0, \Phi(Xs, Vs), \Phi([], 0).$$
$$g(\Phi(E, I), [], \Phi([], 0)).$$
$$g(\Phi(E, I), [\Phi(X, V)|\Phi(Xs, Vs)], \Phi([X|Ys], U)) \leftarrow \Phi(E, I) > 0,$$
$$\Phi(E_1, I_1) = \Phi(E, I) - 1, \lambda.$$

When the occurrences of the variabilization function Φ are replaced with new variables and when the recursive calls are manually generalized taking α into account, this effectively amounts to the generalization g that was depicted in Example 4 on page 7.

The algorithm's termination is guaranteed by the fact that the stack Q eventually runs out of candidate selections. Indeed, at each iteration, a new such selection S of cells is popped. Although more than one extended versions of this selection can be pushed on the stack again, all of these extended versions will comprise at least one more cell than those constituting S, so that the successive stacked selections will be of increasing size, ultimately running out of available compatible cells. While several stacked selections can be composed of the same cells, two different selections will necessarily vary at least in the *order* in which the cells are selected. Since the number of permutations of a finite number of cells (corresponding to the worst-case scenario of the algorithm) is itself a finite number, the process is guaranteed to reach an end in a finite time frame.

The algorithm's runtime depends on the amount of backtracking carried out, which is proportional to the number of cells harboring the same nonzero value. This amount of (potential) backtracking is thus reduced when the matrices are filled with a large number of zeroes. Interestingly, we observe the following result.

Proposition 2. *Given a weight matrix W and a coordinate $i \in 1..\mathcal{N}$ (where $\mathcal{N} = N$ if $W = H$ and $\mathcal{N} = M$ if $W = B$), let us denote by F_i^W the set $\{j \in 1..K | W[i,j] \neq 0\}$, that is the set of non-zero values of line i in W. Then, $\forall W \in \{H, B\}, l \in 1..\mathcal{N}$ it holds that either $F_i^W \cap F_l^W = \emptyset$, in which case $|F_i^W| + |F_l^W| \leq M$; or $F_i^W = F_l^W$.*

Regarding the matrix H, the proposition above stems from the fact that two terms are either based on the same functor (in which case they only unify with the terms based on said functor) or they are not (in which case they do not unify with any term with which the other term unifies). Likewise, in B, two literals are either built upon the same predicate symbol from $\mathcal{L} \cup \mathcal{P}$, in which case the anti-unification weight is strictly positive, or not, in which case it is zero. The implication on our matrix is important: whenever two lines have different non-zero positions, there are at least $N \times K$ (or $M \times K$) zeroes in the two lines combined (the same is true for columns). This situation is expected to occur frequently in H since predicates either use *different* functors in their heads for pattern matching, or do not use pattern matching at all, resulting in all weights being zero. In contrast, in B, it is not rare that the same predicate symbols occur multiple times, particularly for constraint predicates like the equality constraint $=/2$. However, as our running example shows, and in particular in recursive predicates, some clause have empty bodies (typically for the basic case of recursion), resulting in several ignored, $-\infty$-valued cells in B.

5 Conclusions and Future Work

In this work we have studied anti-unification in the context of predicate definitions. We have given an incarnation of what could be called the most specific generalization – as the τ-maximal generalization – whose computation can be formalized as an optimization problem that is computationally hard due to the number of possible clause mappings, argument mappings, and clause body generalizations. To manage this complexity, we have given an approximate algorithm that combines greedy search with a limited amount of backtracking and that constructs the underlying (and interdependent) mappings simultaneously.

While the algorithm *tries* to maximize the resulting generalization's size (as represented by its τ-value), it is clear that it does not necessarily compute a τ-*maximal* generalization. Nevertheless, the resulting generalizations are interesting as they are themselves predicate definitions and the algorithm provides as such the missing link in our own framework for semantic clone detection [16]. In that work, we suppose a given (but undefined) generalization operator to decide, given two predicates under transformation and their generalization, how much code of the predicates is shared and how the differences could be used to steer the continuation of the transformation process. Until now we had no algorithm to concretely compute such generalizations and in further work we intend to investigate our algorithm's performance in that particular context.

As for the time complexity of the algorithm, it is clear that – except for some contrived examples – the matrices H and B are generally sparse and the algorithm can presumably be further optimized by better exploiting the structure of the search space, in particular with respect to the handling of the exclusion zones of a selected position. For practical applications, one could further alleviate the computational intensity of the anti-unification process by reducing the involved search space even more. One approach would be using type and/or mode information for limiting the pairs of arguments from both predicates that need to be considered. More generally, one could use more involved program analysis techniques (and/or take the order of the arguments and clauses into account) to approximate suitable subsets of mappings to consider for α and γ, which boils down to excluding more parts from H and B from the search. An encouraging approach for this is taken in [20], where a dataflow analysis is devised that is capable of ordering predicate arguments based on their involvement in different operations (atoms and unifications). The order of the arguments can then become a significant indicator regarding their roles in the predicates. We suspect that this technique, if properly used, can significantly ease the search for a promising argument mapping α.

In its current form, our algorithm tries to maximize the τ-value of the generalization as a whole. According to the application at hand, other definitions of what constitutes a desirable generalization might be of interest. For example, when generalizing predicates that deal with a lot of unifications in their heads, it might be advantageous to have the algorithm maximize the τ-value of only the heads of the generalized predicate, disregarding the bodies. Or the other way round for predicates that do less processing in the heads of their clauses. Note that this could easily be achieved by a variant of our algorithm, by introducing weights that make the algorithm prioritize positions from H (or B) when selecting the positions of maximal weight.

In further future work, we intend to investigate how we can better integrate the handling of recursive calls, somehow estimating the weight of their potential generalizations (rather than supposing, as we do now, that each recursive call in p anti-unifies with each recursive call in q with weight 1). Doing so is far from straightforward, as the generalization should take the argument mapping– which is under construction– into account. In addition, we plan to develop other variants of the algorithm that go beyond using the quality measure τ alone. One important aspect that is not treated by τ is data flow optimization, which is the process of minimizing the number of variables appearing in the computed common generalizations of each pair of clauses that are mapped during the anti-unification process. As the examples in the paper suggest, different generalizations yielding the same quality (as measured by τ) can indeed exist and be computed by the algorithm; some of these generalizations, however, harbor less different variables than others (thanks to Φ being applied on the same pairs of variables or terms), thereby better capturing the data flow information between different literals in the resulting generalization, which can thus be considered as more specific. To achieve more specific results in that regard, we will need to modify the anti-unification algorithm to dynamically account for the number of "new" variables introduced (i.e. different occurrences of $\Phi(t_1, t_2)$) when selecting a position.

Yet another interesting line of future research would be investigating and formalizing the semantic or operational properties, if any, linking a generalized predicate and its instances. This should allow to better appreciate what is lost and what is maintained during the generalization process.

References

1. Bossi, A., Cocco, N., Fabris, M.: Norms on terms and their use in proving universal termination of a logic program. Theoretical Computer Science **124**(2), 297–328 (1994). https://doi.org/10.1016/0304-3975(92)00019-N
2. Cerna, D.M., Kutsia, T.: Anti-unification and generalization: A survey. ArXiv abs/2302.00277 (2023)
3. De Schreye, D., Glørgensen, J., Leuschel, M., Martens, B., Sørensen, M.H.: Conjunctive partial deduction: foundations, control, algorithms, and experiments. The Journal of Logic Programming 41(2), 231–277 (1999). https://doi.org/10.1016/S0743-1066(99)00030-8

4. Gutiérrez-Naranjo, M.A., Alonso-Jiménez, J.A., Borrego-Díaz, J.: Generalizing Programs via Subsumption. In: Moreno-Díaz, R., Pichler, F. (eds.) EUROCAST 2003. LNCS, vol. 2809, pp. 115–126. Springer, Heidelberg (2003). https://doi.org/10.1007/978-3-540-45210-2_12
5. Jaffar, J., Maher, M.J.: Constraint logic programming: a survey. The Journal of Logic Programming **19–20**, 503–581 (1994). https://doi.org/10.1016/0743-1066(94)90033-7
6. Krumnack, U., Schwering, A., Gust, H., Kühnberger, K.-U.: Restricted Higher-Order Anti-Unification for Analogy Making. In: Orgun, M.A., Thornton, J. (eds.) AI 2007. LNCS (LNAI), vol. 4830, pp. 273–282. Springer, Heidelberg (2007). https://doi.org/10.1007/978-3-540-76928-6_29
7. Li, H., Thompson, S.: Similar code detection and elimination for erlang programs. In: Carro, M., Peña, R. (eds.) Practical Aspects of Declarative Languages, pp. 104–118. Springer, Berlin Heidelberg, Berlin, Heidelberg (2010)
8. Miyani, D., Huang, Z., Lie, D.: Binpro: A tool for binary source code provenance (2017). https://doi.org/10.48550/ARXIV.1711.00830
9. Muggleton, S., de Raedt, L.: Inductive Logic Programming: Theory and methods. The Journal of Logic Programming **19–20**, 629–679 (1994). https://doi.org/10.1016/0743-1066(94)90035-3
10. Plotkin, G.D.: A Note on Inductive Generalization. Machine Intelligence **5**, 153–163 (1970)
11. Rich, C., Shrobe, H.E., Waters, R.C.: Overview of the programmer's apprentice. In: Proceedings of the Sixth International Joint Conference on Artificial Intelligence (IJCAI). pp. 827–828 (1979). https://doi.org/10.5555/1623050.1623101
12. Roy, C.K., Cordy, J.R., Koschke, R.: Comparison and evaluation of code clone detection techniques and tools: A qualitative approach. Science of Computer Programming **74**(7), 470–495 (2009). https://doi.org/10.1016/j.scico.2009.02.007
13. Schmid, U., Wysotzki, F.: Induction of recursive program schemes. In: Nédellec, C., Rouveirol, C. (eds.) ECML 1998. LNCS, vol. 1398, pp. 214–225. Springer, Heidelberg (1998). https://doi.org/10.1007/BFb0026692
14. Sørensen, M.H., Glück, R.: An Algorithm of Generalization in Positive Supercompilation. In: Proceedings of ILPS'95, the International Logic Programming Symposium. pp. 465–479. MIT Press (1995)
15. Storey, M.D.: Theories, Methods and Tools in Program Comprehension: Past, Present and Future. In: 13th International Workshop on Program Comprehension (IWPC). pp. 181–191 (2005). https://doi.org/10.1007/s11219-006-9216-4
16. Vanhoof, W., Yernaux, G.: Generalization-driven semantic clone detection in clp. In: Gabbrielli, M. (ed.) Logic-Based Program Synthesis and Transformation, pp. 228–242. Springer International Publishing, Cham (2020)
17. W. Kuhn, H.: The Hungarian Method for the Assignment Problem. Naval Research Logistic Quarterly 2 (05 2012)
18. Yernaux, G., Vanhoof, W.: Anti-unification in Constraint Logic Programming. Theory and Practice of Logic Programming **19**(5–6), 773–789 (2019). https://doi.org/10.1017/S1471068419000188
19. Yernaux, G., Vanhoof, W.: On detecting semantic clones in constraint logic programs. In: 2022 IEEE 16th International Workshop on Software Clones (IWSC). pp. 32–38 (2022). https://doi.org/10.1109/IWSC55060.2022.00014
20. Yernaux, G., Vanhoof, W.: A dataflow analysis for comparing and reordering predicate arguments. In: Proceedings of the 39th International Conference on Logic Programming (ICLP) (2023)

21. Zhang, F., Huang, H., Zhu, S., Wu, D., Liu, P.: ViewDroid: Towards Obfuscation-resilient Mobile Application Repackaging Detection. In: Proceedings of the 2014 ACM Conference on Security and Privacy in Wireless and Mobile Networks. pp. 25–36. WiSec '14, ACM (2014). https://doi.org/10.1145/2627393.2627395
22. Zhang, F., Jhi, Y.C., Wu, D., Liu, P., Zhu, S.: A First Step Towards Algorithm Plagiarism Detection. In: Proceedings of the 2012 International Symposium on Software Testing and Analysis. pp. 111–121. ISSTA 2012, ACM (2012). https://doi.org/10.1145/2338965.2336767

A Term Matching Algorithm and Substitution Generality

Marija Kulaš(✉)

Knowledge-Based Systems, Faculty of Mathematics and Computer Science, FernUniversität in Hagen, 58084 Hagen, Germany
kulas.marija@online.de

Abstract. We revisit a simple non-deterministic algorithm for term matching and employ it for deciding substitution generality as well, using *witness term* technique. The technique alleviates the need for ad-hoc proofs involving generality of substitutions.

Keywords: substitution · term matching (subsumption) · generality (of terms and substitutions)

1 Introduction

In logic programming literature, there is a certain wariness towards using substitutions, modeled as total mathematical functions and composed in the usual way, for the purpose of describing logic computation [15,19]. This is due to occasional counter-intuitive behaviour of ensuing concepts like *substitution generality.* With common understanding of generality, it comes as a surprise that substituting y for x, written here as $\binom{x}{y}$, is *not* more general than $\binom{x}{a}$, but is more general than $\binom{x\ y}{a\ a}$, and also that $\binom{x}{f(y,z)}$ is *not* more general than $\binom{x}{f(a,a)}$. Yet, these examples (coming from [2] and [19, p. 148], here handled in Subsect. 5.2) comply with the definition, stating that σ is more general than θ if there is a substitution δ whose composition with σ gives θ.

Apart from the choice of name, the problem with this definition lies, in our view, primarily in its practicability. To verify the property of being more general, we need to find an appropriate δ for any given σ and θ, which is not always obvious; in literature, δ appears to be produced on a case-by-case basis. We offer a simple method for this task, obtained by observing that substitution generality can be decided with a *term matching* algorithm. The term matching algorithm we employed originates in its non-deterministic form from [3].

The paper is organized as follows. We start with notation in Sect. 2. Term matching (subsumption) is defined in Sect. 3. Next, in Sect. 4 we present a deterministic version *TMAT* of the term matching algorithm from [3], using *relaxed core* representation of substitutions ([11], here in Subsect. 2.5). To conclude, in Sect. 5 we show some applications. In Subsect. 5.1, *TMAT* is applied to decide

R. Glück and B. Kafle (Eds.): LOPSTR 2023, LNCS 14330, pp. 150–166, 2023.
https://doi.org/10.1007/978-3-031-45784-5_10

substitution generality, on the basis of *witness terms*. This enables checking of substitution equigenerality as well (Subsect. 5.3), and helps with confirming or disconfirming of most general unifiers (Subsect. 5.4).

Beside examples with concrete substitutions, we apply the technique of witness terms to prove two classical results (Legacy 5 and Legacy 6) in a more direct way.

2 Preliminaries

Due to some novel concepts necessary for our algorithm (like *relaxed core* representation) which need to be put in context, and also to the wish for a self-contained presentation, we include a rather detailed notation. Let us begin with the concept of *term*. In this paper, as in Prolog, *term* shall be the topmost syntactic concept: everything is a term.

2.1 Term

Assume two disjoint sets: a countably infinite set $\boldsymbol{V}$ of *variables*, with elements like x, y, z, possibly with indices, and a set ***Fun*** of *functors*, with elements like $f, g, h, a, b, |, []$.[1] Associated with every functor f are one or more natural numbers n denoting its number of arguments, *arity*. For disambiguation, f/n will be used. Starting from $\boldsymbol{V}$ and ***Fun*** we build data objects, *terms*, denoted typically by r, s, t. Any variable $x \in \boldsymbol{V}$ is a term. If $t_1, ..., t_n$ are terms and $f/n \in$ ***Fun***, then $f(t_1, ..., t_n)$ is a term with *constructor* f and *outline* f/n. In case of zero arity, the term is written without parentheses and called a *constant*, like $a, b, []$.

The *ordered pair* of terms s and t is written in McCarthy's dot-notation as $(s \cdot t)$, with s called the *head* and t the *tail* of the pair. A *non-empty list* is an ordered pair whose tail is a special constant *nil* called the *empty list*, or a non-empty list itself. In Edinburgh Prolog notation, the above ordered pair would be written with brackets instead of parentheses and '|' instead of '·', resulting in $[s|t]$, and the empty list as $[]$. A *list of n elements* is a term $[t_1|[t_2|[...[t_n|[]]]]]$, conveniently written as $[t_1, ..., t_n]$.

The set of variables in t is $Vars(t)$. A term without variables is a *ground term*. We may treat a *sequence* of terms as a term in its own right, so e.g. $Vars((s,t))$[2] would be the set of variables in s and t. The list of distinct variables in t, in order of appearance, is $VarList(t)$. If s and t do not share a variable, they are said to be *variable-disjoint*, written as $s \shortparallel t$. If $Vars(s) \subseteq Vars(t)$, then s is *variable-poorer* than t (including equality), denoted by $s \sqsubseteq_v t$.

---

[1] Strictly speaking, there should be two sets of symbols: one for the *object language* (terms themselves), and another for the *meta-language*. We adopt a sloppy approach, where f can be both an object-functor and a meta-variable denoting *any* object-functor, as befits the context. In contrast, '[]' and '|' are object-functors of Prolog with their usual meaning. Note: x, y, z will be used *only* for variables.

[2] The double parentheses in $Vars((s,t))$ serve to distinguish a sequence *as* argument from a sequence *of* arguments.

Regarded as a sequence of characters, a term may have subterms which are terms in their own right; they are called *subterms*. To signify that somewhere within the term t occurs the term s, we write $s \dot{\in} t$, or $t = \boxed{s}$. Since a subterm may occur more than once, *subterm occurrences* must be identified. For that purpose, terms are usually represented as labeled trees, which makes each subterm occurrence a subtree with a unique *access path*. We shall try a more direct way:

Let t be a term and consider a fixed occurrence $\underline{s}$ of its subterm s, identified by underlining it in the term; this picture ($\underline{s}$ within t) is a visual expression of the subterm relationship between $\underline{s}$ and t, so we denote it by $\underline{s} \dot{\in} t$.[3]

The *access path* of $\underline{s} \dot{\in} t$, denoted $AP(\underline{s} \dot{\in} t)$, is built as follows. If $s = t$, then $AP(\underline{s} \dot{\in} t) := r^0$, where r is the *root label* for t (which is t itself, if t is a variable, otherwise the constructor of t). If $t = f(t_1, ..., t_n)$ and $\underline{s} \dot{\in} t_k$, then $AP(\underline{s} \dot{\in} t) := f^k \cdot AP(\underline{s} \dot{\in} t_k)$. By extracting the second components (numbers) from $AP(\underline{s} \dot{\in} t)$, we obtain the *position* of $\underline{s} \dot{\in} t$.

If $\underline{s} \dot{\in} t$ and $\underline{s'} \dot{\in} t'$ have the same access path, except possibly for the last label, then we say that $\underline{s} \dot{\in} t$ and $\underline{s'} \dot{\in} t'$ is a pair of *siblings*. Alternatively, the occurrences $\underline{s}$ and $\underline{s'}$ are *siblings* within t and t'.

For example, let $\underline{s} \dot{\in} t$ be $[f(y), \underline{z}]$. By the list definition, $[f(y), z]$ is an abbreviation of $[f(y)|[z|[]]]$, so

$$AP(\underline{s} \dot{\in} t) = AP([f(y)|[\underline{z}|[]]]) = |^2 \cdot AP([\underline{z}|[]]) = |^2 \cdot |^1 \cdot AP(\underline{z}) = |^2 \cdot |^1 \cdot z^0$$

Hence, the position of $\underline{s} \dot{\in} t$ is $2 \cdot 1 \cdot 0$. Examples of sibling pairs: $[f(y), \underline{z}]$ and $[g, \underline{h(x)}]$, or $f(\underline{a})$ and $f(\underline{x})$.

2.2 Variable Substitution

The central meta-function in this paper is *variable substitution*, replacing variables with terms. For the most part traditional notation will be used, save for writing application of a substitution σ on a term t in the functional way as $\sigma(t)$, despite the meanwhile prevalent postfix notation $t\sigma$. Hence, composition of substitutions shall be applied from right to left.

A *substitution* σ is defined as a function mapping variables to terms which is identity almost everywhere, i. e. the set $\{x \in \mathbf{V} \mid \sigma(x) \neq x\}$ is finite. This finite set is traditionally denoted $Dom(\sigma)$ and shall here be called the *active domain*[4] or *core* of σ, and its (mutually distinct) elements $x_1, ..., x_n$ are the *active variables*[5] of σ. The definition domain of σ is extended in the functor-preserving way to contain *all* terms by $\sigma(f(t_1, ..., t_k)) := f(\sigma(t_1), ..., \sigma(t_k))$. Given a term t, we say that $\sigma(t)$ is an *instance* of t. The *range* of σ is $Ran(\sigma) := \sigma(Dom(\sigma))$.

---

[3] Here we slightly overload the symbol '$\dot{\in}$', for use with subterm occurrences, to mean not only *membership* (in a term), but also its visual *evidence*.

[4] Traditionally called just *domain*. This may be confusing, since in the mathematical sense it is always the whole $\mathbf{V}$ (and by extension, the set of all terms) that is the domain of definition of any substitution. Alternatively, [6] speaks of *finite support*.

[5] The name *active variable* also appears in [10].

Hence, every substitution σ can be represented in a finitary way as $\sigma = \{x_1/\sigma(x_1), ..., x_n/\sigma(x_n)\}$, or alternatively $\begin{pmatrix} x_1 & \cdots & x_n \\ \sigma(x_1) & \cdots & \sigma(x_n) \end{pmatrix}$. This we call the *core representation.* Each coupling $x_i/\sigma(x_i)$ therein is an (*active*) *binding* by σ. The identity substitution $\{\}$ or $()$ is here denoted as ε. Often we identify a substitution with its core representation; e. g., the set of variables of a substitution σ is defined by $Vars(\sigma) := Dom(\sigma) \cup Vars(Ran(\sigma))$.

The traditional concept of *restriction* of a substitution σ to[6] a set of variables M is denoted as $\sigma\restriction_M$ and means: if $x \in M$ then $\sigma\restriction_M(x) := \sigma(x)$, otherwise $\sigma\restriction_M(x) := x$. For an arbitrary term t we put $\sigma\restriction_t := \sigma\restriction_{Vars(t)}$. The restriction of σ to variables outside of t is denoted as $\sigma\restriction_{-t} := \sigma\restriction_{Dom(\sigma)\setminus Vars(t)}$. Restrictions to a core subset are visible: if $Dom(\theta) \subseteq Dom(\sigma)$ and $\sigma\restriction_{Dom(\theta)} = \theta$, then the core representations satisfy $\theta \subseteq \sigma$, and we call σ an *extension* of θ.

Regarding substitutions again as sets of bindings, the *union* $\sigma \cup \theta$ of substitutions σ and θ is the extension of σ with the bindings from θ (or vice versa). Clearly, this is not always possible, because two different bindings for the same variable do not make sense in a function, i. e. $x/s \in \sigma$ and $x/t \in \theta$ with $s \neq t$. We call two substitutions *additive*, if their union is possible. That would be obviously satisfied in case of disjoint cores. In other words, if $Dom(\sigma) \shortparallel Dom(\theta)$, then $\sigma \uplus \theta := \sigma \cup \theta$ exists, and we call it the *sum* of σ and θ.

The composition of θ and σ is defined by $(\theta \cdot \sigma)(x) := \theta(\sigma(x))$. If $\sigma \cdot \sigma = \sigma$, then σ is called *idempotent.* There is a well-known visual criterion for idempotency, first reported in [5]:

Legacy 1 (idempotence). *Substitution σ is idempotent iff $Dom(\sigma) \shortparallel Ran(\sigma)$.*

Another visually recognizable kind of substitution is *renaming*, represented by permutations: ρ is a *renaming* if $Dom(\rho) = Ran(\rho)$. Then for a given term t we say that $s := \rho(t)$ is a *variant* of t, denoted as $s \doteq t$.

2.3 Generality

Definition 1 (more general term). *A term s is* more (or equally) general[7] *than a term t, written as $s \dot{\leqslant} t$,*[8] *if there is a substitution σ such that $\sigma(s) = t$.*

Term equigenerality, even non-trivial, is also possible: $s \dot{\leqslant} t$ and $t \dot{\leqslant} s$ iff $s \doteq t$.

Definition 2 (more general substitution). *A substitution σ is* more (or equally) general *than a substitution θ, written as $\sigma \lesssim \theta$,*[9] *if σ is a right-divisor of θ, i. e. if there exists a substitution δ with the property $\delta \cdot \sigma = \theta$.*

---

[6] cf. Remark 1.

[7] It has also been said that s *generalizes* t [8].

[8] Some authors like [3,17] turn the symbol around. Our bias towards '$\dot{\leqslant}$' stems from the original definition in [18], and also from the observation that a more general term is never bigger (regarded as a tree).

[9] Some authors like [1,10] turn the symbol around. We will stick to the heuristics that a more general object is somehow "smaller".

As with terms, the cases where $\theta \lesssim \sigma$ as well as $\sigma \lesssim \theta$ form an equivalence relation, traditionally simply called *equivalence* and denoted by $\sigma \sim \theta$. We recommend the name (*substitution*) *equigenerality*, likely to evoke more realistic expectations (cf. Example 1).

Legacy 2 (substitution equigenerality, [5, p. 34]). *Substitutions θ and θ' are equigeneral iff for some renaming ρ holds $\rho \cdot \theta = \theta'$.*

2.4 Unification

Let s and t be terms. If there is a substitution θ satisfying $\theta(s) = \theta(t)$, then s and t (as well as the equation $s = t$) are said to be *unifiable*, and θ is one of their *unifiers*. If such a θ has no extraneous variables, i. e. if $\theta \sqsubseteq_v s, t$, then θ is called a *relevant* unifier of s and t. A unifier of s, t is a *most general unifier* (*mgu*) of s, t if it is more general (includes equality) than any unifier of s, t. The set of all mgus for s, t shall be denoted as $MguSet(s, t)$. Since unifiability of the equation $f(s_1, ..., s_n) = f(t_1, ..., t_n)$ entails unifiability of the set of equations $\{s_1 = t_1, ..., s_n = t_n\}$ and vice versa, we also use unary notation $MguSet(E)$, where E is a set of equations. In case of one equation, we drop the braces.

Any two unifiable terms have an idempotent (and relevant) most general unifier, as provided by Robinson's unification algorithm [18] or Martelli-Montanari's unification scheme [14].

2.5 Relaxed Core Representation

Clearly, the traditional (core) representation of substitutions reflects only the aspect of *non-fixpoints*. But if we are also interested in other aspects like *injectivity*, then core representation is not adequate.

For example, assume a substitution σ mapping s to t; it is mapping each variable in s to a subterm of t, so it is possible that a variable stays the same. If we want our mapping to account for *all* variables in s, necessarily x/x would have to be tolerated, say as a *passive binding*. In other words, the core of σ would have to be *relaxed* to allow some (a finite set of) passive variables, raising those above the rest, as it were; this was originally proposed in [11].

Definition 3 (relaxed core). *A* relaxed core *for a substitution σ is any finite set of variables $\{x_1, ..., x_n\} \supseteq Dom(\sigma)$. The corresponding* relaxed core representation[10] *for σ is $\begin{pmatrix} x_1 & \ldots & x_n \\ \sigma(x_1) & \ldots & \sigma(x_n) \end{pmatrix}$; we assume $x_1, ..., x_n$ to be pairwise distinct.*

If we fix a relaxed core for σ, it shall be denoted as $D(\sigma)$; the corresponding range $\sigma(D(\sigma))$ we denote as $R(\sigma)$. To get back to the traditional representation of σ, we use $\|\sigma\|$.

Hence, relaxed core representation generalizes the traditional representation. A relaxed core of σ can be seen as the set of variables σ is currently focused on. Traditionally, only active variables are in focus.

[10] Also: core representation in a relaxed form, for short: *relaxed form*.

The main purpose of relaxed form is to enable *placeholding.* This is especially important when building a substitution and a variable is confirmed as passive, hence may not be bound at some later point.

Actually, the placeholding capability of passive bindings is nothing new, it is implicitly used each time when applying the well-known scheme for composing substitutions and a variable gets deactivated: $\begin{pmatrix} x & y \\ y & x \end{pmatrix} \cdot \begin{pmatrix} x \\ y \end{pmatrix} = \begin{pmatrix} \not{x} & \not{x} & y \\ \not{x} & \not{y} & x \end{pmatrix} = \begin{pmatrix} y \\ x \end{pmatrix}$. Here, x became passive, but it is not *free* (rather, it is *confirmed passive*), therefore x/y cannot be accepted. This is depicted by striking out the column x/y as well[11].

The particular case with only passive bindings can be useful as well. A substitution σ with $D(\sigma) = M$ and $\|\sigma\| = \varepsilon$ is called *M-epsoid,* and denoted ε_M. Strictly speaking, it is just the identity substitution ε, but with a bit "more information", showing which variables are also of interest.

Example 1 (a subtlety of '$\sim$'). Any two renamings ρ, δ are equigeneral, as shown by $(\delta \cdot \rho^{-1}) \cdot \rho = \delta$ and vice versa. Hence also $\rho \sim \varepsilon$, so permuting any number of variables amounts to doing nothing. For example, $\begin{pmatrix} x & y \\ y & x \end{pmatrix} \sim \varepsilon$, which is another often-cited example of counter-intuitive behaviour of substitutions: there is loss of information [15].

As a remedy, using epsoids we could have $\begin{pmatrix} x & y \\ y & x \end{pmatrix} \cdot \begin{pmatrix} x & y \\ y & x \end{pmatrix} = \begin{pmatrix} x & y \\ x & y \end{pmatrix} = \varepsilon_{\{x,y\}}$, instead of just ε, and thus preserve the information.

Passive bindings also give us a chance to rectify a perceived shortcoming of the traditional concept of restriction:

Remark 1 (exact restriction). Observe that $Dom(\sigma \restriction_M) \subseteq M$ but not necessarily $Dom(\sigma \restriction_M) = M$, contrary to expectation, as noted in [3]. For finite M, that can be fixed by using relaxed form. So in addition to the traditional restriction we obtain a "padded" version: $\theta = \sigma \upharpoonleft\!\!\upharpoonleft_M$ would mean that $\theta = \sigma \restriction_M$ and $D(\theta) = M$. As before, $\sigma \upharpoonleft\!\!\upharpoonleft_{Vars(t)}$ is abbreviated to $\sigma \upharpoonleft\!\!\upharpoonleft_t$.

The concepts of extension, union and sum of substitutions can be simply taken over to relaxed representation. For example, if $\sigma = \begin{pmatrix} x_1 & \dots & x_n \\ s_1 & \dots & s_n \end{pmatrix}$ and $\theta = \begin{pmatrix} y_1 & \dots & y_m \\ t_1 & \dots & t_m \end{pmatrix}$ are substitutions in relaxed form with $x_1, \dots, x_n \parallel y_1, \dots, y_m$, then $\sigma \uplus \theta = \begin{pmatrix} x_1 & \dots & x_n & y_1 & \dots & y_m \\ s_1 & \dots & s_n & t_1 & \dots & t_m \end{pmatrix}$.

We shall need substitutions laying claim on all variables of the given term (and on nothing else) like $\sigma \upharpoonleft\!\!\upharpoonleft_t$. So we say that a substitution σ in relaxed form is *t-focused* if $D(\sigma) = Vars(t)$.

More generally, σ is *complete* for t if its relaxed core is variable-richer than t, i. e. $D(\sigma) \supseteq Vars(t)$. In that case, extensions of σ still map t in the same way:

---

[11] We may strike out passive pairs when depicting a relaxed form, like $\begin{pmatrix} \dots & \not{x} & \dots \\ \dots & \not{x} & \dots \end{pmatrix}$, to visually reconcile it with the traditional representation. But as a rule, we depict passive bindings on a par with active bindings. After all, they also belong to the substitution at hand.

Lemma 1 (backward compatibility). *If σ is complete for t, then its every extension $\sigma \uplus \theta$ is complete for t and satisfies $(\sigma \uplus \theta)(t) = \sigma(t)$.*

In this paper, relaxed core representation will be used for incremental construction of a substitution in the matching algorithm *TMAT* (Sect. 4); otherwise we assume substitutions in traditional, non-relaxed representation.

As a visual reminder, a relaxed core of σ is denoted $D(\sigma)$, and the traditional core $Dom(\sigma)$.

2.6 Partial Renaming

In practice, one would like to change the variables in a term without bothering to ensure that this change is a permutation of variables. For example, the term $p(z, u, x)$ can be changed to $p(y, z, x)$ using the mapping $z \mapsto y$, $u \mapsto z$, $x \mapsto x$. Distinct variables must remain distinct after mapping, and some variables may remain the same. This is all we know about the mapping.

One possibility to model this is $\{z, u, x\}$-renaming [5, p. 35], defined as follows: Let $M \subseteq \mathbf{V}$. A substitution σ is an *M-renaming,* if σ is on M both variable-pure and injective. However, it may be arbitrary outside of $\{z, u, x\}$, so let us look at a more focused mathematical underpinning, inspired by [13, p. 22]. An M-renaming σ we call an M!-renaming, if σ is passive outside of M. Due to passivity holds $M \supseteq Dom(\sigma)$. Hence, an M!-renaming is a variable-pure substitution injective on a superset M of its core.

How to represent this? For a finite M, an M!-renaming can be represented visually, using relaxed form with relaxed core M; then we call it an *M-prenaming* [11]. Given a term t, a $Vars(t)$-prenaming is shorter called a *t-prenaming.* Summarily, prenamings are variable-pure substitutions in relaxed form with mutually distinct variables in their range.

3 Term Matching (Subsumption)

Matching of a "pattern" with an "object" is an ubiquitous operation in everyday life, science and technology. *Patterns* are more or less summarized descriptions of things or events (*objects*) that need to be recognized, e. g. regular expressions in text processing or question patterns in AI [12]. Also, patterns are a flexible way to define functions [7] and rewriting rules [3], and of course Prolog predicates (however, in Prolog retrieval is done by two-way matching, unification).

In this paper, we regard a simple kind of pattern matching, illustrated as follows. Intuitively, the terms $f(x)$ and $f(y)$ "match" each other, because each can be made to look the same as the other one (by substituting an appropriate term for its variable), while $f(x)$ and $g(x)$ do not. If asked about $f(x, y)$ and $f(x, x)$, we would probably consent that they match only in one direction, since $f(x, y)$ can be made to look like $f(x, x)$ by substituting x for y, but not the other way around. Hence, it is the following kind of pattern matching:

- both the pattern and the object are terms

- a variable matches any one term (but not two different terms)
- a non-variable matches only terms with the same outline and with arguments matched by its own.

Such a notion appears under the name *subsumption* [18], *generalization* [16,17] or *term matching* [4].

Note the difference to unification: there, a non-variable may match a variable as well. In other words, the pattern and the object of term matching are not on a par: the object is passive, its variables may not be changed (as if frozen).

Thus, in the above example $f(x,y)$ matches $f(x,x)$. But since in the literature both turns of phrase "object matches pattern" and "pattern matches object" can be found, we prefer the asymmetric wording $f(x,y)$ *subsumes* $f(x,x)$.

Definition 4 (term matching, subsumption). *A term s* matches *(or* subsumes*) a term t, if there is a substitution σ such that $\sigma(s) = t$, i. e. if $s \dot{\leqslant} t$. Then σ is called a* matcher *of s on t.*

Similarly to unifiers, a matcher σ is *relevant* if it has no extraneous variables.

In ISO Standard Prolog, there is a stricter notion of subsumption, embodied in the utility `subsumes_term/2` [9, Section 8.2.4]: A term s *strictly subsumes* a term t, if there is a substitution σ such that $\sigma(s) = \sigma(t) = t$.

Thus, $f(x)$ subsumes $f(g(x))$, but does not strictly subsume it, while $f(x,y)$ strictly subsumes $f(x,x)$. Here a matcher $\sigma = \binom{y}{x}$ is easy to find, but how to proceed in general?

Remark 2 (one-way unification). For arbitrary terms s,t it was observed in [18] that matching can be seen as one-way unification: s subsumes t iff s and $\mathit{Freeze}_{s,t}$ unify, where Freeze_r is a meta-function replacing each variable in its argument with a distinct constant not appearing in the parameter r.

Remark 3 (a naïve subsumption check). Prior to the utility `subsumes_term/2`, one-way unification used to be implemented as in Listing 1.1. The counter-examples show why fresh constants are indeed necessary.

```
naive_subsumes_chk(General, Specific) :-
    \+ ( numbervars(Specific, 0, _), \+ General = Specific ).

 ?- naive_subsumes_chk(p('$VAR'(0)), p(Z)). %shrinkage
yes
 ?- naive_subsumes_chk(p(X,X), p('$VAR'(0), Y)). %divergence
yes
```

Listing 1.1. A buggy implementation of strict subsumption

But even though matching can be checked with any unification algorithm, there are algorithms specifically made for matching. An efficient parallel algorithm is proposed in [4], and a very simple non-deterministic algorithm is given in [3]. Our contribution is a deterministic, one-pass version of the latter:

4 The Term Matching Algorithm *TMAT*

With the help of relaxed core representation, we made the term-matching algorithm from [3] deterministic and one-pass. The resulting algorithm, named *TMAT*, is shown in Fig. 1.

It receives three inputs; the first and the second one are terms to be compared, and the third is a substitution (in relaxed form) serving as an accumulator of bindings. The output of the algorithm will be a possible matcher of the first term on the second one, additive to the given substitution.

Given two terms L, R and a substitution δ in relaxed representation, a possible matcher $TMAT(L,R,\delta)$ of L on R additive to δ is computed according to the following rules:

variable
: Let L be a variable. If for some S holds $L/S \in \delta$ and $S \neq R$, then stop with *Failure("divergence")*. Else, $TMAT(L,R,\delta) := \delta \cup \binom{L}{R}$.

failure: shrinkage
: If L is not a variable, but R is, stop with *Failure("shrinkage")*.

failure: clash
: If L and R are both non-variables but with different outlines, stop with *Failure("clash")*.

decomposition
: Let $L = f(s_1,...,s_n)$ and $R = f(t_1,...,t_n)$. If there exist substitutions $\delta_1 := TMAT(s_1,t_1,\delta)$, $\delta_2 := TMAT(s_2,t_2,\delta_1)$, ... up to $\delta_n := TMAT(s_n,t_n,\delta_{n-1})$, then $TMAT(L,R,\delta) := \delta_n$.

Fig. 1. One-pass term matching by $TMAT(L,R,\delta)$

The algorithm can be justified as follows.

Theorem 3 (term matching by *TMAT***).** *Let L and R be arbitrary terms. If $TMAT(L,R,\varepsilon)$ stops with failure, then L does not subsume R. Otherwise, it will stop with a substitution δ that is a relevant matcher of L on R.*

Proof. The algorithm clearly always terminates. The rest of the claims ensue from the following properties:

1. If $TMAT(L,R,\delta)$ stops with failure, there is no substitution μ such that $\mu(L) = R$ and $\mu \supseteq \delta$.
2. If $TMAT(L,R,\delta) = \delta'$, then $\delta'(L) = R$ and $\delta' \supseteq \delta$. Hence, $TMAT(L,R,\delta)$ is a matcher of L on R extending δ. Additionally, δ' is complete for L and holds $\delta' \sqsubseteq_v L, R, \delta$.

For 1., we use two observations, readily verified by structural induction:

- If μ maps L to R, then it maps any $s \mathrel{\dot\in} L$ to its sibling $t \mathrel{\dot\in} R$.
- Each time *TMAT* is reinvoked, its arguments L and R denote a pair of siblings within the original terms.

Thus, in the "L non-variable" failure cases of Fig. 1 there can be no matcher for the original terms, notwithstanding δ.

In the "L variable" failure case, the purported matcher $\mu \sqsupseteq \delta$ would have to map one variable to two different terms (Fig. 2).

For 2., we again use structural induction. In case of a variable, the claim holds. Assume we have a case of decomposition and the claim holds for the argument terms, i. e. $\delta_1(s_1) = t_1$, $\delta_1 \sqsupseteq \delta$, $\delta_2(s_2) = t_2$, $\delta_2 \sqsupseteq \delta_1$, ..., $\delta_n(s_n) = t_n$, $\delta_n \sqsupseteq \delta_{n-1}$, and each δ_i is complete for s_i as well as relevant for s_i, t_i. Due to completeness and Lemma 1, from $\delta_n \sqsupseteq ... \sqsupseteq \delta_2 \sqsupseteq \delta_1$ follows $\delta_n(s_1) = ... = \delta_2(s_1) = t_1$ and so forth. Hence, $\delta_n(L) = R$. Clearly, $\delta_n \sqsupseteq \delta$ and δ_n is complete for L and relevant.

□

Fig. 2. Divergence error: one variable, two values

Moreover, the first rule of *TMAT* ensures that each variable of L will be bound (actively or passively), and only those. Hence, the possible outcome $\delta = TMAT(L, R, \varepsilon)$ satisfies $D(\delta) = \mathit{Vars}(L)$, i. e. it is L-focused.

Owing to the placeholding facility of relaxed form, the algorithm needs only one pass along its two input terms. Actually, *without* the placeholding facility, matching terms in just one pass would, in general, require auxiliary registers (in effect, emulating relaxed core). Example: capturing the failure in matching $f(x, x)$ on $f(x, y)$.

Remark 4 (one-way unification). The non-trivial part of the claim in Remark 2 can now be easily proved. Assuming $s = \mathit{Freeze}_{s,t}$ is unifiable, there is a substitution σ with $\sigma(s) = \mathit{Freeze}_{s,t}$. If $s \not\dot{\leq} t$, then $TMAT(s, t, \varepsilon)$ must fail. From the proof of Theorem 3 we know there must be a pair (or two) of siblings in s and t that cannot be (simultaneously) matched. But each of the three possible failures (divergence, shrinkage or clash) becomes impossible when $\sigma(s) = \mathit{Freeze}_{s,t}$.

5 Applications

The main application of *TMAT* may be for deciding *substitution generality*, a task hitherto being tackled on a case-by-case basis.

5.1 Deciding Substitution Generality

By Definition 2, $\sigma \lesssim \theta$ if there is δ with $\theta = \delta \cdot \sigma$. Clearly, $\varepsilon \lesssim \theta$ for any θ; the claim $\binom{x}{y} \not\lesssim \binom{x\ y}{y\ x}$ may not be so obvious. So how to check for arbitrary σ and θ whether $\sigma \lesssim \theta$ holds?

One possibility would be to look for a counter-example, i. e. try to find a term W such that for no substitution δ holds $\delta(\sigma(W)) = \theta(W)$. Let us call such a term a *witness* of $\sigma \not\lesssim \theta$. How to obtain it?

Intuitively, we may take W to be the list of all variables of σ and θ, i. e. $W := \mathit{VarList}((\sigma, \theta))$, and see if we can find an impasse, i. e. a pair (or two) of siblings in $\sigma(W)$ and $\theta(W)$ that cannot be (simultaneously) matched. This turns out to be sufficient.

Theorem 4 (witness). *Let σ, θ be substitutions and let $W := \mathit{VarList}((\sigma, \theta))$. Then holds: $\sigma \lesssim \theta$ iff $\sigma(W) \dot{\leqslant} \theta(W)$. Additionally, if $\mathit{TMAT}(\sigma(W), \theta(W), \varepsilon) = \delta$, then $\delta \cdot \sigma = \theta$.*

Proof. If for some δ holds $\delta \cdot \sigma = \theta$, then surely $\delta(\sigma(t)) = \theta(t)$ for any t. For the other direction, assume there is a matcher of $\sigma(W)$ on $\theta(W)$. By Theorem 3, we can choose a relevant matcher by setting $\mu := \mathit{TMAT}(\sigma(W), \theta(W), \varepsilon)$, so $\mu(\sigma(W)) = \theta(W)$ and $\mu \sqsubseteq_v \sigma(W), \theta(W) \sqsubseteq_v \sigma, \theta$. If for some $x \in \mathbf{V}$ holds $\mu(\sigma(x)) \neq \theta(x)$, then clearly $x \notin \sigma, \theta$, hence the inequality becomes $\mu(x) \neq x$, meaning $x \in \mathit{Dom}(\mu)$, which contradicts the supposed relevance of μ. □

Theorem 4 shows that $W_{\sigma,\theta} := \mathit{VarList}((\sigma, \theta))$ is the only potential witness term ever needed: if there is an impasse, $\mathit{TMAT}(\sigma(W_{\sigma,\theta}), \theta(W_{\sigma,\theta}), \varepsilon)$ will find it, and if there is no impasse, it will find a matcher. Therefore, we call $W_{\sigma,\theta}$ the *sure candidate* for a witness of $\sigma \not\lesssim \theta$.

As a consequence of the theorem, we obtain a simple visual criterion.

Corollary 1 (witness). *The relation $\sigma \lesssim \theta$ does not hold iff for some W with $W \sqsubseteq_v \sigma, \theta$ any of the following holds:*

1. *At some corresponding positions, $\sigma(W)$ exhibits a non-variable, and $\theta(W)$ exhibits either a variable ("shrinkage"), or a non-variable with a different outline ("clash").*
2. *$\sigma(W)$ exibits two occurrences of variable x, but at the corresponding positions in $\theta(W)$ there are two distinct terms ("divergence of x").*

A few test runs are shown in the following pictures and in the proofs of the two remaining legacy claims. Mostly the sure candidate is used, with the exception of Legacy 6.

5.2 Illustration: Subtleties of "$\lesssim$"

Let us go back to the introductory examples. It has been noted in [2] that $\binom{x}{y}$ is more general than $\binom{x\ y}{a\ a}$, but not more general than $\binom{x}{a}$, assuming $x \neq y$.

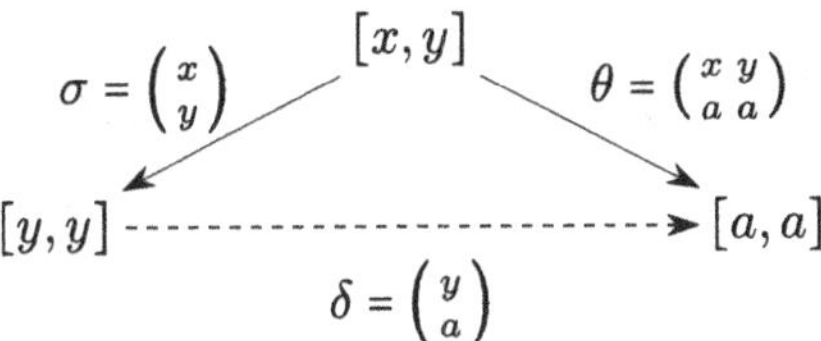

Fig. 3. Example of confirmed $\sigma \lesssim \theta$

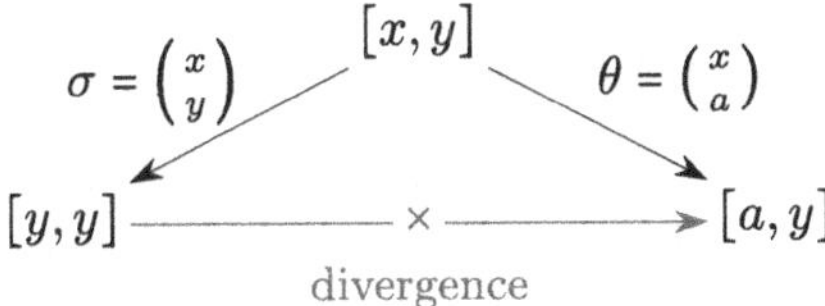

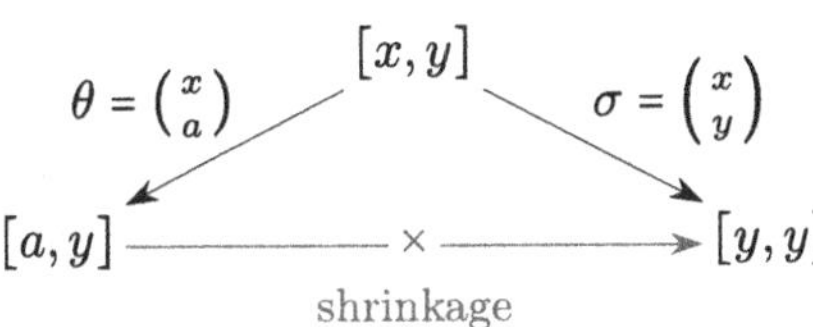

Fig. 4. Substitutions σ and θ incomparable by "$\lesssim$"

The former claim is justified by $\binom{x\ y}{a\ a} = \binom{y}{a} \cdot \binom{x}{y}$. Here, a matcher was not difficult to guess, and the same one was found by *TMAT* (Fig. 3).

The latter claim, $\binom{x}{y}$ not being more general than $\binom{x}{a}$, is much less obvious; the proof by *TMAT* is in Fig. 4. The claim is a simplified form of a counter-example by Hai-Ping Ko, reported in [19, p. 148].

The Ko example was pivotal in showing that the strong completeness theorem for SLD-resolution as formulated in [13] does not hold, which stresses the importance of a decision procedure for substitution generality.

The example claims that $\binom{x}{f(y,z)}$ is not more general than $\binom{x}{f(a,a)}$. For proof, it was observed: if $\delta \cdot \binom{x}{f(y,z)} = \binom{x}{f(a,a)}$, then $\{y/a, z/a\} \subseteq \delta$, therefore even if one of y, z (but not both) were equal to x, at least one of the bindings $y/a, z/a$ would have to be in $\binom{x}{f(a,a)}$.

Notwithstanding the elegance of custom-made proofs like this one, they need some attention. Instead, refuting substitution generality can be delegated to a simple mechanical procedure like *TMAT*, for this example as well (Fig. 5). In short, the witness method alleviates the need to look around for a contradiction (and to put it together afterwards as a logical chain of reasoning).

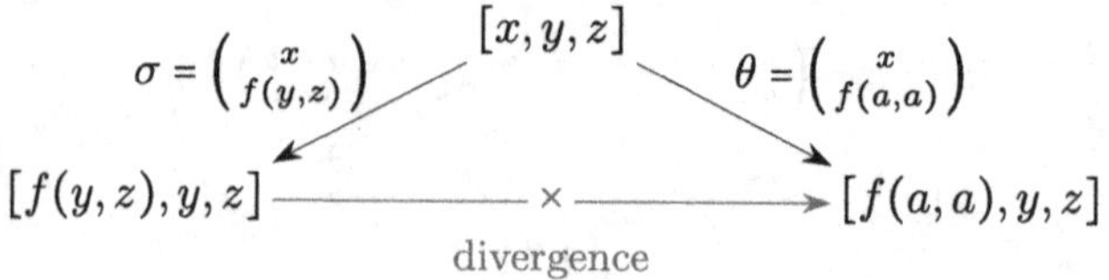

Fig. 5. Example of refuted $\sigma \lesssim \theta$ (Hai-Ping Ko)

5.3 Deciding Substitution Equigenerality

Clearly, if an algorithm decides substitution generality, then equigenerality as well. This gives us an opportunity to showcase *TMAT* in several more examples.

Example 2 ('$\sim$' is not composition-stable). To show that equigenerality is not compatible with composition, [5] uses $\sigma := \binom{y}{x}$, $\sigma' := \binom{x}{y}$ and $\theta := \binom{x}{z}$. Then $\sigma \sim \sigma'$, but $\theta \cdot \sigma = \binom{x\ y}{z\ z} \nsim \theta \cdot \sigma' = \binom{x}{y}$, assuming $z \neq y$. The non-equigenerality is perhaps not obvious, so in Fig. 6 we verify[12] it by *TMAT*.

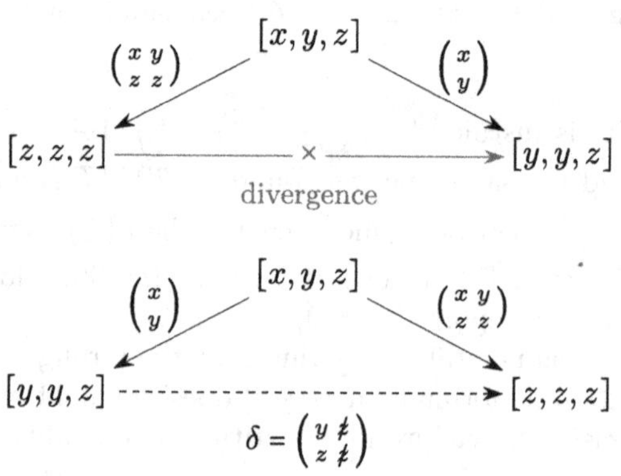

Fig. 6. Checking equigenerality of substitutions

Now let us use the witness method to prove Legacy 2, in a stronger formulation (with added relevance):

Legacy 5 (substitution equigenerality, [2, p. 25]). *Substitutions θ and θ' are equigeneral iff for some renaming ρ satisfying $\rho \sqsubseteq_v \theta, \theta'$ holds $\rho \cdot \theta = \theta'$.*

Proof. If $\rho \cdot \theta = \theta'$ for an invertible substitution ρ, then clearly $\theta \lesssim \theta'$ and $\theta \lesssim \theta'$.

[12] In this case, the second triangle was not necessary. We only include it to show an outcome of *TMAT* with some *passive pairs*.

For the other direction, let $\theta \lesssim \theta'$ and $\theta' \lesssim \theta$, and let $W := VarList((\theta, \theta'))$. By Theorem 4, we know that $TMAT(\theta(W), \theta'(W), \varepsilon)$ must succeed, as well as $TMAT(\theta'(W), \theta(W), \varepsilon)$. Observe that in both of the $TMAT$ calls the *same* two terms are matched, so the case where one of a sibling pair is a variable and the other a non-variable is clearly not possible (shrinkage failure); dito for the case of the same variable in the one vis-à-vis two distinct variables in the other (divergence failure). Hence, any bindings obtained by $TMAT$ are necessarily variable-pure with mutually distinct variables in range, i. e. we obtain a *prenaming* (defined on p. 7).

Now let $\delta := TMAT(\theta(W), \theta'(W), \varepsilon)$. By construction, δ is a $\theta(W)$-prenaming, and satisfies the generality equation $\delta \cdot \theta = \theta'$. Yet δ does not have to be a renaming, and we want one.

So assume δ is not a renaming, i. e. not a permutation of variables, and let us embed it in a relevant renaming. There is $y \in R(\delta)$ with $y \notin D(\delta)$, as in Fig. 7. By construction, $y \,\dot{\in}\, W$, so its whereabouts may be

1. $y \in Dom(\theta)$
2. $y \in Dom(\theta') \setminus Dom(\theta)$
3. $y \in (Vars(Ran(\theta)) \cup Vars(Ran(\theta'))) \setminus (Dom(\theta) \cup Dom(\theta'))$.

Actually, only the first case is possible: In the last case, $\theta(y) = \theta'(y) = y$, so $y/y \in \delta$, which contradicts the assumption $y \notin D(\delta)$ and is thus impossible. In the middle case $\theta(y) = y$ and $\theta'(y) \neq y$, so $y/\theta'(y) \in \delta$, also impossible.

Therefore, y is bound by θ, hence $(\delta \uplus \binom{y}{\_}) \cdot \theta = \delta \cdot \theta$ for every binding $y/\_$, where '_' means arbitrary term. Thus, a binding for y can be added without disturbing the generality equation. The empty places '_' in the (finitely many) added bindings can[13] be populated so as to obtain a permutation of variables. As a final touch, any passive pairs can be discarded, to obtain traditional core representation.

In the example in Fig. 7, there is only one choice for a relevant embedding, resulting in the renaming $\binom{x\ y}{y\ x}$. □

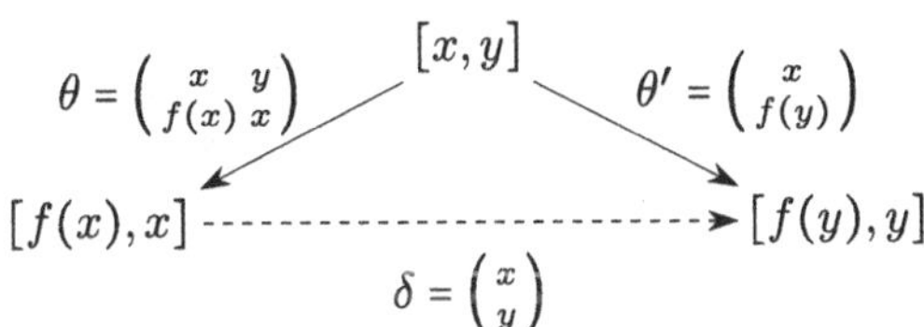

Fig. 7. A variable-pure matcher that is not a permutation

[13] For a "natural" choice of embedding, see [11, Sec. 5.1].

5.4 Most General Unifiers and Their Possible Relevance

Substitution generality is part of the concept of a *most general unifier* too.

Example 3 (simple pair). It is known (e. g. from [2]) that for any $x = t$ satisfying $x \notin t$ holds $\binom{x}{t} \in MguSet(x = t)$. The nontrivial part, maximal generality, can also be proved by the witness method:

Proof. For this, we take an arbitrary $\sigma \in MguSet(x = t)$ and build the witness-method diagram (Fig. 8), starting with $VarList((x, t, \sigma)) = [x, y_1, ..., y_n]$.

Due to $\sigma(x) = \sigma(t)$, the left-hand term of the diagram subsumes the right-hand term. According to Theorem 3, the diagram will commute, i. e. *TMAT* will produce a δ satisfying $\delta \cdot \binom{x}{t} = \sigma$, which proves $\binom{x}{t} \lesssim \sigma$. □

Additionally, we know that the substitutions σ and δ must coincide on $Vars((t, y_1, ..., y_n))$, the set which equals to $D(\delta)$, hence $\delta = \sigma \Downarrow_{t, y_1, ..., y_n}$.

Example: for $t := f(y)$ and $\sigma := \begin{pmatrix} x & y \\ f(z) & z \end{pmatrix}$ we obtain $\delta = \sigma \Downarrow_{\{y,z\}} = \begin{pmatrix} y & z \\ z & z \end{pmatrix}$.

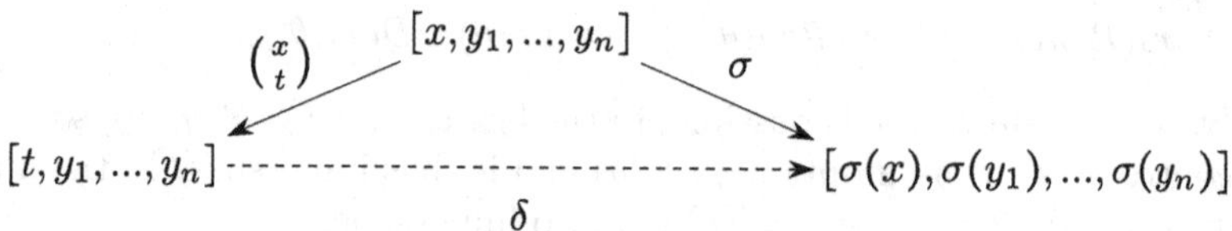

Fig. 8. Proving maximal generality of $\binom{x}{t}$

Example 4 (a non-relevant mgu). Let variables x, y, z be mutually distinct. According to Fig. 6, $\sigma := \begin{pmatrix} x & y \\ z & z \end{pmatrix}$ is not an mgu of x and y, being not more general than their obvious unifier $\mu := \binom{x}{y}$. However, it may come as a surprise that its extension $\theta := \begin{pmatrix} x & y & z \\ z & z & y \end{pmatrix}$ *is* an mgu of x and y (Fig. 9).

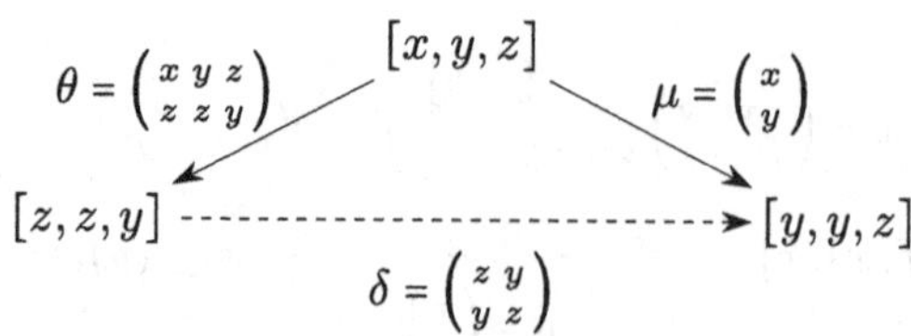

Fig. 9. An extension can be more general

The mgu θ above happened to be non-relevant. Idempotent mgus do not have this option, they are always relevant [2]; this can be proved in a focused way using the witness method:

Legacy 6 (relevance). *Every idempotent mgu is relevant.*

Proof. Assume $\sigma \in \mathit{MguSet}(E)$ is idempotent, but not relevant, i. e. there is $z \in \mathit{Vars}(\sigma) \smallsetminus \mathit{Vars}(E)$. To refute maximal generality of σ, let us find a unifier θ of E with $\sigma \not\mathrel{\dot{\leqslant}} \theta$. Technically, we will construct θ and a witness term w satisfying Corollary 1.

Case $z \in \mathit{Dom}(\sigma)$*:* Here we choose $\theta := \sigma\restriction_{-z}$ (defined on p. 4). If σ is an idempotent unifier of E, then so is θ, by Legacy 1.

Subcase 1: $\sigma(z)$ is ground. Take $w := z$. Then $\theta(w) = z$ is a variable, so we have shrinkage.

Subcase 2: $\sigma(z)$ contains a variable, say x, pictured as $\sigma(z)=\boxed{x}$. By Legacy 1, $x \notin \mathit{Dom}(\sigma)$, so $x \neq z$. Let $w := [x, z]$. Then $\sigma([x, z])=[x, \boxed{x}]$, whereas $\theta([x, z])=[x, z]$. If $\boxed{x}$ is not a variable, we have shrinkage, otherwise divergence.

Case $z \in \mathit{Vars}(\mathit{Ran}(\sigma)) = \mathit{Vars}(\mathit{Ran}(\sigma)) \smallsetminus \mathit{Dom}(\sigma)$*:* There is $x \in \mathit{Dom}(\sigma)$ (and therefore $x \neq z$) with $\sigma(x)=\boxed{z}$. Here we take $w := [x, z]$ and θ to be a relevant mgu of E, e. g. an outcome of the Martelli-Montanari scheme. Then $\sigma([x, z]) = [\boxed{z}, z]$ and $\theta([x, z]) = [\theta(x), z]$, with $z \notin \theta(x)$ due to relevance. Even if $\boxed{z} \mathrel{\dot{\leqslant}} \theta(x)$, we obtain a failure (divergence of z).

□

6 Summary

A simple one-pass term matching algorithm *TMAT* is proposed. It is a deterministic version of the algorithm given in [3], enabled by *relaxed core* representation of substitutions, where passive pairs x/x may appear.

Apart from term generality, *TMAT* also decides *substitution generality*, and hence equigenerality of two substitutions as well, by reducing it to term generality (*witness term* method). This method alleviates the need for ad-hoc proofs involving substitution generality.

Acknowledgements. Many thanks to Ch. Beierle, M. D. Kulaš and the anonymous referees for helpful comments on earlier drafts of this paper.

References

1. Amato, G., Scozzari, F.: Optimality in goal-dependent analysis of sharing. Theory Pract. Logic Program. **9**(5), 617–689 (2009). https://doi.org/10.1017/S1471068409990111
2. Apt, K.R.: From Logic Programming to Prolog. Prentice Hall, Hoboken (1997)
3. Bezem, M., Klop, J.W., de Vrijer, R. (eds.): Term Rewriting Systems, chap. First-order term rewriting systems. Cambridge University Press, Cambridge (2003)
4. Dwork, C., Kanellakis, P., Mitchell, J.C.: On the sequential nature of unification. J. Logic Program. **1**, 35–50 (1984). https://doi.org/10.1016/0743-1066(84)90022-0

5. Eder, E.: Properties of substitutions and unifications. J. Symb. Comput. **1**(1), 31–46 (1985). https://doi.org/10.1016/S0747-7171(85)80027-4
6. Gallier, J.: Logic for Computer Science: Foundations of Automatic Theorem Proving, 2 edn. Dover, Mineola (2015)
7. Hudak, P., Peterson, J., Fasel, J.: A gentle introduction to Haskell. Version 98 (2000). http://www.haskell.org/tutorial
8. Huet, G.: Résolution d'équations dans des langages d'ordre 1,2,...,ω. Ph.D. thesis, U. Paris VII (1976). http://cristal.inria.fr/~huet/bib.html
9. ISO/IEC JTC 1/SC 22: Information technology - Programming languages - Prolog - Part 1: General core. Technical Corrigendum 2. ISO/IEC 13211-1:1995/Cor. 2:2012(en) (2012). https://www.iso.org/standard/58033.html
10. Jacobs, D., Langen, A.: Static analysis of logic programs for independent AND parallelism. J. Log. Program. **13**(2–3), 291–314 (1992). https://doi.org/10.1016/0743-1066(92)90034-Z
11. Kulaš, M.: A practical view on renaming. In: Schwarz, S., Voigtländer, J. (eds.) Proceedings of WLP'15/'16 and WFLP'16. EPTCS, vol. 234, pp. 27–41 (2017). https://doi.org/10.4204/EPTCS.234.3
12. Lally, A., Fodor, P.: Natural language processing with Prolog in the IBM Watson system. Newsletter of ALP (2011). http://www.cs.nmsu.edu/ALP/2011/03
13. Lloyd, J.W.: Foundations of Logic Programming, 2 edn. Springer, Heidelberg (1987). https://doi.org/10.1007/978-3-642-83189-8
14. Martelli, A., Montanari, U.: An efficient unification algorithm. ACM Trans. Prog. Lang. Syst. **4**(2), 258–282 (1982). https://doi.org/10.1145/357162.357169
15. Palamidessi, C.: Algebraic properties of idempotent substitutions. In: Paterson, M.S. (ed.) ICALP 1990. LNCS, vol. 443, pp. 386–399. Springer, Heidelberg (1990). https://doi.org/10.1007/BFb0032046
16. Plotkin, G.D.: Automatic methods of inductive inference. Ph.D. thesis, University of Edinburgh (1971). http://homepages.inf.ed.ac.uk/gdp
17. Reynolds, J.C.: Transformational systems and the algebraic structure of atomic formulas. In: Meltzer, B., Michie, D. (eds.) Machine Intelligence, vol. 5, pp. 135–151. Edinburgh University Press (1970)
18. Robinson, J.A.: A machine-oriented logic based on the resolution principle. J. ACM **12**(1), 23–41 (1965). https://doi.org/10.1145/321250.321253. J. H. Siekmann and G. Wrightson (eds.): Automation of reasoning: Classical papers 1 (1957-1966), Springer-Verlag (1983)
19. Shepherdson, J.C.: The role of standardising apart in logic programming. Theor. Comput. Sci. **129**(1), 143–166 (1994). https://doi.org/10.1016/0304-3975(94)90084-1

Knowledge Representation and AI-Based Learning

A Novel EGs-Based Framework for Systematic Propositional-Formula Simplification

Jordina Francès de Mas[1(✉)] and Juliana Bowles[1,2]

[1] School of Computer Science, University of St Andrews, St Andrews KY16 9SX, Scotland, UK
{jfdm2,jkfb}@st-andrews.ac.uk
[2] Software Competence Centre Hagenberg (SCCH), 4232 Hagenberg im Mühlkreis, Austria

Abstract. This paper presents a novel simplification calculus for propositional logic derived from Peirce's Existential Graphs' rules of inference and implication graphs. Our rules can be applied to arbitrary propositional logic formulae (not only in CNF), are equivalence-preserving, guarantee a monotonically decreasing number of clauses and literals, and maximise the preservation of structural problem information. Our techniques can also be seen as higher-level SAT preprocessing, and we show how one of our rules (TWSR) generalises and streamlines most of the known equivalence-preserving SAT preprocessing methods. We further show how this rule can be extended with a novel n-ary implication graph to capture all known equivalence-preserving preprocessing procedures. Finally, we discuss the complexity and implementation of our framework as a solver-agnostic algorithm to simplify Boolean satisfiability problems and arbitrary propositional formula.

Keywords: Simplification · Existential graphs · Equivalence-preserving preprocessing · Propositional satisfiability · Diagrammatic reasoning · Knowledge representation · Implication graphs · Hypergraphs

1 Introduction

Propositional logic simplification is closely related to the reduction of complex Boolean algebraic expressions, logic circuits' minimisation, and Boolean satisfiability (SAT) preprocessing techniques. Simplification is crucial to reduce the complexity of a problem, which makes it easier to understand, reason about, and work with. Minimising the size of a problem also reduces memory usage and speeds up solving times [30], as fewer steps are required to reach a solution or

J. Bowles—Bowles is partially supported by Austrian FWF Meitner Fellowship M-3338 N.

R. Glück and B. Kafle (Eds.): LOPSTR 2023, LNCS 14330, pp. 169–187, 2023.
https://doi.org/10.1007/978-3-031-45784-5_11

proof. Unfortunately, existing minimisation algorithms for Boolean expressions such as Karnaugh maps [18] or the Quine-McCluskey algorithm [22] become increasingly inefficient as the number of variables grows, making them unusable for large formulas. To minimise larger Boolean problems, we can only resort to suboptimal heuristic methods, such as the ESPRESSO logic minimiser [27]. Intuitively, all equivalence-preserving simplifications can also be achieved by applying the axioms of Boolean algebra or rules of inference in nontrivial ways, or by utilising proof systems such as sequent calculus or natural deduction; however, there are currently no known generic or systematic methods of doing so.

Many simplification techniques in the field of SAT use heuristics too, but a greater emphasis is placed on efficiency so that they can be used on very large problems. Preprocessing has actually become an essential part of SAT solving, with some of the most powerful SAT solvers interleaving preprocessing with solving steps, a technique referred to as *inprocessing* [12,17]. Despite the already vast body of literature on preprocessing (see Chapter 9 in the latest Handbook of Satisfiability [7]), there is still much ongoing research into finding efficient rewriting and simplification techniques to expedite or better inform the solving phase (see, e.g., [1,6,20,21]), which evidences the importance and complexity of this topic. However, SAT problems commonly need to be translated into a standard form (usually conjunctive normal form (CNF)) before solving, and most procedures apply to this form only. Consequently, most preprocessing techniques in the literature only study or work on CNF formulae. Moreover, this encoding process can be non-equivalence-preserving, result in bigger problems, or lead to the loss of important structural properties of the original problem, such as symmetries, which can detrimentally impact the preprocessing and solving phases [1,11].

In this paper, we present novel simplification techniques for zeroth-order logic derived from Peirce's existential graphs' rules of inference and implication graphs. Our rules can be seen as SAT equivalence-preserving preprocessing techniques applicable to arbitrary propositional-logic formulae (not only in CNF) that guarantee a monotonically decreasing number of variables, clauses and literals and maximise the preservation of structural problem information. Existential graphs offer a fresh view of preprocessing never explored before that allowed us to independently rediscover many simplification techniques known in the world of SAT preprocessing, understand the underlying connections between apparently distinct methods, and generalise many of them. We compare our rules with the state-of-the-art and discuss their advantages and limitations. In particular, our last rule (TWSR) can efficiently emulate complex combinations of preprocessing techniques, and we propose even more powerful extensions to it.

The remainder of our paper is structured as follows. Section 2 introduces basic concepts and notation on existential graphs, propositional logic and implication graphs that will be used in the rest of the paper. In Sect. 3, we present our simplification rules and explain their properties. In Sect. 4, we discuss the implementation of our approach and point to future work, including a generalisation of our TWSR rule. Section 5 ends the paper with some concluding remarks.

2 Background and Notation

Modern formal logics, including formulations of SAT problems, are usually presented in a symbolic and linear fashion. **Existential graphs** (EGs) [29,31], by contrast, are a *non-symbolic* and *non-linear* system for logical expressions, where propositions are drawn on a two-dimensional sheet, negation is represented by oval lines (aka *cuts*), and all elements contained in the same area (delimited by negation lines) are in implicit conjunction. We say that an area is *evenly* (resp. *oddly*) *nested* if it is enclosed by an even (resp. odd) number of cuts. Note that a blank sheet of assertion denotes *true* ($\top$), has nesting level 0 and therefore it is assumed to be evenly enclosed. In Fig. 1, we present a few introductory examples illustrating that the combination of these simple primitives suffices to express any propositional-logic formula. Extensions of EGs allow for the representation of first-order-logic and higher-order-logic formulas, but these are beyond the scope of this paper (for more details, see e.g. [9,26]).

(a) EG of $P \wedge \neg Q$ or, equivalently, $\neg Q \wedge P$. This EG is also the canonical form of infinitely many equivalent formulas, such as $\neg(P \rightarrow Q)$ or $\neg(\neg(\neg(\neg P \vee Q))) \wedge (R \vee \neg R)$.

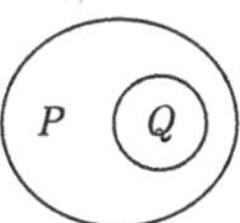

(b) EG of $\neg(P \wedge \neg Q)$ or, equivalently, $\neg P \vee Q$, or $P \rightarrow Q$.

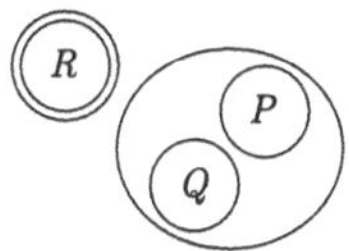

(c) EG of $\neg(\neg R) \wedge \neg(\neg Q \wedge \neg P)$ or, equivalently, $(P \vee Q) \wedge R$, or $R \wedge (\neg P \rightarrow Q)$, or $R \wedge (\neg Q \rightarrow P)$.

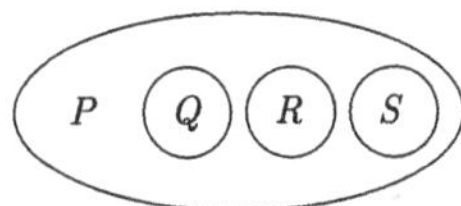

(d) EG of $\neg(P \wedge \neg Q \wedge \neg R \wedge \neg S)$, which can be linearly represented by many equivalent formulations, such as $P \rightarrow (Q \vee R \vee S)$, or $(P \wedge \neg Q) \rightarrow (R \vee S)$, or $(P \wedge \neg Q \wedge \neg R) \rightarrow S$, or $\neg P \vee Q \vee R \vee S$.

Fig. 1. Examples of existential graphs of propositional-logic formulae.

EGs cannot only represent propositional-logic formulae, but they are, in fact, equivalent to sentential languages [25,26,33]. Even if this diagrammatic notation is less commonly used, it offers a simple, elegant, and easy-to-learn alternative that comes with a sound and complete deductive system, which has many advantages over the traditional Gentzen's rules of *natural deduction* and *sequent calculus* and, thus, over all other rewriting methods based on the latter. Most significantly, EGs' inference rules are symmetric, and no bookkeeping of previous steps is required in the process of inferring a graph from another. Furthermore, as illustrated in Fig. 1, EGs' graphical non-ordered nature provides a canonical representation of a logical formula that, in linear notation, can take many equivalent forms. Another key and perhaps underexplored advantage is that the visual representation allows for the recognition of patterns that would otherwise be obscured in nested clausal form. Finally, since EGs are easily transferred to any notation, they can help clarify the relationships between diverse reasoning methods, such as resolution and natural deduction and, ultimately, help understand the foundations of proof theory.

We assume the reader is familiar with basic notions of *propositional logic* and the *Boolean satisfiability problem* (**SAT**). In what follows, we will use a subscript to indicate the size of a clause (e.g. C_8 refers to a clause of size 8) and, given a clause $C_n = (l_1 \vee l_2 \vee \cdots \vee l_n)$, we refer to the set of its literals as $\text{lit}(C_n) = \{l_1, l_2, \cdots, l_n\}$.

As shown in Fig. 1, nested cuts can be interpreted as implication, so it is easy to see that every binary clause, e.g. $C_2 = (x \vee y)$, admits the following two interpretations: $(\neg x \rightarrow y)$ and its logically equivalent contrapositive $(\neg y \rightarrow x)$. Thus, binary clauses provide the information needed to build what is known as the **binary implication graph** (BIG) [2] of the formula, which is a directed graph where edges represent implication, and nodes are all the literals occurring in binary clauses and their negations (see Fig. 2).

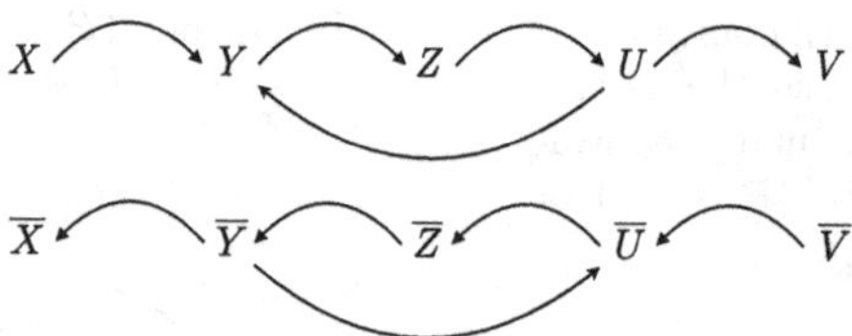

Fig. 2. BIG of $\varphi = (\overline{X} \vee Y) \wedge (\overline{Y} \vee Z) \wedge (\overline{Z} \vee U) \wedge (\overline{U} \vee V) \wedge (\overline{U} \vee Y)$.

If there exists a directed path from vertex x to vertex y, we say that y is a **descendant** of (or *reachable* from) x, and we say that x is an **ancestor** of y. We will denote the set of all descendants (resp. ancestors) of a vertex z by des(z) (resp. anc(z)). We say that two vertices u and v in a directed graph G are strongly connected iff there are directed paths from u to v and from v to u. A subgraph $S \subseteq G$ is a **strongly connected component** if all its vertices are strongly connected and they are not strongly connected with any other vertex of $G \setminus S$ (i.e. every vertex in S is reachable from every other vertex in S and S is maximal with this property wrt G). Every strongly connected component corresponds to an **equivalence class**. Two elements belong to the same equivalence class iff they are equivalent. We can choose one of the elements in the class as a **class representative** to refer to the whole equivalence class.

3 Preprocessing Framework

3.1 Simplification Rules

Charles S. Peirce (1839–1914) provided the following sound and complete set of inference rules for EGs (for more details, see e.g. [9,24,29,31]), where an *EG-element* is any arbitrary clause[1] expressed as an EG:

1. (i) **Insertion:** in an odd area (nesting level $2k+1, k \in \mathbb{N}$), we can draw any EG-element.
   (e) **Erasure:** any EG-element in an even area (nesting level $2k, k \in \mathbb{N}$) can be deleted.
2. (i) **Iteration:** any EG-element in an area a can be duplicated in a or in any nested areas within a.
   (e) **Deiteration:** any EG-element whose occurrence could be the result of iteration may be erased.
3. (i) **Double Cut Insertion:** a double negation may be drawn around any collection of zero or more EG-elements in any area.
   (e) **Double Cut Erasure:** any double negations can be erased.

We investigate the reversibility properties of Peirce's EGs inference rules and their combinations in order to determine which sequences of rule applications and underlying restrictions ensure non-increasing model equivalence. Note that rules $2i$ & $2e$ and $3i$ & $3e$ are mutually reversible and, thus, preserve equivalence, whilst the first two rules are not.

To the best of our knowledge, the EG calculus has only been studied as a proof system and used to prove logical assertions by inference [9,31], but it has never been used as a simplification method nor restricted to equivalence-preserving rules.

In what follows, we present the definitions of each of our rules alongside a visual exemplification and compare them to existing preprocessing techniques. Throughout, let φ be an arbitrary propositional formula and BIG(φ) denote its binary implication graph.

Singleton Wipe. This rule is equivalent to a combination of Shin's *rules 1* and *2* [29], and to Peirce's EGs *deiteration rule* (2e above) restricted to single EG-elements (unit clauses) and extended to account for the generation of empty cuts. Most importantly, it can be seen as a generalisation of *unit propagation* applicable over arbitrary formulae, not only in CNF.

Definition 1 (Singleton wipe rule (SWR)). *Let x be a singleton (i.e. a literal or clause of size 1) in any clause or subclause of φ. Any other instances of x in the same clause or its subclauses can be deleted, and any generated empty subclause (i.e. $\neg()$) results in the deletion of its parent clause.*

[1] We refer here to the generic notion of 'clause', understood as a propositional formula consisting of a finite collection of literals and logical connectives.

From an EG point of view, any copy of a single EG-element in the same or any nested (inner) areas can be erased, and every area containing an empty cut (i.e. a negation oval) shall be deleted.

Note that, in linear notation, clausal levels can be distinguished by parenthesis (either explicit or implicit in accordance with the precedence of logical operators). Moreover, note that empty cuts are generated when the negation of the propagated singleton is encountered.

Example 1. Let $\varphi = P \wedge ((A \wedge D \wedge P \wedge (A \rightarrow B) \wedge (\neg C \vee D)) \vee (P \wedge Q \wedge R) \vee T \vee (S \wedge T) \vee \neg(X \rightarrow (X \wedge Y \wedge Z))) \wedge \neg T$. Several singletons can be propagated at the same or inner levels, namely $A, D, P, \neg T$, and X. This is not easy for a human reader to detect if the formula is expressed in linear form, but it becomes apparent when expressed as an EG (see Fig. 3). If we apply SWR to φ, we obtain the following simplified equivalent form: $\varphi' = SWR(\varphi) = P \wedge \neg T \wedge ((A \wedge B \wedge D) \vee (Q \wedge R) \vee (X \wedge (\neg Y \vee \neg Z)))$. Note that transforming φ to CNF would result in a formula of 30 clauses of sizes 1 to 5 with a total of 124 literals, where traditional unit propagation could only be applied to the unit clauses P and $\neg T$, and the resulting (partially) simplified formula would have 26 clauses of sizes 1 to 5 with a total of 98 literals. Instead, if we transform φ' to CNF, we obtain a formula with 14 clauses of sizes 1 to 4 and a total of 44 literals.

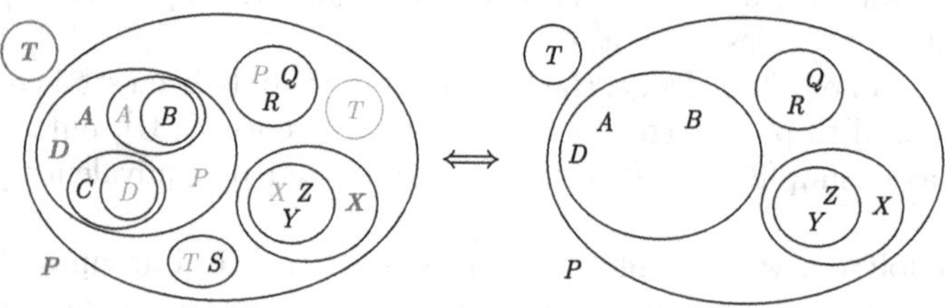

Fig. 3. EG of φ (left), where the EG-elements coloured in orange can be simplified by propagating their outermost instances, marked in blue, to obtain φ' (right). (Color figure online)

Remark 1. SWR effectively tells us that each EG-element (literal, clause, or subclause) contributes to the truth value of the whole EG (i.e. the whole formula) at its outermost occurrence, and the presence or absence of more deeply nested instances is irrelevant.

Equivalence Projection. This rule can be achieved by nontrivial applications of the iteration, deiteration and cut rules (2*i*, 2*e*, 3*i* and 3*e* from Sect. 3.1) and noticing that two propositional variables x and y are equivalent (resp. opposites) whenever we have the following two clauses: $(x \vee \overline{y}) \wedge (\overline{x} \vee y)$ (resp. $(x \vee y) \wedge (\overline{x} \vee \overline{y})$).

This is obvious from the implication interpretation of these clauses as EGs that we saw in Sect. 2.

Trying all possible (de)iterations of binary clauses within each other is clearly impractical, and requires a nontrivial search for candidate EG-elements and backtracking. However, if we use the BIG of the formula to inform our procedure, it becomes straightforward and efficient.

Definition 2 (Equivalence projection rule (EPR)). *Every* strongly connected component *of* BIG(φ) *corresponds to an* equivalence class, *and all same-level or inner-level literals in the equivalence class can be substituted by their* class representative. *If a same-level or inner-level subclause contains multiple elements of the equivalence class, they can all be substituted by a single instance of the representative literal. If a subclause contains both an element of the equivalence class and the negation of an element in the equivalence class, it can be deleted. The* BIG(EPR(φ)) *of the remaining binary clauses is guaranteed to be acyclic and corresponds to the* condensation *of* BIG(φ).

The deletion of literals and clauses in EPR can be seen as a nested application of the SWR rule (see Definition 1) performed immediately after a substitution step. The replacement part of EPR is in fact equivalent to a well-known preprocessing technique called *equivalent-literal substitution* [14,19], but ours does not require a formula to be in CNF form. Moreover, our rule is equivalence-preserving since we keep the information of any equivalence classes, and both substitution and simplification are applied in one step. Additionally, the BIG built and updated in this preprocessing phase will inform other preprocessing techniques, so the effort of building the graph will be reused and further exploited.

Nested Equivalence Projection. Equivalence projection can be applied not only at the formula level but also within nested cuts, which enhances its reduction powers and makes EPR applicable to formulae in forms other than CNF too (see Example 2). To do so, we maintain local implication graphs corresponding to the binary clauses present at each nesting level.

Example 2. Let $\varphi = (\overline{X} \vee \overline{Y} \vee \overline{A}) \wedge \neg((A \rightarrow B) \wedge (B \rightarrow A) \wedge (\overline{X} \vee \overline{Y} \vee \overline{B}))$. We generate the BIG of any area with binary clauses, which in this case is only the big level-1 area. The nested BIG contains a strongly connected component $[A] = \{A, B\}$, so the innermost B can be substituted by the representative A. The resulting ternary clause can then be wiped by the deiteration rule (and our rules to come), leading to the negation of the equivalence found (see Fig. 4). Hence φ can be simplified to $\varphi' = \text{EPR}(\varphi) = (\overline{X} \vee \overline{Y} \vee \overline{A})$ with $[A] = \{A, \overline{B}\}$.

Even higher reductions can be achieved if we consider equivalence—and, as we will see, implication chains—in the union of nested implication graphs (see Example 3).

Example 3. Let $\varphi = (\overline{X} \vee \overline{Y} \vee \overline{A}) \wedge (A \rightarrow B) \wedge (B \rightarrow A) \wedge \neg((C \rightarrow B) \wedge (B \rightarrow C) \wedge (\overline{X} \vee \overline{Y} \vee \overline{C}))$. We generate the BIG of any area with binary clauses, which in this case are the outermost area and the biggest level-1 area. The outer BIG contains

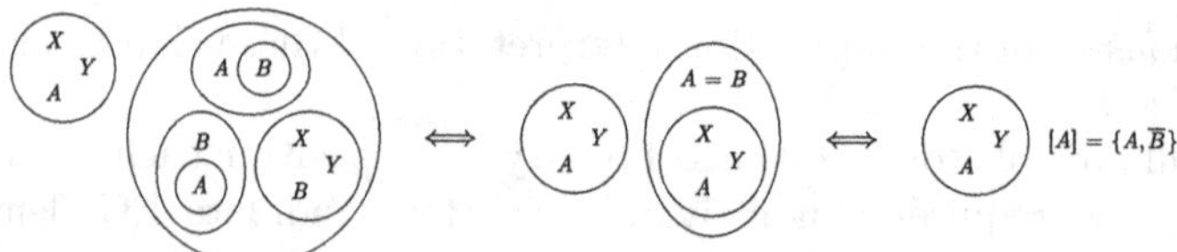

Fig. 4. EGs of $\varphi = (\overline{X} \vee \overline{Y} \vee \overline{A}) \wedge \neg((A \rightarrow B) \wedge (B \rightarrow A) \wedge (\overline{X} \vee \overline{Y} \vee \overline{B}))$ and its reduction to $\varphi' = (\overline{X} \vee \overline{Y} \vee \overline{A})$ with $[A] = \{A, \overline{B}\}$ after nestedly applying EPR and then deiteration.

a strongly connected component $[A] = \{A, B\}$, and the nested BIG contains a strongly connected component $[B] = \{B, C\}$. The union of both BIG results in the strongly connected component $[A] = \{A, B, C\}$, so the inner ternary clause can be wiped by a combination of the EPR and the deiteration rule. Thus, φ can be simplified to $\varphi' = \text{EPR}(\varphi) = (\overline{X} \vee \overline{Y} \vee \overline{A})$ with $[A] = \{A, B, \overline{C}\}$ (see Fig. 5).

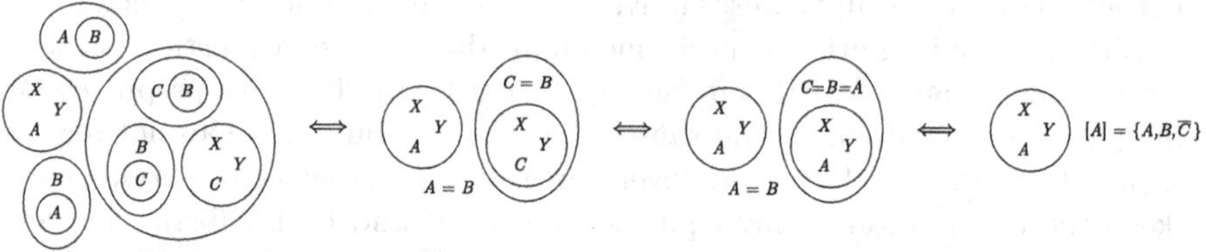

Fig. 5. EGs of $\varphi = (\overline{X} \vee \overline{Y} \vee \overline{A}) \wedge (A \rightarrow B) \wedge (B \rightarrow A) \wedge \neg((C \rightarrow B) \wedge (B \rightarrow C) \wedge (\overline{X} \vee \overline{Y} \vee \overline{C}))$ and its reduction to $\varphi' = (\overline{X} \vee \overline{Y} \vee \overline{A})$ with $[A] = \{A, B, \overline{C}\}$ after nestedly applying EPR to the union of nested BIGs and then deiteration.

Transitive Reduction. After applying EPR until completion, the BIG is guaranteed to be acyclic since all equivalences (and so strongly connected components) have been condensed into a representative literal (or node). However, the formula can still contain redundant binary clauses. In order to remove those, we compute the *transitive reduction* of the BIG (TRR), which in this case coincides with the minimum equivalent graph. As in the EPR, the same results can be achieved by nontrivial applications of the iteration, deiteration and cut rules, but these are only efficient if guided by the BIG. Moreover, the EGs viewpoint allows us to apply this rule in a nested form and so we can detect transitive redundancies in arbitrary formulas (see Example 4).

Example 4. Let $\varphi = (\overline{A} \vee B) \wedge (\overline{B} \vee C) \wedge \neg((C \vee \overline{A}) \wedge X \wedge Y)$. Then the level-0 BIG contains the implication chain $A \implies B \implies C$, and the level-1 binary clause is equivalent to $A \rightarrow C$. Computing the TR of the union of both BIGs shows that the inner binary clause is redundant and can be deleted. As illustrated in Fig. 6, we obtain the equivalent simplified formula $\varphi' = (\overline{A} \vee B) \wedge (\overline{B} \vee C) \wedge (\overline{X} \vee \overline{Y})$.

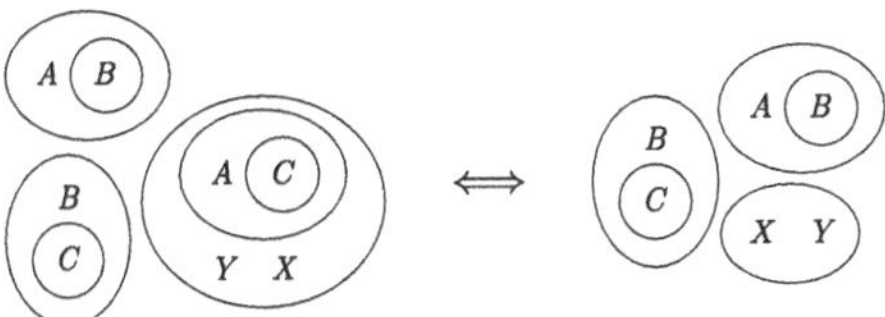

Fig. 6. EGs of $\varphi = (\overline{A} \vee B) \wedge (\overline{B} \vee C) \wedge \neg((C \vee \overline{A}) \wedge X \wedge Y)$ (left), and its equivalent reduction $\varphi' = \text{TRR}(\varphi) = (\overline{A} \vee B) \wedge (\overline{B} \vee C) \wedge (\overline{X} \vee \overline{Y})$ (right).

Opposite Singletons Implication

Definition 3 (Opposite singletons implication rule (OSIR)). *If a directed path in BIG(φ) contains a literal l and later its negation $\bar{l}$, then all the literals including and after the consequent ($\bar{l}$) evaluate to true, and all the literals in the implication path before and including the antecedent (l) evaluate to false. The Boolean variables "collapsing" in opposite chains will be equal by construction, so only one side of the implication path needs to be evaluated. All evaluated literals can be added as singletons and propagated accordingly by the SWR rule.*

Note that this preprocessing step can also be seen as a backtrack-free (i.e. non-look-ahead) exhaustive version of *failed-literal probing* (FLP) [4] over all (implicit and explicit) binary clauses, where we do not need to test candidate literals that might not lead to any new knowledge after a whole round of unit propagation. A strategy to make all possible unit-clause inferences from the BIG was proposed in [13], but their approach may add redundant, unnecessary clauses to the formula. As the previous rules, OSIR can also be applied to arbitrary nesting levels, so it does not require a formula to be in CNF (see Example 5).

Example 5. Let $\varphi = (\overline{X} \vee \overline{Z}) \wedge ((B \wedge \overline{C}) \vee (X \wedge Y \wedge \overline{A}) \vee (A \wedge \overline{B}) \vee (P \wedge A \wedge Q) \vee (C \wedge A))$. The BIG of the 1-nested biggest subformula contains the following implication chain: $A \implies B \implies C \implies \overline{A}$, so we can apply the OSIR to it and derive $\overline{A}$, which can be added as a nested singleton and later propagated using the SWR rule (see Fig. 7 below) to obtain the much simpler formula $\varphi' = \text{OSIR}(\varphi) = (\overline{X} \vee \overline{Z}) \wedge ((B \wedge \overline{C}) \vee (X \wedge Y) \vee A)$.

Tuple Wipe and Subflip. After understanding the basics of Peirce's EGs rules and binary implication graphs, we can now introduce a rule which, in fact, generalises all the previous rules (except the non-reductive part of EPR).

Definition 4 (Tuple wipe and subflip rule (TWSR)). *Let $C_n, D_m \in \varphi$ be two (sub)clauses of size $n \leq m$. Let c be the nesting level of C_n, and D_m be either in the same area as C_n or in a nested area within c. Let* $\text{des}(l)$ *be the set of descendants of a literal l in* BIG(φ). *Let* $\text{lit}(C_n) = \{p_1, \ldots, p_n\}$ *and* $\text{lit}(D_m) = \{q_1, \ldots, q_m\}$. *If for each $i \in \{1, ..., n-1\}$ either $p_i = q_i$ or $q_i \in \text{des}(p_i)$, and: (1) $p_n = q_n$ or $q_n \in \text{des}(p_n)$, then D_m can be deleted from φ; or (2) $p_n = \overline{q_n}$ or $\overline{q_n} \in \text{des}(p_n)$, then q_n can be deleted from D_m.*

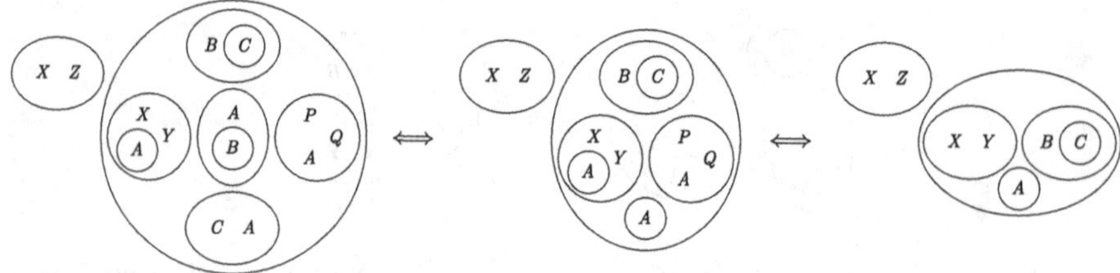

Fig. 7. EGs showing the application of OSIR to $\varphi = (\overline{X} \vee \overline{Z}) \wedge ((B \wedge \overline{C}) \vee (X \wedge Y \wedge \overline{A}) \vee (A \wedge \overline{B}) \vee (P \wedge A \wedge Q) \vee (C \wedge A))$ and the subsequent SWR application where the new singleton $\overline{A}$ is propagated to obtain the equivalent reduced formula $\varphi' = (\overline{X} \vee \overline{Z}) \wedge ((B \wedge \overline{C}) \vee (X \wedge Y) \vee A)$.

Note that we need to specify the cases $p_n = q_n$ and $p_n = \overline{q_n}$ since it is always the case that $x \rightarrow x$ and $\overline{x} \rightarrow \overline{x}$, but these tautologies are not added to the BIG in order to keep it redundancy- and tautology-free.

As before, our rule can be applied to arbitrary nesting levels, and so it does not require a formula to be in CNF (see Example 6).

Example 6. Let $\varphi = (A \rightarrow E) \wedge (B \rightarrow F) \wedge (C \rightarrow G) \wedge \neg((\overline{A} \vee \overline{B} \vee G \vee \overline{H}) \wedge (\overline{A} \vee \overline{B} \vee \overline{C} \vee \overline{D}) \wedge (\overline{E} \vee \overline{F} \vee \overline{G}))$. Note that the BIG of the outermost area applies to the biggest 1-nested subformula. As illustrated in Fig. 8, we can apply TWSR to the clauses of sizes 3 and 4 inside the biggest 1-nested area and obtain the simplified equivalent formula $\varphi' = (A \rightarrow E) \wedge (B \rightarrow F) \wedge (C \rightarrow G) \wedge ((A \wedge B \wedge H) \vee (E \wedge F \wedge G))$. In particular, the clauses $P_3 = (\overline{E} \vee \overline{F} \vee \overline{G})$ and $Q_4 = (\overline{A} \vee \overline{B} \vee \overline{C} \vee \overline{D})$ satisfy condition (1) in TWSR's definition, and P_3 together with $R_4 = (\overline{A} \vee \overline{B} \vee G \vee \overline{H})$ satisfy condition (2).

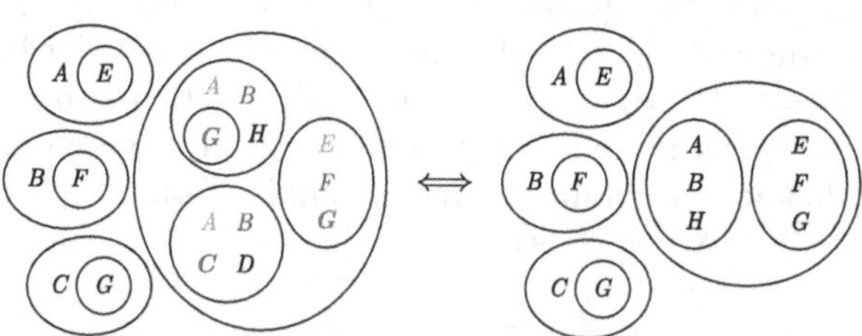

Fig. 8. EG of $\varphi = (A \rightarrow E) \wedge (B \rightarrow F) \wedge (C \rightarrow G) \wedge \neg((\overline{A} \vee \overline{B} \vee G \vee \overline{H}) \wedge (\overline{A} \vee \overline{B} \vee \overline{C} \vee \overline{D}) \wedge (\overline{E} \vee \overline{F} \vee \overline{G}))$ (left), where the literals satisfying TWSR's definition conditions are highlighted in matching colours. The equivalent reduced formula resulting from applying TWSR is shown on the right-hand side.

It is easy to see that TWSR with $n = 1$ is equivalent to SWR. TWSR restricted to binary clauses only (i.e. with $n = m = 2$) is equivalent to the clause deletion part of EPR and computing the TR of BIG(φ) when condition

(1) is satisfied; and to the literal deletion part of EPR together with OSIR when condition (2) applies. However, TWSR cannot fully emulate EPR since it cannot perform the non-reductive substitution step (i.e. substitute a literal by its class representative) nor keep equivalence classes information. Thus, we recommend applying EPR before applying any form of TWSR (including SWR) in order to maximise the preservation of structural problem information. Note that preserving the structural information of the problem is of key importance not only in preprocessing but also for symmetry detection and general solving [1]. Figure 9 shows two examples of TWSR applications for $n = m = 3$ satisfying, respectively, conditions (1) and (2).

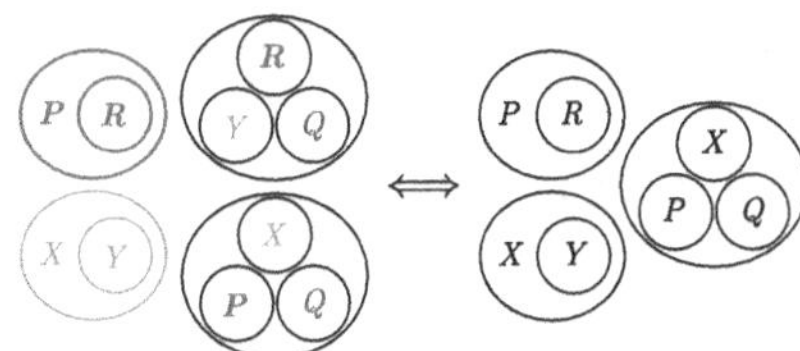

(i) Let $\varphi = (P \to R) \wedge (X \to Y) \wedge (X \vee Q \vee P) \wedge (R \vee Y \vee Q)$. Let $C_3 = (X \vee Q \vee P)$ be the penultimate clause and $D_3 = (R \vee Y \vee Q)$ be the last clause in φ. These satisfy condition (1) in TWSR's definition, so D_3 can be deleted.

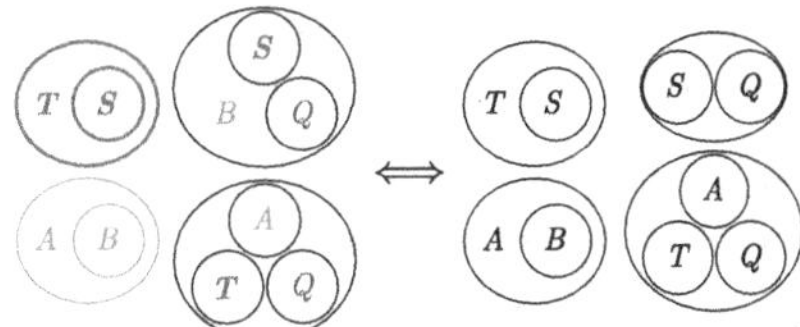

(ii) Let $\varphi = (T \to S) \wedge (A \to B) \wedge (S \vee \overline{B} \vee Q) \wedge (A \vee Q \vee T)$. Let $C_3 = (A \vee Q \vee T)$ and $D_3 = (S \vee \overline{B} \vee Q)$. They satisfy condition (2) in TWSR's definition, so the literal $\overline{B}$ can be deleted from D_3.

Fig. 9. EGs of two applications of the TWSR, where colours highlight related literals (equal –in green– or in the same implication chain –in orange or blue). (Color figure online)

Our TWSR is a generalisation of subsumption and self-subsuming resolution since it removes in one pass not only all the explicitly (self)subsumed redundant clauses but also all the *implicitly* (self)subsumed ones. It also generalises unit propagation, transitive reduction and, since it can be applied to clauses of arbitrary sizes, it is strictly more powerful than binary resolution combined with transitive reduction and unit propagation, while guaranteeing a non-increasing number of variables, literals and clauses (i.e. redundant variables, literals or clauses are never added). TWSR can also be seen as a backtrack-free (non-look-ahead, i.e., with no arbitrary assignments) more efficient version of FLP over all literals in the BIG of the formula.

Moreover, TWSR strictly generalises the combination of *hidden subsumption elimination* (HSE) [15], *hidden tautology elimination* (HTE) [15] and *hidden literal elimination* (HLE) [16] in a manner that is guaranteed to never increase the size of the formula. Note that this is not necessarily the case for the aforementioned rules. For example, in order to deduce that clauses are redundant, HTE adds literals instead of removing them and tests if this leads to a tautology. Note in particular that neither of these rules nor their combination could achieve the reduction shown in Example 6, even if all clauses were at the same nesting level. For formulas in CNF, HTE combined with HSE, computing the transitive closure of BIG(φ) and adding all new binary clauses to φ can achieve the same reduction as TWSR with condition (1) only, but clearly at a much higher cost and space complexity.

3.2 Rules Properties

Visual proofs using the EG calculus are much easier to follow than symbolic ones, and EGs inference rules have been used to establish the results for the two theorems presented below. However, because of space constraints, we only provide symbolic and 'verbal'-EGs skeleton proofs here. Moreover, since the TWSR rule generalises all the others except the substitution part of EPR, we need only provide proofs for these two rules.

Theorem 1. *SWR, EPR, TRR, OSIR, and TWSR are all reversible and so equivalence-preserving.*

Proof (TWSR). Let $C_n, D_m \in \varphi$ be two (sub)clauses of size $n \leq m$ as in TWSR's definition, with $\text{lit}(C_n) = \{p_1, ..., p_n\}$ *and* $\text{lit}(D_m) = \{q_1, ..., q_m\}$*. (1) Let $p_i = q_i$ or $q_i \in \text{des}(p_i)$ for each $i \in \{1, ..., n\}$. We can iterate C_n inside D_m, and all literals in the inner copy satisfying $p_i = q_i$ can be deleted by deiterating their copies in D_m. All literals in the inner copy of C_n satisfying $q_i \in \text{des}(p_i)$ can also be deleted as follows: since $q_i \in \text{des}(p_i)$, it means that we have the binary clauses $(\overline{p_i} \vee x_1) \wedge \cdots \wedge (\overline{x_j} \vee q_i)$, which we can iterate inside D_m, and successively deiterate all the consequents until we obtain $D_m \vee p_i \vee x_1 \vee \cdots \vee x_j \vee \overline{C_n}$. Thus, D_m can be expanded with all p_i's, which can then be deleted from the inner copy of C_n, leaving an empty cut which is either in an even or in an odd area. If the empty cut is in an even area, then we have $\bot$ in a conjunction, which evaluates to* `False`*. This conjunction is contained in an odd area, and so it can be deleted from the disjunction. If the empty cut is in an odd area, then we have $\top$ in a disjunction, and the whole clause evaluates to* `True`*, which can be safely deleted from its implicit surrounding conjunction. (2) Let $p_i = q_i$ or $q_i \in \text{des}(p_i)$ for each $i \in \{1, ..., n-1\}$ and $p_n = \overline{q_n}$ or $\overline{q_n} \in \text{des}(p_n)$. We can iterate C_n inside the nesting area of q_n in D_m (with the insertion of a double cut around it if required). If $p_n = \overline{q_n}$, then $\overline{q_n}$ inside the cut can be deiterated from the inner copy of C_n, and all the remaining $n-1$ literals can be deleted as in (1). If $\overline{q_n} \in \text{des}(p_n)$, we can deiterate the $n-1$ literals from the inner copy as in (1) and are left with $(\overline{p_n} \vee q_n)$. Since we know that $\overline{q_n} \in \text{des}(p_n)$, we can derive $(\overline{p_n} \vee \overline{q_n})$ from the implication chain as in (1), iterate it inside q_n's cut and deiterate its inner q_n and its inner p_n to obtain an empty cut, which results in deleting q_n from D_m, but we then have a $\overline{p}$ in its place. This extra $\overline{p}$ can be deleted by inserting a double cut around it, iterating the $n-1$ implications $q_i \in \text{des}(p_i)$ inside and deiteraiting their $q_1, \ldots, q_{n-1}$. This results in $D_m \vee \overline{C_n}$ from which we can deiterate C_n to obtain $D_m \setminus \{q_n\}$. Since we have only used Peirce's iteration (2i), deiteration (2e) and double cut (3i and 3e) rules, which are all reversible and equivalence-preserving, we know that our rule is too.*

Proof (EPR). *Trivial, since we retain the information on equivalence classes. But, in more detail, the equivalence preservation of the reductive part of EPR follows from TWSR's proof above, and the equivalence of the substitution part can be proved as follows: Let x and y be in the same strongly connected component of a BIG. Then, we have or can easily deduce the following two clauses: $\overline{x} \vee y$ and $\overline{y} \vee x$. For any clause C containing y we can iterate $\overline{x} \vee y$ within C, and deiterate y from it to obtain $C \vee x$. We can then iterate $\overline{y} \vee x$ within the nested area of y (potentially adding a double cut), and deiterate y from it to obtain $y \wedge x$, which can be deleted by an iteration of the copy of x in expanded C, to obtain C with y replaced by x.*

Given that all of our rules can never add any variables, literals or clauses, it is also straightforward to prove the following theorem.

Theorem 2. *The applications of SWR, EPR, TRR, OSIR, and TWSR are guaranteed to be monotonically non-increasing in the number of variables, in the number of clauses and in the number of literals of a propositional formula.*

Proof (EPR). *Trivial, since either (i) the BIG has no strongly connected components and so the formula stays the same, or (ii) at least a strongly connected component is found, and for each component, at least the binary clauses corresponding to all the edges in the component can be deleted.*

Proof (TWSR). *Trivial, since either (i) TWSR does not apply so the formula stays the same, (ii) condition (1) is satisfied and so the number of clauses is reduced by one, or (iii) condition (2) applies and the number of literals is reduced by one.*

4 Discussion and Future Work

Our systematic reduction procedure applies EPR whenever new binary clauses are present, and then prioritises the propagation (by TWSR) of the smallest unprocessed clauses, since these have greater reduction potential than bigger clauses. Our approach might appear to be quadratic in nature, but this is easily avoidable by using existing efficient graph algorithms. For example, finding strongly connected components for the EPR step can be linear [10,28,32] in the number of edges and nodes of the BIG (which is less than $2e + 2n$ with e being the number of binary clauses and n the number of variables present in binary clauses). Additional applications of EPR only need to search for strongly connected components containing any new BIG edges, which is even faster. The substitution step can be done efficiently using occurrence lists [5], or if we condense the hypergraph of the formula instead of searching for equivalent literals to be replaced in every clause. The reachability queries performed in TWSR can be answered in as low as $\mathcal{O}(1)$ time with the right data structure and a preprocessing step of $\mathcal{O}((2n)^3)$ time in the worst case [8], where n is again the number of variables present in binary clauses. In order to avoid a quadratic number of comparisons in TWSR, we can sort clauses and literals, or use known tactics such as the one-watched [35] or two-watched [23,34] literal schemes. Traditional literal occurrence lists would not be as helpful in this case since they do not capture the 'hidden' occurrences. However, other kinds of lists would be helpful, such as lists of clauses containing a given number of BIG nodes (since a clause C_n can only potentially reduce another clause D_m if D_m has at least as many nodes in the BIG as C_n). TWSR could also be guided by the hypergraph of the formula, which can give a first approximation to the (undirected) connectedness of literals and significantly reduce the search for redundant clauses. Finally, processing independent components of the BIG and the hypergraph of the formula would obviously speed up our simplification approach, but parallelisation of preprocessing is still in its infancy [7]. Nonetheless, using any of these known techniques can certainly improve the performance of our method as well as increase its scalability.

Another key advantage of our unified approach is that it eliminates the need to choose between different techniques or their order of application, which can have a major impact on the final level of reduction (e.g. some preprocessing techniques add redundant clauses by resolution, whilst others delete them, which could lead to an infinite loop). It can also be the case that some rules are not applicable at first, but they can provide further reduction if applied after other techniques. This is a nontrivial problem usually resolved by heuristics (e.g. restarts) or by limiting the application and behaviour of the rules according to arbitrary parameters (e.g. apply preprocessing to learned or bigger clauses only). Example 7 illustrates these problems and how our solution addresses them instead. Moreover, note that our approach is guaranteed to terminate since it never increases the size of the problem.

Example 7. Let $\varphi = (A \vee B \vee C) \wedge (A \vee B \vee D) \wedge (B \vee \overline{C}) \wedge (\overline{A} \vee B \vee \overline{C})$. If we apply TWSR to it, our approach first propagates the smallest clause $(B \vee \overline{C})$ and reduces the formula to TWSR$(\varphi) = \varphi' = (A \vee B) \wedge (A \vee B \vee D) \wedge (B \vee \overline{C})$. TWSR next propagates the smallest unprocessed clause $(A \vee B)$, and returns the equivalent formula $\varphi'' = (A \vee B) \wedge (B \vee \overline{C})$. This same result could also be obtained by using other existing techniques combined in many different ways. For example, applying a round of subsumption, then a round of self-subsumption, and then another round of subsumption would achieve the same reduction in this case. We can also obtain φ'' by applying HTE, HSE and self-subsumption in any order. Adding all the possible redundant clauses obtained by resolution and then applying two rounds of subsumption would also lead to φ''. Note, however, that the choice of techniques or their application orders would of course be problem-dependent and not obvious beforehand, so many techniques would probably be unsuccessfully applied before reaching (or not) the desired result.

Some of the existing computationally most expensive preprocessing techniques (namely FLP, *hyper binary resolution* (HBR) [3], *asymmetric subsumption elimination* [15], *asymmetric literal elimination* [7] and *asymmetric tautology elimination* (ATE) [15]) can achieve reductions on CNF formula that TWSR is not able to attain. However, TWSR can reach the same level of reduction if applied to the original nested formula (see Example 8).

Example 8. Let $\varphi = (\overline{C} \vee \neg(\overline{A} \vee \overline{B} \vee \overline{D})) \wedge (\overline{A} \vee \overline{B} \vee \overline{D})$. Let $CNF(\varphi) = (\overline{C} \vee A) \wedge (\overline{C} \vee B) \wedge (\overline{C} \vee D) \wedge (\overline{A} \vee \overline{B} \vee \overline{D})$ be φ expressed in conjunctive normal form. Both FLP and HBR can reduce $CNF(\varphi)$ to $\varphi' = \overline{C} \wedge (\overline{A} \vee \overline{B} \vee \overline{D})$, but TWSR would not be able to do so unless we apply first a nontrivial EG factorisation step to recover its nested form. However, if we apply TWSR directly to φ, we can obtain φ' much more efficiently (see Fig. 10). Note that none of the existing preprocessing methods can be applied directly to φ since it is not in CNF.

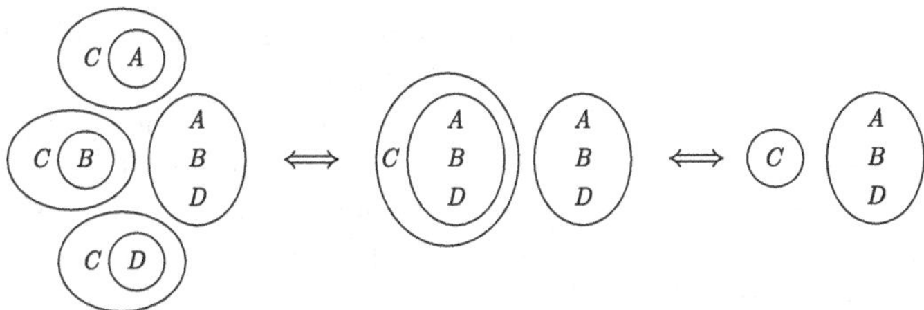

Fig. 10. EGs of CNF(φ) $= (\overline{C} \vee A) \wedge (\overline{C} \vee B) \wedge (\overline{C} \vee D) \wedge (\overline{A} \vee \overline{B} \vee \overline{D})$ (left), its equivalent factorised form $\varphi = (\overline{C} \vee \neg(\overline{A} \vee \overline{B} \vee \overline{D})) \wedge (\overline{A} \vee \overline{B} \vee \overline{D})$ (middle), and its equivalent reduced form TWSR(φ) $= \varphi' = \overline{C} \wedge (\overline{A} \vee \overline{B} \vee \overline{D})$ (right).

In fact, by using EGs and BIGs, we have realised that TWSR and these advanced SAT preprocessing techniques can actually be seen as n-ary versions of TRR and OSIR, where the nodes of the implication graph can be clauses instead of singletons. That is, instead of finding a redundant edge between two singletons, we remove redundant edges between implied clauses (see Example 9), and instead of finding a singleton implying its negation, we uncover an n-ary clause implying its negation (see Example 10). Thus, we are currently working on an extension of TWSR guided by the *n-ary implication hypergraph* of the formula, which we claim will be able to generalise all the aforementioned rules while still guaranteeing a never-increasing problem size.

Example 9. Let $\varphi = (\overline{A} \vee \overline{B} \vee C) \wedge (A \vee \overline{B} \vee \overline{C}) \wedge (\overline{A} \vee B \vee D) \wedge (A \vee B \vee \overline{D}) \wedge (A \vee \overline{C} \vee \overline{D}) \wedge (\overline{A} \vee \ C \vee D)$. These clauses define the following three implication chains (amongst many others): $B \wedge C \implies A \implies \overline{B} \vee C$, $\overline{B} \wedge D \implies A \implies B \vee D$, and $C \wedge D \implies A \implies C \vee D$. These can be combined to form the following equivalent implication chain: $(B \wedge C) \vee (\overline{B} \wedge D) \vee (C \wedge D) \implies A \implies (\overline{B} \vee C) \wedge (B \vee D) \wedge (C \vee D)$, which easily reduces to: $(B \wedge C) \vee (\overline{B} \wedge D) \implies A \implies (\overline{B} \vee C) \wedge (B \vee D)$, meaning that $(A \vee \overline{C} \vee \overline{D})$ and $(\overline{A} \vee \ C \vee D)$ are redundant clauses in φ. Our current version of TWSR cannot find these redundancies, nor can FLP or HBR. From the rules we have mentioned in this paper, only ATE would be able to detect this redundancy.

Example 10. Let $\varphi = (\overline{X} \vee Y) \wedge (\overline{Y} \vee \overline{Z}) \wedge (X \vee \overline{P} \vee \overline{Q}) \wedge (\overline{Y} \vee \overline{P} \vee \overline{Q})$. Remember that we can read $(\overline{X} \vee Y)$ as $(X \rightarrow Y)$ or, equivalently, $(\overline{Y} \rightarrow \overline{X})$. The clause $(X \vee \overline{P} \vee \overline{Q})$ can be interpreted as $(P \wedge Q \rightarrow X)$ or $(\overline{X} \rightarrow \overline{(P \wedge Q)})$, amongst many other equivalent readings. Notice that the reduction obtained from the application of TWSR, $\varphi' = (\overline{X} \vee Y) \wedge (\overline{Y} \vee \overline{Z}) \wedge (\overline{P} \vee \overline{Q})$, can be seen as applying an n-ary version of OSIR to the following implication path: $P \wedge Q \implies \overline{Y} \implies \overline{X} \implies \overline{(P \wedge Q)}$.

5 Conclusion

Reasoning with EGs allowed us to independently rediscover many existing equivalence preserving SAT preprocessing techniques, gain a better understanding of their underlying relationships, and more easily prove and establish many of their properties. EGs also offer a fresh viewpoint which led to a novel approach that generalises many of these techniques with added advantages: it is more efficient, avoids look-ahead backtracking, guarantees a monotonically decreasing number of variables, literals and clauses (and so termination), it is structure-preserving, can be applied to nested formulae, and does not require CNF.

With our approach, it becomes clear why some simplification techniques based on adding redundant clauses or literals sometimes help reduce the problem but other times do not, leading to wasted preprocessing effort and the need for bespoke or contrived heuristics. Since our proposed method generalises a significant set of previously-thought independent techniques, the high complexity and effort associated with finding a suitable application order are drastically reduced. Our rules can also decrease the space complexity of the problem since they may be applied at a higher level before formulas are flattened (e.g. converted to CNF). This can greatly minimise the search space and even prevent potential explosions of the formula size during translation. Our reductions also allow for further problem insight and understanding, which can lead to better modelling, better solving strategies, search heuristics and translations, further symmetry breaking, provide model counting bounds and aid #SAT. Moreover, our techniques are solver-, problem-, and form-agnostic, and apply to propositional logic formula in general, so they can be of use in other fields such as SMT, automated reasoning and theorem proving.

Future work includes extensions of the TWSR rule informed by a novel n-ary implication hypergraph, refining our current implementation and a formal complexity analysis of our working algorithm.

References

1. Anders, M.: SAT preprocessors and symmetry. In: Meel, K.S., Strichman, O. (eds.) 25th International Conference on Theory and Applications of Satisfiability Testing, SAT 2022, 2–5 August 2022, Haifa, Israel. LIPIcs, vol. 236, pp. 1:1–1:20. Schloss Dagstuhl - Leibniz-Zentrum für Informatik (2022). https://doi.org/10.4230/LIPIcs.SAT.2022.1

2. Aspvall, B., Plass, M.F., Tarjan, R.E.: A linear-time algorithm for testing the truth of certain quantified boolean formulas. Inf. Process. Lett. **8**(3), 121–123 (1979). https://doi.org/10.1016/0020-0190(79)90002-4
3. Bacchus, F.: Enhancing davis putnam with extended binary clause reasoning. In: Dechter, R., Kearns, M.J., Sutton, R.S. (eds.) Proceedings of the Eighteenth National Conference on Artificial Intelligence and Fourteenth Conference on Innovative Applications of Artificial Intelligence, 28 July–1 August 2002, Edmonton, Alberta, Canada, pp. 613–619. AAAI Press/The MIT Press (2002). http://www.aaai.org/Library/AAAI/2002/aaai02-092.php
4. Berre, D.L.: Exploiting the real power of unit propagation lookahead. Electron. Notes Discret. Math. **9**, 59–80 (2001). https://doi.org/10.1016/S1571-0653(04)00314-2
5. Biere, A.: Resolve and expand. In: SAT 2004 - The Seventh International Conference on Theory and Applications of Satisfiability Testing, 10–13 May 2004, Vancouver, BC, Canada, Online Proceedings (2004). http://www.satisfiability.org/SAT04/programme/93.pdf
6. Biere, A., Fazekas, K., Fleury, M., Heisinger, M.: CaDiCaL, Kissat, Paracooba, Plingeling and Treengeling entering the SAT competition 2020. In: Balyo, T., Froleyks, N., Heule, M., Iser, M., Järvisalo, M., Suda, M. (eds.) Proceedings of SAT Competition 2020 - Solver and Benchmark Descriptions. Department of Computer Science Report Series B, vol. B-2020-1, pp. 51–53. University of Helsinki (2020)
7. Biere, A., Järvisalo, M., Kiesl, B.: Preprocessing in SAT solving. In: Biere, A., Heule, M., van Maaren, H., Walsh, T. (eds.) Handbook of Satisfiability - Second Edition, Frontiers in Artificial Intelligence and Applications, vol. 336, pp. 391–435. IOS Press (2021). https://doi.org/10.3233/FAIA200992
8. Cormen, T.H., Leiserson, C.E., Rivest, R.L., Stein, C.: Transitive closure of a directed graph. In: Introduction to Algorithms, pp. 632–634 (2001)
9. Dau, F.: Mathematical logic with diagrams – based on the existential graphs of peirce. Habilitation thesis. TU Darmstadt, Germany (2008). http://www.dr-dau.net/Papers/habil.pdf
10. Dijkstra, E.W.: A Discipline of Programming. Prentice-Hall (1976). https://www.worldcat.org/oclc/01958445
11. Een, N., Mishchenko, A., Sörensson, N.: Applying logic synthesis for speeding up SAT. In: Marques-Silva, J., Sakallah, K.A. (eds.) SAT 2007. LNCS, vol. 4501, pp. 272–286. Springer, Heidelberg (2007). https://doi.org/10.1007/978-3-540-72788-0_26
12. Fazekas, K., Biere, A., Scholl, C.: Incremental inprocessing in SAT solving. In: Janota, M., Lynce, I. (eds.) SAT 2019. LNCS, vol. 11628, pp. 136–154. Springer, Cham (2019). https://doi.org/10.1007/978-3-030-24258-9_9
13. Gelder, A.V.: Toward leaner binary-clause reasoning in a satisfiability solver. Ann. Math. Artif. Intell. **43**(1), 239–253 (2005). https://doi.org/10.1007/s10472-005-0433-5
14. Gelder, A.V., Tsuji, Y.K.: Satisfiability testing with more reasoning and less guessing. In: Johnson, D.S., Trick, M.A. (eds.) Cliques, Coloring, and Satisfiability, Proceedings of a DIMACS Workshop, New Brunswick, New Jersey, USA, 11–13 October 1993. DIMACS Series in Discrete Mathematics and Theoretical Computer Science, vol. 26, pp. 559–586. DIMACS/AMS (1993). https://doi.org/10.1090/dimacs/026/27
15. Heule, M., Järvisalo, M., Biere, A.: Clause elimination procedures for CNF formulas. In: Fermüller, C.G., Voronkov, A. (eds.) LPAR 2010. LNCS, vol. 6397, pp.

357–371. Springer, Heidelberg (2010). https://doi.org/10.1007/978-3-642-16242-8_26
16. Heule, M.J.H., Järvisalo, M., Biere, A.: Efficient CNF simplification based on binary implication graphs. In: Sakallah, K.A., Simon, L. (eds.) SAT 2011. LNCS, vol. 6695, pp. 201–215. Springer, Heidelberg (2011). https://doi.org/10.1007/978-3-642-21581-0_17
17. Järvisalo, M., Heule, M.J.H., Biere, A.: Inprocessing rules. In: Gramlich, B., Miller, D., Sattler, U. (eds.) IJCAR 2012. LNCS (LNAI), vol. 7364, pp. 355–370. Springer, Heidelberg (2012). https://doi.org/10.1007/978-3-642-31365-3_28
18. Karnaugh, M.: The map method for synthesis of combinational logic circuits. Trans. Am. Inst. Electr. Eng. Part I Communi. Electron. **72**(5), 593–599 (1953)
19. Li, C.M.: Integrating equivalency reasoning into davis-putnam procedure. In: Kautz, H.A., Porter, B.W. (eds.) Proceedings of the Seventeenth National Conference on Artificial Intelligence and Twelfth Conference on on Innovative Applications of Artificial Intelligence, 30 July–3 August 2000, Austin, Texas, USA, pp. 291–296. AAAI Press/The MIT Press (2000). http://www.aaai.org/Library/AAAI/2000/aaai00-045.php
20. Li, C., Xiao, F., Luo, M., Manyà, F., Lü, Z., Li, Y.: Clause vivification by unit propagation in CDCL SAT solvers. Artif. Intell. **279** (2020). https://doi.org/10.1016/j.artint.2019.103197
21. Luo, M., Li, C., Xiao, F., Manyà, F., Lü, Z.: An effective learnt clause minimization approach for CDCL SAT solvers. In: Sierra, C. (ed.) Proceedings of the Twenty-Sixth International Joint Conference on Artificial Intelligence, IJCAI 2017, Melbourne, Australia, 19–25 August 2017, pp. 703–711. ijcai.org (2017). https://doi.org/10.24963/ijcai.2017/98
22. McCluskey, E.J.: Minimization of boolean functions. Bell Syst. Tech. J. **35**(6), 1417–1444 (1956)
23. Moskewicz, M.W., Madigan, C.F., Zhao, Y., Zhang, L., Malik, S.: Chaff: engineering an efficient SAT solver. In: Proceedings of the 38th Design Automation Conference, DAC 2001, Las Vegas, NV, USA, 18–22 June 2001, pp. 530–535. ACM (2001). https://doi.org/10.1145/378239.379017
24. Peirce, C.: Existential graphs: manuscript 514, with commentary by jf sowa. Self-published by JF Sowa (1909). http://www.jfsowa.com/peirce/ms514.htm
25. Roberts, D.D.: The existential graphs of Charles S. Peirce. Ph.D. thesis, University of Illinois at Urbana-Champaign (1963)
26. Roberts, D.D.: The existential graphs of Charles S. Peirce. Mouton (1973)
27. Rudell, R.L.: Logic synthesis for VLSI design. Ph.D. thesis, University of California, Berkeley (1989)
28. Sharir, M.: A strong-connectivity algorithm and its applications in data flow analysis. Comput. Math. Appl. **7**(1), 67–72 (1981)
29. Shin, S.: Reconstituting beta graphs into an efficacious system. J. Log. Lang. Inf. **8**(3), 273–295 (1999). https://doi.org/10.1023/A:1008303204427
30. Sörensson, N., Biere, A.: Minimizing learned clauses. In: Kullmann, O. (ed.) SAT 2009. LNCS, vol. 5584, pp. 237–243. Springer, Heidelberg (2009). https://doi.org/10.1007/978-3-642-02777-2_23
31. Sowa, J.F.: Peirce's tutorial on existential graphs. Semiotica **2011**(186), 347–394 (2011)
32. Tarjan, R.E.: Depth-first search and linear graph algorithms. SIAM J. Comput. **1**(2), 146–160 (1972). https://doi.org/10.1137/0201010
33. Zeman, J.J.: The graphical logic of C. S. Peirce. Ph.D. thesis, The University of Chicago (1964)

34. Zhang, H., Stickel, M.E.: Implementing the davis-putnam method. J. Autom. Reason. **24**(1/2), 277–296 (2000). https://doi.org/10.1023/A:1006351428454
35. Zhang, L.: On subsumption removal and on-the-fly CNF simplification. In: Bacchus, F., Walsh, T. (eds.) SAT 2005. LNCS, vol. 3569, pp. 482–489. Springer, Heidelberg (2005). https://doi.org/10.1007/11499107_42

From Static to Dynamic Access Control Policies via Attribute-Based Category Mining

Anna Bamberger(✉) and Maribel Fernández

Department of Informatics, King's College London, London, UK
anna.bamberger@kcl.ac.uk

Abstract. We present an algorithm to mine a logic-based, dynamic access control policy from an access control matrix (ACM) or a role based access control (RBAC) policy augmented with principal and resource attributes. Both ACM and RBAC are static (changes in authorisations require the intervention of an administrator) whereas attribute-based policies are dynamic: authorisations change in an autonomous way when attribute values change. Given an ACM or RBAC policy, we obtain a dynamic policy by synthesising category definitions from principal and resource attributes, to our knowledge, the first such mechanism explored. The result is a category-based policy where categories are defined via logic formulas involving attributes and their values. Preliminary experimental results show that the miner provides a foundation for the synthesis of dynamic policies derived from categories.

Keywords: Access control · Policy Mining · Policy Administration · Category-Based Access Control

1 Introduction

Access control policies specify the actions that principals are authorised to perform on protected resources. One of the first and most basic mechanisms employed to protect resources is the access control matrix (ACM), which indicates the authorised actions for each principal and resource. These matrices however are difficult to define and maintain. A wide range of studies have concerned themselves with the conceptualisation and implementation of a stable and easily maintainable access control model, with the most prominent of such models being role-based access control (RBAC [3,13,24,25]) and attribute-based access control (ABAC [17,27,30]). ACM and RBAC are currently the most popular models in practice, however, the static nature of these models makes migrating to a dynamic model such as ABAC a necessity for organisations with complex access control requirements. We address this problem by defining an algorithm to synthesise dynamic *category-based policies* from ACM or RBAC policies.

The category-based access control (CBAC) model [4,6,7] generalises the ACM, RBAC and ABAC models. It provides a skeleton of building blocks,

R. Glück and B. Kafle (Eds.): LOPSTR 2023, LNCS 14330, pp. 188–197, 2023.
https://doi.org/10.1007/978-3-031-45784-5_12

from which dynamically modifiable authorisations arise. The key components in CBAC are the categorisation of the main entities (principals and resources) and the linkage between categories and actions, from which the set of authorisations at each given point in time can be deduced. Categories can be defined using roles, attributes, events, etc. For a more in-depth analysis of CBAC definitions we refer the reader to [5–7].

To aid administrators in the process of creating and maintaining policies, in this paper we propose a proof of concept for a tool capable of synthesising CBAC policies based on attributes. The starting point is an access control matrix or an RBAC policy, together with attributes of principals and resources.

Multiple policy mining mechanisms have been proposed [19,20,23,26,29]. These algorithms translate the theoretical access control model to actual access control policies. Attribute-based mining algorithms significantly reduce the cost of migration to ABAC, by partially automating the development of an ABAC policy [29]. In [2] we defined an algorithm to mine attribute-based category definitions (i.e., logic formulas involving attributes and their values) from access control logs (i.e., from a history of access requests and their associated answers). In this paper we adapt the mining algorithm to synthesise dynamic CBAC policies starting from an ACM or an RBAC policy. Key features of the algorithm are the use of an NLP Doc2vec pre-filter [22] followed by an FP-growth-based check [15]. The proposed CBAC miner increases both the flexibility and autonomy of the access control system thereby reducing the maintenance burden.

Our main contributions are as follows:

1. We present a new approach to mine attribute-based CBAC policies from access control matrices and RBAC policies via a proof of concept as well as its initial implementation technique. The policies synthesised by the miner consist of category definitions (formulas involving attributes and their values) and a list of permitted actions for each category. These, together with the CBAC axioms, define the set of valid authorisations. We discuss an example.
2. The proposed miner seeks to display both dynamic as well as explainable features for policy generation compared with other models such as RBAC or ABAC, due to combining the NLP method with FP-growth.

2 Preliminaries

2.1 The Category-Based Metamodel

A key feature of the CBAC metamodel [4] is the classification into **categories** of sets $\mathcal{E}$ of **entities**, together with sets $\mathcal{R}el$ of **relationships between entities**, and a set $\mathcal{A}x$ of **axioms** that the relationships should satisfy.

The following main generic sets of entities are included in the metamodel and are to be employed alongside any application-dependent and/or environment-specific entities: a countable set $\mathcal{C}$ of categories $c_0, c_1, \ldots$; a countable set $\mathcal{P}$ of principals $p_0, p_1, \ldots$ (we assume that principals that request access to resources are pre-authenticated); a countable set $\mathcal{A}$ of named *actions* $a_0, a_1, \ldots$; a countable set $\mathcal{R}$ of *resources* $r_0, r_1, \ldots$; a finite set *Auth* of possible *answers* to access requests (e.g., grant, deny) and a countable set $\mathcal{S}$ of *situational identifiers* to denote contextual information (situational identifiers might not be needed in some instances of the metamodel).

The assignment of entities to categories is specified via relationships between those entities and their categories, which can be defined extensionally (as a table) or intentionally (e.g., the tuples in a relationship may be obtained by evaluating a condition). The metamodel includes the following generic relationships:

- *Principal-Category Assignment*, $\mathcal{PCA} \subseteq \mathcal{P} \times \mathcal{C}$, s.t. $(p, c) \in \mathcal{PCA}$ iff the principal $p \in \mathcal{P}$ is in the category $c \in \mathcal{C}$;
- *Resource-Category Assignment*, $\mathcal{RCA} \subseteq \mathcal{R} \times \mathcal{C}$, s.t. $(r, c) \in \mathcal{RCA}$ iff the resource $r \in \mathcal{R}$ is in the category $c \in \mathcal{C}$;
- *Permissions*, $\mathcal{ARCA} \subseteq \mathcal{A} \times \mathcal{C} \times \mathcal{C}$, s.t. $(a, c_r, c_p) \in \mathcal{ARCA}$ iff the action $a \in \mathcal{A}$ on resource category $c_r \in \mathcal{C}$ can be performed by principals in the category $c_p \in \mathcal{C}$.
- *Authorisations*, $\mathcal{PAR} \subseteq \mathcal{P} \times \mathcal{A} \times \mathcal{R}$, s.t. $(p, a, r) \in \mathcal{PAR}$ iff the principal $p \in \mathcal{P}$ is allowed to perform the action $a \in \mathcal{A}$ on the resource $r \in \mathcal{R}$.

A reflexive-transitive relation $\subseteq$ between categories is also included (this can simply be equality). The list of relationships is not exhaustive and can be revised to incorporate application-dependent relationships.

Authorisations are derived using the **core axiom** $(a1)$:

$$(a1)\ \forall p \in \mathcal{P},\ \forall a \in \mathcal{A},\ \forall r \in \mathcal{R}, ((\exists c_p \in \mathcal{C}, \exists c'_p \in \mathcal{C}, \exists c_r \in \mathcal{C}, \exists c'_r \in \mathcal{C}, (p, c_p) \in \mathcal{PCA} \land (r, c_r) \in \mathcal{RCA} \land c_p \subseteq c'_p \land c_r \subseteq c'_r \land (a, c'_r, c'_p) \in \mathcal{ARCA}) \Leftrightarrow (p, a, r) \in \mathcal{PAR})$$

Based on this axiom, we can deduce that if a principal p is in the category c_p (i.e., $(p, c_p) \in \mathcal{PCA}$), a resource r is in the category c_r (i.e., $(r, c_r) \in \mathcal{RCA}$), and the category c_p is permitted to perform the action a on resource category c_r (i.e., $(a, c_r, c_p) \in \mathcal{ARCA}$) then p is authorised to perform a on r (that is, $(p, a, r) \in \mathcal{PAR}$). Inherited authorisations can be derived if hierarchies of categories are incorporated. Any derived request that is not authorised by an interaction of the underlying categories is assumed to be prohibited; alternatively, additional relations and axioms can be included to define prohibitions and to deal with more general kinds of answers [6].

The classification of entities into categories can be static (e.g., based on a role label, which can only be updated by the administrator) or dynamic (e.g., a condition on age: a minor may change into the adult category once they passed their 18th birthday). Most of the existing access control models can be defined as instances of CBAC by selecting appropriate sets of entities and relationships and specifying adequate notions of categories [4,5].

Category-Based Specification of ABAC. We now consider the attribute-based access control model ABAC [14] and its category-based specification C-ABAC [11], upon which our practical implementation is based. In C-ABAC, we include the generic sets of entities: $\mathcal{P}$, $\mathcal{A}$, $\mathcal{R}$, $\mathcal{C}$, as well as a countable set $\mathcal{E}nv$ of environment entities and a countable set $\mathcal{A}t$ of attributes ranging over values $\mathcal{V}$. Attributes can assume a non-exhaustive list of values from strings, numbers and Boolean conditions with possible validity constraints (e.g., an age value cannot be negative) as well as a pre-defined range which the values must fit into. Attributes are further split into principal, resource and environmental attributes. The relations linking principals, resources and environment entities to their attributes are referred to as $\mathcal{PATA}, \mathcal{RATA}, \mathcal{EATA}$ in [11]. In addition the following relationship is included in $\mathcal{R}el$ in C-ABAC to link categories with attributes:

- *Category-Attribute Assignment*, $\mathcal{CATA} \subseteq \mathcal{C} \times Cond$, s.t. $(c, cond) \in \mathcal{CATA}$ iff category $c \in \mathcal{C}$ requires attribute values satisfying the Boolean condition $cond \in Cond$; we say that c is defined by *cond*. We write $\Gamma \vdash cond$ if Γ specifies attributes and values that satisfy *cond*.
  We assume $\subseteq$ (the hierarchical relation between categories) is compatible with the conditions defining categories, i.e., $c \subseteq c'$ means that the defining condition for c implies that of c':

$$(c_0)\ \forall c, c' \in \mathcal{C}, \forall \Gamma, ((\exists (c,d)(c',d') \in \mathcal{CATA}, \\ (\Gamma \vdash d \Rightarrow \Gamma \vdash d')) \iff (c \subseteq c'))$$

An entity belongs to a category c if its attribute values satisfy c's definition.

A ***C-ABAC policy*** *is a tuple* $\langle E, Rel\rangle$ *of entities and relationships that satisfy the axioms* $(a1)$ *and* (c_0).

2.2 Policy Mining

CBAC relies on the concept of category to structure authorisations: principals and resources are categorised, and permissions are assigned to specific categories, from which the authorisation relation is derived. A crucial step in the generation of CBAC policies is therefore the definition of appropriate categories of principals and resources. *Since our goal is to obtain dynamic policies, in this work, we consider categories defined on the basis of attributes, i.e., we consider policies in the C-ABAC model* [11,12].

We define the C-ABAC policy mining problem as the problem of generating a C-ABAC policy, given an initial ACM or RBAC policy with accompanying attribute data, such that the authorisation relation $\mathcal{PAR}$ of the generated C-ABAC policy includes the authorisations in the input policy. The challenge is to create the category definitions (i.e., a relation $\mathcal{CATA}$ linking categories with attribute conditions) and the association between actions, resource and principal categories (relation $\mathcal{ARCA}$).

3 Policy Mining Algorithm Overview

We propose a method to mine a C-ABAC policy from an input ACM or RBAC policy in two phases. In the first one we generate access control logs based on the input policy. In the second, we generate a C-ABAC policy from the logs.

To mine C-ABAC policies from logs, we propose to use an algorithm to identify frequently occurring patterns in logs in two stages. Initially natural language processing is proposed to identify initial groups of sufficiently similar entities. Subsequently the FP-growth mining algorithm [15] is used to identify frequently occurring patterns in access control logs based on the similarity groupings identified by the initial NLP stage. This second step is executed to ensure that principals from similarly grouped categories do indeed have the same permissions with relation to the same resource categories. Should this not be the case diverging categories are split into separate groups. We briefly describe each of these phases below and refer the reader to [2] for more details.

Doc2vec. For the initial NLP-based similarity assessment the Doc2vec algorithm has been chosen as introduced in [21,22]. Doc2vec seeks to produce a numerical representation of the underlying document by producing vectors of words, similar to its foundation word2vec [22], the difference being that Doc2vec does not maintain a logical structure in the document but rather introduces another vector named document/paragraph ID to existing word vectors. This is the vector capturing the fundamental concept of the document. Doc2vec has been chosen specifically because of its ability to incorporate the additional document vector on top of the word vectors, so that with each iteration not only words but the entire document concept is updated which is an appropriate procedure to handle one consolidated set of logs.

Doc2vec permits a classification into multiple classes due to its similarity scoring abilities. As a first step Doc2vec requires tagging the data to obtain a tagged document which is the input for the subsequent Doc2vec model. The tagged data can then be used to train the Doc2vec model. Once the model has been trained it becomes possible to conduct a cosine vector-based similarity assessment with the model. Each tag will be associated with a list of the 10 elements with the highest similarity score to the lead tag. This list is then further reduced to only contain members above a specified threshold, e.g., 0.98. The reduced grouping then forms the initial category definition which is then sent through the FP-growth algorithm described below. This is done for auditing purposes: to confirm the validity of the Doc2vec-based grouping and/or to provide remediative action, i.e., splitting and/or merging members of categories, where such action is required following the authorisation assessment by FP-growth.

Frequency Tree. The FP-growth algorithm [15,16] has been chosen as a basis for the validation process completing the NLP-based category mining process due to a logical association of frequently occurring items with a common super class. The FP-growth method uses a bottom-up methodology: it chooses the least occurring prefix, i.e., the lowest leaf of the tree corresponding to the prefix, and builds a frequent pattern for this prefix adding items one-by-one and moving up towards the root. Items not meeting a minimum support are discarded (the support of a pattern A, which is a set of items, is the number of transactions containing A).

Creation of Logs. Now we turn our attention to the case in which the input is not a list of logs but a given access control matrix (ACM) or RBAC policy, together with a list of principals and resources with their attributes (relations $\mathcal{PATA}$ and $\mathcal{RATA}$). If a list of logs does not exist, we generate access request logs as follows depending on whether the input is an ACM or an RBAC policy:

1. For every non-null entry $(principal, resource, [action_1, \ldots, action_n])$ in the ACM, we generate a list of n tuples

$$(principal, action_i, resource, principal\text{-}attributes,\ resource\text{-}attributes)$$

2. Given an RBAC policy consisting of relations URA (user role assignment) and PRA (permission role assignment, i.e., triples of action, resource, role) we generate a list of tuples linking each principal with all the permissions in its roles, obtained by composing URA and PRA:

$$(principal, action, resource, principal\text{-}attributes,\ resource\text{-}attributes)$$

Once the logs have been generated, we apply the NLP-based similarity check followed by FP-growth, as described above.

Summarising, the mining algorithm has two main steps. The first is the generation of logs using as input an ACM or RBAC policy. The second uses the logs as input. If logs are already available (e.g., actual real-life data about access requests is available) then the first step is omitted. The second step is subdivided into two phases as described below.

1. Generation of category definitions:
   The initial category definition is executed via the Doc2vec-based TypeDefinition and mergeCommon functions. TypeDefinition is aimed at identifying candidates with high similarity scores referring to the similar function, those initial candidates are then clustered under an initial assumed common category based on the similarity score. mergeCommon then subsequently merges category duplicates based on commonly found neighbors.
   The next step, the createTree function, constitutes the formation of principal and resource attribute frequency trees via FP-growth. Based on the frequency trees, the algorithm confirms candidate definitions of categories, as well as the assignment of permissions to categories (the $\mathcal{ARCA}$ relation) by ensuring that all candidates assumed to belong to one category are associated with the same permissions and opposite category candidates.
2. Authorisations:
   The dynamic $\mathcal{PAR}$ relation is subsequently derived from the $\mathcal{ARCA}$ relation according to the core CBAC axiom. A final quality audit is carried out to ensure the derived authorisations include the ones in the logs (hence the mined policy is correct). For more details we refer to [2].

4 Category Mining Proof of Concept - Use Cases

The most challenging part of the algorithm is the generation of category definitions once the logs are available. We tested this step using synthetic data and also a real world data set. We describe below the results for the later.

The data set applied to this proof of concept of our proposed tool is a public server log for a university online judge generated for Kaggle [10]. It contains 16008 initial transaction requests, i.e. principal requests for specific actions on resources at a given time stamp. Principals are associated with one IP address each while resources are identified via a given web link. Answers to access requests are given in the form of status codes such as 200 (Successfully found), 206 (Partial content), 302 (Found redirect), 304 (Not modified) or 404 (Not found). For the purposes of this data set the client side status code 404 (Not found) is treated as a negative, i.e., denied request. For the purposes of this use case the principal IP addresses are treated as the principal attributes and the time stamp as the resource attributes.

Our goal is to mine categories for principals and resources which generate the same authorisations as in the logs, and which represent a reduction of information stored thereby providing greater ease of use and maintenance. In this case attribute values that constitute principal and resource category definitions are IP ranges for principals and time stamp groupings for resources. These definitions are obtained from the frequent patterns generated by FP-growth based on the NLP pre-filter applied to the logs. More precisely, category specifications are initially mined by NLP and entities assigned according to the FP-growth confirmation process based on a computation of the principal, resource, action tuple. The final validation step confirming results is the log compliance check. This is to ensure that the generated authorisations match the logs and therefore represent the correct policy. The validated results confirm the achievement of the objective to mine categories representing a reduced amount of information necessary to produce dynamic authorisations: Fig. 1 shows a gradual transition from an initial state of over 16000 granted individual access requests - representing the 16000 tuples $\mathcal{PAR}$ as found in the logs - to a final phase containing just over 360 total resource and principal category definitions.

Because less information is stored due to the grouping into categories, and because the categories are dynamic (i.e., membership depends on attribute values rather than on a manual administrator assignment) the result is a reduction in space usage and maintenance time.

The algorithm permits adding a weight to FP-growth to allow for a match above a certain threshold, e.g., 0.87 which would make further reductions possible. Whether such further reductions based on a wider scope of permissions are appropriate needs to be decided based on organisational safety requirements.

5 Related Work

Mining ABAC policies from RBAC policies has been proposed in [28], we seek to expand the proposed methodology to mining categories based on static policies which include but are not limited to static features such as roles or attributes defined a priori. [9] proposes an analysis of the feasibility of RBAC to ABAC policy mining due to the RuleSet problem defined in [8] which refers to the consistency of ABAC policy generation in an enumerated authorisation system

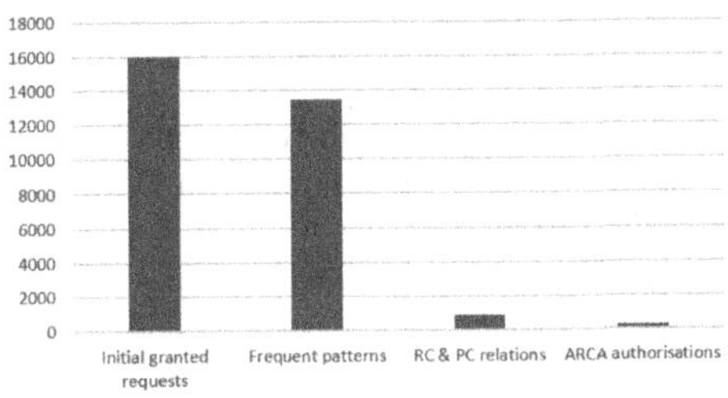

Fig. 1. Results - reduction in authorisation relations

with attribute data. We seek to counter this concern by providing an additional interpretation step rather than terminating at an aggregation of ABAC-based rules. This step represents our final category definitions.

A key distinguisher between ABAC miners such as [29] and CBAC mining as we propose it here is the fact that ABAC produces an aggregation, rather than the CBAC categorisation, of attributes which are then translated to rules from which authorisations are derived. Since ABAC does not provide any mechanism to connect the semantic meaning of attributes this can result in an overabundance of rules which are difficult to manage and understand. We tackle this issue with the initial NLP-based stage of our algorithm which serves as a pre-filter to provide a set of initial category definitions based on semantic relationships. The following validation step via FP-growth aims to ensure all category members deemed similar actually carry the same level of authorisations.

A heuristic search-based ABAC mining method is proposed in [1], by generating n rules with a random combination of attribute values. If a rule is not correct it is swapped by another one which differs just in one attribute value. This computationally expensive method does not help interpret the rules.

In [18] the authors propose an automated log pattern finding approach as well as a policy refinement and pruning algorithm to achieve higher quality of policies. The key differentiators with our work are 1. that input for our method is not limited to attributes and 2. that the authors utilise a manually-driven quality check method as opposed to our automated FP-check.

6 Conclusions and Future Work

We have presented an initial foundation for a CBAC miner that smoothly migrates from ACM or RBAC policies to dynamic, attribute-based CBAC policies, the first such study to the best of our knowledge. The next stage of our work shall analyse the category output with a view to creating an alert system where, e.g. members of the same category are found to have different authorisations as more future logs come in. We seek to establish how our miner can be used to automatically identify inconsistencies in logs, an action traditionally requiring the intervention of administrators; our system may well significantly reduce this burden. The approach can be expanded to include other data (e.g., user stories).

References

1. Aggarwal, N., Sural, S.: RanSAM: randomized search for ABAC policy mining. In: Proceedings of the Thirteenth ACM Conference on Data and Application Security and Privacy, pp. 291–293 (2023)
2. Bamberger, A., Fernández, M.: Mining access control policies from logs via attribute-based categories (2023). https://nms.kcl.ac.uk/maribel.fernandez/papers/CBAC-miner.pdf
3. Barka, E., Sandhu, R.: Framework for role-based delegation models. In: Proceedings 16th Annual Computer Security Applications Conference (ACSAC 2000), pp. 168–176. IEEE (2000)
4. Barker, S.: The next 700 access control models or a unifying meta-model? In: SACMAT 2009, 14th ACM Symposium on Access Control Models and Technologies, Stresa, Italy, 3–5 June 2009, Proceedings, New York, pp. 187–196. ACM Press (2009)
5. Bertolissi, C., Fernández, M.: Category-based authorisation models: operational semantics and expressive power. In: Massacci, F., Wallach, D., Zannone, N. (eds.) ESSoS 2010. LNCS, vol. 5965, pp. 140–156. Springer, Heidelberg (2010). https://doi.org/10.1007/978-3-642-11747-3_11
6. Bertolissi, C., Fernández, M.: A metamodel of access control for distributed environments: applications and properties. Inf. Comput. **238**, 187–207 (2014). https://doi.org/10.1016/j.ic.2014.07.009
7. Bertolissi, C., Fernández, M.: A rewriting framework for the composition of access control policies. In: Proceedings of the 10th International ACM SIGPLAN Conference on Principles and Practice of Declarative Programming, pp. 217–225 (2008)
8. Chakraborty, S., Sandhu, R., Krishnan, R.: On the feasibility of attribute-based access control policy mining. In: 2019 IEEE 20th International Conference on Information Reuse and Integration for Data Science (IRI), pp. 245–252. IEEE (2019)
9. Chakraborty, S., Sandhu, R., Krishnan, R.: On the feasibility of RBAC to ABAC policy mining: a formal analysis. In: Sahay, S.K., Goel, N., Patil, V., Jadliwala, M. (eds.) SKM 2019. CCIS, vol. 1186, pp. 147–163. Springer, Singapore (2020). https://doi.org/10.1007/978-981-15-3817-9_9
10. Online Judge (RUET OJ) Server Log Dataset: Data set weblog. https://www.kaggle.com/datasets/shawon10/web-log-dataset. Accessed 25 Aug 2022
11. Fernández, M., Mackie, I., Thuraisingham, B.: Specification and analysis of ABAC policies via the category-based metamodel. In: Proceedings of the Ninth ACM Conference on Data and Application Security and Privacy, pp. 173–184 (2019)
12. Fernández, M., Thuraisingham, B.: A category-based model for ABAC. In: Proceedings of the Third ACM Workshop on Attribute-Based Access Control, pp. 32–34 (2018)
13. Ferraiolo, D., Kuhn, R., Sandhu, R.: RBAC standard rationale: comments on "a critique of the ANSI standard on role-based access control". IEEE Secur. Priv. **5**(6), 51–53 (2007). https://doi.org/10.1109/MSP.2007.173
14. Ferraiolo, D.F., Atluri, V.: A meta model for access control: why is it needed and is it even possible to achieve? In: SACMAT 2008, pp. 153–154 (2008)
15. Han, J., Pei, J., Yin, Y., Mao, R.: Mining frequent patterns without candidate generation: a frequent-pattern tree approach. Data Min. Knowl. Disc. **8**(1), 53–87 (2004)
16. Harrington, P.: Machine learning in action. Simon and Schuster (2012)

17. Hu, V.C., et al.: Guide to attribute based access control (ABAC) definition and considerations (draft). NIST Spec. Publ. **800**(162), 1–54 (2013)
18. Karimi, L., Aldairi, M., Joshi, J., Abdelhakim, M.: An automatic attribute-based access control policy extraction from access logs. IEEE Trans. Dependable Secure Comput. **19**(4), 2304–2317 (2021)
19. Karimi, V.R., Alencar, P.S., Cowan, D.D.: A formal modeling and analysis approach for access control rules, policies, and their combinations. Int. J. Inf. Secur. **16**(1), 43–74 (2017)
20. Klarl, H., Marmé, F., Wolff, C., Emig, C., Abeck, S.: An MDA-based environment for generating access control policies. In: Fischer-Hübner, S., Lambrinoudakis, C., Pernul, G. (eds.) TrustBus 2009. LNCS, vol. 5695, pp. 115–126. Springer, Heidelberg (2009). https://doi.org/10.1007/978-3-642-03748-1_12
21. Le, Q., Mikolov, T.: Distributed representations of sentences and documents. In: International Conference on Machine Learning, pp. 1188–1196. PMLR (2014)
22. Mikolov, T., Chen, K., Corrado, G., Dean, J.: Efficient estimation of word representations in vector space. arXiv preprint arXiv:1301.3781 (2013)
23. Molloy, I., et al.: Mining roles with multiple objectives. ACM Trans. Inf. Syst. Secur. (TISSEC) **13**(4), 1–35 (2010)
24. Sandhu, R.S., Samarati, P.: Access control: principle and practice. IEEE Commun. Mag. **32**(9), 40–48 (1994)
25. Sandhu, R., Coyne, E., Feinstein, H., Youman, C.: Role-based access control models. IEEE Comput. **29**(2), 38–47 (1996)
26. Schlegelmilch, J., Steffens, U.: Role mining with orca. In: Proceedings of the tenth ACM Symposium on Access Control Models and Technologies, pp. 168–176 (2005)
27. Wang, L., Wijesekera, D., Jajodia, S.: A logic-based framework for attribute based access control. In: Proceedings of the 2004 ACM Workshop on Formal Methods in Security Engineering, pp. 45–55 (2004)
28. Xu, Z., Stoller, S.D.: Mining attribute-based access control policies from RBAC policies. In: 2013 10th International Conference and Expo on Emerging Technologies for a Smarter World (CEWIT), pp. 1–6. IEEE (2013)
29. Xu, Z., Stoller, S.D.: Mining attribute-based access control policies from logs. In: Atluri, V., Pernul, G. (eds.) DBSec 2014. LNCS, vol. 8566, pp. 276–291. Springer, Heidelberg (2014). https://doi.org/10.1007/978-3-662-43936-4_18
30. Yuan, E., Tong, J.: Attributed based access control (ABAC) for web services. In: IEEE International Conference on Web Services (ICWS 2005). IEEE (2005)

Towards a Certified Proof Checker for Deep Neural Network Verification

Remi Desmartin[1], Omri Isac[2(✉)], Grant Passmore[3], Kathrin Stark[1], Ekaterina Komendantskaya[1], and Guy Katz[2]

[1] Heriot-Watt University, Edinburgh, UK
rhd2000@hw.ac.uk
[2] The Hebrew University of Jerusalem, Jerusalem, Israel
omri.isac@mail.huji.ac.il
[3] Imandra Inc., Austin, TX, USA

Abstract. Recent developments in deep neural networks (DNNs) have led to their adoption in safety-critical systems, which in turn has heightened the need for guaranteeing their safety. These safety properties of DNNs can be proven using tools developed by the verification community. However, these tools are themselves prone to implementation bugs and numerical stability problems, which make their reliability questionable. To overcome this, some verifiers produce proofs of their results which can be checked by a trusted checker. In this work, we present a novel implementation of a proof checker for DNN verification. It improves on existing implementations by offering numerical stability and greater verifiability. To achieve this, we leverage two key capabilities of Imandra, an industrial theorem prover: its support for exact real arithmetic and its formal verification infrastructure. So far, we have implemented a proof checker in Imandra, specified its correctness properties and started to verify the checker's compliance with them. Our ongoing work focuses on completing the formal verification of the checker and further optimising its performance.

Keywords: Deep Neural Network · Formal Verification · AI Safety

1 Introduction

Applications of deep neural networks (DNNs) have grown rapidly in recent years, as they are able to solve computationally hard problems. This has led to their wide use in safety-critical applications like medical imaging [33] or autonomous aircraft [19]. However, DNNs are hard to trust for safety-critical tasks, notably because small perturbations in their inputs – whether from faulty sensors or

R. Desmartin and O. Isac—Both authors contributed equally.
R. Desmartin—Funded by Imandra Inc.
E. Komendantskaya—Funded by EPSRC grant AISEC (EP/T026952/1) and NCSC grant "Neural Network Verification: in search of the missing spec.".

R. Glück and B. Kafle (Eds.): LOPSTR 2023, LNCS 14330, pp. 198–209, 2023.
https://doi.org/10.1007/978-3-031-45784-5_13

malicious adversarial attacks – may cause large variations of their outputs, leading to potentially catastrophic system failures [34]. To circumvent this issue, the verification community has developed techniques to guarantee DNN correctness using formal verification, employing mathematically rigorous techniques to analyse DNNs' possible behaviours in order to prove it safe and compliant e.g. [2,9,15,16,21,23,31,32,36]. Along with these DNN verifiers, the community holds the annual competition VNN-COMP [8] that led to the standardisation of formats [3].

Usually, DNN verifiers consider a trained DNN and prove input-output properties, e.g. that for inputs within a delimited region of the input space, the network's output will be in a safe set. Besides verifying DNNs at a component level, verification has the power to verify larger systems integrating DNNs. Integration of DNN verifiers in larger verification frameworks has been studied as well [10], and it requires the DNN verifiers to provide results that can be checked by the system-level verifier.

Unfortunately, DNN verifiers are susceptible to errors as any other program. One source of problems is floating-point arithmetic used for their internal calculations. While crucial for performance, floating-point arithmetic also leads to numerical instability and is known to compromise the soundness of DNN verifiers [18]. As the reliability of DNN verifiers becomes questionable, it is necessary to check that their results are not erroneous. When a DNN verifier concludes there exists a counterexample for a given property, this result can be easily checked by evaluating the counterexample over the network and ensuring the property's violation. However, when a verifier concludes that no counterexample exists, ensuring the correctness of this result becomes more complicated.

To overcome this, DNN verifiers may produce proofs for their results, allowing an external program to check their soundness. Producing proofs is a common practice [4,26], and was recently implemented on top of the Marabou DNN verifier [17,21]. Typically, proof checkers are simpler programs than the DNN verifiers, and hence much easier to inspect and verify. Moreover, while verifiers are usually implemented in performance-oriented languages such as C++, trusted proof checkers could be implemented in languages suitable for verification.

Functional programming languages (FPL), such as Haskell, OCaml and Lisp, are well-suited for this task, thanks to their deep relationship with logics employed by theorem provers. In fact, some FPLs, such as Agda [27], Coq [1], ACL2 [22], Isabelle [30] and Imandra [28] are also theorem provers in their own right. Implementing and then verifying a program in such a theorem prover allows to bridge the verification gap, i.e. minimise the discrepancies that can exist between the original (executable) program and its verified (abstract) model [7].

In this paper, we describe our ongoing work to design, implement and verify a *formally-verifiable and infinitely-precise proof checker* for DNN verifiers. We have implemented an adaptation of a checker of `UNSAT` proofs produced by the Marabou DNN verifier [17,21] to Imandra [28], a programming language with its own theorem prover that has been successfully used in fintech applications [29]. Three key features make Imandra a suitable tool: arbitrary precision ("exact") real arithmetic, efficient code extraction and the first-class integration of formal verification. Support for infinite precision real arithmetic prevents errors due to numerical instability in the proof checker. In the linear case, this corresponds to arbitrary precision rational arithmetic. In the nonlinear case, real computation in Imandra takes place over a canonical real closed field, the field of real algebraic numbers. The ability to extract verified Imandra code to native OCaml improves scalability as it can then benefit from the standard OCaml compiler's optimisations. Finally, with Imandra's integrated formal verification, we can directly analyse the correctness of the proof checker we implement. Capacities of Imandra in DNN verification have already been reported in [13].

Contributions. We improve on the previous implementation [17] in two ways: firstly, our checker can itself be formally verified by Imandra; and secondly, Imandra's infinite precision numbers eliminate the possibility of the usual floating point arithmetic errors. This increases the checker's reliability and overcomes a main barrier in integrating DNN verifiers in system-level checkers. Since reliability usually compromises scalability, our proof checker supports two checking modes: (i) one uses verified data structures at the expense of computation speed; (ii) the other accepts some parts of the proof without checking.

Our ongoing work is currently focused on formally verifying the proof checker. So far, we have managed to verify that our checker complies with linear algebra theorems, and we attempt to leverage these results to verify the proof checker as a whole in the future.

Paper Organisation. The rest of this paper is organised as follows. In Sect. 2 we provide relevant background on DNN verification and proof production. In Sect. 3 and Sect. 4 we respectively describe our proof checker, and our ongoing work towards formally verifying it using Imandra. In Sect. 5 we conclude our work, and describe our plans for completing our work and for the future.

An extended version of this paper is available in [12].

2 Background

2.1 DNN Verification

Throughout the paper, we focus on DNNs with $\text{ReLU}(x) = max(0, x)$ activation functions, though all our work can be extended to DNNs using any piecewise-linear activation functions (e.g. *max pooling*). We refer the reader to the extended version of this paper for a formal definition of DNNs and activation functions [12]. An example of a DNN appears in Fig. 1.

The *DNN verification problem* is the decision problem of deciding whether for a given DNN $\mathcal{N} : \mathbb{R}^m \to \mathbb{R}^k$ and a property $P \subseteq \mathbb{R}^{m+k}$, there exists an input $x \in \mathbb{R}^m$ such that $\mathcal{N}(x) = y \land P(x, y)$. If such x exists, the verification query is *satisfiable* (`SAT`); otherwise it is *unsatisfiable* (`UNSAT`). Typically, P represents an erroneous behaviour, thus an input x satisfying the query serves as a counterexample and `UNSAT` indicates the network acts as expected.

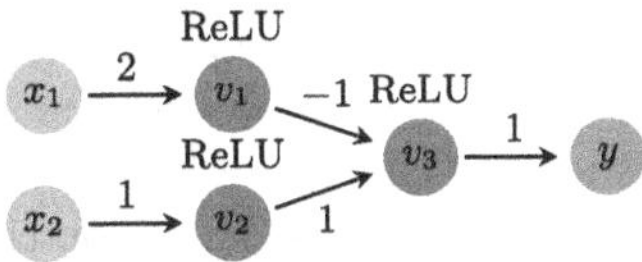

Fig. 1. A Simple DNN. The bias parameters are all set to zero and are ignored. Green denotes input nodes, blue hidden nodes, and red output nodes. (Color figure online)

Due to its linear and piecewise-linear structure, a DNN verification query can be reduced to an instance of Linear Programming (LP) [11], representing the affine functions of the DNN, and piecewise-linear constraints that represent the activation functions and the property. This reduction makes algorithms for solving LP instances, coupled with a *case-splitting* approach for handling the piecewise-linear constraints [5,20], a prime scheme for DNN verification, which we call *LP-based DNN verifiers*.

The widely used Simplex algorithm [11,14,20], is typically used by such verifiers. Based on the problem constraints, the algorithm initiates a matrix A called the *tableau*, a variable vector x and two *bound vectors* u, l such that $l \leq x \leq u$. The Simplex algorithm then attempts to find a solution to the system:

$$Ax = 0 \wedge l \leq x \leq u \tag{1}$$

or concludes that none exists. For clarity, we denote $u(x_i), l(x_i)$ as the upper and lower bounds of the variable x_i, instead of u_i, l_i.

Example 1. Consider the DNN in Fig. 1 and the property P that holds if and only if $(x_1, x_2) \in [-1,1]^2 \wedge y \in [2,3]$. We later show a proof of UNSAT for this query. We assign variables x_1, x_2, y to the input and output neurons. For all $i \in 1,2,3$ we assign a couple of variables f_i, b_i for the inputs and outputs of the neurons v_i, where $f_i = \text{ReLU}(b_i)$. We then get the linear constraints and bounds (where some bounds were arbitrarily fixed for simplicity):

$$b_1 = 2x_1,\ \ b_2 = x_2,\ \ b_3 = f_2 - f_1,\ \ y = f_3 \tag{2}$$

$$-1 \leq x_1, x_2, b_2 \leq 1,\ 0 \leq f_2 \leq 1,\ -2 \leq b_1, b_3 \leq 2,\ 0 \leq f_1, f_3 \leq 2,\ 2 \leq y \leq 3 \tag{3}$$

and the piecewise linear constraints: $\forall i \in 1,2,3 : f_i = \text{ReLU}(b_i)$

Then, an LP-based DNN verifier initiates the input for the Simplex algorithm:

$$A = \begin{bmatrix} 2 & 0 & -1 & 0 & 0 & 0 & 0 & 0 & 0 \\ 0 & 1 & 0 & -1 & 0 & 0 & 0 & 0 & 0 \\ 0 & 0 & 0 & 0 & -1 & -1 & 1 & 0 & 0 \\ 0 & 0 & 0 & 0 & 0 & 0 & 0 & -1 & 1 \end{bmatrix} \quad \begin{aligned} u &= \begin{bmatrix} 1 & 1 & 2 & 1 & 2 & 2 & 1 & 2 & 3 \end{bmatrix}^\intercal \\ x &= \begin{bmatrix} x_1 & x_2 & b_1 & b_2 & b_3 & f_1 & f_2 & f_3 & y \end{bmatrix}^\intercal \\ l &= \begin{bmatrix} -1 & -1 & -2 & -1 & -2 & 0 & 0 & 0 & 2 \end{bmatrix}^\intercal \end{aligned}$$

In addition to the piecewise-linear constraints $\forall i \in 1,2,3 : f_i = \text{ReLU}(b_i)$.

One of the key tools used by the Simplex algorithm, and consequently by DNN verifiers, is dynamic bound tightening. This procedure allows deducing tighter bounds for each variable and is crucial for the solver's performance. For example, using the above equation $f_3 = y$ and the bound $u(y) = 2$, we can deduce $u(f_3) = 2$, and further use this bound to deduce other bounds as well. The piecewise-linear constraints introduce rules for tightening bounds as well, which we call *Theory-lemmas.* For instance, the output variable f_3 of the ReLU constraint of the above example is upper bounded by the input variable b_3, whose upper bound is 2. The list of supported lemmas appears in [12].

The case-splitting approach is used over the linear pieces of some piecewise-linear constraints, creating several sub-queries with each adding new information to the Simplex algorithm. For example, when performing a split over a constraint of the form $y = \text{ReLU}(x)$, two sub-queries are created. One is enhanced with $y = x \wedge x \geq 0$, and the other with $y = 0 \wedge x \leq 0$. The use of case-splitting also induces a tree structure for the verification algorithm, with nodes corresponding to the splits applied. On every node, the verifier attempts to conclude the satisfiability of the query based on its linear constraints. If it concludes an answer, then this node represents a leaf. In particular, a tree with all leaves corresponding to an `UNSAT` result of Simplex is a search tree of an `UNSAT` verification query.

2.2 Proof Production for DNN Verification

Proof production for `SAT` is straightforward using a satisfying assignment. On the other hand, when a query is `UNSAT`, the verification algorithm induces a search tree, where each leaf corresponds to an `UNSAT` result of the Simplex algorithm for that particular leaf. Thus, a proof of `UNSAT` is comprised of a matching proof tree where each leaf contains a proof of the matching Simplex `UNSAT` result. Proving `UNSAT` results of Simplex is based on a constructive version of the Farkas Lemma [35], which identifies the proof for `UNSAT` LP instances. Formally, it was proven [17] that:

Theorem 1. *Let $A \in M_{m \times n}(\mathbb{R})$ and $l, x, u \in \mathbb{R}^n$, such that $A \cdot x = 0$ and $l \leq x \leq u$, exactly one of these two options holds:*

1. *The `SAT` case: $\exists x \in \mathbb{R}^n$ such that $A \cdot x = 0$ and $l \leq x \leq u$.*
2. *The `UNSAT` case: $\exists w \in \mathbb{R}^m$ such that for all $l \leq x \leq u$, $w^\intercal \cdot A \cdot x < 0$, whereas $0 \cdot w = 0$. Thus, w is a proof of the constraints' unsatisfiability.*

Moreover, these vectors can be constructed while executing the Simplex algorithm.

To construct the proof vectors, two column vectors are assigned to each variable x_i, denoted $f_u(x_i), f_l(x_i)$, which are updated during bound tightening. These vectors are used to prove the tightest upper and lower bounds of x_i deduced during the bound tightenings performed by Simplex, based on u, l and A. Constructing the proof vector of Theorem 1 case *2.* allows the proof checker to check the unsatisfiability of the query immediately, without repeating Simplex procedure. This mechanism was designed and implemented [17], on top of the Marabou DNN verifier [21].

Supporting the complete tree structure of the verification algorithm is done by constructing the proof tree in a similar manner to the search tree—every split performed in the search directly creates a similar split in the proof tree, with updates to the equations and bounds introduced by the split. Proving theory lemmas is done by keeping details about the bound that invoked the lemma together with a Farkas vector proving its deduction and the newly learned bound, and adding them to the corresponding proof tree node.

3 The Imandra Proof Checker

Our proof checker is designed to check proofs produced by the Marabou DNN verifier [21], to the best of our knowledge the only proof producing DNN verifier. When given a Marabou proof of `UNSAT` as a JSON [6] file, the proof checker reconstructs the proof tree using datatypes encoded in Imandra.

The proof tree consists of two different node types—a proof node and a proof leaf. Both node types contain a list of lemmas and a corresponding split. In addition, a node contains a list of its children, and a leaf contains a contradiction vector, as constructed by Theorem 1. This enables the checker to check the proof tree structure at the type level. The proof checker also initiates a matrix A called a *tableau*, vectors of upper and lower bounds u, l and a list of piecewise-linear constraints (see Sect. 2.1).

The checking process consists of traversing the proof tree. For each node, the checker begins by locally updating u, l and A according to the split, and optionally checking the correctness of all lemmas. Lemma checking is similar to checking contradictions, as shown in Example 2 below (see [12] for details).

If the node checked is not a leaf, then the checker will check that all its children's splits correspond to some piecewise-linear constraint of the problem i.e. one child has a split of the form $y = x \wedge x \geq 0$ and the other of the form $y = 0 \wedge x \leq 0$ for some constraint $y = \text{ReLU}(x)$. If the checker certifies the node, it will recursively check all its children, passing changes to u, l and A to them.

When checking a leaf, the checker checks that the contradiction vector w implies `UNSAT`, as stated in Theorem 1. As implied from the theorem, the checker will first create the row vector $w^\intercal \cdot A$, and will compute the upper bound of its underlying linear combination of variables $w^\intercal \cdot A \cdot x$. The checker concludes by asserting this upper bound is negative.

The checker then concludes that the proof tree represents a correct proof if and only if all nodes passed the checking process.

Example 2. Consider the simple proof in Fig. 2. The root contains a single lemma and each leaf contains a contradiction vector, which means the verifier performed a single split. In addition, the proof object contains the tableau A, the bound vectors u, l, and the ReLU constraints as presented in Example 1.

The proof checker begins by checking the lemma of the root. It does so by creating the linear combination $\begin{bmatrix}0 \; 0 \; 1 \; 0\end{bmatrix}^\intercal \cdot A \cdot x = -b_3 - f_1 + f_2$. As the lemma is invoked by the upper bound of b_3, the checker uses the equivalent equation $b_3 = f_2 - f_1$, which gives the upper bound $u(b_3) = u(f_2) - l(f_1) = 1$. We can indeed deduce the bound $u(f_3) = 1$ based on the constraint $f_3 = \text{ReLU}(b_3)$, so the lemma proof is correct. Then, the checker certifies that the splits $f_3 = 0 \wedge b_3 \leq 0$

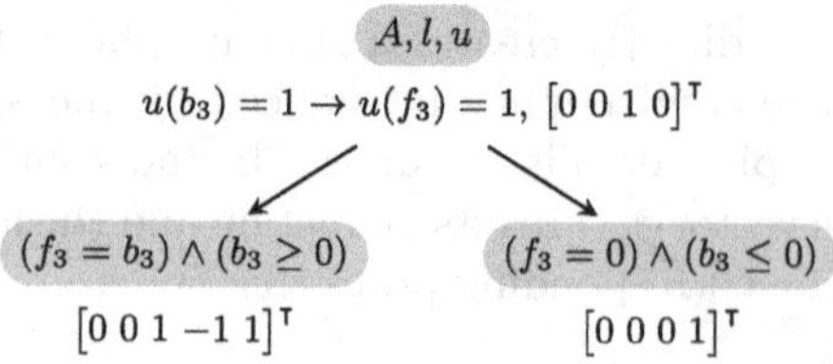

Fig. 2. A proof tree example.

and $f_3 = b_3 \wedge b_3 \geq 0$ correspond to the two splits of $f_3 = \text{ReLU}(b_3)$. The checker then begins checking the left leaf. It starts by updating $l(b_3) = 0$ and adding the equation $f_3 = b_3$ as the row $\begin{bmatrix}0\ 0\ 0\ 0\ 1\ 0\ 0\ -1\ 0\end{bmatrix}$ to A. Then, the checker checks the contradiction vector by computing $\begin{bmatrix}0\ 0\ 1\ -1\ 1\end{bmatrix}^\intercal \cdot A \cdot x = -f_1 + f_2 - y$. The upper bound of this combination is $-l(f_1) + u(f_2) - l(y) = -1$ which is negative, thus proving UNSAT for the leaf according to Theorem 1. Checking the right leaf is done similarly. After checking all nodes, the checker asserts the proof tree indeed proves UNSAT for the whole query.

Implementation in Imandra, OCaml Extraction and Evaluation. Porting the proof checker from C++ to Imandra necessitates taking into account the trade-off between scalability and computation.

The choice of data structures for common objects – like vectors – is essential in the balance between scalability and efficiency [13]. In this work, we experiment with two different implementations for vectors: native OCaml lists, and sparse vectors using Imandra's built-in `Map` data type, based on binary search trees. The latter has better performance but the former makes it easier to verify, so for now our verification efforts focus on the native list implementation (for further discussion of data structure choice, see [12]).

Imandra's logic includes theories for arbitrary precision integer and real arithmetic, which for integers and linear (rational) computations over reals are implemented using OCaml's `Zarith` library [24]. Zarith and GMP, its underlying library, are not verified but trusted. Nonlinear real computations are handled with on-demand field extensions via constructive real closures [25]. As a result, the Imandra implementation of the checker supports arbitrary precision real arithmetic with no overhead.

Executing code within Imandra's reasoning environment is helpful during the implementation and verification process, but is not optimised for performance. To that end, `imandra-extract` is a facility to extract native OCaml code that can be compiled – and optimised – with standard OCaml compilers. The extracted code retains Imandra's semantics, meaning that it still uses infinite precision real arithmetic. An initial comparison of the execution time for checking the same proofs from the ACAS-Xu benchmark [21] in the C++ implementation and in the extracted OCaml code with native lists shows that our implementation is about 150 times slower than the original implementation but stays within a reasonable time, i.e. less than 40 min for all the examples ran (see Table 1). Further optimisations and a comprehensive benchmark are ongoing work.

Table 1. Comparison of the execution speed for checking Marabou proofs for verification tasks from the ACAS Xu benchmark.

ACAS-Xu tasks	C++ [17]	Imandra (native lists)		Imandra (sparse vectors)	
	Full (s)	Partial (s)	Full (s)	Partial (s)	Full (s)
N(2, 9) p3	5.130	167.078	878.075	15.125	4784.866
N(2, 9) p4	5.658	206.675	1019.770	11.208	8817.575
N(3, 7) p3	10.557	299.608	1493.763	24.979	1638.844
N(5, 7) p3	2.568	58.288	311.096	50.365	12276.323
N(5, 9) p3	15.116	424.816	2210.472	30.611	6265.039

4 Specification of the Proof Checker's Correctness

We aim to verify the two main checks performed by the proof checker when traversing the proof tree (see Sect. 3): contradictions and theory lemmas.

Contradictions Checking. We want to verify that our proof checker identifies correctly when a contradiction vector is a valid proof of `UNSAT`, thus satisfying Theorem 1 (case 2). Formally, the specification can be given as:

For any contradiction vector w, tableau A, bounds u, l, and a bounded input $l \leq x \leq u$, if the upper bound of $w^T \cdot A \cdot x$ is negative, then x cannot satisfy the constraints $A \cdot x = 0 \wedge l \leq x \leq u$. The Imandra implementation of this specification is given in Listing 1.1.

```
theorem contra_correct x contra tableau u_bounds l_bounds =
  is_bounded x u_bounds l_bounds
  && check_contradiction contra tableau u_bounds l_bounds
   ==> not (null_product tableau x)
```

Listing 1.1. *High-level theorem formalising correctness of contradiction checking. The function* `check_contradiction` *is a key component of the proof checker which should return* `true` *iff the linear combination of the tableau and contradiction vectors has a negative upper bound.*

Theory Lemmas. We aim to prove that each theory lemma within the proof corresponds to a known theory lemma (see [12] for further details).

Proving the specification necessitates guiding Imandra by providing supporting lemmas, in our case properties of linear algebra. After proving these intermediary lemmas, Imandra's proof automation can apply them automatically, or we can manually specify which lemma to apply.

So far we have defined and proved that our checker is coherent with known properties of linear algebra (e.g. Listing 1.2). Our current work focuses on building on top of these lemmas to fully prove the checker's correctness.

```
lemma dot_product_coeff x y c =
  dot_product x (list_mult y c) = c *. dot_product x y
[@@auto]

lemma dot_product_coeff_eq x y c =
  dot_product x y = 0. ==> dot_product x (list_mult y c) = 0.
[@@auto][@@apply dot_product_coeff x y c]
```

Listing 1.2. *Definition of lemmas proved in Imandra; dot_product_coeff, which defines the homogeneity of the dot-product, is used to prove the second lemma.*

5 Discussion and Future Work

We have implemented a checking algorithm for proofs generated by a DNN verifier in the functional programming language of Imandra, enabling the checking algorithm to be infinitely precise and formally verifiable by Imandra's prover.

Compared to previous work, our implementation presents two new guarantees: it avoids numerical instability by using arbitrary precision real numbers instead of floating-point numbers; and its correctness can be formally verified as it is implemented in a theorem prover. The arbitrary precision linear real arithmetic library, GMP, is standard but it is not itself formally verified.

One limitation of our work is the discrepancy between the initial verified model and the model encoded in the checked proofs: training and verification frameworks use floating point numbers; Marabou uses overapproximation to mitigate the numerical instability, and rounds the values during the proof serialisation; the proof checker then uses exact real arithmetic to reason about the weights. Ultimately though, if the checker validates a proof, it means that the encoded model satisfies the property and can be extracted and deployed.

As expected, adding safety guarantees comes at a cost of performance, but the extraction of native OCaml minimises the overhead compared to the unverified C++ implementation. Furthermore, using an FPL checker to check proofs produced by a DNN verifier is a first step towards integrating DNN verification into the verification of larger systems with DNN-enabled components.

Our immediate future work is to continue the verification of the proof checker. In addition, we intend to identify cases where the existing checker implementation fails (e.g. due to numerical instability) and ours correctly checks the proof. Investigating further optimisations is also a promising direction by implementing better performance data structures, such as AVL trees.

Acknowledgements. We thank the reviewers for their valuable comments and suggestions, which greatly helped us to improve our manuscript.

References

1. The Coq Proof Assistant (1984). https://coq.inria.fr
2. Bak, S.: Nnenum: verification of ReLU neural networks with optimized abstraction refinement. In: Proceedings of 13th International Symposium NASA Formal Methods (NFM), pp. 19–36 (2021)
3. Barrett, C., Katz, G., Guidotti, D., Pulina, L., Narodytska, N., Tacchella, A.: The Verification of Neural Networks Library (VNN-LIB) (2019). https://www.vnnlib.org/
4. Barrett, C., de Moura, L., Fontaine, P.: Proofs in satisfiability modulo theories. In: All About Proofs, Proofs for All, vol. 55, no. 1, pp. 23–44 (2015)
5. Bastani, O., Ioannou, Y., Lampropoulos, L., Vytiniotis, D., Nori, A., Criminisi, A.: Measuring neural net robustness with constraints. In: Proceedings of 30th Conference on Neural Information Processing Systems (NeurIPS) (2016)
6. Bray, T.: The JavaScript Object Notation (JSON) Data Interchange Format (2014). https://www.rfc-editor.org/info/rfc7159
7. Breitner, J., et al.: Ready, set, verify! applying Hs-to-Coq to real-world Haskell code. J. Funct. Program. **31**, e5 (2021)
8. Brix, C., Müller, M.N., Bak, S., Johnson, T.T., Liu, C.: First Three Years of the International Verification of Neural Networks Competition (VNN-COMP). Technical report (2023). http://arxiv.org/abs/2301.05815
9. Brix, C., Noll, T.: Debona: Decoupled Boundary Network Analysis for Tighter Bounds and Faster Adversarial Robustness Proofs. Technical report (2020). http://arxiv.org/abs/2006.09040
10. Daggitt, M.L., Kokke, W., Atkey, R., Arnaboldi, L., Komendantskaya, E.: Vehicle: Interfacing Neural Network Verifiers with Interactive Theorem Provers. Technical report (2022). http://arxiv.org/abs/2202.05207
11. Dantzig, G.: Linear Programming and Extensions. Princeton University Press, Princeton (1963)
12. Desmartin, R., Isac, O., Passmore, G., Stark, K., Katz, G., Komendantskaya, E.: Towards a Certified Proof Checker for Deep Neural Network Verification. Technical report (2023). http://arxiv.org/abs/2307.06299
13. Desmartin, R., Passmore, G.O., Komendantskaya, E.: Neural networks in imandra: matrix representation as a verification choice. In: Proceedings of 5th International Workshop of Software Verification and Formal Methods for ML-Enabled Autonomous Systems (FoMLAS) and 15th International Workshop on Numerical Software Verification (NSV), pp. 78–95 (2022)
14. Dutertre, B., de Moura, L.: A fast linear-arithmetic solver for DPLL(T). In: Ball, T., Jones, R.B. (eds.) CAV 2006. LNCS, vol. 4144, pp. 81–94. Springer, Heidelberg (2006). https://doi.org/10.1007/11817963_11
15. Ferrari, C., Mueller, M.N., Jovanović, N., Vechev, M.: Complete verification via multi-neuron relaxation guided branch-and-bound. In: Proceedings of 10th International Conference on Learning Representations (ICLR) (2022)
16. Henriksen, P., Lomuscio, A.: DEEPSPLIT: an efficient splitting method for neural network verification via indirect effect analysis. In: Proceedings of 30th International Joint Conference on Artificial Intelligence (IJCAI), pp. 2549–2555 (2021)
17. Isac, O., Barrett, C., Zhang, M., Katz, G.: Neural network verification with proof production. In: Proceedings 22nd International Conference on Formal Methods in Computer-Aided Design (FMCAD), pp. 38–48 (2022)

18. Jia, K., Rinard, M.: Exploiting verified neural networks via floating point numerical error. In: Drăgoi, C., Mukherjee, S., Namjoshi, K. (eds.) SAS 2021. LNCS, vol. 12913, pp. 191–205. Springer, Cham (2021). https://doi.org/10.1007/978-3-030-88806-0_9
19. Julian, K., Kochenderfer, M., Owen, M.: Deep neural network compression for aircraft collision avoidance systems. J. Guid. Control. Dyn. **42**(3), 598–608 (2019)
20. Katz, G., Barrett, C., Dill, D., Julian, K., Kochenderfer, M.: Reluplex: a calculus for reasoning about deep neural networks. Form. Methods Syst. Des. (FMSD) **60**(1), 87–116 (2021)
21. Katz, G., et al.: The marabou framework for verification and analysis of deep neural networks. In: Dillig, I., Tasiran, S. (eds.) CAV 2019. LNCS, vol. 11561, pp. 443–452. Springer, Cham (2019). https://doi.org/10.1007/978-3-030-25540-4_26
22. Kaufmann, M., Moore, J.S.: ACL2: an industrial strength version of Nqthm. In: Proceedings of 11th Conference on Computer Assurance (COMPASS), pp. 23–34 (1996)
23. Khedr, H., Ferlez, J., Shoukry, Y.: PEREGRiNN: penalized-relaxation greedy neural network verifier. In: Silva, A., Leino, K.R.M. (eds.) CAV 2021. LNCS, vol. 12759, pp. 287–300. Springer, Cham (2021). https://doi.org/10.1007/978-3-030-81685-8_13
24. Miné, A., Leroy, X., Cuoq, P., Troestler, C.: The Zarith Library (2023). https://github.com/ocaml/Zarith
25. de Moura, L., Passmore, G.O.: Computation in real closed infinitesimal and transcendental extensions of the rationals. In: Bonacina, M.P. (ed.) CADE 2013. LNCS (LNAI), vol. 7898, pp. 178–192. Springer, Heidelberg (2013). https://doi.org/10.1007/978-3-642-38574-2_12
26. Necula, G.: Compiling with Proofs. Carnegie Mellon University (1998)
27. Norell, U.: Dependently typed programming in Agda. In: Proceedings of 4th International Workshop on Types in Language Design and Implementation (TLDI), pp. 1–2 (2009)
28. Passmore, G., et al.: The imandra automated reasoning system (system description). In: Peltier, N., Sofronie-Stokkermans, V. (eds.) IJCAR 2020. LNCS (LNAI), vol. 12167, pp. 464–471. Springer, Cham (2020). https://doi.org/10.1007/978-3-030-51054-1_30
29. Passmore, G.O.: Some lessons learned in the industrialization of formal methods for financial algorithms. In: Huisman, M., Păsăreanu, C., Zhan, N. (eds.) FM 2021. LNCS, vol. 13047, pp. 717–721. Springer, Cham (2021). https://doi.org/10.1007/978-3-030-90870-6_39
30. Paulson, L.C.: Isabelle: A Generic Theorem Prover. Springer, Heidelberg (1994). https://doi.org/10.1007/BFb0030541
31. Prabhakar, P., Afzal, Z.R.: Abstraction based output range analysis for neural networks. In: Proceedings of 32nd International Conference on Neural Information Processing Systems (NeurIPS), pp. 15762–15772 (2019)
32. Smith, J., Allen, J., Swaminathan, V., Zhang, Z.: Refutation-Based Adversarial Robustness Verification of Deep Neural Networks (2021)
33. Suzuki, K.: Overview of deep learning in medical imaging. Radiol. Phys. Technol. **10**(3), 257–273 (2017)

34. Szegedy, C., et al.: Intriguing Properties of Neural Networks. Technical report (2013). http://arxiv.org/abs/1312.6199
35. Vanderbei, R.: Linear programming: foundations and extensions. J. Oper. Res. Soc. (1996)
36. Wang, S., et al.: Beta-CROWN: efficient bound propagation with per-neuron split constraints for neural network robustness verification. Adv. Neural. Inf. Process. Syst. **34**, 29909–29921 (2021)

Author Index

B
Bamberger, Anna 188
Boulytchev, Dmitry 118
Bowles, Juliana 169

C
Carbone, Marco 99
Chailloux, Emmanuel 61

D
De Angelis, Emanuele 39
Desmartin, Remi 198

F
Fernández, Maribel 3, 188
Fioravanti, Fabio 39
Francès de Mas, Jordina 169

G
Gallagher, John P. 28

H
Hermenegildo, Manuel 28, 80
Hu, Zhenjiang 9

I
Isac, Omri 198
Ivanov, Dmitry 118

J
Jurjo, Daniel 80

K
Katz, Guy 198
Komendantskaya, Ekaterina 198
Kosarev, Dmitry 118
Kulaš, Marija 150

L
Lopez-Garcia, Pedro 28, 80
Lozov, Peter 118

M
Marin, Sonia 99
Morales, José 28, 80

P
Passmore, Grant 198
Pettorossi, Alberto 39
Proietti, Maurizio 39

S
Schürmann, Carsten 99
Stark, Kathrin 198
Suzanne, Hector 61

T
Trong, Bach Nguyen 9
Tsushima, Kanae 9

V
Vanhoof, Wim 131

Y
Yernaux, Gonzague 131

R. Glück and B. Kafle (Eds.): LOPSTR 2023, LNCS 14330, p. 211, 2023.
https://doi.org/10.1007/978-3-031-45784-5

Printed in the United States
by Baker & Taylor Publisher Services